Labor Parties in
Postindustrial Societies

Labor Parties in Postindustrial Societies

Edited by
Frances Fox Piven

Oxford University Press • New York
1992

Oxford University Press

Oxford   New York   Toronto
Delhi   Bombay   Calcutta   Madras   Karachi
Petaling Jaya   Singapore   Hong Kong   Tokyo
Nairobi   Dar es Salaam   Cape Town
Melbourne   Auckland
and associated companies in
Berlin   Ibadan

First published 1991 by Polity Press in association with
Blackwell Publishers.

First published 1992 in North America by Oxford University Press,
Inc., 200 Madison Avenue, New York, New York 10016.

Oxford is a registered trademark of Oxford University Press.

Library of Congress Cataloging-in-Publication Data

Labor parties in postindustrial societies / edited by Frances Fox
   Piven.
      p.   cm. — (Europe and the international order)
   Includes bibliographical references and index.
   ISBN 0-19-520926-5
   ISBN 0-19-520927-3 (pbk)
   1. Political parties.   2. Working class — Political activity,
I. Piven, Frances Fox.   II. Series: Europe and the international
order (New York, N.Y.)
JF2011.L33   1992
324.1'7—dc20   91-31554
                                                          CIP

ISBN 0-19-520926-5 (cloth)
       0-19-520927-3 (paper)

Typeset in 10 on 11 pt Baskerville
by Graphicraft Typesetters Ltd., Hong Kong
Printed in Great Britain by TJ Press, Padstow

Contents

Acknowledgments

The chapters which follow originated in a series of papers presented at a conference at the Graduate School and University Center of the City University of New York in February of 1988. The papers have been revised to take account of our joint discussions and mutual criticisms, and to respond to rapidly changing events. This process has been helped immeasurably by the counsel and editing skills of Jeff Escoffier and by Frances Golden, who is my supremely knowledgeable and energetic literary agent. I would also like to thank Brian Waddell for his counsel and assistance throughout this project, and Jeremiah Holland for his help with library research.

The conference at which work on this volume began was sponsored by the Robert F. Wagner, Sr., Institute of Urban Public Policy, of the Graduate School of the City University of New York. It is published as part of the Wagner Institute series on The City in the Twenty-First Century. The volumes in this series are academic studies intended to stimulate interaction between the research community and policymakers. Taken together, they provide a broad perspective of the issues facing the modern city. The general editor of The City in the Twenty-First Century series is Joseph S. Murphy, University Professor of Political Science and Chancellor of the City University of New York from 1982 to 1990. Asher Arian, Director of the Wagner Institute, is editor.

The Robert F. Wagner, Sr., Institute of Public Policy was established at The Graduate School and University Center of The City University of New York in 1987. Its goal is to bring the resources of the academic community to bear upon the understanding and solving of pressing urban and social problems in New York City and other urban centers. The Institute's agenda includes the exploration and analysis of the social, legislative, and political legacy associated with Robert F. Wagner, Sr., a key architect of major components of the American welfare state.

1

The Decline of Labor Parties: An Overview

Frances Fox Piven

The sweeping changes in industrial societies signaled by events of the last decade are making familiar political guideposts unclear. Not least, the prospects of the labor-based political parties that emerged in most industrial countries a century ago, and then grew to become major contenders for governmental power, have faded. The essays in this volume discuss the fate of those parties and their projects, in England, France, Germany, Sweden, Israel, Canada, and the United States.

Of course, there is no single storyline. Each party confronts different national economic and political contexts, and each party is weighted with different internal organizational and ideological legacies. Still, two strong and dualistic themes emerge from these essays. On the one hand, the emerging postindustrial international economic order has generated problems for left parties everywhere. On the other, some common difficulties notwithstanding, labor parties have fared quite differently; the British Labour Party, for example, suffered a steep and precipitous loss of support after 1979, while the Swedish Social Democrats more or less held their own, and returned to power in 1982, as the French Socialists did in 1988. The fate of labor parties in the past decade reveals not only common problems created by a new economic order, but large differences in their ability to weather disturbances to constituencies, party infrastructure, program, and ideology generated by the transformations of postindustrialism. These essays help explain the adaptability of some parties, and the decline of others.

Industrialization and Labor-Based Parties

The life-course of Western labor parties began more or less a century ago, in the aftermath of the emergence of manufacturing economies in the West. As the story is usually told, the growth of factory production and of cities meant that increasing numbers of men and women were no longer dispersed and fragmented by the localisms of traditional village life, but instead came to be concentrated in factories and towns where their common circumstances bound them together in new solidarities, nourished a distinctive political consciousness embedded in what Hobsbawm calls the "common style" of proletarian life,[1] and also led to characteristic forms of workplace struggle and organization, most importantly the trade union and the strike.

The new working class also entered electoral politics. In most industrial countries, the franchise was extended to male workers at the turn of the twentieth century, often as a result of the struggles of workers themselves. The creation of a reservoir of working class votes, in turn, spurred the growth of fledgling socialist or labor parties. As Adam Przeworski and John Sprague report, in Germany the Social Democrats actually won the largest share of the vote immediately after the anti-socialist laws which had disenfranchised many workers were allowed to lapse in 1890. The Austrian Social Democrats won 21 percent of the vote in the first election after the universal male franchise was granted in 1907; and the Finnish Social Democrats won 37 percent, also after the universal male franchise was established in 1907. And as manufacturing advanced, and the industrial working class grew, so did the new political parties. By 1912, the German Social Democrats won 34.8 percent of the vote, twice the share of the next largest party; the Austrian Social Democrats claimed a plurality of 40.8 percent of the vote by 1919; the total Belgian Workers' Party vote rose from 13.2 percent immediately after the introduction of the franchise in 1894 to a plurality of 39.4 percent in 1925.[2]

Of course the pace of these political developments varied among countries, partly because the pace of industrialization varied, and partly because the impact of industrialization on class politics was complexly modulated by the strategies of dominant political coalitions in each country, and also by the pre-existing traditions and organization of the popular classes.[3] Nevertheless, a common pattern can be discerned: for more than half a century – less in some countries, longer in others – the

1   E. J. Hobsbawm et al., *The Forward March of Labour Halted?* (London: Verso, in association with *Marxism Today* and New Left Books, 1981), p. 8.
2   A. Przeworski and J. Sprague, *Paper Stones: A History of Electoral Socialism* (Chicago, IL: University of Chicago Press, 1986), pp. 27–8.
3   The sources of national variations in class politics have been the focus of an enormous literature. For a review, see S. M. Lipset, "Political cleavages in 'developed' and 'emerging' polities," in *Mass Politics: Studies in Political Sociology*, ed. E. Allardt and S. Rokkan (New York: Free Press, 1970), pp. 26–32.

industrial working class, trade union membership and the vote totals of labor-based political parties grew in tandem. To be sure, except in coalition or at moments of crisis, the left parties did not usually control governments. Nevertheless, they became major electoral contenders, and were in most places able to win legal and political protections for their union allies. The growth of unions, in turn, provided the parties with an infrastructure to mobilize the working class vote. Generations of working people came of age in a political world organized to express class interests and class cleavages.[4]

Industrialization generated a working class politics in the United States as well, although the articulation of class politics in electoral arenas was blunted, a fact that has inspired a huge literature exploring the intricacies of "American exceptionalism." Most of this literature fastens on the stubbornly individualistic American political culture which inhibited the development of class identities and solidarities. In turn, individualism is often traced to a variety of distinctive features of the American experience: the absence of a feudal past, the open frontier, rapid economic mobility, regional diversity in a vast country, racial, ethnic and religious divisions, and so on. I am inclined to think that, taken as a whole, these arguments exaggerate the varieties of American distinctiveness, although I will argue in my closing essay that specific political institutions did work to prevent the emergence of a labor party, and the lack of a party vehicle in turn inhibited the subsequent articulation and development of working class politics.[5] Nevertheless, the industrial working class figured in American electoral politics, and for some years after the realignment of the 1930s the Democratic Party was its vehicle. And, at least for a time, the Democrats acted like labor parties elsewhere, supporting new policies which extended legal protections to unions and actually facilitating membership growth, with the result that at the close of the Second World War union density levels in the United States were about as high as in Western Europe. Moreover, as elsewhere, the unions in turn served as an organizing infrastructure for Democratic vote mobilization, so that in these respects, at least, the United States also witnessed the development of something like a labor party.

The rise of new political formations also spurred new theories of how the society that people knew was organized, and how it could be changed. The growth of the industrial working class and its characteristic

---

4 On the importance of class cleavages in structuring and freezing contemporary political alignments, see S. M. Lipset and S. Rokkan, "Cleavage structures, party systems and voter alignments: an introduction," in *Party Systems and Voter Alignments*, ed. S. M. Lipset and S. Rokkan (New York: Free Press, 1967), pp. 1–64.

5 On the critical role of political mobilization in shaping or failing to shape "class sentiments" in the United States, see R. Oestreicher, "Urban working-class political behavior and theories of American electoral politics, 1870–1940," *Journal of American History*, 74, 4 (March 1988), pp. 1268–9.

union and party formations encouraged interpretations of political life which stressed the centrality of the new classes and conflicts created by industrial capitalism. This Marxist intellectual tradition was inaugurated even as industrialization began, in the mid-nineteenth century. In an important sense, it was the Marxist tradition that created the proletariat, and also created its antagonist, the bourgeoisie. And Marxism also posited that, as industrial capitalism advanced, the potential and transforming power of the proletariat would also grow, even as its misery increased. This was a theory about power so compelling that it created power, both by pointing to the institutional levers of worker power in industrial relations, and by enobling the particular struggles of workers with the mission of historical agency.

By the end of the century, with the winning of the franchise and the growth of labor-based political parties, these ideas about class power that inhered in the institutions of industrial capitalism were being reformulated – not only by Eduard Bernstein but by Engels himself – as ideas about electoral power that inhered in the institutions of the national state and representative democracy. In this context, the growing power of the proletariat rested on its numbers. As industrial capitalism advanced, not only would the power of workers as a force of production increase, but so would its numbers grow, as all of society would be absorbed into the two great classes, the bourgeoisie and the proletariat. Growing numbers, and especially numerical majorities, opened another and different route to power for the working class in the influence it could exert on the national state. True, many of the leaders of the Second International furiously disagreed with the notion of an electoral path to proletarian power. However, among the leaders of the trade union and party formations generated by industrial capitalism, the view that labor-based political parties were vehicles for the rise of the proletariat and the transformation of society clearly prevailed.

These twin power analyses, the one focusing on the power that workers could exert because they had leverage in the mass production industries, the other focusing on the power that worker citizens could exert because their votes could be organized to control the state and because the nation state itself was the very nexus of power, were at the ideological heart of labor politics, along with the conviction that the politics of workers was inevitably politics in the general interest.[6] For almost a century, these ideas lent energy and confidence to labor efforts because they showed how workers could exert power on the institutions that dominated social life, and they also lent elan to labor struggles because they asserted that these were struggles on behalf of all humankind.

The main political project of labor parties became the use of state power to develop the welfare state, by which I mean both the range of

6 On the argument that the melding of particularistic claims to the general interest was the "unique and extraordinary" feature of the workers' movement, see Raymond Williams, in Hobsbawm, *The Forward March of Labour Halted?*, p. 144.

income and health programs that shield workers from biographical or market exigencies, and the macroeconomic policies intended to regulate and stabilize growth. There were, of course, other more revolutionary currents in labor politics, and there were moments when these currents seemed ascendant. But for most of their histories, labor parties have responded to the constraints and opportunities of both industrial capitalism and electoral politics by promoting programs to moderate the effects of capitalist markets rather than to transform them. I need to take some care here, since welfare state programs were often initiated and supported by diverse elite alliances. As usual, however, the issue is complicated, since labor disturbances, and the effort to curb the electoral growth of labor parties, no doubt helped spur elite initiatives. It is also true that welfare state programs were influenced by distinctive national traditions, particularly by religious traditions.[7] Different national configurations of welfare state policy show the strong markings of these diverse origins.[8] But whatever the origins, labor party strength in government appears to have ensured the enlargement of the programs, particularly in the 1960s, when the great expansion of the welfare state occurred in most Western countries.[9] And labor parties also used their

7 On this point, and for a more general discussion of the importance of altruistic cultural traditions in shaping welfare state programs, see M. Paci, "The welfare state as a problem of hegemony," *Planning Theory Newsletter* (Summer 1989), pp. 3–22.

8 On the politics of the origins of welfare state programs, see for example H. Heclo, *Modern Social Politics in Britain and Sweden* (New Haven, CT: Yale University Press, 1974); P. Flora and J. Alber, "Modernization, democratization and the development of welfare states in Western Europe," in *The Development of Welfare States in Europe and America*, ed. P. Flora and A. Heidenheimer (New Brunswick, NJ: Transaction Books, 1981), pp. 37–80. Gøsta Esping-Andersen develops a typology of conservative, liberal, and socialist welfare state regimes, reflecting the constellations of power under which national welfare states were constructed in *The Three Worlds of Welfare Capitalism* (Princeton, NJ: Princeton University Press, 1990). And Hans Keman develops another typology, emphasizing differences in social democratic (or labor) parties in different countries, in "Social democracy and welfare," *Netherlands Journal of Social Sciences*, 26, 1 (April 1990), pp. 17–34.

9 For a review of efforts to measure the impact of labor party power on welfare state growth see M. Shalev, "The social democratic model and beyond: two generations of comparative social research on the welfare state," *Comparative Social Research*, 6 (1983), pp. 315–52. See also G. Esping-Andersen, "Power and distributional regimes," *Politics and Society*, 14, 2 (1985), especially p. 249, table 2, which shows the remarkable increase in labor influence on social security expenditures over time. See also W. Korpi, "Power, politics, and state autonomy in the development of social citizenship," *American Sociological Review*, 54, 3 (June 1989), pp. 309–28. I should also point out that the 1960s expansion may also have owed a good deal of its impetus to the historic escalation of labor unrest in that decade, to which neither labor parties nor their trade union allies contributed. On the 1960s surge of worker protest, see G. Arrighi, "Marxism and its history," *New Left Review*, 179, especially p. 49.

governmental power to promote the range of post Second World War economic stabilization policies which, together with income protections, came to be known as Keynesianism. As Przeworski says, Keynesianism was important. It not only provided guidelines for administering capitalist economies, but justified policies that favored the working class, in terms that, like Marxism, "granted universalistic status to the interests of workers."[10]

For a long time, the political landscape created by these developments was taken for granted, as were the predictions that the industrial working class would steadily enlarge, along with its distinctive political formations and its twin sources of power in industrial capitalism and political democracy. It was in a way a momentous development. As Hobsbawm says in retrospect about the British Labour Party, "A class party of labor ... became the mass party of the British working class ... by giving unity to the class consciousness of this class as a whole, and offering, in addition to the defence of material or other special interests, confidence, self-respect and hope of a different and better society."[11] To be sure, after the first decades of the twentieth century, the proportional size of the working class did not actually grow very much, and in some countries it even began to decline.[12] Nevertheless, labor-based parties held their own, sustained on the one hand by the trade union and welfare state infrastructures they had helped to create, and on the other hand by the economic stability and growth yielded by Keynesian policies. Moreover, successful macroeconomic management and the ideological moderation that success encouraged, along with the expansion of welfare state employment, created new sources of support for labor parties in the middle class salariat. The vote totals of labor-based parties remained at least stable through the 1960s, lending credibility to a program of labor reformism through electoral politics.

Deindustrialization and Labor Parties

The story of the decline of labor politics is the mirror image of the story of its rise. If industrial capitalism and the democratic nation state nurtured labor politics, then the economic transformation of industrial societies, together with the declining importance of the nation state in an international economy, spelled trouble. And, indeed, both the political formations and intellectual outlooks associated with industrial era politics are in upheaval. Support for labor-based political parties and the welfare state institutions they helped sustain and expand is eroding everywhere in the West, including in the fabled social democracies of the

10   A. Przeworski, *Capitalism and Social Democracy* (Cambridge: Cambridge University Press, 1985).
11   Hobsbawm, *The Forward March of Labour Halted?*, p. 71.
12   See Przeworski and Sprague, *Paper Stones*, p. 30, table 2.2.

Figure 1.1   The trend in class voting in four western democracies, 1948–83.
Alford index of class voting.

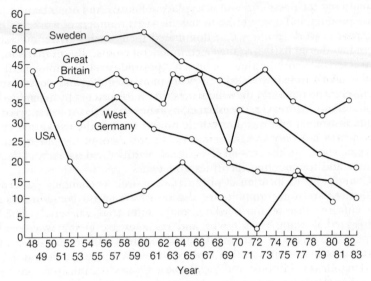

Source: R. Inglehart, "The persistence of materialist and postmaterialist value orientations," *European Journal of Political Research*, 11 (1983), pp. 81–2.

Scandinavian countries, as an aspect of what appears to be a general process of partisan decomposition and fractionalization associated with post-industrial trends.[13] Figure 1.1 illustrates the trend.

The scope of this development is evidence that large-scale influences are at work. The industrial order within which these parties emerged and grew is giving way to a new international economic order, variously characterized as postfordist and postindustrial. This means that in Western Europe and North America, the old working class based in mining and heavy industry is shrinking, and its unions are contracting. True, other sorts of employment are expanding in at least some of these countries, and especially in the United States where low wage service jobs have proliferated. Still, the mass production industries were at the very core of the class politics generated by industrialism, and their contraction inevitably has a telling effect on labor-based political parties.

13   For a discussion of the secular decline in social class voting, see R. J. Dalton, S. C. Flanagan and P. A. Beck, *Electoral Change in Advanced Industrial Democracies: Realignment or Dealignment?* (Princeton, NJ: Princeton University Press, 1984), especially pp. 29–30, 352–3, and 453–5.

The shift from large-scale industrial establishments to more decentralized production locations, and from industrial to service employment, has
also altered the possibilities of workplace solidarity and organization. The
mass production factory brought together vast numbers of workers under
one roof in work routines that dominated their waking lives, and joined
them together in battles against a common antagonist. By comparison, the
characteristic work settings of much "postindustrial" employment are
small and dispersed, work schedules are more irregular, and work routines
themselves do not build the solidarities that were fostered by assembly-line
production.[14] Moreover, the expansion of the service sector has spurred the
influx of women and racial or ethnic minorities into the workforce. All of
this means not only the reduction of the numbers of the old industrial
working class, but the erosion of old class identities and issues, and the rise
of new and fragmenting identities and issues.

Changes in the location of production, as well as changing patterns of
settlement and consumption, are also transforming the communities and
the culture even of those who remain industrial workers.[15] The old
segregated working class towns and enclaves are giving way to more
dispersed patterns of settlement; television and a life organized around
patterns of mass consumption replace the working class pub and insular
working class traditions; and locally based party organizations give way
to national media campaigns. And new generations come of age in a
world where class and class conflict no longer seem salient.[16] Inevitably
as a result of all these developments, the cultural glue of the working
class is dissolved and the old working class organizational bastions in the
trade unions, local parties and government agencies are enfeebled, even
as they are also hobbled by the problems of maintaining schlerotic
organizations in a period of decline.[17]

Perhaps most important, the confidence and elan which labor politics
gained from the twin power analyses which guided and inspired it are
fading, because the analyses do not seem to fit the contemporary world.
The once-stirring idea that the working class could organize to wield

---

14 For a discussion of the variable impact of industrial restructuring on union
strength see D. Kettler and V. Meja, "Social progress after the age of progressiv-
ism: the end of trade unionism in the West?," Working Paper 17, The Jerome
Levy Economics Institute of Bard College, Annandale-On-Hudson, NY, 1989.
On restructuring and unionism in Italy, see R. M. Locke, "The resurgence of
local unions: industrial restructuring and industrial relations in Italy," *Politics
and Society*, 18, 3 (September 1990), pp. 347–79.
15 On this dimension of postindustrial change, see S. Lash and J. Urry, *The
End of Organized Capitalism* (Cambridge: Polity Press, 1987).
16 On this point, see Dalton et al., *Electoral Change in Advanced Industrial Democracies*, p. 353.
17 On the erosion of class attachments among workers, including attachments
to unions, see W. Korpi, *The Working Class in Welfare Capitalism* (London: Routledge and Kegan Paul, 1978).

power over industrial capitalism has lost its force as industrial capitalism has reorganized domestically and dispersed globally, disorganizing the working class and escaping its leverage. Similarly the idea that workers could transform their societies by the power they exercised as citizens in the democratic nation state has lost credibility, because the nation state seems only one player, and often a minor player, in a world dominated by international market organizations. After all, labor party constituencies everywhere watched as the French Socialists gained state power in alliance with the Communists in the early 1980s and rapidly began to implement a left Keynesian "common program," only to be forced to their knees by the combined response of French and international capital. As George Ross shows in his essay, when the Socialists reemerged later in the decade, they had learned the lesson taught by international markets well.

Does Politics Matter?

Still, this market-driven account is not the whole story. I said earlier that historical explanations of the rise of labor politics which focus mainly on the determining influence exerted by economic structures miss important variations in national experience. As the essays which follow make clear, so do economistic explanations miss variations in the course of labor politics in particular nations under postindustrial conditions. I think it indisputable that labor parties as a group have been badly jostled by the impact of shifts in the world economy on the constituencies, infrastructures, and intellectual moorings of labor parties. Nevertheless, the differences between labor parties is large, in ways that are turning out to matter both for the future of labor politics, and for the pattern of postindustrial restructuring in different countries.

One obvious difference is in the extent of labor party losses, which vary in ways not predicted by the impact of postindustrial trends, as table 1.1 shows. Thus, as Ivor Crewe demonstrates in his essay on the British Labour Party, labor party support in Britain slipped much faster than economic change or its correlates would predict. In Sweden it slipped less. In turn, labor parties that have continued to wield government power have been able to buffer the impact of deindustrialization on party constituencies and party infrastructure. Sweden under the Social Democrats, for example, boasted very low unemployment levels even in the 1980s, partly because of its system for creating jobs and retraining workers, and also because it maintained and even expanded its large welfare state programs. (The Swedish political tides have very recently shifted toward greater public austerity, however, as I will momentarily note.)

There is also growing evidence that labor governments are more successful not only in mitigating the costs of postindustrial transformation, but in orchestrating adaptations to an international economy in

Table 1.1 The Left's vote in economically developed democracies, 1944–1978 to 1979–1988

Country	Total Left vote			Social democrat/labor vote			Communist vote		
	1944–78 (%)	1979–88[a] (%)	Change (%)	1944–78 (%)	1979–88[a] (%)	Change (%)	1944–78 (%)	1979–88[a] (%)	Change (%)
(Greece)	n.a.	(51.9)[b]	n.a.	n.a.	(39.8)	n.a.	n.a.	(12.1)	n.a.
Sweden	51.2	49.9	−1.3	46.0	44.3	−0.7	5.2	5.6	+0.4
France	43.3	49.5	+6.2	18.3	30.6	+12.3	23.4	12.4	−11.0
(Spain)	n.a.	(48.9)	n.a.	n.a.	(40.4)	n.a.	n.a.	(6.4)	n.a.
Austria	47.9	48.0	+0.1	44.9	47.2	+2.3	3.0	0.8	−2.2
Denmark	45.4	47.8	+2.4	37.1	32.4	−4.7	3.8	1.1	−2.7
Australia	46.3	47.0	+0.7	45.7	47.0	+1.3	0.6	0.1	−0.5
Norway	50.5	45.9	−0.6	44.0	40.2	−3.8	3.9	0.3	−3.6
Italy	42.7	44.6	+1.9	13.6	11.8	−1.8	25.4	30.0	+4.6
New Zealand	44.9	43.2	−1.7	44.9	43.2	−1.7	0.1	0.0	−0.1
(Portugal)	n.a.	(44.7)	n.a.	n.a.	(27.7)	n.a.	n.a.	(16.7)	n.a.
Israel	48.6	41.3	−7.3	44.6	34.7	−9.9	3.0	3.5	+0.5
Finland	46.5	40.2	−6.3	25.9	24.9	−1.0	20.6	13.9	−6.7
Germany	39.1	40.4	+1.3	37.0	39.4	+2.4	2.1	1.0	−0.9

Luxembourg	46.4	36.8[c]	−9.6	34.0	29.0	−5.0	11.2	7.1	−4.1
Japan	34.3	34.8	+0.5	27.7	25.5	−2.2	5.1	9.3	+4.2
Netherlands	36.1	34.4	−1.7	28.3	30.8	+2.5	4.8	1.5	−3.3
Iceland	33.3	34.0	+0.7	14.5	14.8	+0.3	17.1	16.8	−0.3
United Kingdom	44.7	31.8	−12.9	44.5	31.8	−12.7	0.2	0.0	−0.2
Belgium	35.6	29.9	−5.7	21.1	28.0	−3.1	4.5	1.4	−3.1
Switzerland	28.3	24.3[d]	−4.0	25.4	21.9	−3.5	2.9	1.3	−1.6
Canada	14.5	19.3	+4.8	14.1	19.4	+5.3	0.4	0.1	−0.3
Ireland	12.2	8.3	−3.9	12.2	8.3	−3.9	0.0	0.0	0.0
All (mean)[e]	39.6	37.6	−2.0	31.7	30.3	−1.4	6.9	5.3	−1.6

n.a., not applicable.

"Total Left" includes extreme Left, regional socialist, left radical and "Socialist Peoples" parties and can therefore add up to more than the combined social democrat/labor and communist vote; Green parties are excluded. Right-wing or Centerist breakaways from social democratic/labor parties are excluded (e.g. British SDP; Australian Democratic Labour Party).

[a] Or most recent three elections, if fewer than three held since 1978.

[b] Includes 1977 election.

[c] Includes 1974 election.

[d] Includes 1977 election.

[e] Excludes "interrupted" democracies (Greece, Spain, Portugal).

Source: I. Crewe, "The decline of labour and the decline of Labour," Essex Papers in Politics and Government, 65 (September 1989)

ways that sustain growth levels and market shares over time.[18] All in all,
the evidence suggests that the complex of policies associated with labor
party governments, including government economic planning capacities,
centralized unions, and strong welfare state programs, work not only to
humanize economic transition, but to rationalize it. Both productivity
and market shares seem to be holding up better where labor parties are
strong than under the neo-*laissez-faire* regimes in Great Britain and the
United States.[19] And, of course, successful economic management by
labor governments shores up the electoral support that makes this kind
of postindustrial Keynesianism possible in the first place.

Taken as a group, these essays argue that the political conditions
specific to different countries have mattered a great deal in accounting
for the variable fate of labor parties (see table 1.1) and their policies.
The terrain they explore is complicated, and the authors themselves
have different perspectives. Nevertheless, I think a number of consistent
themes emerge from these accounts. One has to do with a complex
heritage of national political institutions, and of labor party infrastructure and ideologies, which together constitute a kind of historically
accumulated topography of obstructions to new political adaptations to
new conditions. Thus what emerges as the strong argument explaining
differences in the fate of labor parties is the great and constraining
weight of the politics of the past. A historical politics creates institutional
structures, policies, party organizations, and ideologies that have to be
treated as largely given by particular actors at particular times and
places. Political actors are constrained not only by aspects of the economy that are beyond their reach. They are also constrained by the
accumulated consequences of a history of strategic politics. The politics
of the past thus comes to constitute the objective conditions which
confront new generations of political actors, and also helps construct the
collectivities we call political actors.[20]

But politics is not only a legacy of constraints. Strategic political
actors continually try to reshape or overcome old constraints, and to create
new ones. The political topography constantly shifts, as calculating

18   See A. Hicks, "Social democratic corporatism and economic growth," *Journal of Politics*, 50 (1988), pp. 677–704; P. Lange and G. Garrett, "Performance
in a hostile world: economic growth in capitalist democracies," *World Politics*,
38 (1986), pp. 517–45; R. Friedland and J. Sanders, "The public economy and
economic growth in Western market economies," *American Sociological Review*, 50
(1985), pp. 421–37.
19   For a recent discussion, see B. Jessop, K. Bonnett, and S. Bromley, "The
Thatcher balance-sheet," *New Left Review*, 179 (January–February 1990),
pp. 81–102.
20   Peter Hall discusses some of these same factors under the rubric of "organization." Organization, he says, not only facilitates the expression of interests,
but helps shape interests, and also affects the nature of the policies produced in
reflection of interests, and their implementation. See *Governing the Economy* (Cambridge: Polity Press, 1986), especially pp. 232–3.

political actors work to alter features of political institutions, party organization, or the character of symbolic appeals (and also try to use politics to alter economic constraints). I will draw on the essays that follow to illustrate dimensions of what I call the political topography and of strategic efforts to alter that topography.

Electoral institutions and alliances

Labor parties competing in elections have always needed electoral support beyond the working class, in part because the working class never actually became a majority, and in any case the working class was never unanimous in its support for labor parties. As Przeworski proclaims, "The crucial choice was whether to participate."[21] Once the decision was made to compete in elections, the electoral representative system itself, and the principle of majority rule on which it rests, forced labor parties to try to build alliances. But alliances with whom? The impact of economic change on the labor party vote has depended in part on the kinds of alliances which these parties constructed at key turning points in their history. The weakness of labor politics in the United States owes a good deal to the fragility of the alliance on which it rested between the northern working class and a backward and racist rural oligarchy in the south. In contrast, social democratic parties in Scandinavia forged alliances with small farmer parties which posed less restrictive conditions on labor party strategy and were also more durable. Indeed, Göran Therborn's essay on the Swedish Social Democrats attributes at least part of their contemporary success to the distinctive politics of the contemporary successor to the farmers' party which, while it is only a sometimes ally, nevertheless helps to prevent the development of a coordinated bourgeois opposition.[22]

The electoral coalitions on which labor party success depends, however, are not fixed, but the object of strategic maneuvering, especially at a time when exogenous economic and social change makes electoral allegiances unstable. Numerous examples can make the point. The American Republican party worked actively to whip up the racial fears that were undermining the Democratic party, and that in fact destroyed its southern base. For their part, labor parties are not oblivious to the problem and have actively pursued new constituency support, particularly among women, environmentalists, and the middle class salariat, to compensate for a contracting industrial working class. Therborn credits

21 Przeworski, *Capitalism and Social Democracy*, p. 7.
22 The bourgeois parties in Norway have also been plagued by divisions, helping to account for the strength of labor parties there as well. See J. Fagerberg, A. Cappelen, L. Mjoset, and R. Skarstein, "The decline of social democratic state capitalism in Norway," *New Left Review*, 181 (1990), pp. 60–94. Esping-Andersen makes the point that, while Austrian and Swedish labor have comparable resources, the bourgeois block in Austria is unified. See Esping-Andersen, "Power and distributional regimes." p. 226.

the Swedish Social Democrats for their flexible and opportunistic use of environmental concerns and gender appeals to recruit voters. George Ross depicts the French Socialists as supremely adaptive, easily shedding the baggage of their common front with the Communists in favor of neo-liberal growth-oriented policies and a technocratic cadre and style which could win support from the middle class.

State centralization and decentralization

The organization of the state itself also constitutes both inherited topography and an arena of strategic maneuvering. Neil Bradford and Jane Jenson, for example, emphasize the difficulties posed for the Canadian New Democratic Party and its union supporters by state decentralization. The challenge to this minority third party was to develop an electoral strategy responsive to the problems posed by foreign economic penetration and domestic economic restructuring. But the challenge was made far more difficult by constitutional decentralization which forced the party to contend not only with the economic reality of regional diversity, but with the fragmenting political reality of strong provincial governments. Similarly, my account of the travails of the American Democratic party also emphasizes the importance of constitutional arrangements in accounting for the failure of the party to develop along the lines of labor parties elsewhere. A constitutionally fragmented and decentralized government structure not only gave privileged access to sectional and interest group forces, but also had the effect of disorganizing the party, making coherent strategy and organization unlikely if not impossible.

State structures are also the objects of partisan contention. Although these papers do not devote much attention to such strategies, the Thatcher regime was persistent in its efforts to strip local governments of money and authority, in an effort to stymie those local governments which remained Labour Party bastions.[23] The Reagan administration also was persistent in its efforts to shift power in the federal system by promoting changes in federal grant-in-aid programs – some already pioneered by the earlier Republican administration of Richard Nixon – that reduced the funds and authority of the big city bastions of the Democratic Party. The federal contribution to municipal budgets plummeted, from 26 percent in 1978 to 8 percent in 1987.[24]

The welfare state

Labor party policies also contributed to the creation of new structures which then came to be part of the topography of postindustrial politics.

23 For examples of this kind of Thatcher strategy, see Hall, *Governing the Economy*, especially pp. 127–9.
24 D. Kirschten, "More problems, less clout," *National Journal* (August 12, 1989), p. 2030.

Where welfare state institutions were extensive, and not so closely market conditioned, these institutions have worked to shield party constituencies from market exigencies, and simultaneously to limit the strategies of opposition parties and investor interest groups striving to adapt to a new international division of labor. The characteristic elements of strong welfare states include policies which sustain high levels of employment, provide income protections for those who are pushed out of the labor market, and create a large public service sector. Together with strong unions, these policies delimit national adaptations to international competition. Gøsta Esping-Andersen's essay comparing postindustrial labor market patterns in Sweden, Germany, and the United States provides evidence of the bearing of different welfare state systems on labor markets. More generally, where income protections (and strong unions) shield workers from the pressures on jobs and wages which might otherwise be generated by international labor markets (and by national capitalists taking advantage not only of the reality but of the spectre of international wage competition to shore up profits by cutting wages and taxes), the adaptation to postindustrialism is less likely to take the form of expanded low wage employment and public sector cutbacks, and more likely to take the form of capital intensive investment and expanded public employment.[25]

Moreover, a large public sector also means large public employee unions, whose membership is largely female and supportive of the welfare state. The support of these unions has partly compensated for the vote loss that the Social Democrats in Sweden suffered from postindustrial economic change, a pattern that is replicated in other Scandinavian countries. Indeed, the development of a partisan gender gap in a number of Western countries suggests that women voters generally are turning out to be an important potential constituency for labor-based parties, and survey evidence suggests that this is related to their strong support for welfare state policies. Strong welfare states may thus generate important new coalition partners for labor parties in a postindustrial era.

It hardly needs to be pointed out that welfare state programs have been the focus of political battle, particularly in the United States and Great Britain where ascendant conservative parties have succeeded in forcing significant cutbacks in expenditures and coverage. Moreover, welfare state institutions cannot be described on only one dimension, as merely strong or weak, as many studies that measure "welfare state effort" by expenditures imply. There are also important variations among welfare states having to do with the specific structure of programs and the political interests created by these structures. Claus Offe's essay is about the West German welfare state, which is a relatively big spender

25   For comparative data showing the relationship between the institutional and political position of labor and the rate of growth in public employment, see M. F. Masters and J. D. Robertson, "Class compromises in industrial democracies," *American Political Science Review*, 82, 4 (December 1988), pp. 1183–202.

and has not so far been subjected to the relatively large cutbacks that have occurred in the United States. But Offe is not optimistic. He argues that economic shifts are combining with the restructuring of the German programs to marginalize increasing numbers of people, thus undermining popular confidence in the programs and fracturing support, in ways that ultimately pave the way for cutbacks in response to post-industrial pressures.[26]

Party infrastructure

Political parties depend on an infrastructure to create and sustain constituency support. Labor parties have mainly relied on unions, and in some places on branches of the state apparatus that they came to control, particularly local governments. Where this apparatus remains vigorous, it has helped to buffer the impact of postindustrialism. But infrastructures also develop an organizational dynamic of their own which can have perverse effects on the party, as internal oligarchies hobble adaptations to new political conditions. Thus programs and agencies originally created to organize constituency support may ultimately become political liabilities. In his essay on the troubles of the big city Democratic parties, Alan DiGaetano shows that urban development policies in the United States, begun in the New Deal period in part to shore up the big city partners of the national Democrats, were by the 1950s implemented by local "progrowth" regimes in ways that had perverse consequences for the fortunes of the national party.

Asher Arian and Ilan Talmud provide a particularly dramatic example of the costs to the Israeli Labor Party of its party infrastructure. In this instance, the vast apparatus of the Histadrut labor federation and the jobs and benefits it generated for European Israelis helped to foster the deep animosities among newer immigrants that eventually fueled the rise of the opposition Likud coalition. And once the Likud gained power, a Labor Party saddled with the imperative of maintaining the state-dependent Histadrut was forced to participate in a Likud-dominated government for fear of jeopardizing the funds and programs on which its infrastructure depended.

Labor Party infrastructures have naturally become the object of attack by conservative parties, and have often proved vulnerable, in part because the rigidity of the infrastructure organizations themselves has weakened popular support for them. The Thatcher program for the privatization of council housing, for example, was a direct assault on what had been a Labour Party effort not only to provide desperately needed housing to its working class constituency, but to consolidate working class voters and a working class culture in bright socialist

26 Offe's emphasis on status divisions encouraged by contemporary welfare state programs is at least reminiscent of Lipset's much earlier characterization of the importance of status groupings in German politics. See Lipset, "Political cleavages in developed and emerging polities," especially pp. 26–8.

communities. But council housing became something quite different, and privatization initiatives proved popular in part because of widespread dissatisfaction with grim and poorly administered council houses. Similarly, the extraordinarily aggressive campaign against American unions by employer groups and the Reagan administration was as successful as it was because the charge that the unions were merely a "special interest" was not entirely farfetched.

Ideology

The substance of popular politics depends on interpretations which tell people what is within the realm of the politically possible, and what is naturalized as beyond the reach of politics. Interpretations also organize the realm of the political, helping to shape collectivities and cleavages, and to identify issues of contention. The construction of this political culture is in large measure the achievement of political parties who mobilize people around a common set of programs and symbols.[27] Parties in power are especially effective in constructing political interpretations since they have at their disposal the enormous resources of the state to communicate definitions and, indeed, to create realities consistent with those interpretations. But a party culture developed in the context of industrial politics is likely to stress identities and interests that can hobble the mobilization of new constituencies under new circumstances by stressing identities, symbols and arguments that seem old and tired.[28] Thus still another problem of the British Labour Party, as Joel Krieger argues in his examination of the party's future prospects, is that it failed to adapt appeals to take account of the identities and interests of the minorities and women who are its potential constituencies, just as it failed to adapt its productivist political arguments to the more fluid collective problems of a postindustrial era. Overcoming the dead weight of inherited labor party iconography can be wrenching, as illustrated by the extended conflict generated by leadership efforts to rename the Italian Communist party, or by the inability of the French Communist party to adapt its party symbols and arguments, as George Ross shows in accounting for the rise of the French Socialists.

I think, in fact, that the great battle of postindustrial politics is being fought on the terrain of ideology, and it may be here that the future prospects of labor parties are decided. So far, it is the bourgeoisie that has taken the strategic initiative, with an analysis of the power of capital in a global economy, and its transforming mission, that parallels and

27　See Lipset and Rokkan, "Cleavage structures, party systems and voter alignments." On the role of parties in class formation in particular, see A. Przeworski, "Proletariat into a class: the process of class formation from Karl Kautsky's 'The Class Struggle' to recent controversies," *Politics and Society*, 7, 4 (1977), pp. 343–402.
28　On this point, see Z. Bauman, "Britain's exit from politics," *New Statesman and Society* (July 29, 1988), pp. 34–48.

supersedes the ideology of labor power. Postindustrial economic developments have both inspired and justified new and winning arguments by
conservative parties and their business allies about the imperatives of
international markets, and the inevitable need to align domestic wages
and public policies with the terms of those markets. In this ideological
effort, not only is the power of capital and labor reversed, but so is their
moral standing, for it is capital and not labor that is the agency of
progress. The historic political mobilization of the right in the United
States that began in the 1970s is an example. The Republican Party and
its corporate interest group allies mobilized party and class resources to
promulgate arguments to the effect that, whatever else their merits, trade
union demands and welfare state programs constituted a drag on the
competitive position of the United States. And there is enough evidence
in the simultaneous contraction of the old domestic industries and the
proliferation of goods produced in Japan or Korea to make that argument seem very plausible. Indeed, so forceful has this ideological assault
proved that labor parties in most countries are deserting the field,
acknowledging the necessity of adapting to international markets and of
the austerity policies capital has demanded, arguing mainly their own
superior technical capacity to develop and administer the neo-liberal
policies that will match market imperatives. This is the main political
moral of Crewe's account of the changing strategies of the British
Labour Party and Ross's account of the French Socialists.

Future Prospects

This seems the worst of all possible moments to hazard predictions. As
I write these words in the fall of 1990, the Western economies seem to
be sliding into recession, and the electoral fortunes of both labor and
conservative parties are in flux. On the one hand, even such stalwarts of
labor politics as the Norwegian and Swedish parties are clearly faltering
as popular support slips and the parties reconnoiter. The Swedish Social
Democrats alternately promise further expansion of the welfare state and
tax cuts, labor unrest is growing and centralized wage bargaining seems
to be unraveling, and Sweden's share of the world market in manufactured goods is falling as the government searches for ways to translate
the profits of international Swedish corporations into domestic productivity growth.[29] Meanwhile, the rush of events in Eastern Europe has
also weakened social democracy symbolically, by generating a powerful
iconography fusing the ideas of the free market and democracy, as if
the one necessarily entailed the other. But so are the "hypercapitalist"
conservative parties of England and the United States showing evidence

29   See J. Pontusson, "Austerity, government crisis, and political realignment in
Sweden, 1989–90," Paper presented at the Annual Meeting of the American
Political Science Association, San Francisco, CA, September 1990.

of increasing internal disarray as both the Conservatives in Britain and the Republicans in the United States become more fractious in response to the slipping popularity polls and policy quandaries generated by general economic deterioration and the specific failures of national economic policies. And the disarray will surely worsen if the international economy continues its downward slide.

Still, even economic hard times and conservative disarray do not lead me to think a revival of labor politics as we once knew it is likely. Labor parties may win some elections, relying on the repertoire of strategies to cope with postindustrial decline described in these essays, including appeals to environmental concerns and to women, and the perfecting of classless appeals oriented to a generalized public opinion that Crewe calls "image management" and Bradford and Jenson call "contentless populism." But the specific economic and social arrangements which nourished the labor politics of the past have changed too much to expect the revival of class politics in familiar forms. Most telling to my mind, the twin power analyses which fueled the rise of labor politics by revealing the possibilities of worker power over a national capitalist class on the one hand, and over the sovereign nation state on the other, have lost their force because they do not match the institutional realities of the new world order of international capitalism. It is not that class inequities and conflicts of interest have faded. If anything, postindustrial trends have made class divisions sharper and harsher. But the strong articulation of these interests awaits the "construction of a new 'social imaginary,' capable of carrying a whole population forward."[30] Central to that social imaginary will be a new argument about the possibilities of popular power in postindustrial societies which, I firmly believe, the continuing experience of political conflict will begin to delineate. The largest significance of the different labor political configurations discussed in these essays may well be whether they constrain or nurture the new political movements and new political arguments that emerge as industrial era politics fades.

30 C. Leys, "Still a question of hegemony," *New Left Review*, 181 (May–June 1990), p. 128.

2

Labor Force Changes, Working Class Decline, and the Labour Vote: Social and Electoral Trends in Postwar Britain

Ivor Crewe

The history of political parties in the second half of this century is one of remarkable adaptation and continuity in the face of rapid social change. Since the Second World War, the economic structures of the developed democracies have been transformed by, first, the eclipse of agriculture and, more recently, de-industrialization and a "post-Fordist" reorganization of production; their social structures have been marked by urbanization and unparalleled affluence; their ethnic composition has changed through mass immigration; their cultural order has undergone a "silent revolution" of secularism, environmentalism and new cross-national and sub-national loyalties. Yet the party political response has been undramatic. What stands out from the broad long-term picture of party fortunes is the sheer electoral resilience of the major parties and ideological blocs. Christian democracy has overcome the decline of religious faith; agrarian parties have survived rural depopulation; and, despite impressions to the contrary, the Left has weathered – so far – the steady contraction of the industrial working class.

The electoral fate of the Left since the war is displayed in chapter 1, table 1.1. It compares the Social Democratic/Labour, Communist and "total Left" vote in the twenty uninterrupted democracies of the developed world between the three postwar decades (1944–78) and the most recent decade (1979–88). The "total Left" vote did fall between 1944–78 and 1979–88, but by a mere 2 percentage points, from 39.6 to 37.6 percent; the Social Democratic/Labour vote dropped by 1.5 points. This global figure, moreover, masks some recent successes for the non-

Communist Left, notably the Socialists in France and the Labour parties in Australia and New Zealand, and also reflects the solidity of the Left vote wherever the non-Communist Left is the dominant governing party, as in Sweden and Norway, or where it regularly takes office, as in Austria, Denmark, Germany, and the Netherlands. The decline of labor, therefore, does not necessarily mean "the Decline of Labor." Simple sociological reductionism does not work. Almost all labor-based parties have found ways to survive and indeed flourish.

The Electoral Decline of
the British Labour Party

The one, massive, exception is the British Labour Party. Between 1944–78 and 1979–88 the average Labour vote fell from 44.5 to 31.8 percent. No party of the Left has suffered such a sharp decline. The only near parallels are the French Communist party and Israel's Mapai/Labor party. But in France Communist losses have been more than made up by Socialist gains, so that the total Left vote increased; and in Israel the quite exceptional immigrant growth of the electorate, which has no equivalence elsewhere, has played a part. Moreover, the Left's electoral decline in Britain cannot be attributed to the collapse of the Communist vote or to the emergence of the Greens, neither of which has ever been a serious electoral force in Britain. Thus, by the 1980s there were only four democracies with a lower total Left vote than Britain. In two of these, Canada and Ireland, the Left has always been represented by a small minority party, vulnerable to a "third party squeeze" on its support; in the other two, Belgium and Switzerland, linguistic and denominational or religious/secular cleavages cut athwart and weaken the class-based Left–Right allegiances. No such factors apply in Britain.

Part of Labour's electoral slide – we shall estimate how much later – is perhaps the product of exceptional but short-lived political circumstances. But it would be oversanguine to portray Labour's recent electoral losses simply as three unlucky spins on the wheel of political fortune. The evidence, instead, is that Labour's decline is not only internationally unique but long term. As table 2.1 shows, the three recent elections mark a further stage in what transpires to be *more than three decades* of almost unremitting erosion of Labour support. At every election since 1951, with only two minor exceptions (1966 and 1987), an additional slice of the electorate has stopped voting Labour; added together the slices amount to a loss of over two-fifths of Labour's support between 1951 and 1987.[1] This gradual slide has attracted little attention

1   However, it can be argued that the decline in Labour's (and the Conservatives') share of the vote until 1970 was largely due to the increase in the number of Liberal candidates. See M. Linton, *Labour Can Still Win*, Fabian Society Tract 532, November 1988.

Table 2.1   Labour share of vote and electorate, United Kingdom,
1945–1987

General election	Labour share of:	
	Vote[a] (%)	Electorate[b] (%)
1945	47.9	36.4
1950	46.1	38.7
1951	48.8	40.3
1955	46.4	35.6
1959	43.9	34.5
1964	44.1	34.0
1966	48.1	36.5
1970[c]	43.1	31.4
1974 (Feb)	37.1	29.0
1974 (Oct)	39.2	28.5
1979	37.0	28.1
1983	27.6	20.1
1987	30.8	23.2

[a] This table makes adjustment for the number of Liberal and other minor candidates. Their steady increase since 1955 partly accounts for the decline of the Labour (and Conservative) vote, but partly results from it too.

[b] These figures are based on the registered electorate in the United Kingdom, which will have people who had died, emigrated, or moved out of the constituency by the time the election took place. Adjustment for the age of the register at the time of the election would raise the figures (by 4 percent on average) but not alter the direction or magnitude of the trend over the period.

[c] The voting age was lowered from 21 to 18 in 1969.

because it has not precluded Labour winning elections. But on the two postwar occasions that a Labour opposition defeated an incumbent Conservative government – 1964 and February 1974 – it "won" the elections by default: compared with the previous election it actually lost votes, but not by as much as the Conservatives. The long-term element in Labour's decline is also reflected by the fact that it is not confined to, or even concentrated in, the desertion of supporters disillusioned by Labour's record in government. On the contrary, its sharpest drops in support have occurred during periods of Opposition. In this respect, Labour's loss of votes in February 1974 and 1983 were particularly significant because on both occasions Labour was not simply out of office but in opposition to an unpopular government which was attacking the prerogatives of Labour's traditional constituencies – trade unionists, council house tenants, and welfare recipients.

A further reason for believing Labour's electoral crisis to be deep seated is that it encompasses more than the vote. If Labour's electoral decline in the Thatcher decade was simply the product of short-term adversity one would expect the indicators of more enduring loyalties to hold up, or at least to erode more gently. But in fact they have fallen in tandem with the vote. For example, the proportion of Labour "identifiers" in the electorate – a proven indicator of its long-term support – fell by a quarter, from 43 percent in 1964 (the first British election at which party identification was measured) to 32–3 percent in 1983–7.[2] By contrast, the level of Conservative identification in the electorate has barely changed. This ebbing away of Labour identifiers, moreover, has not left a pool of militant loyalists: the proportion of "very" or "fairly" strong Labour identifiers has also dropped, from 37 percent in 1964 to 22–5 percent in 1983–7. The trend in party membership tells a similar story. Expressed as a proportion of its vote, Labour Party membership is a mere 2.9 percent, which is probably lower than in every European democracy except Ireland and the Netherlands.[3]

Labour's electoral decline is internationally unique; it is long term; and it extends deeper than the vote. It may well not be fully reversible in the short term. The three election defeats of the past decade have left Labour so far behind the Conservatives in the popular vote that the electoral turnround needed to restore Labour to office at the next election would have to be extraordinary by historical standards.

Nor is comfort for the Labour Party to be found in the younger generation of electors. One hint (although no guarantee) of a potential Labour revival would be an increasing Labour vote and strengthening of Labour partisanship among successive cohorts of new electors; or, at the very least, a trend line that slopes down more gently than for the electorate as a whole. But the Labour vote, the proportion of Labour identifiers, and the strength of commitment among Labour identifiers has fallen much more sharply among the successive cohorts of new entrants than among Labour identifiers as a whole.[4] Unless these recent entry cohorts strengthen their Labour partisanship as they mature through their twenties and thirties at a faster rate than their predecessors

---

2 See I. Crewe, "The decline of labour and the decline of Labour," *Essex Paper in Politics and Government* No. 44, table 3.

3 See S. Bartolini, "The membership of mass parties: the social democratic experience, 1889–1978," in *Western European Party Systems: Continuity and Change*, ed. H. Daalder and P. Mair (London and Beverly Hills, CA: Sage, 1983), pp. 177–220 (p. 187). The Labour Party's official individual membership fell from 304,000 in 1981 – when reliable figures became available for the first time – to 289,000 by the end of 1987, a drop of 5 percent. See P. Wintour, "Labour recruiters to woo the working class," *The Guardian*, January 16, 1988.

4 Crewe, "The decline of labour and the decline of Labour," table 4.

we may expect a continuing dilution of overall Labour support as older generations die out.

Two qualifications need to be made to this story of decline. The Conservative vote, as well as Labour's, has fallen since the 1950s: its landslide parliamentary majority of 102 seats at the last election rested upon only 42.3 percent of the vote, the smallest share to elect a majority government since 1922. However, the Conservative decline is gentler and more erratic than Labour's, bearing none of the hallmarks of a long-term trend. Falls are confined to periods of Conservative government (notably 1959–64 and 1970–4), followed by recovery in opposition, and have not been accompanied by a parallel decline in the level of Conservative Party identification. Conservative losses are cyclical and short term, Labour's linear and long term.

Second, Labour's decline has been geographically uneven, especially in recent years. Between 1955 and 1987 Labour's share of the two-party vote fell by 6 percent overall: but in the South of England it fell by 9 percent whereas it *increased* by 9 percent in the north and by a massive 19 percent in Scotland. These regional disparities, moreover, have been particularly marked in the past decade.

Whatever their precise cause, they have one consequence of enormous significance for the British party system. The interaction of uneven economic growth, geographical region and prior party strength is drying up the supply of marginal seats, and the drought is likely to continue.[5] This is a decidedly mixed blessing for the Labour Party. On the one hand, its increasingly large majorities in the de-industrializing north and Scotland guarantees it a significant parliamentary presence even if its national vote deteriorates still further. On the other hand, the increasingly large swings required to gain Conservative seats makes its prospects of a parliamentary majority ever slimmer.

Structural Explanations for Labour's Decline

The decline of labor?

To describe Labour's electoral decline is relatively straightforward; to explain it convincingly much more complex. Long-term symptoms suggest long-term causes and the foremost candidate of these is the gradual transformation of Britain's occupational structure since the war, and in particular of Labour's electoral base among industrial manual workers. This part of the chapter, however, will show that, contrary to popular assumptions,[6] these mutations of the labor force can account for only

5 See J. Curtice and M. Steed, "Proportionality and exaggeration in the British electoral system," *Electoral Studies*, 5 (1986), pp. 209–28.
6 See, for example, E. J. Hobsbawm, *The Forward March of Labour Halted?* (London: Verso, in association with *Marxism Today* and New Left Books, 1981), which was particularly influential among the neo-Marxist intelligentsia.

part of the Labour Party's electoral misfortunes. The decline of Labour has proceeded much further and faster than the decline of labor; moreover, some shifts in the labor force have offered the Left opportunities for remobilization which, so far at least, have not been effectively exploited. Even if the decline of labor was the explanation, it would beg the question of why, alone among the major parties of the democratic Left, the Labour Party has failed to cope electorally with structural changes in the labor force. Political "agency" as well as economic "structure" must therefore account for part of Labour's electoral misfortunes.

The main features of Britain's changing occupational structure may be easily summarized. De-industrialization and the reorganization of production have produced a smaller labor force, a smaller working class, a contraction of trade unionism, mass unemployment, and a much larger "peripheral" workforce of part-time and temporary workers. The same processes have produced a rapidly expanding "service class" (or "salariat") of managers, administrators, and professional workers, substantially recruited from the children of the working class, and a "core" working class of skilled, secure, and well-paid workers in the multinational private sector. It has been accompanied by a "pink collar" revolution of women entering the labor force, mainly in routine white collar or lower professional jobs, and disproportionately on a part-time and short-term basis. These changes accelerated in the 1980s under the Thatcher governments, which attempted to return the British economy to the "discipline of the market" in order to reintegrate it into the world capitalist economy.

On the face of it, not all of these changes should necessarily disadvantage the Left. The shrinking of its social base among manual workers and trade unionists is clearly an electoral threat; but the return to high unemployment, the creation of a peripheral workforce and the entry of many more women into work (and trade unions) should be an electoral opportunity.

We turn first to changes within the labor force. Whatever definitions and schemas are employed, the post-war period has witnessed an unremitting and accelerating shrinkage of the manual working class. If the "working class" is conventionally but crudely defined as all manual workers, its size has fallen from 64 percent of the labor force in 1951 to 46 percent in 1986. If it is more narrowly defined as all rank-and-file manual employees (i.e. excluding the self-employed, foremen, and technicians) it has contracted in size from 47 percent of the electorate in 1964 (the earliest year for which figures are available) to 34 percent in 1983.[7] Either way it is now a *minority* class and will decline further in the foreseeable future.

It is worth noting – for the purposes of our later discussion about the Left's strategic options – that although all the nonmanual classes have

7 A. Heath, R. Jowell, and J. Curtice, *How Britain Votes* (Oxford: Pergamon, 1985), p. 36.

grown in size, the managerial and higher professional classes have grown fastest (from 7.4 to 18.5 percent between 1951 and 1981), the clerical employee category has grown least (from 10.4 to 14.5 percent), and the sales employee category has in fact declined. In other words, those occupational classes that are socially and economically most adjacent to the working class also show signs of stagnation or contraction.

But the shrinking of the working class is only partly responsible for the shrinking of the Labour vote. A comparison of the 1959 and 1987 elections makes the point. During this period the working class (here defined simply as manual workers) diminished in size by 18 percentage points.[8] Had its propensity to vote Labour rather than non-Labour remained constant, the Labour vote would have fallen 11 percentage points simply by virtue of the contraction of the working class. In fact, the Labour vote fell by fully 18 percentage points. This was because the Labour vote *within* the working class did not remain constant but itself dropped very sharply, from 63 percent in 1951 to 41 percent in 1987, while the working class Conservative vote remained the same. Nor was this sharp drop simply a function of Labour's across-the-board decline in popularity. Over the same period the middle class (nonmanual) Labour vote fell by a mere 4 percentage points. The diminishing size of the working class explains a portion of Labour's electoral decline. But the diminishing willingness of the working class to vote Labour explains an almost equal portion. The causes of Labour's decline are as much behavioral as structural.

Perhaps the reason is that industrialization has changed the composition as well as the size of the working class. De-industrialization has had four structural by-products for the working class, each with potential electoral significance for the Labour party: greater social mobility, internal migration, mass unemployment, and falling trade union membership. We shall see that social mobility and internal migration add structural reinforcement to the impact of the diminution in the working class but stop short of completing the explanation for Labour's electoral decline. We shall also see that mass unemployment and the fall in trade union membership offered opportunities for a remobilization of voters by the Left which the Labour Party failed to exploit. Let us examine each of the four structural changes in turn.

Social mobility

The postwar growth of nonmanual work, in particular the fast expansion of the "service" class has inevitably been accompanied by a marked increase in upward, intergenerational, social mobility. In 1949 21 percent of men were in a higher occupational class than their fathers; by

8 The figures quoted in this paragraph are taken from Heath et al., *How Britain Votes*, p. 30, and the BBC/Gallup election survey, June 10–11, 1987. See Crewe, "The decline of labour and the decline of Labour," table 7.

1972 the proportion was 32 percent; by 1983 38 percent. Over the same period downward mobility has decreased, from 27 percent in 1949 to 15 percent in 1983. The figures for upward mobility *out of the working class* are even more striking. In 1972 43 percent of working class fathers had sons in nonmanual work (comprising 16 percent in the professional and managerial "service" class); by 1983 the proportions were 53 percent and 22 percent respectively.[9] In other words, over half of the previous working class generation had seen their children move up and out of their class – one-third to the neighboring classes of routine nonmanual work, foremen, and technicians or to self-employment, one-fifth to the established middle classes. Surveys repeatedly show that social mobility undermines Labour's support. The upwardly mobile children of the working class are much less likely to vote Labour than their parents and there are not enough downwardly mobile children of the "intermediate" and "service" classes to compensate for the loss.[10]

Migration

Postwar de-industrialization has had a spatial as well as occupational impact on the British electorate. The "smokestack" areas of central Scotland, the north of England and South Wales have gradually lost population to the high-growth, high-tech service economies of the south. Within regions people have moved from town to country and from inner city to outer suburb.

On the face of it one would expect these demographic changes to erode Labour's popular base further. The Labour party has always been stronger in Scotland, the north and Wales than in the south and Midlands; and it normally polls better in the bigger cities than the smaller towns and villages. Regional and community differences in wealth and class structure are of course the main reason but, independently of that, region and community have exerted an additional influence: where people live, as well as what they do, shapes their vote. There are important "social neighborhood" effects: the more working class a neighborhood the higher the Labour proportion of the working class vote. And

9 The figures for all men are derived from A. Heath, *Social Mobility* (London: Fontana, 1981), p. 86, and J. Goldthorpe, in collaboration with C. Llewellyn and C. Payne, *Social Mobility and Class Structure in Modern Britain*, 2nd edn (Oxford: Clarendon Press, 1987), p. 263. The figures for working class fathers are taken from Goldthorpe, ibid., p. 263 (old scheme).

10 According to the most recent study of social mobility, conducted in March–July 1984, party support was as follows: non-mobile working class, Conservative 22, Labour 63, Liberal/SDP 15; upwardly mobile out of the working class, Conservative 41, Labour 35, Liberal/SDP 24; downwardly mobile into working class, Conservative 27, Labour 53, Liberal/SDP 19. The net impact on Labour support as a result of both upward and downward mobility was a loss of 3 percent. See G. Marshall, H. Newby, D. Rose, and C. Vogler, *Social Class in Modern Britain* (London: Hutchinson, 1988), p. 241.

such neighborhoods are more frequently found in the north than the south. In 1987 the proportion of working class electors living in a working class neighborhood was much higher in Scotland (67 percent) and the north (53 percent) than in the south of England (40 percent); similarly, the proportion living in a high unemployment neighborhood was considerably greater in Scotland (24 percent) and the north (22 percent) than in the south (5 percent).[11] The disappearance of the traditional, tightly knit, working class community around the pit or shipyard or steel works is therefore a double threat to Labour's electoral base. It means the departure of workers from communities with an established Labour culture of local trade unionism, the "co-op," and working mens' clubs; it also means the migration of workers to socially mixed neighborhoods which lack any such sense of working class identity, autonomy, and values.

However, the decline of Labour support cannot be explained in these terms alone: had class rates of voting within regions remained constant, migration would have lost Labour no more than 2 percent of the national vote. In fact, they have remained far from constant: regional disparities in class voting patterns have widened dramatically in recent years. In 1963–6 Labour was the majority choice of the working class in every region. By 1987 the working class Labour vote, following national trends, had declined everywhere, but by much less in Scotland (down 8 percent) and the north of England (down 11 percent) than in the south of England, where it was fully 28 percent lower. Labour remains the majority party (just) for manual workers in Scotland and the north; but in both 1983 and 1987 it ran well behind the Conservatives in the south, and, outside London, behind the Liberal/Social Democratic Party (SDP) Alliance too. In the 1960s Labour was a national class party; in the 1980s it had become a regional class party.

A variety of factors explain why working class voters have abandoned the Labour Party in so much larger numbers in the south than the north. Individual economic circumstances, the local class environment, and regional economic histories (and prospects) combine to reinforce working class identification and Labour support in the north and to undermine it in the South. So long as these regional inequalities persist, and the north–south, urban–rural drift proceeds, we may expect a further, slow, erosion of Labour support.

Unemployment

The rapid de-industrialization of Britain restored unemployment to its pre-war Depression levels. The process began in 1976, when at the prompting of the International Monetary Fund (IMF) the Labour

---

11 See J. Curtice, "One nation?", in *British Social Attitudes: the Fifth Report*, ed. R. Jowell, S. Witherspoon, and L. Brook (London: Gower, 1988), pp. 127–54 (p. 140).

government under Callaghan abandoned Keynesian demand management for monetarism, but it was taken much further by the first Thatcher
government. The official level of unemployment doubled under the
1974–9 Labour government from 2.6 to 5.7 percent, doubled again
to 11.4 percent by 1981 and touched 14 percent in 1983, after which
it trickled to 10–11 percent by 1987.[12] At the same time long-term
unemployment has increased: between 1977 and 1987 the proportion of
the unemployed without a job for at least a year rose from 25 percent to
43 percent. Centers of heavy industry – mainly in the north, Wales and
Scotland – have been particularly hard hit, as have the young and
blacks.

Unlike the two preceding by-products of de-industrialization, the return to mass unemployment should be a potent source of mobilization
for the Left. The proportion out of work at any one time remains small,
but add the recently unemployed, the dependents of the unemployed,
relatives of the unemployed (e.g. parents), and those in fear of redundancy
and the proportion is of course very much higher.[13] Since the 1930s
the Conservatives have been identified as the party of the (means-tested)
dole queue, Labour as the party of near-full employment *and* unemployment benefits for the unfortunate few: fears of a return to the 1930s were
an important source of Labour's election victory in 1945. Opinion polls
consistently show that Labour is the "preferred party" for dealing with
unemployment, by a comfortable margin, even when otherwise unpopular. At the 1983 election, survey respondents' choice of the "most important issue" was, overwhelmingly, unemployment; and of those citing it a
16 percent margin preferred Labour over the Conservatives to deal with
it. Nonetheless, Labour lost the election by a landslide.

What prevented the Labour Party from converting its potential support on the issue into actual votes? Post-election analysis provided
a number of answers. First, the unemployed themselves, unlike other
manual workers, *did* rally – or at least stick – to the Left. Employed
manual workers swung by 3.5 percent from Labour to Conservative;
unemployed manual workers, by contrast, swung by 4.5 percent, square
against the national trend, from Conservative to Labour.[14] Thus there

12   By June 1989 the official unemployment rate had fallen to 6.4 percent and
the proportion of the unemployed without a job for at least twelve months had
dropped to 38 percent.
13   In the BBC/Gallup survey of the 1987 election 9 percent of respondents
reported themselves as currently unemployed but 36 percent reported that they
or a member of their immediate family had "been unemployed or had great
difficulty in getting a job in the last three to four years." The figures for manual
workers were, respectively, 11 percent and 40 percent.
14   See Crewe, "The decline of labour and the decline of Labour," table 9. It is
perhaps worth noting that this figure might have been affected by the unusually
high proportion of the unemployed who voted Conservative in 1979 (38 percent),
itself a reaction against the record of the Labour government.

was an anti-Conservative backlash by the unemployed; but it did not extend to their more fortunate brothers. Moreover, its electoral impact was muted. For one thing, the unemployed have particularly low rates of electoral registration.[15] Apathy and fatalism, not radical dissent, is the typical response of the unemployed, especially the long-term unemployed. For another, concentrations of unemployment occur in what are already safe Labour areas such as Liverpool and Glasgow, where it has produced large swings to the Left but at almost no cost to the Conservatives who held virtually no seats there anyway.[16]

But the main reason that the Left failed to profit electorally from unemployment was that it lacked political credibility on the issue. "Agency" not "structure" was the major culprit. Both the public and the unemployed themselves placed the main blame for unemployment on the "world economy" rather than the government. Partly as a result, there was profound skepticism that a Labour government would do much better in the short term.[17] For most electors unemployment was a problem, not an issue; they saw Labour as the most concerned of the parties, but not necessarily the most competent. In the 1940s and 1950s wartime experience and the spread of Keynesian ideas persuaded voters that Labour's commitment to full employment was credible. In the 1980s, in the aftermath of a Labour government that had seen unemployment levels double, Labour's reliance on old Keynesian nostrums was not plausible. It paid the price for past failures of government and for a continuing bankruptcy of ideas. It lost the political argument.

The decline of union membership

"The Labour party," as Ernest Bevin put it, "grew out of the bowels of the trade union movement." It was largely established by trade unions;

15   A study of inner London found that 34 percent of the eligible unemployed (and 47 percent of those under 30) were not registered to vote, compared with 14 percent of all eligible residents. Nonregistration is likely to be higher in inner London than elsewhere, but the pattern of differences between the employed and unemployed is probably similar across the country. See J. Todd and B. Butcher, *Electoral Registration in 1981* (London: Office of Population Censuses and Surveys, 1982), p. 23.

16   Of the fifty seats with the highest unemployment rates in 1983, all but two were Labour.

17   A survey of the unemployed in September 1982, when unemployment was at its peak, found that 47 percent put the "chief blame" on "nobody/world economy" and 24 percent put it on "Thatcher/this government." See "Britain's jobless," *The Economist*, December 4, 1982. An opinion poll during the 1983 election campaign revealed that the majority of respondents expected the unemployed in two years to number 3.5 million if the Conservatives were re-elected but at least 3 million if Labour won. See I. Crewe, "How to win a landslide without really trying: why the Conservatives won in 1983," in *Britain at the Polls, 1983*, ed. A. Ranney (Durham, NC: Duke University Press, 1985), pp. 155–96 (p. 179).

all the major blue collar and some of the larger white collar unions are affiliated to the Labour Party and collect a political levy on top of their subscription from all members other than those deliberately "contracting out." The trade unions supply 80 percent of the Labour Party's funds, control five-sixths of the vote at the policy-making annual conference, and sponsor over half its members of Parliament (MPs) (129 out of 229 in 1987). In the constituencies they contribute money and personnel to election campaigns and send delegates – often constituting the majority – to the general management committee of the local Labour Party. One would therefore expect trade union membership to mobilize, or at least reinforce and sustain, support for the Labour Party. On the face of it, a decline in trade union membership spells electoral danger to the Labour Party.

The actual situation is more complicated. The trend in trade union membership has not followed the unswerving downward path of the working class. From 1945 to 1979 it rose almost without interruption, both in absolute numbers and in proportion to the eligible workforce and the electorate.[18] Membership peaked in 1979. In the space of seven years it fell by over a fifth from 13.3 million to 10.5 million in 1987 and has since fallen further. Part of the decline is the direct result of unemployment, which was most serious in the old heavy industries (coal, steel, railways, shipbuilding) where the trade unions were traditionally best organized.[19] But unemployment cannot explain all the fall. Trade union "density," i.e. *rates* of recruitment, which gradually rose for most of the postwar period, has itself recently declined.[20] The contributory causes are various: the illegalization of certain forms of "closed shop"; the lowering of the inflation rate, whose double-digit levels in the 1970s had swelled the ranks of trade unions with new members seeking to protect their living standards; the complete failure of trade unions to prevent redundancies; and, above all, the growth of jobs in the service and high-tech sectors which, because of their smaller-scale organization and greater preponderance of part-time work, are much harder for trade unions to organize.

This de-unionization of the electorate, however, can explain only part of it, just as the reduced size of the working class can explain only part of it. A parallel simulation to that carried out on the impact of the changing

18   In the Gallup/BBC survey of the 1979 election, 32 percent of respondents belonged to a trade union; 41 percent belonged to a household containing a trade union member.
19   Between 1979 and 1987 membership declined from 2.1 to 1.3 million (−35 percent) in the Transport and General Workers Union, from 372,000 to 211,000 in the National Union of Mineworkers (−43 percent), from 170,000 to 118,000 in the National Union of Railwaymen (−31 percent), and from 110,000 to 44,000 in the Iron and Steel Trades Confederation (−60 percent). See Central Statistical Office, *Social Trends 19*, 1989 edn (London: HMSO, 1989), table 11.10, p. 179.
20   See Crewe, "The decline of labour and the decline of Labour," table 10.

class structure is revealing. Had union members voted in 1987 as they did in 1964 (treating white collar and blue collar trade unionists separately), the fall in union membership alone would have reduced Labour's share of the national vote by 6.5 percentage points (while increasing the Conservative and Liberal/SDP shares by 3.5 and 3.0 percent respectively). In fact, the Labour vote fell by twice as much – by 13 percentage points. Labour's support among blue collar union members fell by a massive 17.3 percent. Almost the whole of Labour's electoral losses occurred within this group – its traditional base of support.

The link between class, union, and partisanship has weakened appreciably since 1964, at least among manual workers.[21] By the late 1980s union membership appeared no longer to be an agent of class or partisan socialization: among the working class, at least, it was more or less a nonpartisan matter. This diminution of union influence cannot be attributed to the changing composition of manual trade unions. The main changes – the increasing number of women and the growing importance of the public sector – are associated with stronger, not weaker, Labour support.[22] Moreover, the Thatcher governments' legislative onslaught on trade unions' long-established rights – in particular, the pre-entry closed shop, secondary picketing, "show of hands" balloting, and strikes without ballots – gave the Labour Party the opportunity to counter-mobilize trade unionists, especially blue collar members. Once again, the Labour Party failed to profit from a political opportunity.

Since the 1960s there has been a steady expansion of jobs in such high-growth, high-tech sectors of the economy as Luton (but usually in smaller plants) at the expense of the long-established homogeneous "occupational communities" of pit village, steel town, and dockside estate, where more collective, solidaristic, and politicized values have prevailed. A critical factor has been the decline in the big manufacturing plant, where the closed shop and union power was usually entrenched, thus weakening the political ecology and culture that underpinned the traditional union-Labour electoral connection. In 1979 there were 1,104 plants employing more than a thousand workers, accounting for 41 percent of all manufacturing workers; by 1981 the number of such plants had fallen to about six hundred.[23] The electoral implications of these shifts are seen in the much lower Labour vote among trade unionists living in the south than in the north in both 1983 and 1987 and also in the results of the ballots on retaining political (i.e. Labour Party) funds which trade unions were required to hold under the 1984 Trade Union

21 See P. Webb, "Union, party and class in Britain: the changing electoral relationship, 1964–83," *Politics*, 7, 2 (October 1987), pp. 15–21; Crewe, "The decline of labour and the decline of Labour," table 11.
22 See C. Cockburn, *Women, Trade Unions and Political Parties*, Fabian Research Series 349, September 1987, p. 6.
23 A. J. Taylor, *The Trade Unions and the Labour Party* (London: Croom Helm, 1987), p. 251, citing S. Dunn and J. Gennard, *The Closed Shop in British Industry* (London: Macmillan, 1984).

Act. Although every ballot resulted in a substantial majority for retaining the fund, the largest percentage majorities were in such heavy industry unions as ASLEF (train drivers), the NUM (miners), and UCATT (building workers) and the lowest were in unions representing highly paid skilled workers in expanding sectors such as ACTAT (cinematograph and television technicians), TASS (draftsmen), and the NGA (printers).[24] The electoral diagnosis of Eric Hammond, leader of the EEPTU speaks for itself:

> The vast majority of the electorate is white and English and a large percentage are skilled manual workers.... [The remedy for Labour is] to attract young, skilled workers, especially in the South. These are the ones who feel over taxed and ... who see their differentials from other manual workers as under threat. They talk of rewards for skills acquired and are directly concerned with the growth of new technology ... the last election was lost because many of our members voted for self first and self last.[25]

Thatcherism and Political Explanations of Labour's Decline

A property-owning (and Tory voting) working class?

So far we have examined the impact on Labour support of long-term structural changes that have been essentially beyond the control of governments. But some aspects of the social structure can be altered by political agency. The Thatcher administrations have been far more determined than previous Conservative governments to reshape the social structure in favor of individual property-ownership in the name of "self-sufficiency" and "responsibility." The motive has been primarily ideological, but the anticipated economic and partisan side-benefits have played a part too.

The sale of council houses (i.e. houses rented from the local authority) to long-standing tenants at a discount on the market value represents the Thatcher government's most celebrated attempt to turn the working class into property-owners. In the 1930s Herbert Morrison, the Labour leader of London, promised to "build the Tories out of London" by planning large council estates in the London suburbs. Mrs Thatcher's aim was to conveyance the Conservatives back in again by selling the estates to their tenants. Between 1980 and 1988 over 1.1 million council houses were sold. The electoral impact has clearly been favorable to the

---

24 See D. Fatchett, *Trade Unions and Politics in the 1980s* (London: Croom Helm, 1987), especially pp. 121–30. Between May 1985 and March 1986 thirty-seven unions held ballots, all of which upheld the political fund. Altogether 82 percent voted in favor, 18 percent against, on a 51 percent turnout.

25 Quoted in Taylor, *The Trade Unions and the Labour Party*, pp. 256–7.

Table 2.2   Council house sales and the vote,[a] 1979–1987

	1979–1983					
	Council tenants who bought			Council tenants who did not buy		
			Change			Change
	1979[b]	1983	1979–83	1979[b]	1983	1979–83
	(%)	(%)		(%)	(%)	
Conservative	46	56	+10	24	23	−1
Lib/SDP	12	25	+13	14	22	+8
Labour	42	18	−24	63	55	−8
Total	100	100		100	100	
Swing			17% to Con			3.5% to Con

	1983–1987					
			Change			Change
	1983	1987[c]	1983–87	1983[d]	1987	1983–87
	(%)	(%)		(%)	(%)	
Conservative	41	43	+2	30	26	−4
Lib/SDP	28	24	−4	21	19	−2
Labour	31	32	+1	49	56	+7
Total	100	100		100	100	
Swing			0.5% to Con			5.5% to Lab

[a] Three-party vote.
[b] Based on 1983 re-call of 1979 vote weighted by actual 1979 result.
[c] That is, bought in the previous four years. If those who bought before 1983 are included the swing to the Conservatives is 3 percent.
[d] Based on 1987 re-call of 1979 result weighted by actual 1983 result.

Conservatives and adverse on Labour (table 2.2). It is true that, as in the case of shares, the tenants who bought were more likely to be Conservative than those who did not; but, in the early years especially, the Labour tenants who did buy were much more likely to have stopped voting Labour by the time of the next election than those who continued to rent. In 1987 the impact of council house purchases was very much weaker than in 1983 but nonetheless to the disadvantage of Labour: buyers swung by 2 percent from Labour to Conservative (against the national trend) whereas the continuing renters swung by 5.5 percent from Conservative to Labour.[26] To this extent the Conservative govern-

26 Heath et al., *How Britain Votes*, p. 50, argue that in 1983 council house sales had no electoral impact. Their method of analysis was identical to that adopted in this chapter, albeit on a slightly smaller sample interviewed some time after the election. There is no obvious explanation for this discrepancy between our findings.

ment has legislated away part of Labour's electoral base. But one should not exaggerate the overall impact. Sales have so far affected 7 percent of the whole electorate and about 8 percent of manual workers, and are beginning to slow down. Their political significance has been symbolic as much as substantive.

Council house sales, however, merely accelerated a steady long-term growth of house-ownership in Britain. Between 1951 and 1988 the proportion of households owning their home, either outright or through a loan ("mortgage"), more than doubled from 31 to 64 percent. The proportion renting from a private landlord steeply declined from just over half (52 percent) to 6 percent. The proportion renting from a local authority increased from 18 percent in 1951 to 34 percent in 1981 before falling slightly to 26 percent in 1988 as a result of council house sales and a virtual stop to further council house building.

The correlation between housing and vote is dismissed as spurious: owner-occupiers, it is alleged, vote Conservative because they are middle class, not because they are owner-occupiers. The evidence from three-way housing, class and vote tables, however, strongly suggests that housing tenure has a substantial effect independent of class. For example, in 1983 the impact of housing tenure on Labour support within the working class was equal to the impact of occupational class on Labour support among council tenants.[27] This does not mean that housing tenure has replaced occupational class as a basis for partisanship, but rather that it now almost matches it in significance.[28] The main reason for the impact of housing is that the residential segregation of council housing into inner city blocks, large outer-suburban estates, or enclaves of small towns and villages has enabled them to form socially homogeneous communities which reinforce the prevailing working class values – and Labour subculture – of the neighborhood. There is plentiful evidence that "council house" constituencies provide Labour with a bonus vote over and above what it could expect from the class composition of the constituency.[29]

The impact of housing on the working class vote, moreover, has remained fairly constant, after taking into account national fluctuations in the parties' fortunes.[30] In 1964, the Labour vote was 21 percentage points higher among manual workers who rented from the council than

27 There is another way of making the same point: the Conservative vote is higher among working class house-owners (39 percent) than service class council tenants (33 percent). See Heath et al., *How Britain Votes*, p. 36.
28 See also R. Rose and I. McAllister, *Voters Begin to Choose* (London and Beverly Hills, CA: Sage, 1986), pp. 85–93, which suggests on the basis of an AID analysis that by 1983 housing tenure was a stronger influence on the vote than occupational class.
29 See I. Crewe and C. Payne, "Analysing the census data," in *The British General Election of 1970*, ed. D. Butler and M. Pinto-Duschinsky (London: Macmillan, 1971), pp. 416–36.
30 The figures in this paragraph are taken from Crewe, "The decline of labour and the decline of Labour," table 14.

among those who owned their homes; in 1987 it was 23 points. But in
1964 council tenants outnumbered owner-occupiers by 40 percent to 35
percent (the rest were mainly private renters); by 1987 the ratio was
reversed and owner-occupiers outnumbered council tenants by 51
percent to 36 percent. The constancy of the political division between
working class home-owners and council tenants suggests that housing
tenure is an enduring cross-class cleavage; and the gradual postwar
expansion of working class home-ownership implies that this must have
eroded – and will continue to erode – Labour's electoral base.

Strategies for the Future

The Labour Party has largely retained the loyalty of the economically
marginal and dispossessed – the unskilled, the council tenants, the
unemployed, the welfare dependants – as well as the more secure working class living in areas of economic decline in the industrial north and
Scotland. But it has lost those sections of the secure and relatively
prosperous working class who live in areas of economic growth. Labour
continues to be supported by the have-nots in an increasingly polarized
society; but, unlike the 1930s, the have-nots are a minority, albeit a
substantial one. Britain has become a two-thirds/one-third society in
which Labour represents the one-third.

The choice of strategy to mobilize support beyond the one-third
minority must confront certain political realities that are peculiar to the
British situation. The first is the limited capacity of the Labour Party to
lead a crusading missionary movement. The educational institutions of
the labor movement – the Labour Club libraries, socialist Sunday
schools, Fabian summer camps, and workers' educational association –
have almost disappeared along with the traditional working class communities and auto-didactic values that sustained them. The proportion
of the daily press (in terms of circulation) that supports the Left has
declined from 40–5 percent in the period 1950–70 to 24 percent in 1988:
the vast majority of manual workers, indeed the majority of Labour
supporters, daily read a Conservative newspaper.[31] It is true that television is obliged to retain "political balance" but it is also required to
refrain from editorializing; moreover, cable and satellite television will
operate under less strict rules of neutrality. The trade unions offer a
more promising basis for mobilization. In this regard, the 1985–6 ballots
on political funds were a conspicuous success. But otherwise they have
failed to mobilize support for the Left, or for cross-union solidarity. Thus

31   See M. Harrop, "The press and post-war elections," *Political Communications:
The General Election Campaign of 1983*, ed. I. Crewe and M. Harrop (Cambridge:
Cambridge University Press, 1986), pp. 137–49 (p. 139); 1988 figures are from
Audit Bureau of Circulations, published in *Sunday Times*, January 15, 1989. See
also Central Statistical Office, *Social Trends 19*, p. 166.

the Left has little choice in the face of the old dilemma: moving towards the electorate offers better prospects than persuading the electorate to move towards it.

The second reality is the limited capacity of the Left to recreate the social structure in its own image, thus undoing the work of the Thatcher administrations. Most structural trends, such as migration and social mobility, are irreversible in any but a totalitarian system. In opposition the Labour Party can make virtually no impact, of course (except marginally, where it runs the local authority); in government it could effect structural changes only slowly and in the long term. Building new council house estates takes longer than privatizing them; expanding the public sector of the economy is more expensive, and thus riskier electorally, than winding it down. The Labour Party has to take the social structure largely as it is.

The third reality follows from the last two. Discussions of Labour's choice of strategies must be conducted within a numerical framework. If it is assumed that ultimately votes count, then the measure of alternative strategies is to count votes.

Simplifying drastically, the Left has both a social and a political choice. As regards the first, it can seek to recapture the working class votes it has lost or, if it regards them as irretrievable, seek new support from other classes. As regards the second, it can choose to appeal on either traditional or new ideological grounds, irrespective of its social choice. The double pair of choices offers the Labour Party four strategies (figure 2.1), of which three have been adopted, with varying success, by different Labour-led local authorities in the 1980s. We shall briefly discuss each in turn, before outlining a fifth strategy, which the Labour Party appears to be following at present.

Strategy 1:
Class confrontation and worker economism

The first strategy aims to retrieve working class support by appealing, with renewed vigor and imagination, to traditional working class interests (see figure 2.1, top right). The Scargill-led miners' strike in 1984–5 and the Militant regime on Liverpool council from 1984 to 1987 are the most prominent examples. Both involved the mobilized defence of communities in rapid economic decline through uncompromising confrontation with the government, centralized and authoritarian (but not necessarily unpopular) leadership, the suppression of dissenting or autonomous groups within the movement (Nottinghamshire miners, black and women's groups in Liverpool), and simple short-term economistic interpretations of working class interests: rent and price freezes, no redundancies, subsidized job creation. In Liverpool, the local authority attempted to recreate a militant proletariat by a crash programme of council house building and public sector employment.

The evidence on the electoral impact of this strategy is mixed. Militant did not obviously damage Labour support in Liverpool nor did the

Figure 2.1   Four strategic paths towards a Labour Party recovery.

SOCIAL STRATEGY

	Retrieve working-class support	Appeal to other classes
Appeal on traditional grounds **POLITICAL STRATEGY**	e.g. escalating the class war class solidarity, industrial militancy, "struggle," impossibilism (Militant, Scargill) e.g. worker economism price and rent freezes, job protection and creation, import controls, free collective bargaining (Tribune, Liverpool Council)	e.g. updating 1945 social justice, economic reconstruction, "responsible" welfarism, public enterprise (Kinnock, mainstream Labour, Sheffield and Glasgow Councils)
Appeal on new grounds	e.g. populist authoritarianism patriotism, parochialism, immigration control, law and order, traditional morality (Callaghan, some local parties in Labour heartlands, Social Democratic Association)	e.g. coalition of minorities minority rights, pacifism, libertarianism (Livingstone, GLC) e.g. natural party of government competence, efficiency, "white heat of technology," growth, corporatism (Wilson, Benn 1964–70)

NUM in the coalfields (outside breakaway Nottinghamshire). But the strategy undermined Labour support in the country as a whole, first because it was easily labeled as "extremist" and "irresponsible" in the media (Liverpool council rapidly slid towards bankruptcy) and second because, as a result, it divided the labor movement. As a local defensive tactic it worked; as a national offensive strategy it failed, flawed by its parochial exclusivity.

It is difficult to believe that any electoral strategy based on the economically marginalized working class (i.e. rank and file manual employees) can succeed. The percentages are simply not big enough. On the generous assumption that all rank and file manual employees (i.e. excluding supervisors and technicians) belong to the marginalized working class its size (currently about 28 percent of the voting electorate, but falling) would be quite insufficient by itself to put Labour into office. In fact, Labour has not won more than 72 percent of the support of the rank and file manual employees even in its best election years, and this would provide it with 21 percent of the vote – barely half of what it needs. The remainder must clearly be found in other classes, but which, and through what appeals?

Strategy 2: updating 1945

The second strategy is to extend the social democratic Left's traditional appeal to new classes, especially the large class of routine nonmanual workers. This is the course broadly approved by the mainstream of the party, and the strategy adopted by some notably successful Labour councils such as Glasgow and Sheffield. The emphasis is on the social rights of all "citizens" (as distinct from the "working class"), i.e. the right to high quality welfare provision and public services irrespective of market position. At the local level it has taken the form of comprehensive but also efficient welfare services (especially child care and provision for the old) and heavily subsidized low-fare public transport combined with vigorous attempts to attract private industry to the local area.

This strategy makes much more electoral and sociological sense. The two "adjacent" classes to the working class are "foremen and technicians" (a stable 7 percent of the voting electorate) and, crucially, routine nonmanual workers (26 percent of the voting electorate). The latter comprise many office staff whose pay and long-term prospects place them economically close to the working class and who regard the maintenance of the public services (the National Health, state pensions, universities) as in their interest. The potential for a growth of trade union recruitment of white collar workers is considerable, especially in the public sector and where automation has de-skilled and routinized office and shop work. Nonetheless, creating a cross-class commitment to a big-welfare high-spending programme is not as straightforward as it might appear. The "taxes vs welfare" issue serves to divide the welfare-dependent "underclass" from the rest of the working class and, in particular, the foremen and technicians and routine nonmanual workers – many of whom just fall into the tax bracket.

It would be a mistake, too, to regard routine nonmanual workers as a cohesive social formation with a collective interest of a kind comparable with the working class. It is the most fluid social class in terms of life-time and intergenerational mobility and thus the most heterogeneous in class origins and destinations.[32]

32   Goldthorpe et al., *Social Mobility and Class Structure in Modern Britain*, pp. 334–5.

Moreover, even a marked improvement of support from routine non-manual workers might not be enough. On the fancifully favorable assumption that Labour could return to a 70 percent vote among the working class, 60 percent among foremen and technicians and 40 percent among routine nonmanual workers (which it just achieved in its landslide 1966 election victory)[33] that would deliver only 33 percent of the total vote by 1991 because of the rapidly diminishing size of the working class. To win an election Labour must also find substantial support among the salariat. A possible way of doing this would be to mobilize the "new social movements."

Strategy 3: coalition of minorities

The strategy of constructing a "rainbow alliance" of social and political minorities (including the working class) has been advocated by the libertarian Left of the Labour Party (notably Tony Benn) and was seriously attempted by the Greater London Council (GLC) under Ken Livingstone's leadership from 1981–6. The electoral pay-off was, at best, ambivalent. Labour did relatively well, but not exceptionally, in the 1986 London borough elections,[34] but by that time it was identified as the "defender" of the GLC against the Government's unpopular decision to abolish it. A year later, in the general election, Greater London was the only region to swing further away from Labour, even compared with 1983.

As a national strategy, a coalition of minorities has little to commend it in a political system and culture that is deeply majoritarian. Close association with disadvantaged and stigmatized minorities gains activists for the Left but loses it votes. The Afro-Caribbeans and Asian minorities together constitute 4 percent of the electorate. The overwhelming majority already vote Labour and live in Labour areas.[35] In the British electorate racists outnumber blacks. The electoral arithmetic for gays – a larger minority than blacks – is similar: the Labour vote is

33 Labour achieved these levels of support when very few working class Labour seats were contested by the Liberals. The present-day capacity of the Centre (now the Democrats) to contest all seats makes it even more unlikely that Labour could return to its 1966 levels of support among the working class or adjacent classes.
34 There was a 5.8 percent swing from Conservative to Labour since 1982 (when the previous London borough elections were held), a fraction above the overall 1982–6 swing (5.5 percent).
35 See M. Fitzgerald, *Political Parties and Black People* (London: Runnymede Trust, 1984), p. 12. In 1987 the one opinion poll of black voters suggested that 67 percent of Asians and 86 percent of Afro-Caribbeans voted Labour. See Z. Layton-Henry, "Black electoral participation: an analysis of recent trends," paper presented to the annual conference of the Political Studies Association, Plymouth, April 1988.

probably not as high proportionately as for blacks, but the anti-homosexual vote in pre-AIDS let alone post-AIDS Britain is larger.[36]

By contrast, the women's movement offers the Left potentially richer pickings because it represents the interests of a numerical majority. The increasing proportion of women in the labor force, the gradual increase in single-parent families headed by women, and the preponderance of women among welfare dependents are all incipient sources of radicalization among working class and lower middle class women. There is ample evidence, too, that women take positions to the left of men on many issues, notably social welfare, defense, and the environment, and that this has not yet converted itself into a vote for the Left. One possible explanation is that the image and culture of the Labour Party, especially the trade union wing, remains very masculine in terms of personnel, language, and values.[37] A feminized re-orientation of Labour policies on welfare, work, taxation, and the public services, emphasizing, for example, child- and mother-centered benefits, an expansion of permanency and pension rights for part-time and short-term workers, tax allowances for care givers of dependent children and parents (or expenditure thereon), and much larger public investments in health (especially preventative health measures), education, and provision for the elderly would probably bring electoral benefits as well as update the social democratic program. Nonetheless, we should not exaggerate the likely impact.

Strategy 4: popular front of the centre-left

Two remaining strategies are available to the Labour Party. Both acknowledge the difficulties and risks in sectional targeting in a post-industrial society; both abandon a primary reliance on the support of organized labor. One strategy retains the party's primordial bond with organized labor but accepts that this imposes a permanent minority status on the party. The logic of this position is then to form alliances – currently dramatized as anti-Thatcherite popular fronts – with the smaller Nationalist, Centre and Green parties, by means of pre-election pacts, common programs, government coalition, and proportional representation. Such proposals gained advocates across the spectrum of the Left after the 1987 defeat but are fraught with practical problems and are a recipe for deep, electorally damaging, divisions within the party. The idea has been buried since the electoral resurgence of the Labour Party beginning in 1989 but will undoubtedly be resuscitated should Labour be decisively defeated yet again at the next election.

---

36 Reliable evidence on the number and voting patterns of homosexuals is not available. For evidence of a recent growth of intolerance of homosexual relations see Jowell et al., *British Social Attitudes: the Fifth Report*, p. 37.
37 For a development of this argument, see Cockburn, *Women, Trade Unions and Political Parties*.

Strategy 5: from sectional party of
protest to natural party of government

The strategy of electoral recovery that has in fact been adopted by the
Labour Party since 1987 goes further in its acknowledgment of the
decline of labor: it attempts to insulate the party from the trade unions
and all other organized social constituencies of the Left. It might be
summarized as the transformation of the Labour Party from an ideological movement to an electoral organization and from a sectional party
of protest to a national party of government.[38] The three main components of this strategy are interrelated.

1   The abandonment of policies tailored to specific group interests and
    demands in favor of across-the-board appeals to the consensual
    values of the whole electorate: organized groups and movements are
    no longer incorporated in the policy-making apparatus of the party
    (i.e. on subcommittees of the National Executive Committee); even
    the role of trade unions, despite their constitutional entrenchment in
    the Labour Party organization, has been downgraded.
2   The substitution of electoral for ideological criteria in policy-making:
    since 1987 the party has relied heavily on market research for the
    formulation of policy, and in particular for the identification of un-
    popular elements in Labour's traditional program.
3   The elevation of image management above policy detail as the cen-
    terpiece of the party's communications strategy: the party has in-
    vested extensively in "media consultants" and in public relations
    techniques for the conveying of general impressions about the party,
    with an emphasis on "competence," "responsibility," and "respect-
    ability"; at the same time mass communications such as manifestos
    and election broadcasts have omitted specific policy details in favor
    of broad themes and attacks on the government record.

These dimensions of the Labour Party's strategy are all reflected in its
1989 Policy Review, *Make the Change, Meet the Challenge*, the culmination
of three years of policy-making and the "bible" for its future manifesto
and government program. The Review marks the wholesale abandonment of its 1983 and 1987 programs and the least socialist policy statement ever to be published by the party. The complaint of left-wingers
that their party has jettisoned socialism for a diluted social democracy is
perfectly fair. On almost every major issue – macroeconomic policy, the
role of the market, public services, privatization and the public sector,
Europe, trade union democracy, and, most important, nuclear defense –

38 A useful journalistic account of the Labour Party's program for electoral
recovery can be found in C. Hughes and P. Wintour, *Labour Rebuilt* (London:
Fourth Estate, 1990).

Labour's Policy Review has adopted positions barely a millimetre away from the SDP's of 1987.

The precise policy changes are summarized in table 2.3. A few additional points are worth emphasizing here. First, the universal discourse of "citizenship" has superseded the sectional discourse of "class." The phrase "working class" does not appear; it is replaced by "ordinary people," "consumers," "users," or "citizens." "Socialism" does make an appearance but in a brand new guise. "Socialism," the Policy Review says, "is about diffusing power and giving people more control over their lives." This definition is so diluted of any substantive meaning that Thatcherites, Liberal Democrats, and Greens would all be happy to adopt it as *their* slogan.

Second, the Policy Review ignores the Labour Party's constitutional commitment to public ownership to the point of contradicting it. Clause 4 defines the party's purpose as the "common ownership of the means of production, distribution and exchange" and is printed on every party member's card. But the Policy Review rules out any form of renationalization requiring "substantial resources which might be applied to other purposes," which effectively means any public ownership involving the purchase of more than a small number of shares.

Finally, the Policy Review acknowledges the advantages of markets in an unprecedented way. There are references to the "strengths" and "vital role" of free markets, qualified only by the need for the state to correct abuses and failures.

Since the publication of the Review in mid-1989 the Labour Party has enjoyed an extraordinary surge in popular support, reflected in comfortable majorities and sometimes spectacular swings, in the 1989 European elections, the 1989 and 1990 local elections, by-elections (special elections), and opinion polls. In Spring 1990 Labour's national lead in the polls reached 24 percent and it ran ahead of the Conservatives in every social class except the professional and managerial "salariat," among owner-occupiers as well as tenants, in every age group, and in every region except the nonmetropolitan southeast. The magnitude of this recovery suggests something more substantial than the ephemeral Labour revivals in the mid-term of the two preceding Thatcher administrations. Its new pattern of support has transfigured it from a regional class party of dispossessed minorities to a national, majority party. For the first time since 1979 talk of Labour forming the next government sounds plausible and, even if this fails to materialize, there should at the very least be a notable improvement in Labour's share of the popular vote.

This sharp recovery of Labour's fortunes is self-evidently not the result of a sudden shift in Britain's economic and social structure. Much of the recovery undoubtedly arises from the short-term unpopularity of the government and not from any sudden conversion to social democratic policies and values by the electorate. Since early 1989 support for

Table 2.3 How Labour Party policy has changed

1983 and 1987	1989 Policy Review
Defense	
Non-nuclear defense policy in lifetime of Parliament	No timetable for nonnuclear policy
Removal of all nuclear weapons (including Cruise) from British soil	Retention of nuclear weapons until negotiated away in unilateral talks
Close down US nuclear bases within lifetime of Parliament	No plan to close down US bases. Reliance on US nuclear umbrella once British nuclear arms scrapped
Cancel Trident submarine program	Retain three of the four commissioned Trident submarines
Increase spending on conventional forces (1987 only)	Cut spending on conventional forces
Economic strategy	
Massive program of expansion	Public spending to be limited to what Britain can afford
Import controls	No import controls
Price controls	No price controls
Job subsidies (1983)	No commitment about unemployment level: "there is no
Reduce unemployment by 1 million in two years (1987)	reason to believe that it will fall"
Europe	
Withdrawal from EC within lifetime of Parliament (1983)	Seek closer European cooperation and more decisions at EC level
Stay in EC but reject EC interference in Labour's program for national recovery (1987)	Full membership of European Monetary System. Acceptance of Social Charter
Industrial recovery	
1983: Compulsory planning agreements with companies, involving state control of prices, credit, and investment	Public–private collaboration and partnership

Creation of new companies and science-based industries	Revamp Department of Trade and Industry to improve climate for enterprise. Establish Technology Enterprise to invest in advanced technologies
Radical extension of industrial democracy	Promotion of co-determination and information disclosure

Public ownership

1983: Buy back assets privatized by Conservatives; limited compensation to owners	No rationalization requiring "substantial resources"
Take significant public stake in electronics, pharmaceuticals, and building materials industries	Privatized utilities to be converted into public interest companies through tougher regulation and government purchase of "golden share" at market rates. No limit on dividends
1987: Social ownership of basic public utilities by converting private shares into new securities with guaranteed returns or dividends	Government stake in British Telecom to increase from 49% to 51%

Taxation

Shift tax burden to better off	"Fair tax" policy. No return to "the high marginal rates of the past"
Wealth tax on richest 100,000	No wealth tax
Reverse Conservative tax cuts, using extra revenue for job creation	More tax bands, starting at 20% rate, rising to maximum of 50%

Trade unions

1983: Repeal all Conservative employment laws	No commitment to return to pre-1979 position. Switch of emphasis from collective to individual rights
1987: Replace Conservative laws with new laws to strengthen legal rights of representation and bargaining	Restoration of limited secondary action; unions no longer to be subject to *ex parte* injunction of sequestration of funds
Keep ballots before strikes and for election of union executives	Keep ballots before strikes and for election of union executives

Labour has steadily grown in tandem with rising inflation and interest rates (and therefore home loan rates).

We may therefore confidently expect Labour's swell of popularity to subside with equal rapidity if interest rates and inflation take a downturn and the Conservative administration avoids divisions and gaffes. Nonetheless, the renewed capacity of the Labour Party to benefit from the Conservative government's discomfiture is significant. For what distinguishes electoral trends since 1989 from the rest of the decade – and indeed from all periods of Conservative government since 1945 – is a new pattern of anti-Conservative voting. In the past most disillusioned Conservatives switched to the halfway-house of a center party (the Liberals, SDP, Nationalists, etc.) rather than all the way to Labour. This time, quite exceptionally, Labour has been the sole beneficiary of the anti-government protest vote. It has captured the ideological and social "center ground" as well as its traditional left-of-center constituency.

The Labour Party's gameplan looks remarkably similar to the catch-all leader-focused approaches adopted by the democratic Left in Australia, France, and Spain. It might be equally successful in electing a Labour government, especially at a time of economic recession, but almost certainly not one that is recognizably of the Left in the sense of being socialist, or at least radical, or at the very least allied to the interests and values of labor.

3

Class, Consumption, and Collectivism: Perspectives on the Labour Party and Electoral Competition in Britain

Joel Krieger

Careening from a set of strategic blunders and short- or medium-term crises – the poll tax, rising inflation and mortgage rates, and its waffling on Europe – Margaret Thatcher was unexpectedly forced to resign as Conservative Party leader and Prime Minister in November 1990. With John Major's hold on both offices not yet secure, Labour is rebounding from a decade of sorry electoral performances and programmatic reversals. Thus, in the spring of 1991, the chorus of voices that insisted after the 1987 election that the Labour Party was nearly finished as a competitor for national leadership and Britain was fast approaching a single party dominant system have quieted for the time being.

Nevertheless, a crucial point of agreement among post-1987 critics from across the political spectrum has not been lost on the Labour Party leadership: the terms of social conflict, the lines of social cleavage and party opposition, and the means for interpreting social experience have passed Labour by and, indeed, sidestepped productivist politics altogether. The demise of the traditional Labour Party is taken for granted, and the alternatives discussed for the most part reject social democratic politics, the close association between party and unions within a labor movement, and the appeal to productivist solidarities. Nearly everyone calls for a radical break with Labourist tradition and a sustained effort to repudiate an interpretation of history and social life in which class relations play the central role.

The more election minded advance a nondenominational anti-class centrism, a project enshrined in the Labour Party's much heralded policy review[1] and reinforced by Neil Kinnock's up-tempo attacks on the Labour left and its "shopping list socialism."[2] At the same time, radical critics offer variants of democratic socialism based in "new social movements" and segments of the working class beyond the core Labourist constituency of white male workers in manufacturing industries (the British version of a rainbow coalition). Successive electoral defeats and the sorry spectacles of the Callaghan years – creeping monetarism, the collapse of the Social Contract, the "winter of discontent" – have created pressure for a wholesale renovation of the party. From many quarters has come the blunt message: reject the traditional class-collectivist appeals, distance the party from union politics and agendas, trumpet competitiveness and initiative, and, particularly since Labour's victory and the strong showing of the Greens in the June 1989 elections for the European Parliament, embrace 1992, economic and political union, and the environment.

This advice, I want to suggest, is "too smart by half." It is true that the familiar tunes of British Labourism have lost their appeal, and for good reason. To recapture and sustain political initiative, Labour will have to acquire the instruments to create a "narrative" that makes sense of political life in Britain.[3]

For a number of reasons, however, as I hope to demonstrate in this chapter, the advice of the alternative voices is questionable in narrow electoral terms, and confused and contradictory in broader conceptual and political terms. Going too far to distance the party from its shrinking and unfashionable working class base and its tradition of class-based politics, many Labour leaders and observers of the party reject collectivism in any form and "turn to the religion of individualism in the hope that it will provide the route to salvation."[4]

In so doing they go beyond what in my view is the urgent and necessary task of reducing the privilege of traditional (male and white) proletarian politics in the Labour Party. Rather than embracing a wider interpretation of social needs and a more focused and grounded understanding of today's complex and fluid patterns of solidarity and collectivity (more on this below), they cede the interpretive ground and effectively succumb to the prevailing Thatcherite ethos.

Moreover, the advice relies too heavily for its intellectual justification on a set of claims about "consumption cleavages," a uniquely British

1 *Meeting the Challenge/Make the Change: A New Agenda for Britain* (London: Labour Party, 1989).
2 P. Webster, "Kinnock hits at 'shopping list socialism'," *The Times*, May 9, 1989, p. 1.
3 See F. Jameson, *The Political Unconscious: Narrative as a Socially Symbolic Act* (Ithaca, NY: Cornell University Press, 1981), ch. 1, pp. 17–102.
4 H. Wainwright, "The limits of Labourism: 1987 and beyond," *New Left Review*, 164 (July–August 1987), p. 43.

contribution to the discourse about postindustrial societies. Because of the sheer vigor of the academic debate that these claims have fostered, their use in wholesale and highly political efforts to devalue *any* version of productivist or collectivist politics, and their centrality to the consolidation of Thatcher's narrative of political life in Britain, the consumption arguments will receive particularly close attention here.

In the chapter which follows, first, I shall consider the break-up of Labourist Britain, the emergence of Britain's new right agenda, and the advance of an anti-collectivist Thatcherite vision. Second, I shall discuss and critique efforts to explain the declining fortunes of Labour in structural terms, particularly those which assert the displacement of productivist by consumption politics. Finally, I shall propose some tentative and necessarily uncertain points of departure for a renewal of collectivist politics in Britain.

The Break-Up of Labourist Britain[5]

Before the age of Thatcher signaled a dramatic rightward shift in Britain's policy agenda, a broad postwar consensus for "Keynes–Beveridge social-democratic collectivism"[6] oriented a cross-party and interclass consensus. It privileged the Labour Party vision of politics and provided the "master code"[7] for explaining the mysteries of postwar reconstruction, political regulation of the market, and class compromise within a context of positive-sum cooperation.[8]

Writing in 1952 of a "post-capitalist society" in the United Kingdom, with Labour its natural party of government, Anthony Crosland provided a key political narrative. The new society was distinguished from the old by a broad set of changes: greater equality of incomes and enhanced opportunity through governmental intervention in economic affairs; an increased level of social services; full employment; an improved standard of living; class struggle "softened" by the "rise of the technical and professional middle class"; and a shift in emphasis from "the rights of property, private initiative, competition, and the profit

5 This discussion follows in part from previous work. See J. Krieger, *Reagan, Thatcher and the Politics of Decline* (New York: Oxford University Press; Cambridge: Polity Press, 1986), pp. 36–58; "Britain," in *European Politics in Transition*, ed. M. Kesselman and J. Krieger (Lexington, MA: D. C. Heath, 1987), pp. 25–125; "Social policy in the age of Reagan and Thatcher," in *Socialist Register 1987*, ed. R. Miliband, L. Panitch, and J. Saville (London: Merlin, 1987), pp. 177–98.
6 R. Martin, "The political economy of Britain's north–south divide," in *The North–South Divide*, ed. J. Lewis and A. Townsend (London: Paul Chapman, 1989), p. 47.
7 Jameson, *The Political Unconscious*, p. 58.
8 See A. Przeworski, *Capitalism and Social Democracy* (New York: Cambridge University Press, 1985).

motive ... to the duties of the state, social and economic security, and the virtues of co-operative action." Thus, Crosland's new society – what has been regarded as British social democracy with a Labour Party signature (Labourism) – was a rich and appealing hybrid. As Crosland explained, it was "non-capitalist to the extent that market influences are subordinated to central planning ... [and] the power of the state is much greater than that of any one particular class"; socialist in its distribution of income; and "a pluralist society."[9]

However conceptually amorphous the *New Fabian Essays* of Crosland and his Labour "revisionist" comrades, they helped crystallize an interpretation which had sustained Labour's landslide victory in 1945, informed Labour practice during the Atlee government, and justified allegiance in the aftermath of defeat in 1951. Labour worked to preserve the interpretive high ground and, despite a string of electoral defeats, succeeded to a considerable degree in providing the "text" for understanding the transformation of society through the class compromises and institutional arrangements for corporatist bargaining and economic steering associated with the postwar settlement, and the institutionalization of Beveridge and Keynes throughout the postwar period and into the 1970s.

So long as Crosland's social democratic vision represented the moderate, but still impassioned, mainstream of Labourism, then Labour largely interpreted the societal consensus (such as existed) and preserved its role as the central interlocutor between "the state" and "the people," whatever the electoral vicissitudes.

Labour revisionism held sway throughout the period of the postwar settlement, sustained by the shallow but generally consistent economic growth which reduced distributional conflicts until the Wilson–Callaghan era. So long as these circumstances held, the more Marxist fundamentalist visions of socialism – ownership and control of the commanding heights of production, radical redistribution of resources in society, and "workers control" – could be contained within the party. Fundamentalism and Crosland-inspired revisionism could effect an intra-party electoral alliance and organizational truce at crucial junctures and keep trade union, constituency, and parliamentary elements from the full expression of their centrifugal tensions. And during the height of Labourist social democracy political loyalties and constituencies conformed to a predictable pattern as electoral behavior displayed a strong correlation with occupation. In the 1950s and early 1960s, those not engaged in manual labor voted Conservative three times more commonly than Labour; and more than two out of three manual workers, by contrast, voted for Labour.

Viewed against this backdrop, the 1970s appear as a crucial turning point. It was not only the decade of dealignment in terms of party

9 C. A. R. Crosland, "The transition from capitalism," in *New Fabian Essays*, ed. R. H. S. Crossman (New York: Praeger, 1952), pp. 38–45.

competition,[10] but a period of the nullification of the Labourist social democratic vision.

In an era marked, for the first time, by the previously inconceivable combination of increases in wages/prices and reduced growth (stagflation), core constituencies (both natural allies and increasingly restive adversaries) rebelled against the Heath government of 1974–9. There were strikes by workers from dockers, to local authority employees, to mineworkers, enraged by the Industrial Relations Act, and strikes by investors, which proved particularly frustrating for Heath. And there was Heath's famous U-turn in 1972 in a corporatist direction. Heath could not sustain a Tory centrism/social democracy in a context of intensifying economic constraints, proliferating political opposition, and his own vacillating popular messages. In the end the government was defeated not exactly by the miners, as is often said, but by a failed economic strategy which was forced by a spate of strategic miscues to its ultimate political denouement.

The period of the 1974–9 Labour government of Wilson, Callaghan, and Healey underlined the loss of vision, reinforced the impression of governments out of control of the surrounding events, and completed the destruction of British social democracy/Labourism.

In the genealogy of Britain's transformation from a social democratic to an anti-collectivist orthodoxy[11] few developments are more significant than the failure of the Social Contract during the last Labour government, the cornerstone of its industrial relations and, in a sense, macroeconomic policies, and the political–institutional instrument which symbolized its unique claim as a party of government.

Planning for its chance at national leadership during the period of the often bitter confrontations over Heath's 1972 industrial relations policy, Labour hoped to present a clear contrast in both approach and results. The new Labour strategy, it was hoped, would stabilize the economy by involving the Trades Union Congress (TUC) in an expanded agenda of shared responsibility for economic and social policy. The Social Contract agreed to by the TUC–Labour Party Liaison Committee in February 1973 called for wage and price controls "within the context of coherent economic and social strategy designed both to overcome the nation's grave economic problems and to provide the basis for cooperation between the trade unions and the Government."[12]

In the end, nothing was further from the truth. The pressure of economic exigencies, such as mounting inflation and a substantial run on the pound, quickly removed the more expensive (and expansive) elements of

10 See B. Särlvik and I. Crewe, *Decade of Dealignment* (Cambridge: Cambridge University Press, 1983).
11 See S. Hall, *Thatcherism and the Crisis of the Left: The Hard Road to Renewal* (London and New York: Verso, 1988), pp. 46–8.
12 TUC–Labour Party Liaison Committee, *Economic Policy and the Cost of Living* (February 1973).

the Social Contract. Promises of expanded social provision were jettisoned, and the discussion of industrial and economic democracy was
shelved indefinitely. What remained after Labour's victory in February
1974 was a set of formal but voluntary incomes policies which were
bargained for in each of four annual phases, with decreasing TUC, trade
union, and rank-and-file support. In the aftermath of Wilson's resigna-
tion and replacement by Callaghan in April 1976 and the government's
promise to the International Monetary Fund (IMF) to further restrain
incomes and reduce social expenditure as collateral for its $3.9 billion
credit later that year, trade unionists became increasingly restive under
the pinch of wage restraints. The government was forced to go it alone
during Phase Three as the number of unofficial work stoppages
increased.

In Phase Four, the Social Contract fell apart, and with it the social
democratic collectivist era in British politics ended. In a confrontational
stance, the government insisted on a 5 percent pay norm for the fourth
year of the incomes policy. Affronted, the TUC overwhelmingly rejected
any "arbitrary pay limit" at its September 1978 conference, despite the
expectation cultivated by Callaghan that the announcement of a general
election was only days away. The Labour Party itself reconfirmed the
labor movement's rejection of the Social Contract at its own conference
in October, as both rank-and-file work stoppages and official strikes,
fueled by a seemingly endless series of leapfrogging pay demands,
erupted throughout the "winter of discontent."

As Thatcher's victory in May 1979 would make clear, Labour's
political survival and, beyond simple party politics, the Labourist/social
democratic/collectivist narrative of British political life required successful corporatist interest intermediation and economic steering by the
Wilson–Callaghan government. As its name implies, the Social Contract
took on considerable normative significance in political debates and its
demise figured centrally in the obituaries to social democracy that have
followed. By the end of the 1970s it was clear that the defeats, in turn, of
Heath in the quasi-corporatist stage of his government after the 1972
U-turn and of Callaghan five years later had exhausted the options of
party alternation and programmatic continuity within a Keynesian welfare state perspective. Like the complex symbiosis between parts of the
Labour Party – constituency, parliamentary party, and trade unions
– the set formula of two-party competition between mainstream/
collectivist representatives of the Conservative and Labour parties rested
on the political perseverance of a growth coalition. This in turn required
more growth, high productivity, an increasing standard of living, and
a shared "one-nation" narrative of politics not very far removed from
Crosland's Labourist vision.

A new vision of politics, which had begun to eclipse Labourism in the
course of the 1970s, gained full voice with the Conservative campaign in
the 1979 general election. The new right themes of anti-collectivism and
anti-statism which had begun to pervade academic common rooms, the

perspectives of senior civil servants and bodies like the Institute for Economic Affairs, gained new prominence and increasingly colonized the press from *The Times* and *The Economist* to the tabloid dailies.[13] With Thatcher's rise to the leadership of the Conservative Party, Hayek and Friedman and these loosely identified new right currents received powerful institutional backing.

Keynesianism was everywhere in retreat and with it the class compromise–welfarist ethic that it had intellectually legitimated throughout the postwar period. Not simply "monetarism" or the "social market economy" were at issue, nor electoral politics in the narrow sense, but a conception of political community: what it meant to be British, how social and political life was to be interpreted. "Neither Keynesianism nor monetarism ... win votes as such in the electoral marketplace," observes Stuart Hall. "But, in the discourse of 'social market values', Thatcherism discovered a powerful means of translating economic doctrine into the language of experience, moral imperative and common sense, thus providing a 'philosophy' in the broader sense – an alternative *ethic* to that of the 'caring society'. This translation of a theoretical *ideology* into a populist *idiom* was a major political achievement."[14]

From the start the "Thatcher revolution" involved a coordinated assault, with electoral appeals, policy agendas, and discourse united to reconstitute common sense, redefine the nation, and shatter traditional Labourist–collectivist solidarities. On the one hand, there is Thatcher's famous 1978 remark on "World in Action" expressing sympathy for those who feel "swamped" by the flow of immigrants. The fear and racial hostility were played upon throughout the 1979 campaign, and were codified in the British Nationality Act 1981 that tightened restrictions on entry and settlement of New Commonwealth citizens, formalized a new hierarchy in citizenship levels, and deepened the principles of patriality and gender bias in the determination of status for entry. On the other hand, there is the sale of council housing at subsidized rates, sold to the mass of British citizens in language which resonated closely with Hayek:

> Socialists actually *want* to keep thousands of families trapped (at great public cost) in what has been called "the serfdom" of municipal estates. We offer the much more attractive prospect of a choice – a free choice between ownership and a less restrictive kind of tenancy.[15]

Both these starkly drawn issues in the 1979 campaign are of a piece with crucial gestures to follow: the legislative and industrial attacks on

13 Hall, *Thatcherism and the Crisis of the Left*, pp. 46–8.
14 Hall, ibid., p. 47.
15 *The Right Approach: A Statement of Conservative Aims* (London: Conservative Central Office, 1976), pp. 53–4.

the trade union movement culminating in the 1984–5 miners' strike and Thatcher's characterization of the miners as the "enemy within" (by way of comparison with the Argentine external enemy in the Falklands/ Malvinas war); the privatization campaigns and the creation of a "share holding democracy"; the multiform changes in the administration and quality of social welfare provision. They are all part of a strategy to reinforce particularism and individual property rights over citizenship status and universalist appeals: not only to tarnish Labourism and sully collectivist sentiments, but to divide citizens into highly valuative categories of "us" and "them." "We" are the solid citizens who feel swamped, can afford to buy the better range of council flats, buy British Telecom stock, and are outraged by the violence of miners and by welfare cheats. "They" are blacks, the unemployed, the renters, the clients of the welfare state, the strikers.

In the end, according to Thatcher's "master code" all solidarities, class and otherwise, are obliterated, for in the prime minister's oft repeated observation: "There is no such thing as society, only individual men and women and their families."[16]

Consumption vs Class

At this stage, the leap to consumption-based politics is not big but it is very significant. The politics of consumption assumes an important role in the anti-collectivist narrative because, like monetarism in economic policy, it seemed to translate political–electoral behavior into the language of experience.

On its face, the translation is simple and direct. Both in terms of identity and material advantages, the Thatcher years helped create a majority of "haves" and a minority of "have-nots" defined by a private/public distinction in how people acquire services like health care and fulfill their shelter requirements. Increasingly, it is argued, distinctions based on patterns of consumption rather than class influence political behavior. As Peter Saunders puts it, "we are moving [in Britain] towards a dominant mode of consumption in which the majority will satisfy most of its consumption requirements through private purchase ... while the minority is cast adrift on the waterlogged raft of the welfare state." As Saunders notes, "Whereas the class system is constituted in such a way that a minority excludes a majority from its power and privileges, the divisions arising out of consumption reveal an inverted pattern."[17]

Despite the intuitive force of this argument, I hope to show below (i) that conceptual problems weaken the consumption cleavages model and confuse important issues about class and class politics; (ii) that the

16 S. Hall and D. Held, "Left and rights," *Marxism Today* (June 1989), p. 16.
17 P. Saunders, *Social Theory and the Urban Question*, 2nd edn (New York: Holmes & Meier, 1986), p. 318.

effects of consumption patterns on British elections have been exaggerated, and that the advantages that consumption politics offers to the Conservatives have, for the most part, come and gone; (iii) that consumption politics is likely to tilt *toward Labour* in the future (unless, as is always possible, Labour manages to squander the opportunity to turn the issue to its advantage); and (iv) that despite the conceptual nonidentity between consumption and class, a renewal of a collectivist politics may lie in a recognition of their potential programmatic compatibility.

The decline of class in interpretations of British politics

Political attitudes and behavior are no doubt influenced by interpretations which explicitly privilege some experiences, interests, and intuitions about "the way the world works" over others. An understanding of class which overestimates the effects of consumption cleavages on politics is neither innocent nor inconsequential. As with texts that leave race and gender silent, the disappearance of class helps construct a political world in which the experiences of work hierarchies and solidarities do not matter.

Unless very carefully distinguished, the multiple objects of study to which the term class, itself, has been applied in the analysis of party competition and electoral behavior in Britain equates the unequal and therefore helps silence any politics which includes a productivist element. In British electoral studies the concept "class" has been applied to occupation within a manual/nonmanual divide, private/public cleavages in consumption, and ownership of the means of production and control over other people's labor in the workplace.[18] Moreover, none of the camps has offered a convincing causal model of the relationship between class identity/position, however defined, and voting patterns. As Elinor Scarbrough has observed about Dunleavy and Husbands' effort to integrate social class distinctions with private/public cleavages in consumption and production, it "is suggestive about sources of social diversity, [but] it lacks any mechanism by which to understand how experiences in a social location provide a grounding for partisan decisions."[19] With little modification the same could be said to describe the explanatory gap between sociological condition and political behavior which remains

18 Dunleavy and Husbands, for example, integrate these two dimensions of social class with a more conventional third dimension based on the manual–nonmanual divide. They acknowledge the influence of Erik Olin Wright's treatment of class, and it is likely that they intend the manual–non-manual distinction to correspond to Wright's distinction based on skill assets (P. Dunleavy and C. Husbands, *British Democracy at the Crossroads* (London: Allen & Unwin, 1985), p. 122). See E. O. Wright, *Classes* (London: Verso, 1985).

19 E. Scarbrough, "The British electorate twenty years on: electoral change and election surveys," *British Journal of Political Science*, 17, 2 (April 1987), pp. 231–2.

unbridged in party identification and issue voting models which begin
from occupational class formulations, despite increasingly thoughtful
applications of a variety of rational choice models.[20]

The distinctiveness of the different meanings of class is obscured by a
tacit assumption that incompatible definitions and classificatory schemes
can be made commensurate through "negotiation." But should the
general uneasiness about the definition and influence of class which
characterizes British electoral studies lead to the conclusion that social
identities and collectivities based in productive relations have become
irrelevant?

The studies do not actually suggest that this is so, but any such tacit
conclusion not only obscures the category of social class by default but,
in so doing, privileges (and encourages) the anti-collectivist Thatcherite
vision of political life without society. This problem arises even if one
leaves aside the manual/nonmanual distinction as too crude and focuses
on the distinction between consumption sector/class and social class.
Despite efforts by Saunders, Dunleavy and Husbands, and others to
develop analytical distinctions between class and sectoral concepts,[21]
both the form of the argument and the conclusions tend to spill the two
concepts together.

For example, in an effort to view comprehensively both "production-
side" and "consumption" influences on voting alignments in the 1983
general election, Dunleavy and Husbands look at the effects, in turn, of
social class and "consumption locations" on voting patterns. Thus, conceptual equivalence is created between location in a system of production and "consumption locations" defined by privatized or commodified
"participation" in five consumption processes: home-ownership, access
to a car, use of a private old-age home, private medical care, and past
or prospective private schooling by a family member.[22] Rejecting
individualistic assumptions, Dunleavy and Husbands rely upon "aggregate social phenomena" that define the "social structure" or "social
location" and these include both "production influences (such as social
class, economic activity status, sectoral location, unionization and
gender) and consumption influences."[23]

20 For example, see D. Butler and D. Stokes, *Political Change in Britain: The
Evolution of Electoral Choice*, 2nd edn (London: Macmillan, 1974); D. Butler and
D. Kavanagh, *The British General Election of 1983* (London: Macmillan, 1984); D.
Butler and D. Kavanagh, *The British General Election of 1987* (London: Macmillan,
1988); B. Särlvik and I. Crewe, *Decade of Dealignment* (Cambridge: Cambridge
University Press, 1983). For a discussion of the problem, see Scarbrough,
pp. 230–7.
21 See V. Duke and S. Edgell, "Public expenditure cuts in Britain and consumption sectoral cleavages," *International Journal of Urban and Regional Research*, 8, 2
(1984), pp. 181–3.
22 Dunleavy and Husbands, *British Democracy at the Crossroads*, p. 140.
23 Dunleavy and Husbands, ibid., pp. 18–19.

From this perspective, collectively sorted and interpreted ideological messages condition voting, as people in different "social locations" assess party association with or distance from salient issues linked to their social locations. As a consequence, in the resulting analysis of voting patterns, a "cumulative consumption sectors approach"[24] conceptually equates as a structural influence access to a car and social class location. Any such implication of equivalence in terms of characteristic influence on life experience and political behavior seems far-fetched, as does the characterization of consumption choices as structural (although the term "consumption location" may sound quite permanent and fixed). Whatever the intent, a process of political individuation which helps underwrite anti-collectivism is unjustifiably enhanced.

By contrast, Saunders' method and empirical forecasts assert the difference between class and consumption sectors. Thus "the boundaries of consumption sectors bear a necessary non-correspondence to class boundaries (in Weberian terms they are 'status groups'), nor do they necessarily exhibit any significant degree of overlap with each other."[25] From this premise, Saunders develops what he calls a "dualistic theory of politics" which maintains corporatist interest intermediation at the level of the nation-state within a framework of productivist politics, and projects the greatest influence of the politics of consumption at the local level where "imperfect pluralism" leaves authorities and local officials open to sectoral pressures.[26] Nevertheless, in a neo-Weberian effort to swallow class theory, Saunders concludes that a process of restratification is taking place: consumption cleavages "are important in shaping material life chances, in structuring political alignments, and in shaping cultural experiences and identities,"[27] and people in consumption sectors "share certain fundamental material interests in common."[28] At this point, sector has effectively been transmuted into class in both subjective

24 The cumulative sectors approach assumes a differential influence of consumption location based on the number of privatized or commodified consumption options (from the list above) employed by respondents who are grouped accordingly (none, one, two, three, or more). Dunleavy and Husbands, ibid., pp. 140–1.
25 A. Cawson and P. Saunders, "Corporatism, competitive politics, and class struggles," in *Capital and Politics*, ed. R. King (London: Routledge & Kegan Paul, 1983), quoted in Duke and Edgell, "Public expenditure cuts," p. 182. Saunders is very clear that separate "theoretical and conceptual tools" should be employed to analyze class relations/divisions (production based) and sectoral relations/divisions (consumption based). See P. Saunders, "Beyond housing classes: the sociological significance of private property rights in means of consumption," *International Journal of Urban and Regional Research*, 8, 2 (1984), pp. 202–23; and M. Harloe's reply, "Sector and class: a critical comment," *International Journal of Urban and Regional Research*, 8, 2 (1984), pp. 228–37.
26 Saunders, Beyond housing classes," pp. 306–7.
27 Saunders, ibid., p. 319.
28 Saunders, ibid., p. 321.

terms (regarding cultural experiences and identities) and objective terms (regarding common material interests). In forging such an equivalence, the category of social class is obscured once again, the experiences which ground social class are devalued, and the *structural* status of consumption options and individual choices is overblown.

This criticism of the explanatory tilt toward consumption politics should *not* be viewed as an effort to resurrect an anachronistic class model that denies the structural transformations (such as "de-industrialization") which represent profound limiting factors on Labour and other processes (like the "feminization of the labor force") which represent new opportunities. Rather, it is in part an effort to debunk a powerful intellectual instrument which has helped explain the world in a way that justifies the "Thatcher revolution." It is also an attempt to preserve what sociologists sometimes call "agency" and political scientists call "behavior." Given the current volatility of the British electorate, the complex and ungovernable factors that are recasting British politics, from Green politics to Europe, and the vicissitudes of leadership and even organizational form in contemporary party competition, it seems only sensible to question claims that electoral–political outcomes have been foreordained by structural factors which have created a two-thirds–one-third society with Conservatives inevitably dominant.

The politics of consumption: structure or behavior?

Ivor Crewe is exactly right to observe about the shrinking of the working class vote for Labour, "the causes of Labour's decline are as much behavioural as structural."[29] The political–electoral implications of the politics of consumption are likewise as much behavioral as structural, the use to which they can be put in party competition dependent upon the policy options that drive them, the vision of politics that frames them, and the contemporary popularity of the party and the leader who enunciate them. Through the 1987 general election, all these factors played to the advantage of the Conservatives, but important cross-currents have begun to emerge as the European elections of June 1989 may indicate.

Does "consumption location" represent a fundamental structural force at play in British politics or do consumption patterns and choices have more limited and open influences on British politics? It is my contention that group perceptions of sectoral consumption interests that result in individual cross-pressures in voting have a short time horizon and are likely to have only relatively circumscribed pass-through consequences on electoral behavior and little long-term effect on the alignment of party competition.

Even with the issue of housing, where the consensus is greatest and the influence on recent electoral behavior most convincing, there is little

---

29   I. Crewe, this volume, p. 26.

to support a claim that consumption location has reached the status of a structural factor. The sales of council houses have mainly involved the preferred category of semi-attached houses with gardens, which amount to roughly one-third of the housing stock;[30] they are typically occupied by those with the means necessary to buy their housing and the majority have already done so. So, as a campaign issue, the importance of housing tenure is likely to recede in the future. Moreover, even stalwarts of the consumption cleavage approach admit that by 1983 housing patterns had begun to stabilize, their influence on political alignments were lessening, and the effects on the electorate had declined. As the most forceful advocates of a consumption sector approach, Dunleavy and Husbands should be taken seriously in their cautionary advice that it is the *transition* (the move from public to private) not the *condition* that seems to affect electoral behavior:

> If these patterns of change in housing ... have begun to stabilize, we may then expect to see a concomitant settling of their influence on alignments, especially if other consumption sector cleavages become progressively more important in economic and ideological terms.... The extent to which the electorate is fragmented by the housing cleavage is already beginning to decline.[31]

Studies of electoral behavior support the view of reduced influence: according to Crewe, by 1987 the swing by buyers from Labour to Conservative was down to 2 percent over the national trend.[32]

While it is hard to predict with certainty what effects housing consumption will have on electoral behavior in the future, it is safe to say that those effects are not structurally set, but rather subject to change in policy and perception linked to broader political–cultural messages. For the Conservatives, with the political gains for the most part behind them, both the material and "narrative" demands of the housing issue may prove difficult to sustain. In fact, there are signs that housing policy is beginning to cut the other way, eroding Conservative support. On the one hand, deductibility of mortgage interest is capped at £30,000, the Treasury is opposed to deductibility altogether, and the value of the deduction is rapidly declining as a proportion of the price of houses. On the other hand, the increase in mortgage interest rates of some 6 percent in 1988–9, fuelled at least in part by the Chancellor's policy of encouraging higher interest rates to reduce overheating of the economy, has significantly raised the monthly payments for home-owners' mortgages (which are mainly adjustable mortgages).

The combination of significantly increased out-of-pocket expenses and

30 P. Taylor-Gooby, *Public Opinion, Ideology and State Welfare* (London: Routledge & Kegan Paul, 1985), p. 80.
31 Dunleavy and Husbands, *British Democracy at the Crossroads*, p. 143.
32 Crewe, this volume, p. 34.

a static housing market (particularly in London and the southeast) squeezes both Conservative converts among the new ownership class who bought their council houses and "Thatcher's children" in the south. An "anti-collectivist" vision girded by Hayek's notion of the serfdom of municipal states has come up against the lived experience of an increasingly onerous slavery to the bank or building society. It is no surprise that discussions of the Conservatives' poor showing in the European elections are full of references to interest rates and mortgages,[33] nor is there any great puzzlement over the fact that the swing to Labour was greatest in London, the Southeast, and the Midlands where the housing pressure is also greatest.[34] Although the picture is neither clear nor fixed (governments can always manipulate tax benefits and mortgage rates), there are signs of a consumption politics backlash. Housing-cost pressure on the Tories may become like wage-push pressures on Labour during the era of the ill-fated Social Contract: they cannot be met by a government facing broader macroeconomic pressures and, as a result, a rebellion by natural constituents builds up to embarrass a government and cloud the shared vision which had sustained it.

Looking elsewhere, there seems little reason to suppose that other consumption-based issues will acquire even the short-term political significance that housing achieved in the 1980s, nor that any will achieve structural status. Moreover, as with housing, time may not be on the Conservatives' side.

First, the state provisions in which privatization is considered the most likely – health care and pensions – rank highest in the public judgment (98 percent or higher in one study) that services should be provided by the state, although many in Britain (four-fifths in the same study) oppose a policy of preventing people from "paying extra for themselves for services they need."[35] Second, the impact of privatization in these areas has been minor and is likely to remain limited. The likelihood of expansion of private old-age pensions is limited by the preferential employee opportunities which are required, and, similarly, the popular outrage unleashed in November 1988 by government consideration of a plan to introduce means testing for many pensioners' rights suggests that for the foreseeable future old-age pensions will remain a predominantly public provision.

In health care, private hospital beds accounted for only 6 percent in 1981 and rates of growth in private subscriptions fell from 26 percent in the boom year of 1980 to 3 percent in 1982.[36] Private health care is limited for the most part to specialized aspects of medical care, particularly short-term hospitalization with outpatient emphasis, and private

---

33 See, for example, P. Jenkins, "A difficult ballot paper to contemplate," *The Independent*, June 15, 1989, p. 29.
34 "While those behind cried forward," *The Economist*, June 24, 1989, p. 56.
35 Taylor-Gooby, *Public Opinion*, pp. 29–40.
36 Taylor-Gooby, ibid., p. 80.

health insurance is concentrated in heavily employer-subsidized group plans among predominantly privileged employee clientele. In addition, the pressure for expansion of private health provision is heavily associated with the insurance providers, who pay for 80 percent of private medical expenses. Not surprisingly, insurance coverage drops off very sharply as one goes down the table of socioeconomic groups: 23 percent of the professional and managerial socioeconomic groups benefit from private medical insurance plans, while only 2 percent of semi-skilled and unskilled manual socioeconomic groups have coverage.[37]

Extensive growth of private provision therefore seems unlikely[38] and the political–electoral gains to the Conservatives of privately based consumption in health care, which very seldom surfaces outside core Conservative socioeconomic groups, seem very modest. Health care contributes very little to the creation of a "majority of haves" whose reliance on private provision helps cement a sectoral identity, particularly since a large percentage of those with private benefits "have built up a 'mixed bundle' of welfare provision in which they depend on the National Health Service (NHS) for serious conditions while relying on the private sector to bypass the NHS waiting list for non-urgent treatment."[39] On the contrary, the strategic selection of a mix of public and private health care services by those with the wherewithal to have consumption choices underscores the problems associated with terminology like "consumption location" which imputes a fixed structural character to a fluid set of options and hybrid choices.

More to the point, for those who argue that consumption politics in this anti-collectivist age invariably ("structurally") strengthens the Conservatives, the early returns on the current package of market-based reforms to the NHS presented by Kenneth Clarke, the Health Secretary, on behalf of the government must be disheartening. According to surveys taken by the Royal College of Physicians and the British Medical Association (BMA), most medical consultants reject the government's plan to encourage hospitals to become self-governing, and their representatives voted overwhelmingly in June 1989 to oppose the plan claiming that it "would lead to greater inequality in care and threaten comprehensive services."[40]

The proposals have generated opposition by every organization of health care professionals in the country, and motivated the usually staid and establishment BMA to launch an unprecedented advertising campaign which goes beyond disagreement over policy to challenge the fundamental principles of Thatcher's anti-collectivist political narrative. A remarkable cultural text, the campaign affirms values such as equality

37 S. Curtice and J. Mohan, "The geography of ill health and health care," in Lewis and Townsend, *The North–South Divide*, p. 187.
38 Harloe, "Sector and class," p. 230.
39 Curtis and Mohan, "The geography of ill health," p. 189.
40 "Consultants reject hospital opt-out," *The Times*, June 16, 1989, p. 2.

and fairness and debunks the core anti-collectivist virtue of competition. Read one advertisement: "Mr Clarke wants to introduce a new spirit of competition within the NHS – the health of the patient versus the cost of the treatment."[41] Health is a crucial consumption issue with far reaching implications, but far from advancing a permanent Conservative majority linked to growing privatization and sustained by anti-collectivist values, the health care proposals have doubly hurt the government. They gave strong institutional voice to resurgent collectivist values, contributed to Thatcher's setbacks in the European election, as many observers have noted and her aides have conceded, and very likely contributed to her demise.[42]

If the above observations are true, then four conclusions follow. First, no consumption location issue is likely to achieve the political–electoral salience that housing possessed at the height of its significance. Second, insofar as the issues of old-age pensions and health care influence individual voting through complex processes that match interest and party, barring maladroit Labour handling of these issues, the politics of consumption is likely to advantage the Labour Party.

Third, it seems likely that Saunders is going too far in arguing that consumption sector developments are leading to an "inverted triangle" with the majority of "haves" who can sustain private consumption options pitted against the minority of "have-nots" who remain dependent on the state for consumption options. It has become clear, in fact, that very extensive direct and indirect state subsidies are involved in the "private" provision of housing, health care, and pensions.[43] Discounts and mortgage tax relief, the reliance on NHS hospitals and laboratories, and tax relief to employers (and employees) on contributions to health care insurance and occupational pension schemes ensure continued dependences for the relatively prosperous. In that sense, the society remains populated almost universally by "have-nots."

Finally, I hope that I have shown why claims that consumption sectors have become a central structural force for the remodeling of the British electorate and the marginalization of Labour should be viewed with considerable skepticism. Housing policy enjoyed considerable pass-through influence for the Conservatives in 1983, was much reduced in significance in 1987, and, for reasons explained above, began to show signs of benefiting Labour in the European elections of June 1989. No other consumption issue has demonstrated political–electoral influence in the same way and early indications are that pensions and health care may naturally be tipping towards Labour.

None of the above four points is intended to suggest that changes in the public/private balance in consumption options have not conditioned

41   C. R. Whitney, "Thatcher's new health plan: an outcry rises on all sides," *New York Times*, June 26, 1989, pp. A1, A10.
42   Whitney, *New York Times*, p. A1.
43   See Taylor-Gooby, *Public Opinion*, pp. 82–7; Harloe, "Sector and class," pp. 228–31.

the *behavior* of voters and thereby influenced elections in the 1980s and it is not my purpose to adjudicate the complicated claims of combatants in the ongoing debate about "the British electorate." Rather, only a more limited, essentially negative, claim is made at this juncture: that there is nothing in the nature of consumption cleavages to recast political alignments in Britain in structural terms nor to mandate an anti-class centrism or a Lib–Lab pact. And nothing foreordains the decline of a party which refuses to deny that experiences of production powerfully influence political behavior and help form collective identities in society, whatever Thatcher's efforts to discredit the very concept of society. Simply put, Labour's future as a serious contender for national leadership has not been determined by inexorable structural forces and may rely instead on its ability to contest the pervasive anti-collectivism that Thatcher spawned and develop an alternative narrative to explain British political life.

Consumption, Class, and Collectivism

In Britain, Thatcherism has involved a concerted effort in discourse and policy to advance consumption-based politics strategically to legitimize an anti-collectivist vision, and to demobilize and discredit production-based politics and social solidarities. The political significance and institutional pervasiveness of the Thatcherite onslaught on collectivism and the drift of the academic controversy over consumption cleavages have obscured an important point. Consumption cleavage and social class are neither identical nor equivalent, but nor are they necessarily antagonistic principles of social identity.

Postindustrial society involves the novel and fluid interplay of consumption (which remains collective in significant ways) and production politics. This creates the possibility for a *new collectivism* and the first job of the Labour Party is to frame collective consumption in its master narrative of political life, and to use it programmatically to help motivate new solidarities and reconstruct core constituencies. Success in this project would require an abrupt reversal in the tendency of party leaders to endorse the principles of individualism, effectively assume leadership for Thatcher's anti-collectivism, and decide to orient their appeal even further "to the individuals who own their own house, a car and perhaps £500 worth of shares,"[44] as the Labour Party's Campaign Coordinator explained shortly after the 1987 election. It would also involve several critical departures both from traditional Labourist social democracy and from Kinnock's more centrist approach.

For a start, class must be recast: it loses its ontological privilege and some (but not all) of its strategic priority. On the one hand, the claim that "consumption location" is a social structural characteristic comparable with social class is unconvincing. The term is an effort to impute to

44 Wainwright, "The limits of Labourism," p. 43.

a set of unconnected market choices a cohesive, external, and impersonal force. Individual choices/capacities to buy a house or use a private car might be used, as like measures have been before, as a measure of poverty or deprivation, not as a demonstration of emergent structural properties in society. But, on the other hand, traditional class theory overreaches the mark, asserting that labor is not only "a fundamental category of human existence ... and a scheme both of action and of apprehending the world"[45] but *the* fundamental category. It is possible to affirm that the social relations forged in production have considerable importance for political life and the formation of collective solidarities without "accepting the elision of labour and *Praxis*,"[46] that is, without accepting the claim that all socially constitutive human activity involves production.

Second, consumption should be stripped of its Thatcherite under-pinnings and recast as part of a collectivist politics. It has been argued by theorists of collective action that "a state is first of all an organization that provides public goods for its members, the citizens; and other types of organizations similarly provide collective goods for their members."[47] As "consumption cleavage" theorists emphasize, the Thatcher govern-ment's numerous privatization measures diminish the reservoir of public goods, shift resources from the state to other organizations, and privilege membership in specific groups over citizenship in the fulfillment of basic social needs (shelter, health care, etc.) – hence the claim that Britain has become a "two-thirds society," echoed in Labour's recent policy review.[48] Consumption theorists overlook or underplay, however, the fact that if the condition of a public good is kept in mind (it is "in some degree indivisible and non-excludable" with respect to a given group[49]), then the goods at issue are a set of *mixed types*: hospitals are indivisible but with the government's proposed changes potentially excludable; housing is divisible but the associated benefits (the subsidies granted in the sale of council houses or the more general mortgage interest deducti-bility) are nonexcludable with respect to the relevant group. Classic Labourism stresses universal citizenship rights for the provision of social needs, while Thatcherites and many consumption cleavage theorists stress societyless individualism as the field of provision. With some exceptions, both camps ignore the crucial collective dimension of even "privatized" social provision which stems from the mix of divisible–indivisible/

45 J. Habermas, *Knowledge and Human Interests* (Boston, MA: Beacon Press, 1971), p. 28.
46 A. Giddens, *A Contemporary Critique of Historical Materialism*, vol. 1, *Power, Property and the State* (Berkeley and Los Angeles, CA: University of California Press, 1981), p. 53.
47 M. Olson, *The Logic of Collective Action: Public Goods and the Theory of Groups* (Cambridge, MA, and London: Harvard University Press, 1971), p. 15.
48 *Meeting the Challenge/Make the Change*, p. 29.
49 M. Taylor, *The Possibility of Cooperation* (Cambridge and New York: Cam-bridge University Press, 1987), p. 5.

excludable–nonexcludable elements. The rise of mortgage interest rates, like the shutting down of a general purpose inner-city hospital due to the "success" of the internal market for health services, affects specific collectivities: not universal citizens nor merely individuals. It is Labour's job to identify these fractional collectivities and help spawn new solidarities and constituencies associated with these "mixed" consumption goods that are neither perfectly private nor perfectly public but collective in ways strictly delimited by state policy: health care, education, housing, child care, etc.

Third, the understandings of class and consumption politics must be reconstituted with a full appreciation of their gender-specific character in contemporary societies. This project begins with an understanding that "feminine and masculine gender identity run like pink and blue threads through the areas of paid work, state administration and citizenship ... [and] gender identity is lived out in all arenas of life."[50] Yet gender identity is experienced quite differently in various arenas of social life, a fact which greatly complicates the interactive effects of class, gender, and consumption on political attitudes and behavior. Can Labour mobilize support in part by recasting its narrative to help women make sense of their changing lives in all three arenas?

Changes in *paid work* may be the most profound, the easiest to interpret, and the most difficult to acknowledge organizationally. Whatever the resistance in union and party organizations, the expansion of the service sector, the decline of "industrial" employment, and the active participation of women in paid work make the traditional appeal to "full employment" based on the privileged position of male "proletarian manufacturing" implausible if not impossible.[51] This crucial structural change provides the rationale for a challenge to deeply entrenched patterns of job discrimination and segregation and unequal pay,[52] and the impetus to confront gendered and sex-segregated models of women at the workplace and in the labor market.[53] Thus far, however, neither the Labour Party nor trade unions have done much to challenge the gendered character of social class and the experience of production. To date, the "masculine subtext of the worker role is confirmed by the vexed and strained character of women's relation to paid work in male-dominated

50   N. Fraser, "What's critical about critical theory?," in *Feminism as Critique* ed. S. Benhabib and D. Cornell (Minneapolis, MN: University of Minnesota Press, 1988), p. 45.
51   A. Barnett, "Is Labour for turning?," *New Statesman and Society*, September 30, 1988, p. 14. See also D. Coates, *The Context of British Politics* (London: Hutchinson, 1984), pp. 63–75.
52   S. Perrigo, "The women's movement: patterns of oppression and resistance," in *A Socialist Anatomy of Britain*, ed. D. Coates, G. Johnston, and R. Bush (Cambridge, Polity Press: 1985), pp. 132–44.
53   R. Feldberg and E. N. Glenn, "Male and female: job versus gender models in the sociology of work," in *Women and the Public Sphere*, ed. J. Siltanen and M. Stanworth (London: Hutchinson, 1984), pp. 23–36.

classical capitalism" – as service workers and members of the "helping professions," poorly paid and relatively unprotected workers in sex-segregated occupations, part-time workers, "working wives" and "working mothers."[54]

Similarly, the collective identities fashioned by the administration of the welfare state and the needs fulfilled through "public consumption" are interpreted and experienced in gendered terms: labor-market-based programs are "masculine" and family/household-based programs are "feminine."[55] By contrast to the secondary character of women's relationship to paid labor, the gendered character of the consumer role cuts the other way, with primary responsibility for consumption assigned to women, both in its general domestic forms and in particular with regard to health and child care, and in other social welfare related to "collective goods." Changes in eligibility and reductions of provision tend to re-absorb women into the private sphere of responsibilities as mother/wife/daughter.[56] Under these circumstances, the often precarious situations of female heads of household are particularly endangered and, likewise, women in multiple-earner households face reductions in labor force participation, their contributions to and control over the household budget, and their autonomy and control within the household.

Certainly gender-based experience is not a solvent that washes clean all differences of interest based on consumption sector or social class. Nevertheless, a recognition of the gendered character of each may provide some tentative directions for a revitalization of Labour's appeal and the creation of a new narrative to replace Labour's post-1945 social democratic vision and challenge Thatcher's anti-collectivism.

One way to pose the alternative might be termed "new collectivism," a perspective which emerges from an appreciation of the partial and overlapping identities that help constitute collectivities. By contrast with classic postwar social democratic collectivism, this variant refuses to privilege white male manufacturing labor, attempts to explicate the pink and blue threads that run through public policy, work space, and house-hold life, and looks to identify policies that reinforce the collective condition-based solidarities and group identities that constitute society.

From a stance that accepts that both labor and other forms of social activity constitute identities, it is far easier to value both work relations which are the core of social class and issues of housing tenure – which involve not only property acquisition but also changes in community, leisure patterns, and often household responsibilities and interactions –

54 Fraser, "What's critical about critical theory?," pp. 42–3.
55 See N. Fraser, *Unruly Practices: Power, Discourse and Gender in Contemporary Social Theory* (Minneapolis, MN: University of Minnesota Press, 1989), pp. 144–60.
56 J. Dale and P. Foster, *Feminists and State Welfare* (London: Routledge & Kegan Paul, 1986), pp. 59–61.
57 See Crewe, this volume, p. 36.

as pervasive and enduring elements of people's lives.[57] With an understanding that crucial areas of social consumption involve "mixed" goods which are neither private/individual nor public/universal but strictly delimited by state policy, it is possible to make sense of the terribly significant difference between *universal* citizenship rights and the resources necessary to substantively achieve the relevant goals of good housing or quality education that implicate *selective collectivities differently* on the basis of conditions such as location, access, and financial resources.[58]

From an appreciation of the gendered character of social class experiences and collective consumption, it is easier to present policies like pay equity and social service provision that affirm the feminine subtexts of worker and family experiences. While interest-based policies directed at constituencies defined at the nexus of collective consumption and social class may help motivate crucial areas of support, it may be even more important to present a narrative of contemporary life that makes sense to the female nonmanual workers (and their male counterparts at home and on the job) who are crucial to Labour's appeal outside the economically marginalized residue of the party's traditional base. Labour is in a serious bind, and there is more at issue in the fate of socialism in Britain than what market research may say about the most expedient course to pursue in the next general election.

Labour's chances

From any reasonable perspective, the desertion of over two-fifths of Labour's support between 1951 and 1987[59] and, more particularly, the significant north–south divide in the geography of voting create a formidable obstacle to Labour's success at the next general election. If Labour won all the seventy seats where it came within 10 percentage points of the Tory tally in 1987 it would still remain fifteen seats behind the Conservatives in the House of Commons; if the Social and Liberal Democrats (or a centrist alliance of whatever shape) also won in all twenty-eight constituencies in which the Alliance came second to the Conservatives by 10 percent or less in 1987, then the Labour party would be the largest party in a hung Parliament.[60] Despite what the opinion polls may suggest, and despite results of by-elections and the elections for the European Parliament, the obstacles make a Labour victory at the next election uncertain. It may be Kinnock's job to rally

58 For a useful discussion of this point with regard to reproductive rights, see Committee for Abortion Rights and Against Sterilization Abuse (CARASA), S. E. Davis (ed.), *Women Under Attack: Victories, Backlash, and the Struggle for Reproductive Freedom* (Boston, MA: South End, 1989).
59 Crewe, this volume, p. 21.
60 R. J. Johnston, C. J. Pattie, and J. G. Allsopp, *The Electoral Map of Great Britain 1979–1987: A Nation Dividing?* (London: Longman, 1988), pp. 305–6.

the troops, but as with most generals he should be warned off the proclivity to fight the last war.

The most pressing question for Labour supporters is not "how do we win the next election?" but "how do we win the argument?" If the premise is accepted that the central task *now* is to set the preconditions for success *whenever it may come* (whether in the next or the subsequent general election), then counting the votes to evaluate alternative strategies[61] becomes a questionable approach. If for no other reason, the expanded time horizon multiplies the uncertain influences of leadership and organizational capacity and "externalities" to the usual run of things in British elections (environmentalism, Europe, etc.).

"Simplifying drastically, the Left has both a social and political choice," writes Crewe. "As regards the first, it can seek to recapture the working class votes it has lost, or if it regards them as irretrievable, seek new support from other classes. As regards the second, it can choose to appeal on either traditional or new ideological grounds, irrespective of its social choice."[62] These either–or alternatives are not persuasive, however, in part because the discourse and practice of Thatcherism have altered the boundaries and both fragmented and reconstituted social identities.

Thus the options for Labour recovery designated in each cell of Crewe's figure 2.1 (see page 38) have a "freeze frame" quality that preserves political images taken out of context and fails to capture some crucial developments which create identities that merge production experiences and consumption interests. Many of Scargill's Yorkshire miners who provide the iconography of Strategy 1 (see top left corner) have bought their council houses, are vying with each other for redundancy payments as the industry is run down in the northeast, are consuming in a frenzy, and are buying up pubs and other small businesses. They remain as "class conscious" as anyone, but they have also entered the alleged "two-thirds society" with abandon.

Similarly, I would suggest that Strategy 3 (see bottom right corner, "Coalition of minorities") does not fully reveal the dynamics of the "rainbow alliance" politics or its extensive overlap with the preferred appeal to expanded social rights of citizenship which is central to Strategy 2 (see top right, "Updating 1945"). Before the abolition of the Greater London Council (GLC) and a set of metropolitan councils in March 1986, a number of multifaceted action committees and groups were spawned in a host of London boroughs and women's committees sponsored by local authorities were created in some twenty-two other cities in England and Scotland.[63] Autonomous feminist organizations, politically motivated councillors and local government officials, members

61 See Crewe, this volume, p. 37.
62 Crewe, this volume, p. 37.
63 J. Gelb, "Feminism and political action," in *Challenging the Political Order*, ed. R. Dalton and M. Kuechler (New York: Oxford University Press, 1990), pp. 141–4.

of trades councils and Labour Party activists allied in a number of cases (such as the GLC and the Sheffield Council) to develop approaches to economic planning, and in Walsall, thirty-three neighborhood offices were set up with housing departments and repair teams with considerable local access and immediate accountability.[64] In bringing together white women and women of color, and by developing alliances with occasional trade union allies like the National Union of Public Employees (NUPE) in London, the local campaigns focused attention on crucial structural properties of British society, notably the feminization and racial asymmetry of poverty and the difficulties faced by female-headed single-parent households. "Despite media emphasis on funding of 'radical' projects," notes one observer, "in fact child care subsidies comprised the bulk of GLC funding efforts."[65] The identification of the GLC activities with a "coalition of minorities" strategy as distinct and separate from (and by implication at cross-purposes with) an appeal to nonmanual workers associated with the expansion of the social rights of citizenship (the "updating 1945" strategy) is not helpful for a number of reasons. It fails to explain that the core constituency of the "coalition of minorities" was defined by gender not race or sexual preference (and is therefore potentially majoritarian), that it was mobilized by collective concerns for social consumption/social rights of citizenship that motivate a core constituency of nonmanual workers, and that it brought together (partially and for a time) trade union/productivist and consumption-based agencies.

Whatever may be said to challenge the validity and potential of pre-existing alternative strategies, it is much more difficult, of course, to suggest what interpretation would make sense of things from a broadly socialist perspective and have the potential in the medium run to mobilize majoritarian support. But if the central task for Labour's revitalization is to get the interpretation right so that Labour can once again make sense of political life, then historically repetitive choices based on a definition of social identities trapped in discrete binary oppositions will not do the trick. A "postindustrial" and "post-modernist" politics of fragmented partial identities based in diverse social relations and animated by both productivist and consumption influences requires a different mapping of the social–political world, a set of political strategies which challenge the old definitions, and a programmatic agenda which confirms new collective identities.

Unfortunately, the Labour Party leadership does not see it this way. "Being part of a collective is not as strong as it used to be," observed Neil Kinnock a few weeks after the 1987 election. "Our initial approach

64   D. Massey, L. Segal, and H. Wainwright, "And now for the good news," in *The Future of the Left*, ed. J. Curran (London: Polity Press/*New Socialist*, 1984), pp. 216–21.
65   Gelb, "Feminism and political action," p. 142.

has got to be from the party to the individual. They have got to be told that socialism is the answer for them because socialism looks after the individual."[66] If the individuals are individual property owners, private consumers, and shareholders, then conservatism looks after them well enough and the Conservative party helps them stake their claim. Structural factors aside, unless Labour can convincingly present a collectivist narrative for contemporary times, British socialism will continue its disheartening fade, whatever the opinion polls (or even electoral results) may suggest to the contrary.

66 Wainwright, "The limits of Labourism," p. 43.

4

The Changing Face of
Popular Power in France

George Ross

Introduction

The mysteries of popular power in modern France are best introduced
with a few facts. To begin with, on the political front, the parties of the
Left in France did not win a single national election between 1956 and
1981, when François Mitterrand became the first Left President of the
Fifth Republic and brought, in his wake, a Left parliamentary majority.
For more than two decades, therefore, the Center-right controlled both
the French presidency and Parliament. After 1981, however, except for a
brief interlude in 1986 and 1987 when Mitterrand and a Center-right
parliamentary majority coexisted, Left-leaning parliamentary majorities
dominated (table 4.1).

The economic context is equally interesting. The French economy
grew very rapidly – more so, indeed, than almost all its competitors –
from the later 1950s to 1973, averaging nearly 6 percent annually.
Growth rates for the rest of the 1970s slipped to 3.25 percent per year
and averaged below 2 percent for most of the 1980s (moving back to 3
percent after 1988). French inflation levels over the same years were
consistently quite high comparatively – twice those of West Germany,
France's most important European competitor, in the 1960s and 1970s,
and then three times as high during the first half of the 1980s (table 4.2).
From 1984 to 1985 France's inflation rate fell precipitously towards a
deflated European norm, however. On the labor market front, postwar
France had close to full employment through 1973, a still modest rate of
4+ percent unemployed by 1979, rising to around 10 percent by the
second half of the 1980s (table 4.3).

By combining these political and economic indicators one can infer a

Table 4.1   Left–Right electoral balances

Election	Left (%)	Right (%)	Majority
1956 Legis.	50+/−	50	Left
1958 Legis.	45.2	56.2	Right
1962 Legis.	43.7	56.2	Right
1965 Pres.	45.5	54.5	Right
1967 Legis.	43.6	56.4	Right
1968 Legis.	40.5	58.9	Right
1969 Pres.	Two Right candidates		Right
1973 Legis.	45.8	54.2	Right
1974 Pres.	49.2	50.8	Right
1978 Legis.	50.2	47.5	Right
1981 Pres.	51.8	48.2	Left
1986 Legis.	44.5	55 (45 moderate, 10 National Front)	Right
1988 Pres.	54.0	46.0	Left
1988 Legis.	50+	49+	Left

Table 4.2   Inflation, France versus West Germany

	1959–67	67–70	70–73	73–79	82	83	84	85	86	87
Fra	3.5	5.6	6.2	10.5	11.8	9.6	7.4	5.8	2.7	3.1
FRG	2.4	3.3	5.9	4.7	5.3	3.3	2.4	2.2	−0.2	3

Source: INSEE, *Tableaux de l'économie française*, 1987

Table 4.3   Unemployment in France (percentage of labor force)

1964–73	74–79	80	81	82	83	84	85	86	87
2.2	4.5	6.3	7.8	8.7	8.4	9.7	10.1	10.4	10.8

Source: INSEE, *Tableaux de l'économie française*, 1987

number of things. In France, the Right presided over, shaped, and, presumably, benefited politically from the postwar economic boom while the French Left *never* held power during the boom years. But because the Right *also* presided over the coming of economic "crisis" after 1973, it was blamed by the electorate for changing economic circumstances, allowing the Left to install itself in power in the 1980s. When the French

Left finally did break through, however, circumstances obliged it to administer an enfeebled economy which could produce but minimal growth. The French Left thus adopted austerity policies rather quickly once in power, squeezed down inflation levels precipitously, allowing unemployment to rise ever more rapidly and, as income distribution statistics show, put the brakes on wage growth.[1] The meaning of the sharp decrease in strikes which occurred in the 1980s is harder to intuit. One might suspect, erroneously, that the Left in power brought pacifying "neo-corporatist" arrangements. In fact, declining levels of industrial conflict in 1980s France, with the Left in power, indicate a general weakening of organized labor.

One more set of facts will help. Unlike many other European Lefts, the official Left in twentieth-century France has never been unified under an umbrella social democratic party and trade union confederation. Its life instead has involved persistent pluralism, largely between competitive Communist and Socialist political worlds which, during the 1960s and 1970s, had more or less equal resources. Something dramatic occurred in the 1980s to the relative strengths of these two "families," however: the Communists have very recently and very suddenly been eclipsed. Communist voting strength – just one index – which had been roughly 20–21 percent as of 1979, had fallen to below 10 percent by the later 1980s, while the Socialist voting strength went up by roughly the same amount. In a crudely electoral sense, then, the Left which exercised power in the 1980s was a different Left from that which came before it.

The chapter that follows pursues two interconnected arguments. The first is comparative. France has been different from those many advanced capitalist societies where the social democratic Left and conservative Right alternated in power during the boom years. And it has certainly not resembled those countries like Britain, the United States, West Germany, and Canada where "the crisis" produced a shift to the Right. In France the Right presided over the boom *and* the first years of the post-1974 downturn. The electoral volatility caused by changed economic circumstances thus benefited the Left, bringing it to power in the 1980s to face the worst moments of crisis. The second argument has to do with the changing nature of popular power in France itself. What

1 Between 1979 and 1982, in the wake of the second oil shock, the share of household disposable income in national value added rose 3.8 percent while the share of national value added going to firms declined by 2.3 percent. From 1982 to 1985, the first period of Left austerity, the figure for household income was −2.4 percent and for firms 1 percent while for the years 1985–7 the numbers were −2.3 percent and 2 percent respectively. See J.-M. Jeanneney, "Salaires, prix et répartition," in *L'Economie Française depuis 1967* (Paris: Seuil, 1989), ch. VIII and pp. 142–3, table 17. The figures for the 1960–83 period can be found in CERC (Centre d'Etude des Revenus et des Coûts), *La Croissance et la crise: Les revenus des français, 1960–1983* (Paris: La Documentation Française, 1985), and CERC, *Constat de l'évolution récente des revenus en France, 1984–1987* (Paris: La Documentation Française, 1988).

happened in the 1980s, in part because of the difficult economic context which the French Left faced when it finally did come to power, was that the experience of government coincided with a dramatic change in the nature of this Left itself. In effect, an "old" *ouvriériste* and radical Left gave way to a new one dominated ideologically by a technocratic modernism and administered politically by new middle strata. Popular power in France has been irremediably transformed by this change. The analysis of this dramatic transition from one Left to another by attempting to portray the complicated interactions between changing economic and labor market structures and organizations trying to define and redefine the ideological content of French Left politics is the main purpose of this chapter. The text is organized chronologically, first reviewing the trials and tribulations of the "Old Left" as it faced Left pluralism, the transition from postwar boom to crisis and longer-run social changes, and then describing the coming of a New Left in the 1980s.

Oppositional Popular Power in the 1970s

In the late 1940s France still had many of the features of an agrarian, protected, empire-oriented, and nineteenth-century society. In the twenty years that followed France expanded industrially, there were major shifts from traditional to modern sectors, productivity vastly increased, and service sector employment exploded. Economic growth was sudden and rapid.[2] In these years the French built houses, installed central heating and indoor plumbing, and bought refrigerators, washing machines, television sets, and automobiles at a tremendous pace.[3] The shape of French trade shifted away from old empire to advanced industrial societies, Western Europe in particular.

Economic change began more despite than because of French capitalists, with administrative elites helping post-1944 France toward a state-led and partly planned economic trajectory.[4] The presidentialism of the Gaullist Fifth Republic after 1958 allowed greater space for these technocrats to pursue their indicative planning, industrial policies structured around state incentives and resources, manipulation of credit and the like. Technocrats were helped, as well, by the stabilization of a quasi-

2 With the index set at 100 for 1938, gross national product was 109 in 1949, 333 in 1970, and 400 by 1975. Value added grew 5.5 percent annually from 1950 to 1957, 6 percent from 1957 to 1964, and 5.9 percent for the decade thereafter.
3 See J. Fourastié, *Les Trente glorieuses* (Paris: Fayard, 1979), p. 282, Graph 4 (household equipment, automobiles), p. 127, table 32 (vacations), p. 130, table 33 (housing).
4 After 1947 until 1958 the absence of any politically continuous majority forced Fourth Republic modernizing technocrats to pursue their strategies through state agencies, bypassing the legislature as much as possible.

permanent Center-right parliamentary majority. Perhaps most important was de Gaulle himself, a genuinely charismatic leader who added his political weight to the technocrats' modernization strategy. The General was no economist, nor was he a particularly modern man, but he had ambitious geopolitical plans which dovetailed well with the technocrats' vision.[5]

The return of the Old Left

The consolidation of a Right-leaning parliamentary majority around General de Gaulle repolarized French party politics in the 1960s.[6] At this point the Parti Communiste Français (PCF) had a solid electoral base, the support of the majority of workers, control over the strongest union, an army of militant members, substantial local governmental power, and great ideological influence over Left politics and the intelligentsia. Its major rival, the Socialist SFIO, was in electoral and membership decline, based primarily among local notables and stodgy municipal socialists with a discredited leadership.[7] The situation thus gave the Communists major strategic opportunities. The PCF's strategic choice, united frontism, involved coalition manipulation with the non-Communist Left. The initial step in this approach was to seek a "common program" with the Socialists. The Communists foresaw this program as continuing the plans of the Resistance from the 1940s – nationalizations, strengthening the labor movement, economic planning, achieving international independence – all cast in nationalistic language. Given the PCF's relative advantage over the Socialists, it was this programmatic vision and, by and large, the *ouvriériste* social map which

5 J. Lacouture, *de Gaulle*, vol. 3 (Paris: Seuil, 1986), part II, is especially good on de Gaulle's geopolitical pretensions.
6 The Fourth Republic had been founded by a very uneasy Resistance-based coalition of Gaullists, Christian Democrats, Socialists, and Communists. The crystallization of ultra-parliamentary institutions in 1946 had pushed the Gaullists out, while the coming of the Cold War in 1947 did the same to the Communists. Both groups continued to be strong electorally, however. The consequence of this, in the context of Fourth Republic institutions, was that parliamentary majorities could only come from Center-left and Center-right combinations.
7 The Section Française de l'Internationale Ouvrière (SFIO) was instrumental, among other things, in making the Cold War in Europe possible, in breaking the forward momentum of French labor after 1947 and thus allowing French capital to restore a position which had become very precarious as a result of the late 1930s and Vichy, in installing France in quasi-permanent colonial warfare (from Vietnam to Algeria), and in helping the Right to rehabilitate itself. See H. Portelli, *Le Socialisme français tel qu'il est* (Paris: PUF, 1980), especially ch. 3; D. Ligou, *Histoire du socialisme en France depuis 1900* (Paris: PUF, 1961); R. Quilliot, *La SFIO et l'exercice du pouvoir* (Paris: Fayard, 1972).

underlay it, that established the predominant vocabularies of French popular power for the next two decades[8] – hence the "return" of old Left ideas and approaches to popular power in the 1970s which we shall presently discuss.

The electoral setting of the 1960s obliged the Socialists to change their perspective on alliances[9] away from the Center-left deals which had isolated the PCF during the Cold War. The relative success of François Mitterrand's first Presidential campaign in 1965 was the initial turning point. Between 1965 and the events of 1968 the Left made slow progress toward clearer agreement on program and toward greater electoral strength. In May–June 1968, a massive rebellion against the tensions created by rapid social modernization within the conservative authoritarian political framework of Gaullism caused only a brief interruption in this evolution.[10]

May–June 1968 changed the political world faced by French capital, however. General de Gaulle's 1969 departure foreshadowed the loss of charismatic political resources for France's modernizing project and, more importantly, weakened and redefined this project itself.[11] De Gaulle's successor, Georges Pompidou, was less visionary and more conservative than the General, concerned with jettisoning *dirigisme* and clipping the wings of the modernizing high civil service to give capital new space

8 The PCF's strategic thinking and reflexes had not changed much since the 1930s, despite the emergence of an entirely new political and institutional situation. The party belligerently refused to recognize that French society might be different from what it had been in Popular Front years, as, for example, was illustrated strikingly by its insistence well into the 1960s, flying in the face of the reality of economic growth, that French workers were undergoing relative absolute pauperization and in its pro-natalist positions on birth control which signaled Communist to social changes transforming the family and labor force. Its blunt refusal to hear and heed calls for destalinization coming from the international Communist movement indicated sclerosis of yet another kind, as did the continuation of rigidly undemocratic democratic centralism inside the party.

9 In the aftermath of the end of the Algerian War in 1962 electoral and institutional movements strongly comforted the PCF's decision to reassert alliance politics. At 26 percent of the vote in 1956, the PCF suffered a net electoral loss of 25 percent in the transition to the Gaullist Republic in 1958, but its vote nonetheless remained at around 22 percent after the new Republic normalized in the early 1960s, while that of the SFIO nosedived.

10 May 1968 was also a dramatic first indicator that not all of the social forces which the official political Left sought to represent found the resurrection of a Socialist–Communist United Front around a reedition of a classically "Old Left" program to their liking. Young members of the intelligentsia were skeptical of the Socialists because of their record on decolonization and their stodginess and disliked the PCF because of its unwillingness to destalinize and its own moderation in opposing the Algerian War. And, to be sure, one found in France the general anti-authoritarian, anti-bureaucratic themes which were found in student movements elsewhere.

11 Lacouture, *de Gaulle*, ch. 27, discusses the last 300 days of de Gaulle. See also G. Pompidou, *Pour rétablir la vérité* (Paris: Flammarion, 1982).

in the European and international market. The relaxation of certain dimensions of French statism occurred at a moment of powerful renaissance for French organized labor such that new efforts to de-politicize labor relations seemed politically advisable. Efforts at mild "social democratization from the Right," to encourage decentralized collective bargaining and a neo-corporatist public sector incomes policy, foundered, however, because of opposition from both capital and labor.

These policy failures obliged capital to face an insistent and demanding working class during a moment of intense economic expansion. Real wages also began to go up rapidly, as did inflation, fed by international pressures and an exceptionally high rate of French saving. Corporate profits thus began to decline.[12] Simultaneously, French capital, dragged into the twentieth century by the state, had to begin facing the consequences of a process of modernization which had not appreciably bettered its international position. The benignly expansionist international economy of the boom years began to disappear in the early 1970s and warfare over market shares broke out between France, newly industrializing countries, and more successful, better endowed advanced capitalist economies.

The first oil shock, coinciding with the beginning of Giscard d'Estaing's presidency in 1974, brought little recognition of the minefield that French capitalism had begun to cross.[13] Government and capital both responded to inflationary pressures as just another cyclical movement susceptible to short-term Keynesian techniques.[14] Rapidly rising unemployment levels, even higher inflation rates, and the end of pre-1974 levels of growth were the results.

For the Left, the first major event in the immediate aftermath of May–June 1968 was the construction, from an assortment of non-Communist fractions including SFIO, of the new Parti Socialiste (PS), completed in 1971.[15] The new PS was a cleverly structured organization whose internal pluralism had the advantage of allowing the new PS to appear to be almost all things to all people and therefore to reach out

---

12 On the evolution of real wages and profits see J.-C. Delaunay, *Salariat et plus-value en France, depuis la fin du XIXe siècle* (Paris: Presses de la Fondation Nationale des Sciences Politiques, 1984), especially pp. 221ff.

13 Giscard continued Pompidou's de-emphasis on *dirigisme*, with the official economic planning apparatus itself gradually assuming the status of a public policy dodo.

14 See C. Stoffaës, *La Grande menace industrielle* (Paris: Calmann-Lévy, 1978), ch. III, for a description of this period and A. Cotta, *La France et l'impératif mondial* (Paris: PUF, 1978), part II, ch. 1.

15 One has an *embarras de choix* for sources on this process. In English, see D. Bell and B. Criddle, *The French Socialist Party* (Oxford: Clarendon Press, 1984), ch. 3; R. W. Johnson, *The Long March of the French Left* (London: Macmillan, 1982). In French see H. Portelli, *Le Socialisme français tel qu'il est*, and J. Kergoat, *Le Parti socialiste* (Paris: le Sycomore, 1983). For some of the flavor of the smoke-filled back rooms, see A. Du Roy and R. Schneider, *Le Roman de la rose* (Paris: Seuil, 1982).

widely both leftward and to the center.[16] Its forward movement was nonetheless purposeful, following François Mitterrand's strategy of Left Unity, to the signature, in June 1972, of a PCF-PS Common Program. Except for vagueness on issues of defense and foreign policy (where the two parties agreed to disagree), this quite radical document was simply a tamer reproduction of what the Communists had been advocating for some time. The new coalition would expand the welfare state, raise wages and benefits, operate extensive nationalizations and install democratic management at firm level coordinated with democratic planning nationally, greatly increase the rights of unions and workers, and engage in a host of other reforms to increase democratic participation locally and regionally.

In short order, then, the French Left seemed to acquire the unity and agreement on program which it had long lacked. And, indeed, an official Left political vocabulary and tone for the 1970s were established at this point. Appearances were deceiving, however. The underlying logic of Left unity meant that, if the Left as a whole was likely to grow in strength, one party's gain would come at the other's expense. The circumstances of the 1970s greatly favored the Socialists. François Mitterrand, concerned primarily with coming to power himself by strengthening the Socialists electorally at the PCF's expense, saw the Common Program more as an instrument to exploit flaws in Communist strategy than a commitment. By allying leftwards and giving in to the PCF on issues of program, Mitterrand was buying a new certificate of good Left conduct which would blur political distinctions between the PS and PCF. This certificate would then help the PS to win new support from soft – protest – sectors of the PCF electorate more attached to the Left than to the PCF. Movement towards the PS might then be magnified by the presidential effect that produces tactical voting for the party which appears more plausible. Mitterrand could also count on attracting much fresh support from leftward-moving new middle strata, politically homeless after May–June 1968.

The PCF's face-lifting responses to the perceived dangers from the Socialists proved too little and too late. Much of the PCF leadership was aware that any Communist united front success would depend on rapidly modernizing many of the party's traditional postures. Thus the party worked to change its theoretical perspectives,[17] tried, painfully and partially, to take some distance from the Soviet model, and also relaxed its

16   Since strength inside the party depended upon the support and attention garnered in mobilization, each tendency or *courant* which composed the party was encouraged to do its own politics and produce its own rhetoric.
17   The party's miserabilist absurdities were abandoned in the interests of "state monopoly capitalism" theory, an attempt to change the PCF's vision of the working class which considerably modified traditional *ouvriérisme* and re-theorized the material foundations for an alliance between workers and intermediary strata. The work was first presented in *Economie et Politique* in the later 1960s and then gathered together into a new party manual, *Traité d'économie politique (manuel), Le Capitalisme monopoliste d'état* (Paris: Editions Sociales, 1972), 2 vols.

organization somewhat to solicit greater debate and increase recruitment. In consequence, members flocked to the party, particularly from
the new middle strata, while public interest in the party's politics and
leaders grew significantly.[18] Such measures were not enough, however,
to overcome the institutional and coalitional logics upon which François
Mitterrand and the Socialists were counting. The rejuvenated PS soon
began to overtake the Communists electorally. In the 1973 legislative
elections the PCF outpolled the PS, but not by much and for the last
time. In the presidential elections of 1974 François Mitterrand, once
again the Left candidate, came within 1 percent of winning. United frontism was indeed propelling the Left toward success, but the PS was
benefiting disproportionately, making serious inroads into the PCF's
own electorate. This evidence that part of its electoral base was now in
Mitterrand's sights pushed the PCF into one of the most turbulent
periods in its history.[19]

The 1977 Municipal Elections – when the United Left first won a
majority – marked the beginning of a turn. The PCF's leap forward into
doctrinal Eurocommunism had failed to halt growing Socialist gains.
Reflection on this caused the PCF's unstable leadership compromise to
come unglued[20] and in Summer 1977 the PCF broke completely with the
Socialists. The tactical logic which led the PCF to this renunciation
proved even more costly than the alliance politics which had preceded it,

18   According to opinion poll evidence, by the mid-1970s the PCF had become
more legitimate than at any other point in its history.
19   The party moved first in 1974–5 to a year of attacks on the Socialists as
potential traitors to Left ideas and program. Next, in 1976, the PCF lived a
frenzied moment of doctrinal and political innovation – its Eurocommunist
period, when it moved closer to the Italian and Spanish Communists and joined
them in questioning Soviet hegemony in the international Communist movement. Much in this represented divisions in the party leadership about how to
respond to this challenging new situation. Some leaders pushed for further
facelifting while others advocated abandoning united frontism altogether. The
result came close to strategic and tactical incoherence. For good illustrations for
the 1974–5 period, see F. Hincker, *Le Parti communiste au carrefour* (Paris: Albin
Michel, 1981). On international matters, there were several spectacular visits by
party leaders to one another during this time, but the most important specific
event was the Eurocommunist coalition's resistance to Soviet strategic goals at
the September 1976 Berlin Conference of European Communist Parties. Jean
Kanapa, Marchais' major advisor, was the PCF's tactician in all this. Moreover,
at its 22nd Congress in 1976 – weeks after Georges Marchais had sprung the
change on its membership – the party officially abandoned the dictatorship of the
proletariat, in effect jettisoning traditional Marxist–Leninist theories of the state.
20   A recent book, purported to be based on documents of a leading PCF figure,
claims that the abandonment of united frontism occurred on Soviet initiatives.
See J. Fabien, *La Guerre des camarades* (Paris: Olivier Orban, 1985). There are
solid reasons to believe that the Soviets did not like united frontism but to move
from this to argue that the party's shift was *only* because of the Soviets is to deny
the very real logic of the situation. From a purely domestic point of view, united
frontism, as the party had defined it, had turned into a political disaster.

however. The PCF – justifiably or not – received the bulk of the blame
for the Left's defeat in the 1978 legislative elections. François Mitterrand
and the Socialists, presenting themselves as *unitaire pour deux* and standing by the Common Program, gained relatively. In addition, the abrupt
strategic shift of 1977–8 proved an utter organizational disaster for the
PCF, leading to a huge explosion of internal dissent and massive exodus
of intellectuals from the party.[21]

Ironies abounded in the Left's political situation after 1977. Having
worked for decades for a new alliance with the Socialists, the Communists had finally succeeded. The 1972 Common Program was the PCF's
program, by and large. The new united front had come into being
carrying much of the ideological and conceptual baggage which the PCF
had insisted upon. Yet the Communists paid an enormous price for their
success. Faced with a loss of Left supremacy to the Socialists, the party's
solution of renouncing the alliance which it had worked so hard to create
then achieved nothing except even greater losses. Visible electoral decline would not come until 1981, but the causes of it were readily
apparent after 1978.

The Socialist response to the PCF's twists and turns was to pose as the
only remaining defenders of the 1972 Common Program. This tactic,
promoted by François Mitterrand, was designed to maximize defections
from the PCF electorate towards the PS. Yet at the same time that the
PS was winning predominance on the Left, opposition inside the PS was
increasing to Mitterrand and the strategy of *Union de la Gauche* that he
represented, the approach of the Common Program and the discourse of
"Old Left" popular power which the PS had adopted with such tactical
success. Center-left elements within the PS who had never really
accepted *Union de la Gauche* and the Common Program gained strength,
in part by borrowing *autogestionnaire* ideas from the 1968 movement and
superimposing them upon a neo-Mendesist technocratic modernism.[22]
Beyond such political circles, large segments of the new middle strata

21 More than two decades of united frontism, however ill-conceived, not only
had been convincing to the *peuple de gauche*, but had made a substantial number
of Communists into believers as well. Perhaps more important, the years of
Union de la Gauche had attracted hundreds of thousands of new Communists,
particularly from the intelligentsia and urban middle strata, who believed themselves part of a massive project to rebuild French Communism and the French
Left. The change of 1977–8, decreed from above, and accompanied by a return
to miserabilist rhetoric of a transparently electoralist kind, galvanized these
groups into an inner-party movement of dissent the magnitude of which the PCF
had not known for decades. We have written ethnographically about how this
period was lived "from below" in the Paris party in J. Jenson and G. Ross, *The
View From Inside: A French Communist Cell in Crisis* (Berkeley, CA: University of
California Press, 1985).
22 Their leader in the later 1970s was Michel Rocard, whose challenge to
Mitterrand's PS leadership after 1978 fell short. At the center of this challenge
was an appeal to economic "realism" against the "archaic" statist radicalism of

and intelligentsia, despite continuing to vote on the Left, began to conclude that neither the PCF nor the PS, nor *a fortiori Union de la Gauche*, really addressed their concerns.[23]

These movements coincided with the spiral of ideological hysteria and post-modern skepticism of the "new philosophers." By the end of the 1970s the intellectuals as a category had turned away from the kind of politics embodied in the Common Program. Marxism collapsed as a viable intellectual paradigm, *ouvriérisme* as a broader outlook was rapidly discarded, and many of the Left intelligentsia had begun an orgy of anti-Sovietism and anti-socialism – a category which included classical social democracy as well.[24] In almost any other advanced capitalist society such intellectual movements would hardly have mattered to anyone but the intellectuals themselves. Given France's cultural centralization, the importance of intellectuality in the daily practice of French political life, and the overlap between intellectual, communications, and political elites these things mattered a great deal in France.[25]

The hidden logic in all this would play itself out later. In the dramatic 1970s the Socialists had reembraced an "Old Left" political approach proffered to them by the Communists. This embrace was meant to, and did, inflict mortal wounds on these same Communists. As the Communists began to decline, however, the conditions which had obliged the Socialists to embrace this approach began to evaporate. The French Left, as it turned out, was headed for power in the 1980s committed to a program whose economic, social, political, and ideological bases were rotting away.

---

the Common Program and rejection of alliance with the Communists in the interests of a new Center-left project.

23 Important institutions from which the intelligentsia and new middle strata got their cues like Libération, *Nouvel Observateur* and Parisian publishing houses (such as Editions du Seuil) also went to work disseminating technocratic modernist politics.

24 The high intellectual attack, shared by new philosophers and real philosophers like Foucault, Deleuze, Derrida et al., was on the Enlightenment thought which underlay socialism. Some of the ironies in these developments are truly cruel. From virulent rejections of Anglo-Saxon developments in the 1950s and 1960s the French intelligentsia turned in the 1970s and 1980s to reproducing virtually the same intellectual trends for which they had damned the Americans and British earlier. One would be only mildly uncharitable in labeling the "new philosophy" as plagiarized Popperism and the rediscovery of Tocqueville as borrowed American Cold War pluralism.

25 There is no really definitive sociological work on the place of intellectuals and intellectuality in French life. A general perspective may be gleaned from J.-F. Sirinelli and P. Ory, *Les Intellectuels en France* (Paris: Armand Colin, 1986), and E. Ritaine, *Les Stratégies de la Culture* (Paris: Presses de la Fondation Nationale des Sciences Politiques, 1983). See also G. Ross, "The decline of the Left intellectual in modern France," in *Intellectuals in Liberal Democracies*, ed. A. Gagnon, (New York: Praeger, 1987).

Economic and social contexts

The history of the French trade union movement until 1981 was, in many ways, parallel to that of the political Left. There were *five* important French union organizations as of the 1960s. The CGT (Confédération Générale du Travail), controlled by the PCF, was by far the most powerful (with slightly under 50 percent of union allegiance at this point). Force Ouvrière, a Cold War anti-Communist split-off from the CGT, was much weaker. The Catholic CFTC, about as strong as FO, "deconfessionalized" in 1964 to become the CFDT (Confédération Française et Démocratique du Travail). Finally, there were independent teacher's unions (gathered into the FEN, the National Education Federation) and a separate white collar workers group (the CGC). Until well into the 1960s collaboration between these organizations was rare. FO refused to work with the CGT, had little love for the "Cathos" of the CFTC, and behaved rather moderately in industrial action. The CFTC had little taste for deals with either the CGT or FO until, in 1964, it became the CFDT. The CGT attacked the others for being tools of the bourgeoisie.

In this context employers were free to divide and rule, pursue sweetheart deals, and, more generally, circumvent unions altogether. Historically, French unionism had also developed a propensity to seek political substitutes – partisan and state actions – for the base level trade unionism which weakness made so difficult, a bias which tended to overstress politics at the expense of the labor market and ultimately perpetuated labor market weakness. In consequence of such things, labor was excluded from serious influence over the process of modernization. And as employers consistently withheld concessions to labor, aggregate economic growth figures considerably outstripped wage increases.[26]

The success of Gaullist modernization and the high point of postwar boom nonetheless brought change. The economy grew and changed rapidly in a context of relative labor shortage, leading to persistent near-full employment which was propitious for working class pressure and wage growth. Modernization also created a volatile labor force characterized by massive in-migration from agriculture plus an important immigration (female labor force participation did not really begin to rise until the end of the 1960s).[27] Moreover, the modernization experience, which included the replacement of declining industries by more modern ones and rapidly changing regional industrial balances, was profoundly disorienting for many of those who had to live through it,

26 Indeed, real wages went up only rather slowly until the later 1960s. See A. Gauron, *Histoire économique et sociale de la cinquième république*, vol. 1 (Paris: Maspero, 1983), p. 31, graph 1.
27 For a good brief source on labor force evolution see D. Gambier and M. Vernières, *L'Emploi en France* (Paris: La Découverte-Repères, 1988). Female labor force participation declined generally by an average of 22,000 per year from 1962 to 1968, and then began to rise quite dramatically (69,000 a year

further fueling working class militancy. Given such raw materials, France's weak unions began to grow stronger, as evidenced by a substantial rise in union activity, mobilization, and strikes in the three years prior to 1968. Both cause and effect of this was the development of a limited but important agreement between the CGT and a newly militant CFDT in 1966, the first major step taken to limit the effects of union division in France since the later 1940s. Government anxiety about inflation plus its general authoritarian propensities led it to resist most dealings with organized labor, extensive agitation notwithstanding, and to encourage the French *patronat* to behave in similar ways. Increasing union and rank-and-file militancy thus elicited no response and recognition, a combination which set the stage for the explosion of 1968.

Despite their alliance, important divisions persisted between the CGT and CFDT. The CGT, powerful enough to shape much CGT–CFDT common activity, was based in heavy industry and thus directly in the line of fire of economic modernization. It consistently reacted with militancy and activism, denouncing capitalism in theory and rhetoric, and striking whenever the balance of forces made it feasible. But the ways in which the CGT defined its tasks, so as to be congruent with the PCF in the political realm, created difficulties.[28] Moreover, nested inside this political vision were shorter-run economistic demands which made the day-to-day workplace CGT behave much like more moderate unions elsewhere, pushing for centralized bargaining, employment security, wage increases, and improved working conditions. It also tended to downplay local struggles which did not fit[29] and to overlook the needs and militancy of new categories in the workforce.[30]

---

between 1968 and 1975, 124,000 a year between 1975 and 1982). Participation of women from 24–54 years of age had nonetheless already begun to rise substantially in the early 1960s, constituting the most important growth component in the labor force from then on.

28 Workers were told, for example, to expect a new order to come from the top from the activities of politicians. This, and other approaches, was because the CGT wanted to shape and direct working class action towards consciousness of the need for a united front. The CGT tried to use its organizational power to promote unity around simple, very general, and national demands, communicating a message that only major political change, beginning with a united front, could bring lasting solutions.

29 Overly militant struggles of a narrow kind might divide rather than unify, the CGT believed. For similar reasons, it had a tendency to downplay the particular struggles of segments of the workforce – minorities, job categories with few members, youth, women, immigrants. It could not, of course, ignore these groups altogether but it would consistently try to assimilate their demands to those of the large working class aggregates which the CGT was trying to create and maintain.

30 This was partly because the CGT "reflected" a specific base and partly because it desired, for doctrinal reasons, to inculcate very simple political themes which unified the working class.

The CFDT, the CGT's ambitious "young" rival, was less well based in mass production industry, and, largely for organization-building purposes, much more interested in militancy. It favored decentralized and multifaceted mobilization of a much less economistic and "Fordist" outlook than the CGT, while rejecting the CGT's political *arrière pensées*. It was these differences which in 1968 – when, lest one forget, the largest strike in the history of French capitalism took place – led to a temporary tarnishing of the CGT's credibility. In the effervescence of the "events" the CGT appeared stodgy, bureaucratized and somewhat out of touch. The CFDT, its major rival, was thus allowed to make considerable gains from, and embrace the *autogestionnaire* mantle of, the student movement.[31]

The CGT and CFDT continued to collaborate uneasily into the mid-1970s and the French labor movement grew stronger in consequence. The economic and political turbulence of the mid-1970s changed this, however. The economic circumstances following the first oil shock made it more and more difficult to mobilize workers on the shopfloor while the political situation tempted both the CGT and the CFDT to take refuge in high level, very general, actions to enhance the Left's electoral chances. In the overpoliticization which followed conventional union activities were overlooked in the hope that a change in government would bring political solutions to new problems which were in fact local and economic. The demobilizing effects of this *fuite politique* were dramatically compounded by the divisions between the Left parties in 1977–8. The CGT openly took the PCF's side and the CFDT, less openly, the PS's.

In response both major unions began in 1978 to "recenter" their activities back to the shopfloor, but in dramatically different ways. The CFDT started first, beginning a long retreat away from radical *autogestionnaire* positions towards advocacy of collectively bargained work sharing – in particular through reducing the length of the working week – as a way out of threatening new economic circumstances. The CGT's new labor market focus initially aspired to something like the kind of *autogestionnaire* radicalism which the CFDT was abandoning.[32] But the PCF was unwilling to allow its union ally to follow through. Instead, by 1979 the CGT had been pushed back towards a classic defensive posture accompanied by support for the PCF's strident anti-PS politics.[33] These new inter-union divisions immeasurably worsened as the presidential elections of 1981 approached. The PCF continued to push its new sectarian strategic concerns onto the CGT, up to and including support

31 I have discussed all this in considerable detail in G. Ross, *Workers and Communists in France* (Berkeley, CA: University of California Press, 1982).
32 See P. Lange, G. Ross, and M. Vannicelli, *Unions, Crisis and Change: French and Italian Trade Unions in the Political Economy, 1945–1980* (London: Allen & Unwin, 1982), ch. 2.
33 The party's response followed largely from fear that the CGT's new course would lead it away from strategic subordination to the party at a moment that the party deemed critical.

for the Soviet invasion of Afghanistan.[34] The CGT also began to excoriate the CFDT as irremediably reformist, a charge which the CFDT's strategic turn away from earlier radicalism made more plausible. In the downward spiral of acrimony which resulted further CGT–CFDT united action quickly became impossible.[35]

Thus at the very moment when economic crisis was challenging trade unionism everywhere, the forces of progressive unionism in France fractured. Union membership and mobilizing power, already slipping by 1977–8, declined even more rapidly afterwards – with the CGT suffering the most. For its part the CFDT was quite unable to find the negotiating partners needed to bargain the work sharing which it believed would alleviate growing unemployment. The only major union which managed to salvage something was *Force Ouvrière* (FO). Employers, eager to exploit the divisions between "radical" unions, sought out FO to sign sweetheart deals.

These changes occurred in an ever more dangerous economic context. The electoral balance between Left and Right which prevailed after 1974 – Left and Right were virtually equal in opinion polls and in various elections, with the Left tending over time to move slightly ahead – made it extremely difficult for the Right to do things which the situation might otherwise have dictated. Worse still, the French Right, like most other coalitions in power when economic crisis appeared, had considerable difficulty in perceiving the new parameters. This combination of factors meant that from 1974 through 1981 French policy responses to crisis, to unemployment, inflation, declining growth and investment, were hesitant and contradictory.

The first half of this period, the high moment of stagflation, was marked by British-style, "stop–go" movements in which inflationary demand stimulations and deflations succeeded one another. At the same time, French governments moved to protect the labor market situation of workers more than ever before, largely out of an electorally driven desire to preserve social peace.[36] The only mildly "conservative" labor market measures enacted involved shutting down immigration. The consequences of all this for the economy were quite negative. In essence, governmental policy actions obliged private sector firms to absorb the

34 This process was not as easy as we make it sound. The CGT leadership was profoundly divided about following the PCF's lines out of quite correct anticipation of the negative effects it would have on prospects for trade union action. A difficult internal struggle ensued in which the PCF position ultimately prevailed. See Ross, *Workers and Communists*, ch. 10, and G. Ross, "The CGT ...," in *The French Workers' Movement*, ed. M. Kesselman and G. Groux (London: Allen & Unwin, 1984).

35 See H. Hamon and P. Rotman, *La Deuxième gauche* (Paris: Ramsey, 1982), and R. Mouriaux and G. Groux, *La CFDT* (Paris: Economica, 1989).

36 In 1974–5 very stringent new administrative limits on layoffs and firings were imposed, making it extremely difficult for private sector French employers to shed labor. At the same time governments encouraged indexation of wages to inflation levels. Unemployment compensation levels were also augmented.

adjustment costs of crisis.[37] Profits and investment levels declined while unit labor costs shot up. The policy package did not diminish inflation, while growth stagnated at around 3 percent – about half of 1960s levels. Unemployment continued to rise, partly for economic reasons but partly also because of changing labor force demographics.

There were slight shifts in emphasis after 1977–8 when the surprising Right election victory gave the Giscard regime a bit more breathing space (prior to the 1981 presidential elections). The government of Raymond Barre turned towards monetarism, devoting much of its attention to defending the currency and the balance of payments by allowing the franc to rise slowly.[38] At the same time it attempted to cut down on wage rises, in particular by tougher attitudes on public sector wages, freed some prices, and shifted the costs of increasing social benefits away from firms to the national budget. Interest rates rose precipitously to control inflation levels – France being a member of the European Monetary System (EMS) at this point – even though France's inflation levels remained dangerously higher than those of its most important European competitor, West Germany. The second oil shock in 1979 made things much worse. Growth screeched to a halt.

Perhaps the most dangerous consequence of these policies was the rapidly declining international competitiveness of French industry, seen dramatically in 1980 when France began to be flooded by imports in critical industrial sectors.[39] Squeezed by high taxation, an overvalued currency, inflation, zero profitability, and debt, which became a complete trap when interest rates shot up, French private sector firms simply ceased investing – virtually all important investment in the French economy in the later 1970s and early 1980s came in the public sector.[40] This was particularly dangerous during a crisis which involved both general international downturn and important international restructuring. The French economy was not particularly successful at restruc-

---

37   Labor market inflexibility was enhanced. The various dimensions of the "social wage" which, in France, was paid in large part by employers (as opposed to direct taxation or by workers) grew rapidly. And the general level of French *prélèvements obligatoires*, as the French call them, taxes plus social welfare and other overhead costs, rose from 37.4 percent of gross domestic product in 1975 to 42.5 percent in 1980, while remaining more or less stationary at lower levels in other competitor countries.

38   On monetary policy over the longer term see Jeanneney, *L'Economie Française*, ch. XV.

39   See "Le commerce extérieur," in Jeanneney, ibid., ch. XIII.

40   Giscard committed a huge amount of public money to a long overdue modernization of France's telecommunications system during this period, to which heavy construction programs in nuclear energy and railroad transportation must be added. Quite as important, large amounts of public money was spent on projects which allowed public sector employment to be maintained. Only some of these projects made economic sense, while others followed a political logic. See also "L'investissement," in Jeanneney, ibid., ch. XII.

turing, a shortcoming which was superimposed on France's already precarious position in the international division of labor (France's international trade pattern was stronger in those middle level industrial sectors which the newly industrializing countries could threaten than in the advanced sectors which were the key to the industrial future). Growing industrial weakness because of failure to restructure thus meant that France was thus destined to lose trading power to the newly industrializing countries in traditional industrial areas while also losing ground to the West Germans, Japanese, and Americans in more advanced areas.[41]

The irony in all this, of course, was that despite the fact that much of what the Right did in the economic policy realm in the later 1970s was politics driven, aimed at holding onto power and keeping the Left from winning elections, the Left nonetheless won in 1981. In consequence, when the Left did come to power it faced empty coffers and industrial disaster areas. Trends in the labor force compounded this legacy. Baby boomers began to flood the labor market beginning in 1975, while, given the small size of interwar-born cohorts, the number of retirements was small. Quite as important, female labor force participation rates continued to rise.[42] Job creation in France would have had to accelerate to provide enough employment for this expanding labor force, other things being equal. The opposite occurred. Industrial employment in France had grown steadily into the early 1970s, but thereafter an important de-industrialization began – about 750,000 jobs were lost between 1974 and 1981.[43] By the later years of the boom, growth in industrial employment had not kept up with the growth of the active labor force, but the shortfall had been largely covered by rapid expansion of tertiary work. Between 1974 and 1981 this coverage ceased. Even though 1,450,000 more workers came to be employed in tertiary activities in these years, it

41 Indeed, the few major international trade successes of the French in this period tended to be massive "turnkey" projects of either an industrial or military nature which were often as much the product of diplomatic muscle as of competitiveness.

42 See Gambier and Vernières, *L'Emploi en France*, ch. 1, for generalities; see also Gauron, *Histoire économique*, pp. 42–52. Census figures presented by Jacques Freyssinet in *Le Chômage* (Paris: La Découverte, 1988) are eloquent. Between 1968 and 1975 the major components of an average annual general labor force growth of 203,000 were 170,000 new demographic entrants, 58,000 new immigrants and 69,000 new women, largely in the 25–54 year age group (whose labor force participation increased annually by an average of 113,000). Disparities in the totals are attributable, of course, to declining labor force participation in other groups, particularly in young people, both male and female, staying in school for longer, and in older workers taking earlier retirement. From 1975 to 1982 the average annual labor force growth figure increased to 242,000, with 201,000 due to demographic growth, 10,000 to immigration (which was largely shut down) and 124,000 to women (156,000 women in the 25–54 year age group). See p. 62, table IV.

43 In a total labor force which grew *in toto* by about 160,000. Gambier and Vernières, *L'Emploi en France*, p. 47, table XI.

was not enough to compensate for de-industrialization, continuing decline in the agricultural labor force, and total labor force growth.

Rising unemployment followed, impacting differentially. Although the
growth of male unemployment was more rapid than that of female
unemployment, at least until 1980 slightly more women than men were
unemployed.[44] Layoffs and firings were the major creators of new unemployment, particularly in industry. A substantial minority of the newly
unemployed were young people, many of whom were unable to find a
first job at all. And as the general outlook worsened, those unemployed
remained so for longer periods of time. Governmental responses involved, for the most part, trying to get people out of the labor force –
early retirement, helping immigrants to return, enticements for women
to return home, different ways of "sheltering" young people (longer
schooling, new apprenticeship programs, and makework schemes), etc.
Employers responded in different ways, using the slackening labor market to use more part-time work and to experiment with new, more
individualized, employment strategies to cut out unions.[45] Unions,
simultaneously threatened by the effects of growing strategic differences
and organizational divisiveness, as we have noted, saw their rank and
file begin to thin out dramatically.[46]

A New Left for the 1980s?

The circumstances of the Left's victory in 1981 as well as the detailed
story of its subsequent policies has been well told.[47] The Left's project
claimed to seek "rupture" with capitalism. At its core were massive
nationalizations, the strategic use of public funds for investment, state
economic planning, and industrial policy. The wise and coordinated use
of this large armory of economic power would liberate economic creativity from the Malthusianism of private capital and stimulate the French

44 This was largely because of the troubles in heavy industry where male
employment dominated.
45 Here see P. Morville, *Les Nouvelles politiques sociales du patronat* (Paris: La
Découverte, 1985).
46 This was especially true for the CGT because it was most firmly based in
those areas of traditional industry where de-industrialization hit hardest.
47 For the Left years between 1981 and 1986 in general, see the collected
articles in G. Ross, S. Hoffmann, and S. Malzacher, *The Mitterrand Experiment*
(New York, Oxford University Press, 1987), and P. McCarthy, (ed.), *The Mitterrand Years* (New York: Praeger, 1987). For the electoral story, which is very
important since it demonstrates the tenuousness of the 1981 electoral shift and
how much it was contingent on divisions on the Right, see A. Lancelot, in Ross
et al., ibid. For reviews of economic policy, in addition to the above, see P.
Bauchard, *La Guerre des deux roses* (Paris: Grasset, 1986), A. Fontaneau and P. A.
Muet, *La Gauche face à la crise* (Paris: Presses de la Fondation Nationale des
Sciences Politiques, 1985), and P. Hall, *Governing the Economy* (New York: Oxford
University Press, 1986).

economy to modernize and grow rapidly. France would thus emerge triumphant in new and advanced sectors of international competition while saving and updating traditional industries like steel, shipbuilding, and coalmining.[48] Reforms to give workers and unions more power in the workplace and a degree of governmental decentralization would generate additional energy for this voluntaristic effort. As it succeeded, outstanding problems such as unemployment, discrimination against different categories of workers, e.g. women, and abusive patterns of employment, e.g. the use of part-time workers to lower wages and circumvent social programs, could be obliterated through more regulation combined with the "boat raising" effects of a higher tide of growth. Finally, success would enable further growth and reform of the French welfare state.[49]

Policy failure and political success

If such pious hopes and voluntaristic rhetoric have often been the Left's verbal currency, the French Left after 1981 was unusual in the degree to which it tried to translate them into reality. The government nationalized nine major industrial groups plus all banks (except for only a few investment houses) and various ministries geared up to transform this into a national economic crusade for competitiveness and growth. Money flowed to declining sectors. The government produced a package of redistributive demand stimulation including rises in the minimum wage, family allocations, and old-age pensions. In the labor market area it promoted various work-sharing programs.[50] It honored its commitment to use the expanded public sector to stabilize unemployment, by keeping people in work, no matter what. It legislated limited decentralization of certain government activities away from Paris and, in early

48   In the words of Jean-Pierre Chevènement, Minister of Industry and Research at the time, "there is no such thing as an obsolete industry, only obsolete technologies."
49   It is important to note, in the welfare state area, that the Left's economic voluntarism essentially allowed it to avoid any profoundly new reflections about reforming the welfare state. The appearance of new resources following the resumption of strong growth would simply allow rapid expansion of programs. Reforms might follow this expansion, even if they were not spelled out much in Left thought. But the expansion of the welfare state as is was the core of the program. See G. Ross, "The Mitterrand experiment and the French welfare state," in *Remaking the Welfare State*, ed. M. Brown (Philadelphia, PA: Temple University Press, 1988).
50   Included were reduction of the retirement age to 60 (55 for hazardous occupations), "solidarity contracts" in which the state helped out companies which were willing to retire older workers earlier to make places for younger ones, 200,000 new public sector jobs, a complex new program to treat the youth unemployment problem (training programs, new job information sharing agencies, new apprenticeship arrangements, etc.) plus a commitment to reduce the legal work week from 40 to 35 hours (which collapsed at 39 hours in disputation over the ties between reduced working time and compensation).

1982, industrial relations reforms to increase workers' and unions' rights and to enhance their legal positions.

The reasons why all this failed were complex. The Reagan recession – leading a transnational macroeconomic policy shift towards monetarism – was not a good time to reform and reflate. In consequence, while everyone else's inflation levels dropped in this period, France's continued to rise, rapidly increasing the differential between the franc's value and that of the deutschmark and other currencies in the "basket" of the EMS. Increased purchasing power in France in a context of French industrial weakness meant a flood of imports. Mitterrand's initial choice to avoid devaluation in 1981 was probably mistaken given the effects of these subsequent policies.[51] Perhaps more important, the new Left government was quite unclear about what the effects of its policies would be, an indicator of the degree to which the Left's commitment to its radicalism had been abstract.

The Left's radical first year thus led to an impasse. In springtime 1982 a "temporary" turn to austerity was initiated. In early 1983 a new international trade crisis led to another, and deeper, round of austerity policies.[52] By mid-1984 the Communists, confronting precipitous electoral decline and unhappy with the Socialists' new directions, had left the government. A change of prime ministers and program in 1984 did not prevent the Right from winning the legislative elections in 1986, however. The Left might have paid a very high price for its failures and changes had not Mitterrand's Machiavellian ability to manipulate in his favor the political situation of "cohabitation" – involving complex coexistence between a prime minister of the Right and president of the Left – allowed him to win reelection in 1988. The Left was then able to win back control of Parliament, which it will retain at least through elections in 1993.

Redefining the Left – how much power, how popular?

More than a policy impasse, the French Left's failure after 1981 was the end of the long collapse of a certain definition of popular power. The agenda for the remainder of the 1980s thus involved a redefinition, indeed almost a reinvention, of the French Left. After two years in power, therefore, the Socialists – who, given the decline of the PCF, were the key actor – began a cultural revolution.[53] The aim of their new

51 Mitterrand's refusal to act has often been contrasted, of course, with the choices made by Olaf Palme in Sweden in 1982, which turned out to be enormously successful.

52 The second austerity period occurred after Municipal Elections in March 1983 revealed that the Left had become quite unpopular.

53 Daniel Singer's *Is Socialism Doomed?* (New York: Oxford University Press, 1988) is particularly good in tracing the evolution of this conversion experience prior to 1986.

politics was to place the PS in a strategic position for proposing and implementing a hegemonic project for national economic restructuring, or "modernization" as François Mitterrand called it, beginning in 1983.

The new politics

Perhaps the best way to begin describing the new politics is to contrast its general political goals with the old. Earlier, capitalism was to be rejected and transcended. Henceforth a "mixed economy" would rebuild France's competitiveness in the – capitalist – international economy. Earlier, *dirigiste* statist politics – highly focused efforts to plan – driving a vast public sector were to produce new growth, the fruits of which could then be redistributed to workers and the disadvantaged. Henceforth the state would be an important facilitator for private sector profitability and innovation and would also work hard at de-statizing and deregulating the economic environment. Earlier "the people" and their political representatives would provide the energy and ideas for change. Henceforth the "enterprise" would be the locus of economic and social creativity – French capitalists were rehabilitated, in other words, after having been scorned for years by the Socialists as incompetent, risk aversive, conservative, and generally useless. Finally, whereas earlier the nation was the essential locus of economic and social regulation, beginning in the mid-1980s Europe as a regional economic bloc became the broader envelope within which the French nation would survive and thrive – the Socialists were thus instrumental in regenerating European integration through the European Community Single Market Act 1992 process.

Contrasts between the old and new were equally vivid concerning the deeper nature of the social world. Earlier the "class interests" of workers dictated strengthening working class power against capital in the workplace. Henceforth class interests were to be replaced by national interests. Workers would be exhorted to collaborate in the great new national crusade for competitiveness and to accept the new "flexibility" dictated by it. The old project of the PS had had a conflictual dynamic – the Left would propose a project of basic change and win over a majority to its implementation, isolating capital and the Right. Now the Left presented itself as a better leader, and manager, of the society and nation's *common* interests. For all this, however, the new Socialist discourse was not completely "neo-liberal." It reserved an important role for the central state, even if a very different one from the Left's earlier visions. Moreover, it was careful in announcing that social "solidarity" and fairness were to be preserved in France's "modernization." If sacrifices were necessary, they were to be shared out equitably. Most importantly, the welfare state would be protected and preserved, even if certain changes in the interests of "flexibilization" were needed.

Finally, the new Socialist project involved a changed repertory of political techniques. The Left projects of the 1960s and 1970s had been premised upon traditional Left models of mobilization. To be sure, what had ultimately counted was political success, votes, and election victories. But conceptions about how to achieve such things had involved issues of class and mobilization around class struggles, ideally through class-based membership organizations like unions and parties whose activities would touch and penetrate different aspects of the lives of ordinary people. The new Socialist discourse replaced vocabularies of class with an elite politics of the "good technocrat," sophisticated opinion polling techniques, professional uses of television, public relations technologies, advertising, and heightened emphasis on personalities, all approaches which the presidentialization of French politics encouraged.

In the old project, relationships of politicians to policy and decisions were mediated by explicit "representation" of various interests which were either organizationally real, like unions, or conceptually real, like classes. The new one brought much less mediated relationships with the social world in which politicians and the Socialist Party spoke directly to the people, primarily as electorate. The major advantage in this was that it allowed a direct tailoring of political offer to evidence about political demand produced by polling techniques and, additionally, a direct targeting of this offer on segments of the public whose favorable response seemed essential. One might put all this in another way. Earlier Left political techniques had seen a highly structured political world and sought to create, nourish, and mobilize certain group identities. The new package saw the political world essentially as an unstructured open market and targeted individuals.

Rethinking policy

The creation of a new politics by the French Socialists after 1983 involved policies as well as philosophy. Devotion to the package of nationalizations, economic planning, and statist-generated economic change abruptly ceased. Deflation and the maintenance of a strong *franc* – monetarism, in fact – became central economic policy goals. From this point on wages were de-indexed from inflation – something which the Right would surely have been unable to do politically. A rigorous *de facto* incomes policy was followed, anchored in the public sector, to keep wage growth at or below productivity growth. Income redistribution from higher to lower income earners, begun in 1981, was reversed, albeit gently. The growth in working class per capita income, which in France had not ceased despite the crisis, finally stopped and, more generally, wages as a share of national income began to decline.[54] Profits and, eventually, investment began to rise. The level of *prélèvements obligatoires* – taxes plus social program costs – taken out of the economic flows by the

<hr>

54 See CERC, *Les Français et leurs revenus: Le tournant des années 80* (Paris: La Découverte/La Documentation Française, 1989), for the best review of these changes.

state was pushed downwards, after having risen sharply throughout the 1970s until 1983.[55]

In the labor market, market mechanisms henceforth were to set the general level of employment. "Modernization" implied a cessation of state-induced employment maintenance in threatened sectors and an end to state efforts to cap unemployment whatever the costs. Nationalized corporations were enjoined to restructure and shed labor as needed. Massive earlier commitments to coalmining, steelmaking, and shipbuilding capacity were abandoned. Private sector companies were also encouraged to shed labor and, to this end, the government encouraged high-level negotiations to increase labor market "flexibility."[56]

Such deregulatory steps had predictable employment consequences.[57] The Left's initial policies had more or less stabilized the growth of unemployment at around 2 million, i.e. 8 percent. Steep rises began again in 1983, peaking at around 2.7 million in 1986 (nearly 11 percent).[58] Labor market policy also became more "active," shifting from work sharing to retraining and relocation efforts to encourage mobility.[59] A number of new programs were put into place to promote what the French call the "social" treatment of unemployment. Certain economic disaster areas – the coalmining and steel regions and shipyard towns – were designated as "conversion poles" where displaced workers might choose between early retirement (with buyouts), extensive retraining programs, or lump sum payments to encourage mobility. Special funds enticed immigrants to leave. Perhaps most important, new

55 In the mid-1980s, partly in consequence, the French Stock Exchange boomed more than it had ever done in its history.

56 With the purpose of replacing the somewhat rigid administrative control over firing and hiring which the Right had installed in the 1970s. The negotiations ultimately collapsed, but were followed by legislation by the Right in 1986 to achieve the same goals.

57 For a good review see J.-M. Delarue, "A propos du chômage et les politiques d'emploi," *Echanges et Projets* (June, 1988).

58 See C. Thélot, "La mesure de l'évolution récente du chômage," *Economie et Statistique*, 205 (December 1987); P. Bouillaguet-Bernard, "L'évolution des politiques de l'emploi en France de 1975 à 1987," *Problèmes Economiques*, 2068 (March 30, 1988); J.-L. Beaud, "Pour une approche stratégique du chômage," *Le Revue Politique et Parlémentaire* (September–October 1987). The Chirac government commissioned François Dalle, Chief Executive Officer of Oreal and an important figure in the French economic sphere, to do a report on unemployment, called *Pour Développer l'Emploi*. A précis of this can be found in *Liaisons Sociales*, June 11 1987.

59 Encouraging early retirement and work-week reduction simply stopped in 1983, as did resort to additional public sector unemployment. Anthony Daley provides an excellent summary of these changes in his "All worked up again: employment policy under Mitterrand II" delivered to the 1990 Meetings of the American Political Science Association.

programs, often in local government and public services, were developed to keep young people off the unemployment rolls.[60]

The change in Socialist approaches to the welfare state was less dramatic. The "new" Socialists, like the old, wanted to protect the welfare state. Emphasis did shift from earlier optimism about expanding welfare programs and using them as redistributive mechanisms to more careful management. In the main, benefit growth leveled off while, on occasion, small new charges were institutionalized and, in particular for unemployment compensation, costs were shifted from payroll contributions to the national budget. In general, there was political mileage to be gained from the new posture of "modernization with a human face" directed against neo-liberal growls from the Right, however much protecting the welfare state also flowed from deeper principles. Opinion polls indicated clearly that if the French had abandoned earlier passions for radical transformational policies their attachment to the welfare state remained strong.

When the Socialists returned to governmental power after the elections of 1988 – after two years of "cohabitation" – most of these policy lines continued. The Chirac government had privatized a number of large public corporations and banks during this interlude and the new Rocard government showed no inclination to challenge this.[61] Stress on de-statizing and deregulating economic decisions continued, as did monetarist determination to maintain the *franc fort*. The Right had repealed the Left's mild "wealth tax," but the government proceeded to reinstate it in milder form. The welfare state remained untouched except for an addition, the legislation of a minimum income (the so-called *revenue minimum d'insertion*) to cope with the "new poverty" (and homelessness) created by long-term unemployment.[62] And, despite a significant economic upturn in 1988, the government held firmly to austerity guide lines for wage growth in the hope of generating greater profits and investment.[63]

60   There is a voluminous literature on the employment question in these years. For a good start, look at the special issue of *Les Temps Modernes* "Chômages et Chômeurs," (November–December 1987), especially articles by V. Merle and M. Gaspard. On the TUCs and other youth unemployment programs, see O. Marchand and E. Martin-LeGoff, "Avec le développement des stages, La France ne perd plus d'emplois depuis 1985," *Economie et Statistique*, 209 (April 1988).

61   The only thing which was tempting was action to dislodge the *noyaux durs* of neo-Gaullist financial interest which the Right had installed to keep control of the newly private firms in the hands of reliable political friends.

62   Which also involved a structure of incentives to reenter the labor market to go along with the minimum income.

63   It refused to redistribute the fruits of new growth despite an extensive public sector strike movement in the autumn of 1988, for example. See G. Ross and J. Jenson, "Strikes and politics," *French Politics and Society* (Winter 1988–9).

Labor and its changed surroundings

We have earlier reviewed the basic labor market tendencies of the 1970s – the baby boom expansion of the labor force and changing patterns of female labor force participation, de-industrialization for which tertiarization was less and less able to compensate, plus "the crisis." Initial Socialist policies to check these tendencies and provide new growth and jobs failed. The Socialists then turned towards more classical approaches aimed to free the labor market plus "flexibilization" which brought their own predictable consequences. Beyond a rapid rise in the numbers of those unemployed, a "new poverty" arose,[64] and young people – despite the special attention which they received – faced inordinate difficulty in finding work, let alone work with adult dignity.

This labor market situation helped upset a precarious capital–labor equilibrium in which labor, with difficulty, had gained relative job security and a share in the fruits of growth in exchange for allowing capital to shape the organization of work and investment. The state's roles in this old equilibrium had been central and the Left's first "radical" period, with its multiple labor market initiatives, sought to consolidate this equilibrium. The cultural and policy revolution after 1983 opened up a much less regulated and diversely organized labor market which allowed employers many more options.[65]

The "crisis" has involved both downturn *and* restructuring, of course. And restructuring brought an important recasting of employer strategies. Neo-Japanese methods came to France, especially to larger firms.[66] Quality circles spread like wildfire.[67] Here the *Auroux laws*, the Socialists'

---

64 R. Foudi and F. Stankeiwicz, "La lutte contre le chômage de longue durée ...," *Revue Française des Affaires Sociales* (July–September 1987); R. Foudi, "L'avenir des chômeurs de longue durée," *Travail et Emploi* (June–September 1988). The statistics demonstrate a clear connection between the long-term unemployed and what the French have come to call the "new poor." Undoubtedly the Socialists' determination after the 1988 elections to legislate on a minimum income follows from such evidence.

65 For a rapid and sophisticated introduction into the issue of flexibilization and new labor market policies in France, see *La Flexibilité du Travail, Les Cahiers Français*, 231 (May–June 1981). For a deeper, comparative treatment from the "regulation school's" leader on such matters, see R. Boyer (ed.), *La Flexibilité du travail en Europe* (Paris: La Découverte, 1986), especially chapter 2 by P. Petit and chapters 9–12. See also R. Boyer, "La flexibilité du travail," *Revue Politique et Parlementaire* (October 1987).

66 For example, methods like "just-in-time" components supply and extensive robotization have been widely deployed in production.

67 Morville, *Les Nouvelles politiques sociales du patronat*, provides the best sophisticated introduction to this general discussion. See Also B. Bunel and J. Saglio, "La redéfinition de la politique social du patronat français," *Droit social* (December 1980); H. Weber, *Le Parti des Patrons* (Paris: Seuil, 1986).

1982 reforms to strengthen unions and workers at firm level, have worked largely to the advantage of employers.[68] There has also been movement towards an individualization of the wage relationship.[69] New techniques have also been developed for "protecting" a core workforce and "hiving off" cyclical labor either through part-time work or through subcontracting to smaller firms (a practice that engenders smaller firms with considerably tougher patterns of industrial relations). Finally, de-centralization of collective bargaining from branch to firm level has occurred, encouraged by Socialist attempts to de-statize, leading to a flood of firm-level bargaining about "flexibilizing" work away from rigidly defined classification schemas and work weeks.[70]

The larger situation played into new employer strategies. The Left in power, however benevolent its intentions, presided over a further weakening of French organized labor.[71] Union membership, mobiliza-tion capacity, and ideological credibility continued to decline, in part because of unions' inability to protect their supporters in crisis in a context of ideological onslaught on *ouvriérisme* more generally. Changing structures of the labor force played a role. Traditionally based in the male industrial workforce and the public sector, French unions had a difficult time adapting to de-industrialization and the growing importance of service sector, often feminized, labor. The situation was made even worse by further union disunity. When, after 1984, the PCF went into a new moment of strident opposition to the Socialists, the CGT moved with it into a period of minority defensive protests.[72] The CFDT, for its part, moved even further towards a moderate "concession bargaining" posture.[73] FO identified doctrinally with the CGT's defensive doctrine

68 Among other things, the laws provided for the institutionalization of em-ployee "rights of expression." Given union weakness at firm level, these new rights could be turned by employers into information exchanging and morale boosting media paralleling quality circles to localize employee attitudes and loyalties at firm level while also further isolating unions.

69 See D. Eustache, "Individualisation des salaires et flexibilité . . . ," *Travail et Emploi* (September 1986).

70 Much of this bargaining might be called "concession" dealing, since it has involved deals in which unions trade work time and productive flexibility for relative employment security. See Morville, *Les Nouvelles politiques sociales du patronat*, part II.

71 We have discussed this weakening and its policy context in some detail in G. Ross, "Le social in Mitterrand's France, from one left to another," in Ross et al., *The Mitterrand Experiment*.

72 This move could not be worked without considerable resistance from the CGT leadership, understandably afraid of the effects on an already weakened organization of another bout of union sectarianism overdetermined by transpa-rent political concerns.

73 This elicited few positive results while chronically dividing the organization internally.

and rejected the CFDT's new concessionist posture but its anti-Communism and moderation made collaboration out of the question. One important consequence of all this was a dramatic decline in the occurrence of strikes.

To some commentators this combination of changes in the structure of the labor force – chronically high levels of unemployment, an enhanced degree of dualism, weakened and divided unions, the decentralizing (de-Fordization?) of bargaining and industrial decision-making, new "participative" employer strategies designed to localize employee outlooks to firm level (and thus fragment class identity), the effects of a general decline in *ouvriérisme* in French culture, and, last but not least, the thrust of the Socialist Party's cultural revolution – has reformulated the system of capital–labor relations. The core of the new system is, they suggest, firm-level collaborative negotiating about the resolution of firm-level problems. These negotiations are moving progressively away from "traditional" problems of wages, hours, job classification, and security towards the inclusion of "flexibility" issues about working time, multivalent job definition, and productivity enhancement. Moreover, the ideology surrounding such negotiations – which are often carried on despite, rather than with, unions – is that of a positive, rather than a zero-sum, game. Accompanying this tendency there is a new state refusal to step in and resolve outstanding issues politically where negotiation has failed – in other words a serious attempt to break with France's old habit of politicizing labor market problems.[74]

It would be mistaken to accept this projection as a crystallized model. Too many details are unclear. Still, we do know enough to realize that old forms are gone for good. *Some* form of de-statized, decentralized and more flexible dealings between capital and labor is emerging in France. What the place of unionism in this new order will be is uncertain. Will a cooperative employer–union relationship built on a new shopfloor culture and premised on collectively bargained restructuring develop, as the CFDT seems to hope? It seems extremely unlikely at this point, given union division and CFDT weakness, but it is not to be excluded.[75] Or will a new decentralized corporate culture around restructuring be developed *despite* unions – via company unions and alternative structures of communication on shopfloors – based on employer skills and initiative (a dynamic which would involve the virtual extinction of French unionism in the private sector)? This "American" scenario also seems unlikely, even though the present weakness and division of unionism undoubtedly tempts employers in such directions.

74 A good summary of these tendencies is found in G. Groux, "Industrial relations in France from crisis to today," in *Contemporary France*, vol. 3, ed. J. Howorth and G. Ross (London: Frances Pinter, 1989).
75 It would be contingent on a form of farsightedness and skill on the part of French employers and the state which has never existed.

Conclusion: Popular Politics in the
Post-Fordist Era?

France in the 1980s demonstrates that it is not possible to "read out" directly the effects of changing economic-structural circumstances on labor's political power. Similar economic circumstances have had different effects in France from those in other societies. Enhanced market internationalization, economic crisis, restructuring of production, and capitalist political offensive have not led either to a strengthened Right or to neo-liberal triumph in France. Economic-structural changes *do* lead to political and labor market regulation changes, but they do not always lead to the *same* changes.

Still, France has felt, in its own ways, all the disorienting processes which other advanced capitalist democracies have experienced in the last two decades. The consequences have involved a reconfiguration of "popular power," both in terms of general discourses and policy outlooks and in the labor market. This reconfiguration did *not* include a decline of the Left, however. Indeed, by the later 1980s the Socialists' electoral potential made them by far the most popular party in postwar France, capable of scoring upwards of 40 percent in legislative elections and of winning two consecutive presidential elections. But the Left did not gain without being profoundly affected by the underlying tendencies of these years. The price of its success was basic *change* in the nature of popular power.

The French Left has moved from a mode of representation which privileged the mediation of class and class organizations to one involving a direct relationship between Left electors and Socialist elites to whom were entrusted the definition of discourses, interests, and policies. In the labor market the capacity of organized labor to defend its interests clearly declined. Of equal importance, however, the decentralization and de-statization of industrial relations undercut *class* solidarity and the capacities of labor organizations to represent a class were truncated. What has happened, it seems, is that a mode of representation premised on social democratic workerism has been replaced by one dominated by the outlooks of the technocratic new middle strata.

The "old" official Left in France was "Fordist" in the sense that its programs, appeals, and outlooks were congruent with a strongly reformist approach to the great Keynesian–Taylorist–mass consumerist postwar boom. The "new" official Left may well be the European vanguard of a "post-Fordist social democracy" placing greatest weight on the regeneration of national economic capacities – through change to produce new international competitiveness – in the face of a rapidly moving and threatening international economic environment. The new project is vastly less redistributional than its Fordist predecessor, since the recognition of narrow international economic constraints has been read as precluding ambitious domestic reform plans. The domestic political game, in other words, has become much more zero-sum. The new Socialist path beyond deadlock involves a national mission to promote international economic advance which, as it succeeds, will then facilitate whatever redistribution is possible.

The new Socialists are more managerial and technocratic than their predecessors. Their major political claim is that capitalism will be better coordinated and more rational if central political tasks are taken away from capitalists and given to state managers who are both technically and politically skilled. Resolutely "modernist" in an economic sense, the new Socialists promise first of all to produce the kind of state-of-the-art, "international best practice" capitalism which, they submit, capitalists themselves cannot usually produce on their own. Given its desire to preserve the welfare state, new social democracy is not a complete capitulation to neo-liberalism. Still, it is much less "workerist" in outlook, relatively uncommitted to class analytical visions of the political world, much less beholden to union movements, and rather more willing than its predecessor to allow relatively elevated levels of unemployment. Finally, it is "European," as French involvement in creating the 1992 Single European Market process has amply shown.

Changing formulations of popular power ultimately bring with them their own characteristic structures of opposition and rebellion. There are always alternative discourses whose advocates try, as best they can, to generate the resources needed to challenge what has become convention. And modes of representation which include some interests must, by definition, exclude others. In the right circumstances, the excluded will assert themselves. In the interests of allegedly ineluctable international economic constraints, the post-Fordist reformulation of social democracy in France undercuts traditional reformist appeals to subordinate social groups. Whether the "new" Socialists will be able to maintain their electoral prominence in consequence is one important question for the future, of course, since their new policy package may not prove sufficiently seductive to groups which earlier supported the Left. Some evidence that this will be a problem is already clear in the willingness of working class protest voters to support the extreme Right, but populist, Front National. Beyond this, as we have mentioned, the Communists, with every reason to develop and assert alternative discourses to those now manipulated by the Socialists, have not disappeared – yet. They can be counted upon to oppose the macropolitical formulation of what has come to predominate on the French Left. "New social movements" were unusually weak in France after the 1960s because of the "vacuum cleaner" effects of the development of the French Left in the 1970s, but concerns about the environment, nuclear issues, urban matters, racism, and feminism, to name but a few, have not completely disappeared.[76]

76   We have written briefly on the social movements matter with L. Frader; see "From Mao to Mitterrand," *Socialist Review*, 100 (1988). On the women's movement, see J. Jenson, "Ce n'est pas un hasard: the varieties of French feminism,"

Will there be new openings for such movements in France's changed Left political environment? In the labor market we simply cannot yet foresee what the characteristic forms of opposition and rebellion may be in the new decentralized setting which is emerging, nor can we gauge their effects on larger politics. But we will be bold enough to hazard the prediction that *there will be* such characteristic forms and that they will have effects.

---

in *Contemporary France* vol. 3, ed. J. Howorth and G. Ross (London: Frances Pinter, 1989). On the Greens, who enjoyed a notable breakthrough in the 1989 elections to the European Parliament, see *Politix*, 9 (1990), special issue on the Greens, especially articles by D. Boy.

5

Swedish Social Democracy and the Transition from Industrial to Postindustrial Politics

Göran Therborn

The politico-economic changes of the past two decades have had the character of an epochal transition – the culmination of industrial society and industrial class politics and the emerging of a postindustrial society with its new patterns of cleavages and conflicts. The outcome of the transition process is likely to crucially affect, if not determine, the foreseeable future of the politics of Western nations. The socioeconomic transformations in Sweden have been major by comparative cross-national standards, but politically there has recently (in 1988) been a reaffirmation of social democratic continuity. In contrast with many other countries, the dislocations, polarizations, and new inequalities accompanying the entrance into postindustrial society have been minor in Sweden; indeed in most respects the country has continued (slowly) to become more egalitarian. A second crucial condition of the transition process has been the legacy of the Swedish system of elections and parties with its bias against any turn to free marketeerism.

Industrialism and Class Politics: Parametric Change into Postindustrial and Nonindustrial Societies

The extraordinary continuity of social democratic power in Sweden is not due to lack of great socioeconomic change. Sweden fits the characteristically European pattern of an economic and employment structure dominated by industry. North America, Oceania, and Japan have never been industrial societies where industrial activities (manufacturing, construction, mining) clearly dominated both agricultural and service work. In these non-European advanced societies industrial employment never exceeded 35 percent of the labor force.[1] Nor is it likely that Third World countries will ever become industrially dominated societies either.

We can, then, distinguish two historical trajectories of industrial structure. One is the familiar European pattern from agricultural to industrial to postindustrial society. The other pattern seems to develop from agricultural society to a society of services-cum-industry, and from there to more services and less industry.

Britain was the first industrial society of the world. The first census that recorded the dominance of industrial employment was taken in 1821.[2] In Belgium and Switzerland this occurred in 1890–1900, and in Germany in 1907. Around 1910 industrial employment comprised about 41 percent of the labor force in Germany, 45 percent in Belgium and Switzerland, and 51 percent in Britain. In Sweden, industrial employment overtook agricultural employment only in 1940, and the relative preponderance of the former in relation to services was small until 1960.

The other trajectory first emerged around the turn of the century in Holland, Australia, and somewhat later in New Zealand; and in the United States, in the 1920s, followed by Canada, when the industrial structure was no longer dominated relatively by agriculture but employment in industry was almost on a par with and soon overtaken by employment in services. On the eve of the Depression it was clear that a major center of capitalism, North America, was not taking the European route to an industrial labor market.[3] For the OECD area as a whole the historical peak of industrialism (measured by the relative size of industrial employment) was circa 1970, when 37 percent of the civilian employment of OECD countries was industrial. Thereafter decline set in, first slowly, and then markedly in the troughs of the new crises in 1975 and the first years of the 1980s. The Swedish crest was in 1965, at 42.8 percent.[4] Comparing different nations, de-industrialization has been very uneven.

Relative de-industrialization in Sweden is dramatic if we count from the peak year of industrial employment. The decline in industrial employment as a proportion of civilian employment is 12.9 percentage

1 H. Kaelble, *Auf dem Weg zu einer europäischen Gesellschaft* (Munich: Beck, 1987), pp. 25ff; P. Bairoch (Supervisor), T. Deldycke, H. Gelders, J. M. Limbor, with G. Lefevere, G. Thorn, and G. Vandenabeele, *The Working Population and its Structure* (Brussels: Ed. de l'Institut de Sociologie, 1968).
2 E. H. Hunt, *British Labour History 1815–1914* (London: Weidenfeld & Nicolson, 1981), p. 26.
3 Bairoch et al., *The Working Population and its Structure*, national tables.
4 OECD, *Labour Force Statistics 1965–1985* (Paris: OECD, 1987), pp. 40–1; OECD, *Historical Statistics 1960–1985* (Paris: OECD, 1987), p. 36; Bairoch et al., *The Working Population and its Structure*.

points, surpassed only by Belgium (15.9), Holland (14.6) (all three countries peaking industrially in 1965), and Britain, whose industrial share culminated in 1911 but stayed rather stable from 1921 to the 1960s and then dropped by 14.3 percentage points between 1965 and 1985. The absolute decline in industrial employment has also been large in Sweden: 18.9 percent between 1965 and 1985 (although this was less dramatic than in Belgium where the drop was exactly one-third, than the 32.5 percent drop in Britain, the 26.1 percent Dutch decline for 1965–83, or Denmark's 19.1 percent decline between 1970 and 1985). In the European Economic Community (EEC) the absolute decrease in industrial employment since its culmination in 1970 has been 18.1 percent. North American and Japanese industrial employment, on the other hand, was higher (in absolute numbers) in 1985 than at any time before 1973–4.[5] Currently (the fall of 1988), industry employs 29.4 percent only of the Swedish labor force.[6] In two decades Sweden has become a postindustrial society, only slightly more industrial than the United States.

Industrial class politics

Class politics has not emerged directly from industrial class structures. Although in the 1830s Britain had history's first mass working class movement (Chartism), the center of socialism was first France and later Germany, and the world's first elected labor governments appeared in nonindustrial(ly dominated) Australia and in pre-industrial Finland. The British Labour Party emerged late and has not been among the most successful working class parties in democratic politics. Swiss working class politics has always been a rather pathetically minority phenomenon, never even reaching 30 percent electorally, which may only in part be explained by the dependence of Swiss capital on imported disenfranchised labor from the 1890s on.[7] Nor have Belgian parties claiming to represent the working class been able to get much leverage from Belgian industrialism. Twice only, in 1946 and 1954, have they been able to muster the support of more than 40 percent of the electorate, and never have they reached 45 percent.[8]

Nevertheless, industrial and advanced industrial-cum-services societies generated various forms of industrial class-collective action, organization, and politics. Trade unions, employers' organizations, strikes and lockouts, class-based political agendas, and parties appeared everywhere (save in the United States). In most countries (exceptions

5 OECD, *Labour Force Statistics 1965–1985*, pp. 36–7.
6 SCB, *Arbetskraftsundersökningen* (Stockholm: SCB, 1988), 3rd quarter, p. 40.
7 G. Therborn, "Migration and Western Europe: the Old World turning new," *Science*, 237 (September 4, 1987), pp. 1184–5.
8 T. Mackie and R. Rose, *The International Almanac of Electoral History*, 2nd edn (London: Macmillan, 1932).

being the United States, Canada, Ireland, and Switzerland, on a federal level) party systems developed that were polarized between a party claiming to represent the working class and having some relation to a socialist tradition on the one hand and an avowedly anti-socialist party on the other.

Moreover, the high point of international industrialism, 1965–75, is also the historic peak, with various time lags, of labor movement influence in the advanced capitalist world. From the late 1960s to the early 1980s there was a record level of industrial action, of the extension of workers' rights at the point of production, of trade union growth, of labor party votes, and of labor governments.[9] In the 1980s, however, the international tendencies have demonstrated a weakening of labor and of the labor movement.

Industrial politics grows out of the class needs of industrial workers and of the owners and managers of capital. Its typical issues are issues of the relative rights of capital and wage labor, the rates of capital accumulation and economic growth, and the distribution of income and wealth. No political system has ever been completely industrial, however. Nonindustrial issues, and their appeal across class, society, or nation, have always been important – national rights and status, foreign and military policy, law and order, health, education, and freedom of expression.

Postindustrial politics may mean, then, either that nonindustrial politics has gained in importance at the expense of industrial politics, or that new postindustrial issues and new patterns of alignments and cleavages have emerged. Both cases, however, should be distinguished from pre-industrial politics, and from the cleavages between industrial and pre-industrial politics – from agrarian class cleavages, agrarian–industrial and rural–urban conflicts, and issues involving inherited identities, such as ethnicity and religion. Postindustrial politics is first a politics of *choice*, rather than of belonging, rights, or progress. On one hand, choice of the direction of societal development (in contrast with arguments about the means of growth in a predetermined direction) and of the content and form of the individual life-course (in distinction to strivings about the rights of given social positions) emerge as the political issues of social organization. On the other hand, political action is on the bases of chosen identities and agreements, rather than on the basis of realization of interests common to a set of given social positions or of a sense of cultural belonging. Environmentalism, gender politics, homosexual politics, and, more generally, collective action based on chosen lifestyles exemplify postindustrial politics most clearly.

Swedish politics has been class politics. Electoral behavior is much more directly explicable in class terms in the Nordic countries than in other developed countries. Among the Nordic polities the Swedish and

9 G. Therborn, "The prospects of labour and the transformation of advanced capitalism," *New Left Review* 145 (1984), pp. 5–38.

the Finnish are clearly and equally the most class patterned. In terms of the index of class voting Sweden scores higher than any other country. The average index of class voting (the proportion of workers voting Left minus the proportion among the upper and middle classes) for the three ordinary parliamentary elections in 1956–64 is 50, for the three elections of 1968–73 39, and for the four of 1976–85 35.[10] Membership of the Social Democratic Party (SAP), high and growing until a few years ago, dropped significantly in 1987, and at the end of 1987 was below the 1979 level. Nevertheless, the class character of Swedish electoral politics is still pronounced by comparison with other countries.[11]

The rise to political domination of the Swedish labor movement coincided with the emergence of a predominately industrial society. The highest electoral share of social democracy and communism in Sweden occurred in 1940, the election in which the working class proportion of the electorate peaked historically. Almost 55 percent of the voters then were manual workers and their families. From 1956 on, manual workers, active or in retirement, and their nonemployed family members comprised about half of the voters until 1976. Thereafter came a significant decline down to 43 percent in 1985.[12] Other things being equal, then, de-industrialization and the arrival of postindustrial society should have led to a decomposition of labor politics in Sweden. In fact, labor politics has been reaffirmed. The average vote for Social Democrats and Communists together – in Sweden officially named "the socialist bloc" – in the three elections in the 1980s was 50.1 percent in a multiparty system with proportional representation. (The tendency is declining, though, from 51.2 percent in 1982 to 49.0 percent in 1988.) The point is, of course, that other things are not equal.

Routes to postindustrial and other advanced nonindustrial societies

The extent to which a political pattern of industrial class politics could be carried over into a new social constellation should depend significantly on the amount of social dislocation involved in the process. Three dimensions seem to be of particular relevance. One is labor market dislocation, as indicated by unemployment. Another is regional dislocation, expressed in divergent patterns of regional decline and expansion. A third is organizational dislocation, expressed in large transfers of job supply from large-scale organizations to small service enterprises. All three dimensions of dislocation can be expected to divide, uproot, and fragment the working class collectives of industrial society and industrial

10 M. Gilljam and S. Holmberg, *Väljare och val i Sverige* (Stockholm: Bonniers, 1987), p. 184.
11 R. Dalton, S. Flanagan, and P. A. Beck (eds), *Electoral Change in Advanced Industrial Democracies* (Princeton, NJ: Princeton University Press, 1987), pp. 30, 352.
12 Gilljam and Holmberg, *Väljare och val i Sverige*, p. 185.

politics. In all three respects, Sweden has made a smooth entry into postindustrialism.

Unemployment in Sweden in 1988 was 1.6 percent, at the end of the year 1.1 percent, and labor scarcity is a major problem of the Swedish economy, both for private industry and for public services. The internationally standardized annual rate of unemployment never surpassed 3.5 percent in Sweden, and only in 1982–4 was it above 3.0 percent.[13] The low Swedish unemployment is not the manifest outcome of a restriction of labor supply, although it is true that the Swedish labor market has not expanded as much as that of the United States. Low or high unemployment in international crises has not been a predetermined effect of the vicissitudes of the world market. Nor is the unemployment rate derivable from indicators of competitive market strength. Rather, as I have elaborated at some length elsewhere,[14] cross-nationally divergent rates of unemployment follow from national institutions, in particular from whether full employment was an institutionalized public policy commitment before the outbreak of the crises or not.

In a somewhat longer historical perspective Sweden's labor market path into a postindustrial society is rather remarkable. Since 1929 the volume of paid work, measured in annual hours, had been declining in Sweden, slowly but rather continuously. A peculiarity about the Swedish labor market was the upward bend in the curve with postindustrialization. In Western Europe, the volume of work has dropped importantly during the crisis. But the volume of paid work reached a historic trough in Sweden in 1978, after which it has slowly begun to grow again. If the 1950 Swedish work volume is put at 100, it was 108 in 1929 and reached 91 in 1978. In 1986 the index stood at 98.[15] The volume of work is still growing according to regular labor force surveys. The 1970 level of work volume has now been overtaken. In brief, Sweden's transition to postindustrialism is occurring without unemployment and with a historical upward turn of the job supply curve.

Moreover, by international standards, the regional and local dislocations caused by the transition from industrialism to postindustrialism have been minor in Sweden. The major pattern in the 1970s to 1980s is one of equalization, among regions and among municipalities. Unemployment, moderate as it was, did hit peripheral provinces and municipalities and some industrial areas harder. But a drastic national equalization of the employment and income of women has produced an overall equalization of income and employment across Sweden's 274

13 OECD, *Economic Outlook*, 44 (1988), p. 182.
14 G. Therborn, *Why Some Peoples are More Unemployed Than Others* (London: Verso, 1986).
15 G. Therborn, "Tar arbetet slut? Och postfordismens problem," in *Sociologer ser på arbete*, ed. U. Björnberg and I. Hellberg (Stockholm: Arbetslivscentrum, 1987), pp. 116–17 with references; SCB, *Arbetskraftsundersökningen*, p. 177.

municipalities between 1975 and 1985.[16] Child-care, care of the elderly, dental care, and general health services have also become more evenly distributed.

In contrast with the rest of the world, growth in Swedish and Nordic services employment has been overwhelmingly in the public sector.[17] Public employment means large-scale organization, broad employee collectives, and generally a pro-union environment. Sociopolitically, the impact of a shift from a mainly industrial labor market to a chiefly non-industrial one is minimized if it occurs within the organizational framework of the public sector.

The ease of Sweden's transition on all three dimensions is due mainly to the importance and effectiveness of steering rather than which party held office. Crucial measures of employment stabilization, regional support, and public sector expansion were taken in the period of bourgeois government in 1976–82.

Total government outlays, as a percentage of gross domestic product, jumped from 51.7 in 1976 to 66.6 in 1982. In 1960, total government outlays in Sweden were only marginally above those in the OECD as a whole, 2.4 percentage points, 0.2 above the OECD without the United States. By 1976 the difference had grown to 14.4 and 11.8 respectively. But when the bourgeois parties returned to the benches of the opposition six years later, the difference stood at 25.0 and 21.4 percentage points respectively.[18] True, 39 percent of the increase in total government outlays in 1976–82 were disbursed by local governments,[19] but local governments also provided 87 percent of the new public sector jobs.[20]

Political institutions can significantly affect vast processes of socio-economic transformation, such as those of de-industrialization and the rise of postindustrial society. But institutional outcomes need themselves to be explained in terms of actors and actions maintaining, using, or changing institutions. In this Swedish case, the outcome indicated above is not what most people would expect from an explicitly bourgeois government.

The Politics in Sweden of the 1970s

Swedish politics of the 1970s may be seen in terms of two major offensives, involving intense mass mobilization and bold political moves. One

16   H. Magnusson and N. Stjernquist, *Den kommunala självstyrelsen, jämlikheten och variationerna mellan kommunerna* (Stockholm: Civildepartementet DS, 1988), p. 36.
17   Therborn, *Why Some Peoples are More Unemployed Than Others*, p. 87 with references.
18   OECD, *Historical Statistics 1960–1985*, p. 64.
19   OECD, *National Accounts 1972–1984*, vol. 11 (Paris: OECD, 1986), pp. 451, 458.
20   SCB, *Arbetsmarknaden 1970–1983* (Stockholm: SCB, 1984), p. 64.

was industrial, the other postindustrial. No detailed picture of them will be attempted here, but their broad outlines will be sketched and contrasted.

The industrial labor offensive

The first offensive was undertaken by the labor movement, with the industrial unions, Metall in particular, as the main source of ideas and organizational impetus, and SAP as the major political vehicle. It was a radicalization of industrial class politics. The industrial labor offensive had three major goals.

The first goal was *"increased equality."* The theme of persisting, unacceptable inequality had come onto the official political agenda in 1965, when a public Low Income Investigation was set up. Trade union leader Arne Geijer, head of the Landsorganisationen (LO) confederation, former chairman of the Metall, emphasized Sweden's enduring class character at the extraordinary SAP congress in 1967. The party congress of 1968 set up a joint SAP–LO "working group for equality issues," chaired by Alva Myrdal. The two lengthy reports of the group, to the party congresses of 1969 and 1972, covered most parts of social life, but with a clear and, in the second report, overwhelming emphasis on industrial class issues, wage structure, employment opportunities and policies, working conditions, and workplace relations. (The SAP congress reports and debates are published.) The industrial muscles of LO were used for bringing about a very substantial compression of wage and salary scales. The differentialist professional union SACO was defeated by the government as employer in 1966, and in 1971 by the government as legislator. The social democratic cadre and the low-ranked majority of the white collar confederation were won for the egalitarian line.[21] The bite of progressive taxation was sharpened in 1970, and further toughened by the effects of the ensuing inflation. In the 1968 election, which resulted in an absolute Social Democratic majority, the goal of increasing equality was accepted even by the right-wing opposition.[22] The egalitarian campaign culminated in the elections of 1970, when the slogan "Increased equality" was on every Social Democratic poster. It could draw upon the realignment of the 1960 election – pro-Social Democratic, pro-welfare state – and was, of course, reinforced by the international radicalization in 1968–70.

The second goal of the industrial working class offensive was *industrial legislation* of job security, job safety, and trade union rights at the workplace. This meant a clear change of policy of the party and of LO from a line of principled reluctance to use legislation, a principled preference for

21 N. Elvander, *Den Svenska modellen* (Stockholm: Publica, 1988), pp. 39ff.
22 G. Therborn, "Electoral campaigns as indicators of ideological power," in *Rethinking Ideology*, ed. S. Hänninen and L. Paldan (West Berlin: Argument, 1983).

collective agreements as regulators of the labor market, and a *de facto* lack of serious trade union concern with job and workplace entitlements. A more critical appreciation of modern industrial working conditions began to appear at the 1966 LO congress, corroborated by findings of sociological research presented to the congress. In 1969 the traditional vanguard of the Swedish trade union movement, Metall, swung round to a line in favor of using the political clout of the labor movement for extending workers' and local union rights. The SAP congress of 1969 made the new trade union line into the party line.[23] The LO congress in 1971 then laid the programmatic basis for a spate of industrial legislation. The centerpiece of this was the Co-Determination Act of 1976, the basic sense of which was that in principle the employer was legally obliged to negotiate with the unions about all decisions affecting the workplace.[24]

The third and most ambitious goal of the industrial labor offensive aimed at a *transfer of the property rights* of the major corporations to trade union ownership through collectively held "wage-earners' funds." This was the first time that Sweden's social democratic labor movement presented a concrete and immediate – albeit with an intended long process of maturation after legislation – proposal of socializing the major means of production. Again the unions took the initiative, formulated the basic ideas, and had the party adopt them in preparation for legislative action, and electoral combat.

The party leadership was caught by surprise,[25] but the 1978 party congress accepted the idea without committing the party to a concrete proposal, which was left to an LO–SAP joint working group. After a number of drafts and revisions, a watered down bill of public investment funds, explicitly barred from ever acquiring more than a clear minority of shares in any corporation, was presented by a returned Social Democratic government and passed by Parliament at the end of 1983.

The egalitarian campaign met little overt and explicit resistance, except from the confederation of professional employees (SACO) who lost badly. Since economic egalitarianism focused on personal income, capital accumulation was not adversely affected by the campaign – indeed the most profitable corporations even benefited from egalitarian wage restraint. The employers were more unhappy with the new pieces of industrial legislation, but the tradition of consensual employer–trade union relations was not broken. Against the illegal wildcat strikes that developed from 1969–70 – pioneered by two groups of classical militancy, the Gothenburg dockers and the far north iron ore miners – employers, unions, and government stood guard together around legally backed institutionalized forms of industrial relations. The bourgeois parties

23   J. Pierre, *Partikongresser och regeringspolitik* (Lund: Kommunfakta, 1986), pp. 186ff.
24   Arbetslivscentrum, *1970-talets reformer i arbetslivet* (Stockholm: Tiden, 1982).
25   R. Meidner, personal communication, 1986.

carefully avoided making worker–employee entitlements and local union rights into a political issue. It was on the property issue, the wage-earners' funds, that the employers' confederation SAF and the bourgeois parties decided to fight. Herein they were successful, forcing the SAP to withdraw from the original position of the trade union again and again, until the whole idea became discredited. The SAP government managed to cover its retreat fairly well with the innocuous 1983 Act.

A brief guide to Swedish bourgeois politics

While the industrial labor offensive was in full swing, the bourgeois parties launched an offensive of their own. They opened up a postindustrial front. While Swedish Social Democracy is a well-known star on most stages of comparative politics and policy, Swedish bourgeois politics is much less known. So, a brief introduction may be needed. First, in Sweden "bourgeois" (borgerlig) is neither an insult nor a controversial Marxist term. It is official political parlance, and (frequently, if not always) it is used as the self-designation of the non-Social Democratic, non-Communist political forces of the country. In fact, one of the problems for Swedish bourgeois politics is that it is only partially "bourgeois" in any Marxist or French sense. Twentieth-century non-socialist politics in Sweden has consisted of four different strands which, with the development of parliamentary government and proportional representation, were manifested in party form. One came out of traditional, royalist, State Church conservatism, reinvigorated by (mainly agrarian) protectionism at the time of the post-1873 Depression. Until 1970 this tendency frankly presented itself as the Right or the Right Party most of the time. Now it calls itself Moderate. While originally harboring strong statist elements, after democratization the Right became increasingly suspicious of the state, and today's Moderates are mainly right-wing liberal free marketeers, if rather moderately so by international standards. Against the right stood two lines of liberalism. One was urban, parliamentarist, free trade, nonreligious or lukewarmly religious, rather pro-defense, intellectual, and modern business. The other was rural, also parliamentarist and free trade, but including religious dissenters, teetotallers, antimilitarists, artisans, small farmers of grain-importing areas, small or medium-size businessmen, rural intellectuals, and religious workers. The second liberal component was before the Second World War by far the largest. After a split into two parties in 1923 – over Prohibition – the liberal currents were reunited in 1934, with a long-term trend towards urban domination.

The fourth major tendency of Swedish bourgeois politics can be found, as an independent political force, only in the other Nordic countries and in Switzerland. It was developed by propertied farmers, constitutionally conservative with the abolition of aristocratic and other "higher" estate privileges; culturally also conservative, suspicious of all "isms," including conservatism and liberalism, but concerned above all with the medium-sized propertied farmer. In contrast with their Danish class comrades, the bulk of Swedish farmers produced overwhelmingly for the domestic market in the twentieth century, which accounts for their protectionist orientation. The parliamentary history of these currents has to be summarized too, in order to make the politics of the 1970s and 1980s comprehensible to non-Swedish readers. The Right and the Liberals, with their two components, were the bitter traditional enemies. In cooperation with the Social Democrats the Liberals forged the "democratic breakthrough," in December 1918, when the Right finally gave way to revolutionary pressure in the wake of the crumbling of the Wilhelmine empire. The 1920s were a period of minority governments, Social Democratic, Right, and Liberal. The Farmers' League never took part in any government, but was regarded as a farmerist annex to the Right. The Depression of the 1930s led to lasting realignment of Swedish politics.

The farmers had one interest in common with the workers, they were reflationist, although the higher food prices had to be paid by the workers. In the Nordic countries there was both a strong Social Democracy and an independent farmers' party, and in all of them a sort of workers–farmers alliance was struck. For two generations a relationship of deep mutual trust and respect existed between the top leaders of Social Democracy and the Farmers' League, in coalition in 1936–9 and in 1951–7, and again in a national government together during the Second World War.[26]

The Right, now turned Moderates, is normally the favored party of capital. In the 1985 elections, the latest for which calculations have been made, 61 percent of the members of the bourgeoisie (owners of medium to big business and business executives) voted Moderate. More bourgeoisie voted for the Social Democrats than for the two other bourgeois parties together, 20 percent for the SAP, 17 percent for the Liberals, and 2 percent for the Centre Party.[27] A few prominent business leaders are active Liberals, though. The currently most well known is Pehr Gyllenhammar, the head of Volvo.

The problems of bourgeois parliamentary politics on the eve of the 1970s can be summed up thus. Against a powerful Social Democracy, that could count upon the support of the Communist Party if need be, stood three bourgeois parties of currently rather equal size but with volatile internal proportions. None of them had ever scored more than 30 percent of the vote in any parliamentary election since the democratic breakthrough in 1918, and since the SAP takeover in 1932 none had even reached a fourth of the vote. They had never governed together,

26   G. Therborn, "The coming of Swedish social democracy," in *L'Internazionale Operaia e Socialista tra le due guerre*, ed. E. Collotti (Milan: Feltrinelli, 1985) (Annali della Fondazione Giangiacomo Feltrinelli 1983–4), pp. 527–93.
27   S. Svallfors, *Vem älskar välfärdsstaten?* (Lund: Arkiv, 1989), p. 127.

and between them were old and deep traditions of mistrust. The Farmers' League since the late 1950s had rather successfully de-agrarianized itself into the Centre Party, but it still represented rural small folk and their urban descendants.

Only jointly, as three parties in collaboration in one form or another, could they hope to unseat the Social Democrats. However, in the three-party constellation one party was always tempted to defect, preferring an immediate deal with the Social Democrats to an uncertain longer-run governmental position, perhaps then marginalized by the other bourgeois parties. The Right/Moderates could hardly defect, given their clearly delineated flank position. But for the liberal People's Party and, in particular, for the Centre Party, defection from the bourgeois camp was always a feasible and rather attractive option. The Farmers' League/Centre Party had a redistributionist low-income earner interest in common with Social Democracy, a cautious neutralism, and a rural popular organization tradition. The People's Party had become a party largely of white collar employees, and the rapprochement in the late 1960s and early 1970s between the manual workers and the white collar trade union confederation stimulated one between the People's Party and Social Democracy too. Both parties harbored a cultural radicalism and feminist concerns about the equality of women and men.

Alongside the parliamentary politics of the Swedish bourgeoisie, weak and divided, was its industrial politics, which was the opposite. The Swedish Employers' Confederation SAF, founded in 1902, is probably the world's most resourceful employers' organization. It currently covers most of Swedish private business, including all the large corporations, and it is the direct bargainer with the unions – although its powerful branch organization, the Engineering Association, is now negotiating on its own – and all agreements between SAF branch organizations or member enterprises have by statute to be accepted by the central SAF leadership. Fines are *de facto* applied as sanctions against violations of the statute.[28]

The 1970s did not look very promising to Swedish bourgeois politics. The industrial labor offensive was being launched. In the 1968 election, the three bourgeois parties together gathered 42.9 percent of the votes, as against 50.1 percent for Social Democracy. The Centre Party advanced to 15.7 percent, the People's Party retreated to 14.3, and the Moderates to 12.9. Ideologically, the bourgeois parties were clearly on the defensive. A battle on the industrial class terrain was hard to deliver as long as the vital interests of property and capital were not at stake, which they were not and had never been since democratization opened the constitutional route to Social Democratic power. The immediate economic interests of state-dependent farmers were not the same as those of the export industry. Nor were they the same as those of the small rural farmers with their

---

28   A. Gladstone and J. Windmuller (eds), *Employers' Associations and Industrial Relations* (Oxford: Clarendon Press, 1984).

low nominal incomes or the urban middle strata grumbling of high taxes. There was never an anti-feminist backlash of any significance in Sweden, but sociocultural issues divided non-Left opinion between radical Liberals and a conservative Centre Party, cutting across socio-economic cleavages. However, a new terrain of politics was emerging, and the non-Left parties were the first to seize the time.

The bourgeoisie trumps with postindustrial politics

Given the tradition of Swedish politics since 1932, the most immediately dangerous threat to Social Democratic power would occur if the Centre Party/Farmers' League emerged as the main alternative to the SAP. That would mean a direct challenge to Social Democracy's legitimacy as *the* representative of the country's popular tradition, and it would make it extremely risky (to put it mildly) for the liberal People's Party (not to speak of the Moderates) to defect towards collaboration with Social Democracy. The snag was that this could hardly be brought about in industrial class terms. On that terrain, the Farmers' League/Centre Party fought a rearguard action, more akin to Social Democratic notions of security and equality than to market competition and efficiency. Nor could any nationalist card be played. The neutralist tradition, in current choices expressed in staying out of NATO and out of the EEC, had the bulk of the population behind it, and was most deeply rooted in the Farmers' League/Centre Party and in Social Democracy. In contrast with Norwegian and Danish Social Democracies, Swedish Social Democracy never abandoned the go-it-alone course of foreign policy.

On the other hand, the precarious anchorage of the Centre Party in industrial society was a decisive advantage in taking the opportunity to develop a postindustrial kind of politics. The party was less bound than others, both to industrial labor and to industrial capital. The transformation, in the late 1950s, from Farmers' League to Centre Party had been moderately successful. In joint declarations with the People's Party, a notion of "middle-of-the-road politics" (*mittenpolitik*) had been established in the Swedish political spectrum, and in the Social Democratic landslide in 1968 the Centre emerged as the largest of the three bourgeois parties and the only one with a widely popular and confidence-inspiring leadership in the opinion polls.

A new political terrain was opened up in the 1970 election. Two themes were stressed – decentralization and the environment. Decentralization was couched in terms of regional equality, deconcentration and participatory democracy. It was not argued from individualist principles, but it did carry anti-bureaucratic connotations. Environmental concern was still expressed in rather vague and general forms. The two parties in the middle both struck those chords, the Centre most strongly and credibly. The message was favorably received. The Centre and the liberal People's Party advanced 6.1 percentage points, while SAP lost 4.8. With the recovery of the Communist Party after Czechoslovakia (whose invasion the Party had roundly condemned) and various Maoist splits, what now was called "the socialist bloc" lost 3.0 percentage points.

The environment was one of the leading concerns of the electorate in 1970, and it had become by far the most important political question to young people. In the fall of 1969 SAP had begun to slide backwards in the polls, and the Centre to advance steadily.[29] In the 1973 election the party leaped forward to 25.1 percent, the highest score of a Swedish bourgeois party since 1928. In Parliament the three bourgeois parties got exactly half of the seats. Nuclear energy became the main environmental issue. The Centre took the lead in an increasingly intense campaign against nuclear power. The conflicting demands upon it in its novel role as the major force of opposition wore upon the Centre after 1973 and it reached its zenith in the polls in early 1974. The classical bourgeois property issues were also activated by the wage-earners' fund proposal.

However, with these reservations it is clear that it was the 1976 Centre Party mobilization on nuclear energy which, after 44 years, tipped the electoral scales against Social Democracy. The same last minute mobilization also saved the bourgeois government in 1979.[30] In other words, the party of industrial labor, industrial progress, and industrial equality was finally defeated when to the usual bourgeois opposition was added a new, postindustrial basis of politics. A new line of political cleavage seemed to appear. Two parties, the Centre and the Communist Party, took a strong and united antinuclear and pro-environmentalist stand, and cooperated in the 1980 referendum on the future of nuclear power stations. The Moderates were clearly pro-nuclear, although in as tactful a manner as possible, and pro-industrial economic growth. The People's Party was also pro-nuclear and pro-industrial, but its sympathizers were seriously divided. How was the outcome of the two competing cleavage patterns, the industrial class and the postindustrial opinions, decided?

The international economic crises and social democratic tactics decide

During the first half of the 1970s the Swedish economy was out of step with the international cycle. An over-restrictive economic policy had generated a domestic recession in 1971–2, which had undermined confidence in Social Democratic capacity to safeguard full employment. In the "lottery parliament" of 1973–6 – a constitutional amendment later added one more seat in order to always ensure a formal majority – the Social Democratic government and the bourgeois-dominated parliamentary Finance Committee pursued in tandem a vigorously expansionist

29   SIFO, *Indikator*, May 1971, October 1972.
30   O. Pettersson, *Väljarna coh valet* (Stockholm: SCB/Liber, 1977); S. Holmberg, *Svenska väljare* (Stockholm: Liber, 1981); S.-E. Larsson, *Regera i koalition* (Stockholm: Bonniers, 1986); H. Bergström, *Rivstart* (Stockholm: Tiden, 1987).

policy, for which both parties congratulated themselves in 1976. Both sides expected a new boom, and regarded the international crisis as successfully kept off Swedish shores.[31] In fact, of course, the crises worsened and struck Sweden after the 1976 election. Economically, the bourgeois parties were extremely unlucky when their time finally came after forty-four years. The bourgeois government then continued a full-employment-above-all economic policy. In labor market terms it was eminently successful. Unemployment was kept below 3 percent until 1982, when it rose to 3.2 percent. The historical trend for the total employment volume – measured in hours of paid work per year – to fall was also stopped in 1979.[32] But the costs were a rapidly rising budget deficit, above average inflation, and a deteriorating competitive position.[33] The latter were hardly issues around which to mobilize a militant anti-bourgeois opposition, however. The new workplace rights took effect with the official benediction of the bourgeois government. The property issue kept the bourgeois bloc together, while labor leaders faced increasing difficulties combining trade unionist demands for power and a technical, gradualist strategy with something concrete to mobilize a rather indifferent and increasingly skeptical working population. The new turn of the tide started with the detonation of the nuclear question. However tactful and judicious for governmental power, the Moderates and the Liberals were not prepared to close down the nuclear power plants just built, and they underestimated the depth and intensity of the antinuclear convictions of Centre leader and Prime Minister Fälldin. In 1978 the three-party government fell apart, succeeded by a weak Liberal minority government. After the Harrisburg accident all Swedish parties united around the idea, launched by Palme, of a referendum on nuclear energy, which opened the way for a new bourgeois three-party government in 1979.

The SAP leadership skillfully avoided a nuclear front. The party line was that existing power plants should be used until their lifetime was ended, after which nuclear energy should be phased out, around 2010. A minor issue was used to prevent the Moderates from adopting the same label as the Social Democrats, and so there were three alternatives presented to the electorate, depolarizing the issue. A massive mobilization of the party and trade union machine finally succeeded in winning a plurality for the option favored by the SAP leadership, just ahead of the antinuclear Line 3. After the March 1980 referendum, nuclear energy rapidly disappeared from the political agenda. By depolarizing the question and by allowing the internal antinuclear opposition – which

31 Bergström, *Rivstart*, pp. 57–8.
32 G. Therborn, "Tar arbetet slut? – Och postfordismens problem," in *Sociologer ser på arbete*, ed. U. Björnberg and I. Hellberg (Stockholm: Arbetslivscentrum, 1987), pp. 109–30; SCB, *Arbetskraftsundersökningen*, p. 177.
33 G. Therborn, "Sweden competitive welfare," in *Can the Welfare State Compete?*, ed. A. Pfaller, I. Gough, and G. Therborn (London: Macmillan, 1991).

included ex-ministers Alva Myrdal and Ulla Linsdtöm – to express and organize itself freely, Palme and the SAP leadership avoided any deeper divisions of the party. Centrist environmentalism lost its momentum and became bitter and demoralized. The advance of the antinuclear Communist Party, which had scored post-1947 records of electoral sympathy in the final phase of the referendum campaign, was stopped.

Industrial class politics returned to the forefront by Mayday 1980. Sweden experienced her largest industrial conflict ever, with strategically coordinated strikes met by mass lockout. On May 2nd, 900,000 workers and employees, about 25 percent of all workers and employees in the country, were locked out or on strike.[34] The issue was wages, complicated by private and public sector union rivalry, and everything was disciplined and peaceful. But Social Democracy was dramatically reunited, and in the end the employers soon had to yield.

The enduring and deepening economic crisis forced socioeconomic issues into the center of party politics. The economic costs of the government policy mentioned above were piling up, and so also were the political costs. The bourgeois electorate had so far got little or nothing from its first governments in forty-four years. The issue of tax reform, of reduction in marginal tax rates in particular, was coming up. Bourgeois politics demanded lower income taxes; the longer-term economic credibility of the government required that something be done to the soaring deficit and debt, in other words, that public expenditure be cut. Social Democracy took advantage of both. The reduction in marginal income tax rates was pushed by the Moderates and the Liberals, while the Centre, with its low nominal income rural electorate, was rather lukewarm. The political basis for a tax reform was thus fragile. In this situation, the Liberals reasoned that a deal with the Social Democratic opposition was the best way to ensure a lasting tax reduction. A late night deal was struck between the Liberal Finance Minister and his counterpart in the Social Democratic opposition. The Centre accepted it, but the Moderates regarded it as betrayal and walked out of the government in 1981.

The proposed cuts were rather modest, but they affected central areas of the welfare state, and SAP was quick to seize upon the most sensitive issues. While sharply criticizing the bourgeois governments for financial laxity and economic incompetence, and accepting the necessity of fiscal restraint and reform, SAP made four popular promises in the 1982 electoral campaign to undo bourgeois-proposed cuts. State subsidies to municipal day-care should be fully restored, the temporary partial de-indexation of pensions should be done away with, there should be no cuts in the state finance of the union-run unemployment insurance, and the re-introduction of waiting days in the sickness insurance should not be effectuated. The still remaining property issue could not prevent the divided bourgeois parties from losing the 1982 election, economically as well as socially discredited.

34   Elvander, *Den Svenska modellen*, p. 52; SCB, *Arbetskraftsundersökningen*, p. 178.

The first period of postindustrial politics was over. Classical socio-economic issues and cleavages took back the center stage. Social Democracy was back in office on a program of keeping social commitments plus offering competent state management of Swedish capitalism. A successful competitive devaluation, backed up by trade union wage restraint, immediately after the 1982 election gave the open Swedish economy a push forward. Improvements in the international economy from 1983 on underlined Swedish Social Democracy's pact with the economic gods. Exactly as fifty years earlier, it had come into office in the trough of the Depression, just before the turn to better times. As fifty years earlier, SAP had gotten its position, not just through luck, but by a superior tactical ability and unity.[35]

The 1985 election demonstrated the tenacity of Social Democratic class politics. The right-radicalized Moderates called for a "system shift" of the Swedish model of welfare capitalism in a right-wing liberal direction. They were forced on the ideological defensive already in the spring of 1985, six months before the election, after a national round of debates with SAP. The Liberals and the Centre both defected and rallied to the defense of the existing welfare state. The right-wing advance was turned into a setback, and the SAP government was re-elected.

In the three-party system of bourgeois Swedish politics it is almost impossible for a right-wing liberal alternative to gain the upper hand in the country. There will almost always be some other currents of bourgeois opinion, and in Sweden they have their outlet in one or both parties located to the left of the Right. These parties have good rational reasons to differentiate themselves from the far Right, which is thus exposed and/or isolated.

Social Democratic Options and Constraints

After 1985 SAP had three basic options. One was continuity, consolidating and further extending the welfare state, linking up with the radical thrust of the 1970s, trying to find new ways to "economic democracy" by limiting property rights and capital concentration. De-industrialization had made the basis for such an option uncertain, and international conjunctures were strongly against it. The still intact and strong trade union movement, in particular the public sector union, were certainly capable of vigorous defense of the welfare state, but by the mid-1980s they were ideologically exhausted. The report to the 1986 LO congress on "The trade union movement and the welfare state" concluded that the construction of the welfare state was coming to its finishing stage and that the next task was to develop its effectiveness; on that point, however, the report had little to say. The inglorious end of the wage-earners' funds project did not immediately inspire new visions of economic democracy. In the labor market, the collective co-determination perspective of

35   Therborn, "The coming of Swedish social democracy."

the 1970s, while not rolled back, was being circumvented by corporate division into market-governed subunits, by profit-sharing schemes and various new managerial forms of individual employee mobilization and involvement. Public sector organization now began to take its models from private business management, in particular from Scandinavian Airlines, SAS.[36]

The second option was a kind of mirror image of the first, offering competent post-Keynesian economic management and a trimmed and revamped welfare state, a kind of market social democracy. For this option, ideas, visions and leadership could be provided by Finance Minister Feldt and his collaborators. And there was a favorable international conjuncture for it. But it was a risk option, exposed to opposition from the public sector unions and potentially to popular criticism from both the Centre and the Communist Party.

A third option was to try to bring about a new majoritarian constellation that aligned labor with new, postindustrial issues – particularly non-distributive issues. The latter implied a Social Democratic environmentalism. But it also was not an option without risks and problems. The SAP could not afford to break its links with industrial labor and industrial capital, thus undermining its core electorate and its credibility in the eyes of private business. Although they fit poorly with prevailing Green currents, the public service welfare state and the government of private capital accumulation are the accumulated assets of Social Democratic reform politics.

For a time SAP chose the third option. That became clear at the 1987 party congress, where environmental protection and antipollution measures emerged as the most popular issues. The government announced the phasing out of the nuclear power plants. Party leader Prime Minister Ingvar Carlsson talked on several occasions in 1988 of preservation of the environment as "the fourth historical task of Social Democracy," after universal suffrage, full employment, and the building of the welfare state.

The 1988 election signaled the success of the environmentalist option, wedded to an expanded welfare state perspective which included an extension of public day-care and the parental leave insurance.

The Environment Party entered parliament for the first time, with 5.6 percent of the vote. It is not a Left party like the German Greens. The new party has drawn voters both from the left and the right as well as first-time voters, but its leadership represents a breakaway from the failed bourgeois environmentalism of the 1970s. It shares a certain affinity with the Centre and Communist Parties.

While the Environment Party rejects the right–left division of politics, the Social Democratic third option has made cooperation with SAP easier than with either of the two parties of market liberalism. In the two largest cities, in the two most important university towns, and in most

36   B. Czarnawska-Joerges, *Reformer och ideologier* (Lund: Doxa, 1988).

other municipalities where it holds the political balance, the Environment Party has made a Social Democratically led government possible.
The main concession, in relation to previous policies, which SAP has
had to make in order to bring about these urban coalitions concerns
restrictions of auto traffic and extension of public transportation.

By the time of the Swedish elections in September 1988, Social Democracy had governed the country for fifty-three of the sixty-seven years
since the breakthrough of parliamentary democracy in the country.
For forty years without interruption (1936–76), the Prime Minister of
Sweden had been a Social Democrat. After six years in opposition, the
Social Democratic Workers' Party of Sweden (SAP) has been in office
again since 1982. The September 1988 verdict of the Swedish citizens
meant that SAP was reaffirmed as the governing party. The enthusiasm
of the electorate was not overwhelming. SAP got the support of 43.2
percent of the voters, an outcome well below its long-term trend –
45.5 percent for 1944–88 – and continuing the 1985 slide downwards.
However, for conservatism – in the American sense, right-wing liberalism in the European sense – the election was a historic defeat. The only
two consistent right-wing opposition parties, the (right-wing) Moderates
and the (liberal) People's Party, received together only 30.5 percent,
down 5 percentage points since 1985. The political editor of the leading
Moderate newspaper commented sadly that a "50/30 pattern" seemed to
be a basic feature of Swedish party politics, that is, around 50 percent of
the vote for Social Democrats and Communists together and about 30
percent for the bourgeois opposition.[37]

Another perspective might be to focus on the entry into Parliament of
the first new political party – splits and mergers of existing parties
uncounted – since 1917. Since 1940 the proportionally elected Swedish
Riksdag had contained the same five parties only. Now a sixth was
added, the Environment party. But the financial market did not react as
bourgeois politics and journalism might have predicted. The day after
the election the Swedish currency went up, interest rates went down, and
the Stock Exchange surged.[38]

The outcome of the 1988 Swedish election was a new alignment of the
classical party of industrial labor with environmentalist currents of different kinds. The losers were the parties of market liberalism, for the time
being isolated in powerless opposition.

In Spring 1989 an attempt by the government at technocratically
cooling down an inflation-prone, very tight labor market economy
backfired seriously. The once loyal unions protested publicly against a
proposal of higher indirect taxation. The Social Democratic standing in
the polls started to decline. It has now come down to a third of expressed
sympathies, but the number of "uncertain" has soared. The winners
have been the right-wing Moderates, the centrist Christian Democrats,

37 *Svenska Dagbladet*, September 25, 1988, p. 2.
38 *Svenska Dagbladet*, September 20, 1988, p. 1.

support for a new right-wing populism, and, to a smaller extent, the (now ex-Communist) Left Party. A second austerity package in February 1990 got a prior benediction from the union leaders, but both the latter and the government had to beat a sudden retreat in the face of a rank and file uproar. Faced with increasing alienation among its working class base the SAP has found it necessary to backtrack on big city auto restrictions, which in turn has broken up the coalition with the Environmentalists in Stockholm. The possibility of a Greenish, postindustrial reform alliance has been ground to pieces, for the time being, by the friction between the marketeers of the Ministry of Finance and the unions, as the resources created by the devaluation boom are petering out. When the clouds gathered, the perspective of social services reform, environmentalism, the quality of work, and participatory decentralization had no shelter from which to fight, unlike market austerity and redistribution. On the other hand, internal division and rivalry among the bourgeois parties continue unabated. Swedish politics remains suspended between different nonradical entries into postindustrialism.

Why is there no conservatism in Sweden?

The reasons why there is no strong radically right-wing current in Sweden comparable with Thatcherism and the shock troops of the Reagan revolution may be grouped in the way that Werner Sombart[39] grouped his classical answer to the question "why is there no socialism in the United States?", i.e. into the political, the economic, and the social position of the Swedish bourgeoisie and the Swedish middle classes. Two characteristics of the political set-up make it very difficult for radical right-wing tendencies to become strong, and even more difficult for them to form a government democratically. One is the proportional electoral system which was buttressed after the Second World War by a high rate of electoral participation. This electoral framework makes radical minority governments, of the left as well as of the right, virtually impossible. It has a strong inertia force which in the current Swedish circumstances tilts the balance in favor of the traditionally strong Social Democracy. Probably only a severe external shock would break the gradualist, majoritarian character of politics in Sweden.

The second political reason is more deeply rooted historically and was a crucial part of the process which made possible the uniquely long-lived Social Democratic governance from 1932 to 1976. This is the independent political organization of the farmers as farmers, the political autonomy and representation of a significant social force not confinable within the two brands of bourgeois politics, "conservatism" and "liberalism." A certain intrinsic affinity between farmers' and ruralist politics, on the one hand, and contemporary Green environmentalist politics, on the other, paved the way for the political leaders and activists who have created

---

39 W. Sombart, *Why is there no Socialism in the United States?* (White Plains, NY: M. E. Sharpe, 1976).

today's Centre Party and "ex-bourgeois" Environment Party. Commodification of nature and of social relationships, capital accumulation and consumerism were as alien to the old farmers' tradition as to current environmentalists. The Swedish party system, in contrast with most others, provided a conveyor belt from the former to the latter.

The economic position of Swedish capital is strong and favorable. Only Switzerland has more large private corporations per capita than Sweden. After the return to office of Social Democracy, profitability has risen steeply in the wake of the competitive devaluation and riding with the international tide.[40] The 1970s and 1980s have seen the successful replacement of several of the old leading families of finance capital by a crop of new wealthy capitalists, who have made their wealth and corporate power mainly on the Stock Exchange and in real estate.[41] While voting right, Swedish business leaders have also expressed great confidence in the competence and reliability of Social Democracy. In February 1988, 39 percent of Swedish big business executives believed that a Social Democratic government took care of business interests better than a bourgeois government. Only 18 percent of the same group, however, said that they actually wanted a Social Democratic government to win the 1988 election.[42]

The position of capital is enhanced by the respect accorded it for entrepreneurial and executive acumen, by the SAP, the union leadership, and the SAP governments. This social position is reinforced by an informal pattern of personal contact between the top echelons of Social Democracy and private business that was first established during the First World War and reaffirmed in the 1930s and since. The world market has provided an open frontier to Swedish capital, export oriented and led since the domestic industrial revolution. Though Swedish business would prefer Swedish entry into the European Community, earlier as well as now, staying out has so far had no visible negative consequences, neither on Swedish exports nor on Swedish corporate acquisitions in Europe.

The middle strata, on the other hand, have few economic reasons to be very happy with their lot. Nor have small nonfarm entrepreneurs, but they are too few to matter much. The income after tax of, say, middle level managers or high school teachers is significantly lower than that of their equivalents in the rest of Western Europe, and their advantage over workers is also much smaller.[43] They *are* also largely critical of Social Democracy. One of the reasons for the enduring high rate of class voting

40   G. Therborn, "Pillarization and popular movements: two varieties of welfare capitalism," in *Comparative History of Public Policy*, ed. F. Castles (Cambridge: Polity Press, 1989); Therborn, "Sweden competitive welfare."

41   SOU, *Ägande och inflytande i svenskt näringsliv* (Stockholm: Allmänna Förlaget, 1988), ch. 4, p. 38.

42   *Dagens Nyheter*, February 18, 1988, p. 13.

43   Näringslivets Ekonomifakta, *Aktuell information* (Stockholm: Näringslivets Ekonomifakta, July 1988).

is that a smaller proportion of the salaried middle strata in Sweden support the SAP than West German middle strata support the SPD or Austrian salaried middle strata the SPÖ.[44] In the 1979–85 elections (1988 data of comparable size and quality are not yet available), more middle level salaried employees supported the Moderates and the Liberals than the SAP. The decline of the SAP/CP bloc between 1968 and 1970 was mainly due to a defection of white collar voters.[45] However, given the bite of egalitarian tax policies into salaried incomes, the more interesting question is why as many as 35 percent of the total middle classes support the Social Democrats and the Communists as did 42–43 percent of the salaried middle class in 1982 and in 1985.[46]

While there are, no doubt, a number of reasons, including family background, occupational and trade union traditions and ideological convictions, for middle classes to vote left, two related factors seem to be of special weight in Sweden. They are the high proportion of women in the labor force (91 percent in the age span 25–54) and the large size of the public sector (a good 37 percent of total employment).[47]

The egalitarian policies of the unions and of the welfare state have clearly benefited women in general, and women lower-level office employees, female semi-professionals, and women workers in particular. Since the 1979 election SAP has a female edge, 1 percent in 1979 and a 5 percent higher proportion of the female vote than of the male vote in 1985. Correspondingly, the most right-wing Swedish party, the Moderates, now has a strong male preponderance, 4 percent in 1976 and 1982, 7 percent in 1985.[48] The net effect of these gender gaps will be a weakening of the middle class effect. With regard to the second factor, there are in Sweden more middle- and high-ranking salaried employees in the public sector than in the private sector. In one sense the former have been hit harder by the income equalization, but they also have an interest in defending the welfare state, which provides their livelihood. At those levels of rank, sector employment has strong effects on political sympathies, with more socialist sympathies in the public sector.[49]

The white collar strata began to emerge en masse and to organize themselves in the 1930s and early 1940s at the peak of Social Democratic electoral strength and when the organized working class imprint upon the labor market and upon social culture was very strong. A second spectacular wave of white collar growth came with the expansion of the welfare state after the mid-1960s. While never fully socialized into Social Democratically shaped industrial and sociopolitical relations, the middle

44   G. Therborn, "Vägen till ständig (?) makt," in *Socialdemokratins samhälle,* ed. K. Misgeld, K. Molin, and K. Åmark (Stockholm: Tiden, 1989).
45   Gilljam and Holmberg, *Väljare och val i Sverige,* pp. 181, 188.
46   Gilljam and Holmberg, ibid., pp. 184–5.
47   SCB, *Arbetskraftsundersökningen,* pp. 2, 38.
48   Gilljam and Holmberg, *Väljare och val i Sverige* p. 174.
49   Gilljam and Holmberg, ibid., p. 193.

strata in Sweden were nevertheless largely formed by them.[50] In brief, the unusually large proportion of the salaried middle strata in Sweden who are women and employed in the public sector have economic, as well as other, reasons to support the so-called Socialist Bloc rather than right-wing liberalism.

By "socialism" Werner Sombart[51] meant a mass working class movement embracing "the 'spirit' of Socialism as we now understand it in continental Europe, which is essentially Socialism with a Marxist character." It is in the corresponding sense that I have talked of conservatism as a mass middle class movement embracing the "spirit" of Thatcherism and Reaganism. The ideological reappraisals and the sociopolitical alignments accompanying Sweden's entry into postindustrial society have only just started. Will the former in the end amount to a political turn? Sombart ended his book by predicting one in the United States:

> all the factors that till now have prevented the development of Socialism in the United States are about to disappear or to be converted into their opposite, with the result that in the next generation Socialism in America will very probably experience the greatest possible expansion of its appeal.

The sign of a change in the prospects of right-wing liberal conservatism in Sweden are much more visible than the forebodings which Sombart perceived. Nevertheless, whatever the government, a Conservative postindustrial Sweden remains unlikely.

50 G. Therborn, "The coming of Swedish social democracy," pp. 527–93; G. Therborn, "Vägen till ständig(?) makt."
51 Sombart, *Why is there no Socialism in the United States?*, p. 18.

6

Smooth Consolidation in the West German Welfare State: Structural Change, Fiscal Policies, and Populist Politics

Claus Offe

The German welfare state, as it was originally established in the 1880s and continuously expanded and adapted without major alterations of its basic principles, is an institutional system that stands in an almost ideal correspondence with an industrial society characterized by the features of full employment, strong families, large and homogeneous corporate collective actors, and a balanced demographic structure. The German welfare state was originally uniquely designed to generate compliance, to be effective, and hence to provide stability within the parameters of this type of industrial social structure. Under present structural conditions it is far less capable of meeting these criteria. The remarkable historical robustness and continuity of the German system of social security, which has survived, since its beginnings in Bismarckian social reform, more than one century and four vastly different political regimes, must not be mistaken for a sign of continued adequacy for present conditions; on the contrary, it must be seen as a sign of institutional rigidity, with the consequence that the system fails to generate both compliance and effectiveness under the conditions to which it is now exposed. In this sense, the German welfare state can be seen as the present victim of its past success; its perfect adaptation to past conditions and ends hinders its adaptation to present conditions. These institutionally built-in rigidities

The author wishes to acknowledge insightful comments that he has received from a number of colleagues, among them in particular Karl Hinrichs, Stephan Leibfried, Frances Fox Piven, and Adrienne Windhoff-Héretier.

are the prime factor responsible for the current symptoms of inadequacy and decline – much more so than the economic turbulence that social policy-making has had to deal with since the mid-1970s or the conservative, liberal, or populist goals and values of political elites that came to power during that period.

More specifically, I shall explore three questions.

1 Which institutional features served to guarantee a high level of both compliance and effectiveness in the past?
2 To which structural social changes can we attribute the decline in the ability to generate rational support and the decline in effective goal attainment?
3 Finally, by what strategies and interpretations have political elites responded to the emergent tension between rigid institutional structures and the social environment of social policies?

The German Welfare State: Its Basic Features and Stabilizing Mechanisms

The institutional features of the German social security system[1] can be interpreted as the outcome of a strategy to maximize both the trust in the system (i.e. the condition for compliance) and the system's effectiveness, or its capacity to reach its limited goals. It generates those signals and perceptions which work as self-stabilizing cognitive feedbacks from which a high degree of "trustworthiness" of the institutions result.

What could be the potential causes of distrust, and how are the potential consequences of these causes precluded by the institutional arrangement. The greatest concern of a rational participant in an insurance system is, of course, that he might not receive (in case of the incident against which he wishes to be insured) the service or payment to which he expects to be entitled. This might possibly happen, first of all, if the insurance funds are insufficient to honor all claims. Such concerns are precluded, in the case of a social security arrangement such as the German one, by the principle of mandatory insurance, as well as by the fact that the liquidity of the fund is guaranteed through subsidies coming from the state budget, and that all members of the insurance

---

1 Recent accounts of the institutional structure of the German social security system and its evolution are given by J. Alber, *Der Sozialstaat in der Bundesrepublik 1950–1983* (Frankfurt: Campus, 1989), V. Hentschel, *Geschichte der deutschen Sozialpolitik 1880–1980* (Frankfurt: Suhrkamp, 1983), and M. G. Schmidt, *Sozialpolitik. Historische Entwicklung und internationaler Vergleich* (Opladen: Leske, 1988); see also G. A. Ritter, *Social Welfare in Germany and Britain* (Leamington Spa and New York: Berg, 1986), F. Tennstedt, "Sozialgeschichte der Sozialversicherung," in *Handbuch der Sozialmedizin*, vol. 3, ed. M. Blohmke (Stuttgart: Enke, 1976), pp. 385–492.

enjoy an unconditional legal entitlement to cash transfers, independent of any need tests, means tests, or other restrictions.

Another rational concern might be that the funds, even though sufficient, might be diverted for purposes other than for covering the proportional entitlements of the insured – be it for (egalitarian) redistribution among the insured, or for distribution in favor of persons other than the insured and their dependents. One of the distinctive features of German social security is its "administration by para-public insurance funds,"[2] the function of which is to build trust among the insured by limiting the scope of potential political (i.e. redistributive) interference with their collective property in the common fund. Again, the system is designed to give as few reasons as possible for this kind of fear; for it guarantees the equivalence of relative status (which means that the level of benefits and the level of contributions stands in a fixed relation to the level of wages). It thus precludes concerns that either "deserving" claimants do not get what they are entitled to or that, conversely, funds are illegitimately appropriated by "undeserving" categories of people.

It also keeps the "collective private property"[3] out of the reach of governments and legislatures since the largest part of the fund is financed through contributions (not taxes, which would provide legitimate reasons for the state's interference). The use of the insurance funds and the administration of its benefits and services is organized according to the principle of "self-government," the bearers of which are a great and complex variety of semi-autonomous corporatist associations and agencies, not a centralized state administration.[4] Both these features help to insulate the system from political contingencies.

Furthermore, the whole system is centered around the core institutions of the labor contract and the family. Contributions are evenly shared by the employees and the employers in proportion to wages (except for accident insurance), and only employees who have "earned" benefits as deferred wages, together with the dependent members of their families, have access to them. The system also establishes a security premium designed for all those who, as employees, lead an ordinary and orderly work life by "earning" a full (and preferably uninterrupted) employment record. As such, the social security system contains a "hidden curriculum" which declares labor and employment to be much more than a legal and economic category, namely a form of respectable and even

2 P. Katzenstein, *Policy and Politics in West Germany* (Philadelphia, PA: Temple University Press, 1987), p. 172.
3 Cf. the discussion of the economic nature of social security funds in A. de Swaan, *In Care of the State* (Cambridge: Polity Press, 1988).
4 Cf. F. X. Kaufmann, "Die soziale Sicherheit in der Bundesrepublik Deutschland," in *Deutschland-Handbuch. Eine doppelte Bilanz 1949–1989*, ed. W. Weidenfeld and H. Zimmermann (Bonn: Bundeszentrale für politische Bildung, 1989), pp. 308–25.

dignified social existence.[5] Implicit in this curriculum is the gender division of labor in which the male breadwinner spends his economically active life in full-time employment and thus acquires the employment record necessary for full pension and other security rights, while his wife does not spend her life in (full-time) employment and hence does not earn any independent social security entitlements. The male bread-winner's wife relies on the legal rights and claims that she derives, directly or indirectly, from her institutional status within the family.

Thus the employment-centered nature of the German social security system largely implies a logic of restitution rather than one of either redistribution or investment. Restitution implies that transfers are obtained to replace market income after it is no longer earned (because of old age, disability, sickness, or unemployment), and are not an optional alternative to market income (as would be the case with basic in-come schemes) or designed to maintain or improve earning capacities (through human capital investment measures such as schooling, train-ing, preventive health measures, and measures promoting social, occu-pational, and geographic mobility). The social security system is thus "status-maintaining" rather than "opportunity-creating,"[6] a feature which minimizes its effects upon social inequality, and hence its poten-tial for generating status conflict.

Not only is the system insulated from political interference with social inequalities but it is also ambiguous and "overdetermined" as to the ideological principles on which it relies. Conservatives[7] accept it as an arrangement which keeps social security issues out of the arena of class conflict by giving workers a "stake in the system," and it encourages

5 Cf. U. Mückenberger, "Die Krise des Normalarbeitsverhältnisses – Hat das Arbeitsrecht noch Zukunft?," *Zeitschrift für Sozialreform*, 31 (1985), pp. 415–34, 457–75, "Zur Rolle des Normalarbeitsverhältnisses bei der sozialstaatlichen Umverteilung von Risiken," *Probleme des Klassenkampfes*, 16 (1986), pp. 31–45, and "Der Wandel des Normalarbeitsverhältnisses unter den Bedingungen einer 'Krise der Normalität'," *Gewerkschaftliche Monatshefte* (1989), pp. 211–23; A. Gorz, *Métamorphoses du travail. Quêtes du sens. Critique de la raison économique* (Paris: Editions Galilée, 1988).

6 To be sure, a new emphasis has been placed upon preventive – and in that sense "human capital forming" – measures and programs, particularly in the late 1960s and early 1970s. They aim at the preventive elimination of accidents and other health hazards, and at the retraining of labor and the upgrading of skills. The fact that these programs are also financed out of the funds of health and unemployment insurance, however, rather than general taxes, has severely limited their effectiveness, as they have to compete against strong pressures to use these funds for income maintenance and medical treatment. Cf. Katzenstein, *Policy and Politics in West Germany*, pp. 179f.

7 Cf. the discussion of the legacies of conservatism in social policy in G. Esping-Andersen, *The Three Worlds of Welfare Capitalism* (Princeton, NJ: Prin-ceton University Press, 1990), pp. 38–41 and *passim*.

employers to take some interest in the protection and maintenance of the employees' physical ability to work. Socialists may welcome it as a form of institutionalized class solidarity; and Roman Catholics or, from a different point of view, political liberals may value it for its built-in precautions against egalitarianism and state intervention. The ideologically overdetermined nature of the social security system explains the fact that basic controversies over social policies have been extremely rare in the history of the Federal Republic. The evolution of social security was mostly a bipartisan matter. Disagreements between the two major parties were limited to matters such as the timing and percentage points of increases in benefits or contributions. The policy debate has never (at least since the Federal Republic's consolidation period in the second Adenauer administration between 1953 and 1957) extended to matters of principle and basic institutional features.[8] This peculiar style of the politics of social security reflects the fact that social policy-making has consistently involved only a tiny group of legislative specialists and academic experts who mastered the vast complexity of legal, fiscal, and economic factors and who thus were able to determine the possible range and priorities of reform.

Social security benefits were originally granted as a privileged status to the "aristocracy" of industrial workers alone. The institutional features of the early system were extended, however, in the smooth and continuous inclusion of new groups (white collar workers, farmers, professionals and other self-employed groups, veterans, students, housewives), the coverage of new risks and needs (unemployment insurance, family allowances, eventually at some point in the near future also insurance covering long-term care), and the dramatic increase in benefits, in particular in old-age pensions which (since 1957) are indexed to the development of average earnings. It is as if the institutional system of social security had provided for the formation of an orderly queue which conveys to each worker-citizen what to expect, how much, and in which order.

The general picture that emerges from this brief review of the basic features of the German social security system is one of depoliticized rigidity. Social security is encapsulated in a set of principles, procedures, and institutions that seem to make it virtually immune from major changes concerning levels and sources of revenues, on the one hand, or the level of benefits and the scope of entitlements, on the other. The

---

8   The observation of this fact in German postwar politics has led Otto Kirchheimer to far-reaching generalizations about the "vanishing opposition" in democratic welfare states: O. Kirchheimer, "Germany: the vanishing opposition," in *Political Opposition in Western Democracies* ed. R. A. Dahl (New Haven, CN: Yale University Press, 1966), pp. 237–59, and "The transformation of the Western European party system," in *Political Parties and Political Development*, ed. J. LaPalobara and M. Weiner (Princeton, NJ: Princeton University Press, 1966), pp. 177–200.

system is morally undemanding in its stated objective of "security"; no one needs to believe in lofty principles of solidarity, justice, or equality to become – and remain – a rational supporter of the system. It is simply not a vehicle for the promotion of such values. Its modest goal is the guarantee of income – and of relative income status! – for employees and their dependents.[9] As a consequence, rational self-interest on the part of the "internal constituency" of the insured is sufficient as a base for consent. It can be assumed that this base of consent will remain solid even under conditions of financial strain. For, as the pension funds are seen by employees as "our" collective property, sacrifices that become necessary to restore the financial balance (such as higher contributions and/or delayed increases in benefits) will be rather readily accepted as a means to cope with temporary employment and demographic conditions and in order to prevent the premature depletion of the fund.[10]

On the other hand, the system with its property-like features is sufficiently "separated out" and insulated from pressures for intervention and reform from the "external constituency" of the democratic political process with its parties, elections, legislative process, and executive powers to preserve its "path-dependence." It is essential to understand the system's institutionally protected rigidity if we want to account for its amazing historical robustness. But when the structural environment in which the system operates is undergoing rather dramatic changes it is exactly this robustness that turns from an asset into a liability because it is not sufficiently equipped to respond or adjust.

Social Change and Social Security

In this section, I wish to pursue the following argument: the capacity of the social security system to regenerate its basis of support and its capacity to achieve inclusive social security are put in question by

9 As this system – in contrast, for instance, with the Swedish welfare state model of *folkhemmet* or "home for the people" – refrains from pursuing any inter-class redistributive or egalitarian goals, its potential for generating consent rests, so to speak, on the simple rule of "the fewer commitments made, the fewer reasons to be concerned or to complain."

10 Alber quotes survey data to this effect and commends citizens for the "understanding" and "flexible" attitudes with which they are prepared to accept cuts in social expenditures: J. Alber, "Der Wohlfahrtsstaat in der Wirtschaftskrise. Eine Bilanz der Sozialpolitik in der Bundesrepublik seit den frühen siebziger Jahren," *Politische Vierteljahresschrift*, 27 (1986), pp. 28–60, especially pp. 50–3. Ganßmann points out that the fiscal imbalance of social security may itself serve as a stabilizing mechanism, as it strengthens the preparedness of members to make sacrifices in terms of increased contributions and decreased benefits: H. Ganßmann, "Der Sozialstaat als Regulationsinstanz," in *Der gewendete Kapitalismus*, ed. B. Mahnkopf (Münster: V. Westfälisches Dampfboot, 1988), pp. 74–98, especially 84ff.

ongoing changes in its social and economic environment. This environment differs sharply from what the system presupposes as "normal conditions" of work, employment, patterns of labor market participation, and security needs in an industrial society. As a consequence, the system fails to "make sense" to those whom it covers – and it also fails to cover all of whom it is meant to cover. For the first of these reasons, and as its rational sources of support begin to crumble, the social security system may become less "secure"; for the second, it may become less inclusive and "social."

Moreover, general political support for the particular arrangements of social security as they have evolved in Germany may suffer not only from the frustration of "individual utility maximizers," but also from a sense of frustration of Left political forces and movements that the "social state" ("Sozialstaat," as postulated by the Federal Republic's Basic Law in its sections 20 and 28) has failed to live up to its promise of social justice and universally inclusive security. The perception of such failure[11] is based upon the observations that a shrinking portion of the working population actually enjoys "social" security; that the way in which the system deals with its clients is alienating, incapacitating, and undermines forms of solidarity; and that it has failed to alter the system of production in progressive ways.

Moreover, the disenchantment of much of the German political Left with issues of social security and social policy may have to do with a new urgency of "post-materialist" and "anti-productivist" concerns superseding[12] the traditional emphasis of socialists on social policy and redistributive issues. On the other hand, any changes away from the core institutional features of the German welfare state (such as arguably are called for by the new conditions of labor markets, employment, and economic growth, and gender and family relations) are consistently and strongly discouraged by the industrial trade unions.

What are the structural changes, political repercussions, and support-shaping effects that attenuate and sap the rational disposition of large groups of actors to vigorously defend the social security arrangements against proposed cuts, or even to support institutional changes that would increase the scope and the political security of these institutions? In order to answer this question, we must concentrate on the changing ways in which labor markets and social policies interact and the way that this interaction is perceived and evaluated by the key actors.

Social security and the labor market interact, as is well known, in two

11 An often quoted statement indicating this feeling of frustration and disappointment is the claim made by Jürgen Habermas that "the development of the welfare state (*Sozialstaat*) has entered a dead end alley" and that its utopian energies are exhausted: cf. J. Habermas, "Die Krise des Wohlfahrtsstaates und die Erschöpfung utopischer Energien," *Die Neue Unübersichtlichkeit* (Frankfurt, Suhrkamp, 1985), pp. 141–63.
12 Cf. C. Offe, "Democracy against the welfare state? Structural foundations of neoconservative political opportunities," *Political Theory*, 15 (1987), pp. 501–37.

ways. First, labor markets and the position of individuals in labor markets (as to their income, employment security, and working conditions) determine the size of their contributions as well as the size, kind, and incidence of needs that are to be covered according to legal stipulations and program parameters. The labor market thus determines the size and nature of the problems which the social security system will have to absorb, as well as the financial means that the system has at its disposal. Second, social security arrangements also determine quantitative and qualitative aspects of labor market developments. The features of the system of social security and the costs and benefits it is perceived to impose upon the parties in the labor market shape the strategies of the participants and thus the overall structure of employment.[13]

This "backward linkage" between the social security system and the structure of the labor market has two effects. First, the social security system and its mode of financing increase the costs of labor and thus decrease the demand for labor by providing employers with a significant incentive to adopt labor-saving technical change ("dynamic flexibility"). Alternatively, they may find ways to escape and bypass these costs of social security by employing low-paid, poorly protected, low-skilled, "flexible," and easily fired labor in appropriately designed jobs ("static flexibility"[14]). Second, and paradoxically, the benefits of social security increase the attractiveness for (potential) employees of acquiring "full welfare state citizenship" through full-time labor market participation. At any rate, they increase the opportunity costs (among other things, in terms of social security status) of nonparticipation in formal employment. The social security system thus appears not only to be vulnerable to labor market imbalances but also to contribute to this imbalance.[15]

---

13   This is not, of course, to imply that the social security system is the only factor that determines the level and quality of employment.

14   The distinction of "dynamic" versus "static" flexibility as well as the general idea that social policies and their mode of financing may affect quantitative and qualitative features of employment is taken from J. Myles, "Decline or impasse? The current state of the welfare," *Studies in Political Economy*, 26 (1988), pp. 73–107.

15   An indirect indicator of the significance of these perverse steering effects that originate from the social security system itself may be seen in specific reform initiatives that have been taken by both major political parties, the Social Democrats and the Christian Democrats. In order to check the social security system's demand effect to price some labor, particularly in labor-intensive industries, out of the market, the Social Democrats favor a shift in the mode of financing social security from payroll deductions to value-added deductions which would move the financial burden of social security from the volume of employment to the volume of output. Conversely, and in order to check the undesired supply effects, the Christian Democrats have proposed and legislated since 1983, with a view to strengthening the family as an institution and to improving the long-term demographic balance, various measures to make the effect of nonparticipation in the labor market on losses in old-age pension more affordable to mothers.

Apart from such endogenous paradoxes and unintended incentive effects of social security, there are a number of structural changes which render the system both less inclusive in its coverage of all labor and less able to maintain "sufficient" levels of benefits. Instead, social security seems to be in the process of becoming a "core working class fortress" discriminating against and excluding all those rapidly increasing social categories that do not conform to assumedly "normal" standards of work life and family life. Two interrelated debates on these issues have become dominant in the German social policy discourse since the mid-1970s: one of them concerns the shifting role of women, the family, and the design of the female life cycle; the other the vanishing of what has been termed the "standard employment relation"[16] (*Normalarbeitsverhältnis*). As a result, both of these debates – and the empirical findings, predictive analysis, and normative considerations that entered into them – have led to the conclusion, now widely accepted, that the structural assumptions and premises on which social security was built can no longer be taken as valid.

This applies, most importantly, to the rapid spread of "precarious" forms of employment, i.e. forms of employment which, because of their part-time character, their insecurity and lack of protection, or their low level of pay, do not involve full social security status and the entitlements derived from it. Apart from the extreme case of outright illegal ("black") employment, these forms include *de jure* self-employment (where a regular employment relation is transformed into a nominal subcontracting relation), part-time employment (in particular, employment below the threshold of nineteen hours per week beyond which compulsory social security contributions become effective), fixed-term employment, labor "rented" for short-term jobs, "telework" in "electronic cottage industries," and employment that is interrupted by stretches of voluntary unemployment. Employees working under such conditions are typically unable to build up an employment record that would provide them with sufficient claims to old-age pensions and to other transfers on which they can rely in cases of unemployment or illness. The same applies to the long-term unemployed, most of whom are transferred, after having lost their job and failed to find a new one for more than one year, from the unemployment insurance to the social assistance, or welfare, system.

The spread of these "deviant" forms of labor market participation must be explained as the synergistic effect of at least four factors. First, in response to the high and stable registered unemployment rates that

16 Cf. R. G. Heinze, J. Hilbert, and H. Voelzkow, "Qualitative Perspektiven eines Umbaus des Sozialstaates," unpublished paper, Bochum, 1989, and Hinrichs for recent summaries of these findings and related policy debates: K. Hinrichs, "Irregular employment patterns and the loose net of social security: some findings on the West German case," Center for Social Policy Research, Bremen, 1989.

reached levels unprecedented in the history of the Federal Republic (9–10 percent in the mid-1980s), the Christian Democratic administration initiated a number of measures deregulating the supposedly overly rigid German labor market. Second, employers in both the more and the less competitive sectors, partly in response to the unions' work time reduction drives in the 1980s, have adopted employment strategies which were designed to make working time more flexible and to rely more strongly on part-time employment. This form of employment is significantly less well covered than full-time employment by protective collective agreements. Similarly employers were exposed to strong incentives to escape the significant nonwage cost burdens of social security contributions and other protective regulations by resorting either to nominal subcontracting or to "cheap" labor employed for less than 19 hours per week. Third, high levels of unemployment forced many people seeking jobs to accept relatively deregulated, unprotected, and insecure forms of employment for lack of a better alternative. Fourth, cultural changes of lifestyles, orientations towards employed work, and biographical patterns contributed to the formation of preferences for "deviant," discontinuous, and less than full-time forms of employment on the part of many female and male workers. These shifts have provided opportunities, and even a measure of apparent legitimacy, for employers' inventive experimentation with forms of "flexible" manpower utilization.

Workers willing to accept such substandard forms of labor market participation may or may not be aware of the fact that what they sacrifice by partially or temporarily "opting out" of employment is not just income from work, but also social security status that is tied to continuous full-time employment. But often the line between "opting out" and "opting in" is not easy to draw. This refers, in particular, to married women who enter the labor market (or indicate the wish to do so if there were an acceptable opportunity) in increasing numbers. This phenomenon has been referred to as an "autonomous supply"[17] effect – a phenomenon that resulted in the simultaneous increase in several years during the 1980s of the total number of unemployed and the total of those employed within the West German economy. The behavior underlying such seemingly paradoxical aggregate effects may be informed by the reasoning that, since employment in general and the employment status of the household's breadwinner in particular is perceived as precarious and endangered, it is a good idea to secure a second source of labor market income which might be used as an intra-household safety net. In this way, the perception of sluggish demand for labor might perversely contribute to its increased supply. This type of motivation has probably replaced another one that prevailed under tight labor market conditions: the wish to "top up," through easily available part-time employment,

---

17 Cf. B. Lutz, "Notwendigkeit und Ansatzpunkte einer angebotsbezogenen Vollbeschäftigungspolitik," in *Resonanzen. Arbeitsmarkt und Beruf – Forschung und Politik*, ed. L. Reyher and J. Kühl (Nürnberg: IAB, 1988), pp. 275–89.

the male breadwinner's income in order to make higher levels of consumption affordable to the household. Another way of accounting for the autonomous supply effect would be to assume that for many married women employed work plays the role of an intrinsically desirable form of activity, or of a "consumption item," which – largely regardless of the level of pay, employment security, and social security it provides – is valued for the challenge, social contact, and esteem it affords and is therefore preferred to unpaid and full-time family and household work.[18] This type of motivation is of special interest to employers, since it is assumed to be less wage elastic than that of "ordinary" labor. The continuing influx of (married) women (and mothers) into the labor market is certainly inspired also by egalitarian feminist values as well as by the rational economic consideration by married women of gaining independent access to income and social security in view of increasing rates of divorce and family breakdown. Otherwise access to social security is conditional upon the marriage relationship and the husband's income.[19]

Irregular types of employment and the loss of social security status are likely to involve the risk of (old-age) poverty if they occur outside the institutional setting of marriage and family relations. Often the family functions as a "capillary" social security system, as dependents and survivors are usually entitled to "derived" benefits of the family's breadwinner. Thus the decline of the family as an institution undermines the scope of effective social security still further. This decline, however, is one of the most consistent long-term trends to be found in German sociological and demographic time series data – whether it is measured in terms of the share of family households in all households, the number of children per married couple, the number of new marriages per 1,000 inhabitants per year, or the number of divorces per 1,000 marriages per

18   One factor that gives rise to this ordering of preferences might not be so much the intrinsic attractiveness of employed work but the lack of acceptable opportunities and the requisite social networks for "informal" work. For traditional forms of socially recognized and status-conferring activities outside formal employment (i.e. within the extended family household, associations, churches, clubs, part-time self-employment, "third sector," etc.), which used to – and might today – serve as a labor market supply buffer, have largely fallen victim within most West European societies to secular processes of modernization, urbanization, and bureaucratization; their decline causes an influx of (mostly) female labor power into the ranks of the employees and the employment seekers. For an elaboration of this line of argument, see Lutz, "Notwendigkeit and Ansatzpunkte" and *Der kurze Traum immerwährender Prosperität* (Frankfurt: Campus, 1984); see also C. Offe and R. G. Heinze, "Am Arbeitsmarkt vorbei. Überlegungen zur Neubestimmung 'haushaltlicher' Wohlfahrtsproduktion in ihrem Verhältnis zu Markt und Staat," *Leviathan*, 14 (1986), pp. 471–95.
19   Cf. D. Schäfer, "Gegenwärtige Probleme und Fragen sowie langfristige Zukunftsperspektiven der Sozialpolitik in der Bundesrepublik Deutschland," *Zeitschrift für Sozialreform*, 35 (1989), pp. 28–36.

year. These powerful trends affect both the capacity of the family to substitute for the lack of social security and, in its quality as a micro social security network, to extend the scope of social security to "inactive" or "precariously" employed dependents.

Social and labor market policies, employers' strategies, cultural changes in the conception of a desirable life course, and emerging uncertainties concerning the social role of women, men, and the family all contribute to the growth of relatively insecure and unprotected segments of the labor market and hence, conversely, to the shrinkage of that part of total labor that is covered by effective, reliable, and sufficient levels of social security. Not only in terms of pay and job security, but also in terms of social security, the distance between "good" jobs and labor market positions versus "bad" ones, or "standard" patterns of labor market participation and "irregular" ones, is increasing – a fact that is often referred to in the German labor market and social policy discourse by the suggestion of an emerging "two-thirds society" (*Zweidrittelgesellschaft*). The failure of trade unions to effectively defend the inclusive and universal nature of social security has also contributed to the rise of these disparities. This failure is due to both objective constraints and the strategic reluctance of the unions to vigorously defend, through their wage demands and collective agreements, the interests and needs of the irregularly employed who make up an increasingly important segment of the representational domain (although not of the actual membership!) of organized labor.[20]

The Politics of Adapting Social Security to the Employment Crisis

It follows from the basic institutional characteristics of an employment-centered and contributions-financed system of social security that its long-term equilibrium is particularly vulnerable to two adverse events: high and lasting levels of unemployment and demographic imbalance. Both of these disturbances hit the German welfare state in the decade 1975–84. As a consequence of the first, there will not be enough current earned income to pay for current entitlements. The second, as it becomes manifest in declining birth rates and increasing life expectancy (with its related increases in health and care needs of the aged), will exacerbate this disequilibrium – or so it came to be widely anticipated for the

---

20   The male-dominated German trade unions, in this respect faithful in their general policy orientation to the built-in assumptions of the German social security system, have also tended, at least until very recently, to consider only the male, skilled, full-time employed worker and family head as the model case whose interests are to be defended through union action, and virtually everyone else as a deficient deviation from this "normal" worker. Cf. Mückenberger, "Der Wandel des Normalarbeitsverhältnisses."

foreseeable future – by increasing the financial burden per capita of the currently employed.[21]

The unprecedented coincidence of these two long-term problems has set the agenda for German social policy during the entire period since 1975 that interests us here. It is important to understand, however, that the simultaneous employment and demographic crises did no more than that: they called for some adequate response, but did not dictate one particular response as the only one practical and feasible. How such critical facts are responded to and coped with depends entirely upon actors, preferences, and institutions. Deterministic explanations of public policies seem to suggest that "politics did not matter," and that actual developments were in fact dictated by economic events and trends. This deceptive suggestion derives from the fact that the policy response was substantially similar whether it occurred under governments led by the Social Democrats (1975–82) or Christian Democrats (since 1982–3). In both cases, the effort was to adapt the welfare state in general, and the social security system in particular, to the emerging new conditions by preserving its institutional foundations (rather than changing or dismantling them) and by steering a careful course of austerity and financial consolidation. This means that the politics of adaptation were basically uncontroversial between the two party elites that otherwise, concerning policy areas such as foreign and defense policies, stood in sharp opposition to each other. Nevertheless, my contention is that it was not economics but politics that shaped social policies after 1975, and the false impression to the contrary derives from the fact that it happened to be bipartisan and largely uncontroversial politics. Its principles and strategies were widely shared by Christian Democrats, Social Democrats, and all major actors such as the unions, the employers' associations, the para-public social security agencies, the major representatives of the health-related industries, as well as the social policy experts. The dramatic changes taking place in the socioeconomic environment of social policy did not translate into similarly vehement political controversies. On the contrary, almost all the cuts, innovations, and adaptations that were put into effect from the "budget structure act" of 1975 to the bipartisan "old-age pension reform act" of 1989 (to become effective in 1992) were passed in a conspicuously and unusually smooth political process.

The range of policy choices that was actually considered was, from the start, much smaller than the entire "feasible set" of possible and practical responses to the crisis. In principle, the following choices were available:

21 English language summaries of the German data substantiating these twin challenges are to be found in K. H. Jüttemeier and H. G. Petersen, "West Germany," in *The World Crisis in Social Security*, ed. J. J. Rosa (Paris: Fondation Nationale d'Economie Politique, 1982), pp. 181–206, and J. Alber, "The West German welfare state in transition," in *Testing the Limits of Social Welfare*, ed. R. Morris (Hanover: Brandeis University Press, 1988), pp. 96–134.

1   cut benefits and increase burdens in negative proportion to the polit-
    ical clout of those negatively affected by such measures;
2   increase contributions to levels that are sufficient to cover existing
    entitlements and predictable future needs;
3   decrease benefits according to need, thus shifting the basis of entitle-
    ment from equivalence to need;
4   cover the deficit in social security out of general taxation, thus
    gradually shifting the financial base of social security from contribu-
    tions to taxes.

Of these options, only the first was seriously pursued. It became the
dominant response to the twin challenge. This choice cannot be explained by adverse economic and demographic conditions, and neither
can it be justified as superior economic rationality. It must be explained,
or so I wish to argue, by the realistic assessment and anticipation, on the
part of political and corporate elites, of the standards of solidarity,
popular sentiments, conceptions of group interest, and parameters of
acceptability of the political culture of social policy that has evolved
within the fragmented and "individualized"[22] West German society in
the 1980s. The policies and innovations by which the German social
security system was adapted to the new conditions that prevailed after
1975 was not uniquely "rational" in the use it made of scarce resources
or in terms of the fiscal and labor market effects it brought about. If
anything, it was "rational" in terms of the popular sentiments it catered
to and the fears it was designed to placate. The conservatism of the
adaptive moves was not a traditionalist but a strategic conservatism. Its
logic was to quell the potential for popular welfare state backlash by
pioneering a moderate version of it.

The policies of social policy adaptation and consolidation adopted by
federal governments since 1975 show a rather clear pattern of selective
protection and discriminatory exclusion which, apart from its substantive redistributive effects, has also played the role of a "hidden curriculum" by projecting images and symbolic demarcations as to which
social categories "deserve" to enjoy undiminished benefits and levels of

22 The term "individualization" has gained a currency within the German
social sciences that is itself rather symptomatic. Being the opposite of what in
British sociology has been termed "collectivism," it captures structural as well as
cultural changes that include the decomposition of encompassing moral and
associational frameworks of (class) solidarity, the erosion of biographical patterns and traditions and the certainties based upon them, and a culture of
"selfishness" that oscillates between "autonomy" and "anomie." Affinities of
this social scientific current to French debates on "postmodernism" and Anglo-
American "methodological individualism" are evident. Important sources of the
German debate include U. Beck, *Die Risikogesellschaft. Auf dem Weg in eine andere
Moderne* (Frankfurt: Suhrkamp, 1986) and W. Zapf, S. Breuer, J. Hampel,
P. Krause, H.-M. Mohr, and E. Wiegand, *Individualisierung und Sicherheit. Unter-
suchungen zur Lebensqualität in der Bundesrepublik Deutschland* (München: Beck, 1987).

security and other social categories that can justly (as well as safely, in terms of their potential for resistance and conflict) be deprived of some of their status rights. Behind the practice of adaptation, there stands an implicit theory about the kind of social justice that the renovated welfare state is meant to serve.[23]

The overall pattern is clear enough. The underlying strategy is to remove cuts and austerity measures from institutional locations where they can easily become the focal point of collective action to locations where they remain largely imperceptible to the wider public, and difficult to interpret as a collective condition and experience on the basis of which organized action might become possible. It is as if the maxim had been followed to make it more difficult to pinpoint the winners, the losers, and those responsible for the transaction. Within this pattern of adaptation to turbulences, eight components can be detected.

1   Unburdening the federal budget: in order to escape the liabilities generated by rising unemployment, more frequent early retirement, and worsening demographic balance, and to keep social security issues out of the arena of the politics of taxation and tax reform, the need to stimulate growth and employment, to lower taxes, to avoid crowding-out effects of the federal debt, and to improve the ratio of capital-forming versus consumptive components of the federal budget were cited as justifications for a strategy of "uncoupling" social security budgets from the federal budget through eliminating the federal budget's liabilities for social insurance deficits.

2   Horizontal subsidies: as the federal government is no longer, or only to a very limited extent, subsidizing the pension, health, and unemployment insurance systems, a highly complicated and opaque system was introduced according to which they are to subsidize each other.[24]

3   Cuts in preventive measures and "operative" budgets: as a balance of revenues and expenditures cannot be fully restored through horizontal redistributions, cuts in some of the programs were introduced, such as the preventive training measures of the unemployment insurance agency and some of the rehabilitative services and programs of the health insurance system. The logic of this type of consolidation measure is to

---

23   This two-tiered (instrumental and symbolic/expressive) nature of political communications can be illustrated in one of the favorite slogans of the conservative and market liberal political Right in the early 1980s, namely *"Leistung muß sich wieder lohnen!"* ("effort is to become worthwhile again!"). At its instrumental surface, this slogan serves to advocate the demand for lowering taxes and tax progression; it designates a desirable future. But on a deeper level it expresses something about the deplorable present which must be brought back to order "again": effort does not pay today, because those making "efforts" are not properly rewarded and people are rewarded without making an appropriate effort (e.g. to find a job).

24   Cf. K. J. Bieback, "Leistungsabbau und Strukturwandel im Sozialrecht," *Kritische Justiz,* 17 (1984), pp. 257–78, especially p. 262.

disperse risks in time, as current needs which are neglected will often cause greater costs in the future.

4 Cuts in entitlements to cash payments, including delayed increases to compensate for inflation, and increases in contributions: these measures make individual employees and social security recipients pay in terms of their current income for some of the costs of adaptation.

5 Shifting the burden to local governments: as the number of long-term unemployed (who are no longer entitled to unemployment insurance benefits[25]) increases and as the real income from the lowest range of old-age pensions falls below the poverty line, the local state is made to carry the burden of increasing expenditures for social assistance (*Sozialhilfe*), which in turn prevents it from spending its budget on (presumably employment-generating) investment programs.[26]

6 Selective termination or reduction of programs funded by the federal government: these have mostly affected high school and university students and the long-term unemployed, thus shifting the burden to either families or individuals.

7 Local and state experiments with secondary and unprotected labor markets: these programs have mostly been targeted at unemployed youth and other "marginal" workers, as well as recipients of local social assistance, thus creating a new status of "deregulated" labor.

8 Cuts in local expenditures on social services and the reintroduction or increase of user-fees.[27]

The overall logic of these fiscal and legislative measures can be compared with that of a giant domino effect which starts in the labor market and goes on to affect the federal budget, the social security systems, local governments, marginal segments of the labor force, families (in particular women within families), clients of services, and individuals. This immensely complex process of adaptation, retrenchment, and carefully designed consolidation explains why social policy expenditures have indeed remained roughly constant in absolute terms – though certainly not in proportion to the dramatically increased levels of need that were caused by unemployment and demographic factors. What still remains to be explained, however, is the fact that these cuts and substantial

25 As early as 1982, 1.3 million registered unemployed no longer received any benefits from the unemployment insurance; as a consequence, a majority of them became dependent upon federal and local support.

26 A growing number of local governments have adopted an ingenious strategy in this game of "vertical dispersion" that is being played between the unemployment insurance and local governments: they fight back by nominally employing unemployed persons for a limited period of time in order to make them eligible for unemployment benefits, and then laying them off and thus making the Federal Employment Agency liable for their income – until the point where the next round of "recycling" the fiscal burden of unemployment may start.

27 Cf. H. Zacher, "Der gebeutelte Sozialstaat in der wirtschaftlichen Krise," *Sozialer Fortschritt*, 33 (1984), pp. 1–12, especially p. 3.

relative losses in no way provoked a significant level of opposition or social and political conflict.

In order to come to terms with this question, we turn from the policies of consolidation to the politics of social policy and the conspicuous absence of polarized conflict about reform and retrenchment. The adaptation has taken place in a slow and gradual rather than sudden and abrupt manner, beginning with restrictive regulations of the unemployment insurance in 1975 and fiscal consolidation laws adopted in 1977 and 1978, and the cuts were dispersed across social categories and institutions. This pace stands in sharp contrast with, for instance, the British sea change in public policy after 1979.[28] Moreover, most of the changes were adopted by a *de facto* bipartisan coalition. In making these cuts, both the Christian Democrats[29] and the Social Democrats were rationally inclined to grant relative protection to active labor market participants[30] and thus the constituency of trade unions. Under these tactics of careful,[31] gradual, and largely consensual[32] management of

28 Cf. H. Michalsky, "Sozialstaat als Programm und Praxis. Die Sozialpolitik der SPD als Regierungspartei (1966–1982), Habilitationsschrift," unpublished, Heidelberg, 1985, chs VI and VII; also Alber, "The West German welfare state in transition," who observes that "the mid-1970s stand out as a watershed in social policy development" (p. 104) – not the coming-to-power of the conservative–liberal coalitions government in 1982–3.

29 The party itself contains a significant Christian socialist (mostly Roman Catholic) minority which is very careful to present itself as based in the working class and representing its interests; this is particularly the case as the Christian Democratic Minister of Labor and Social Affairs, Norbert Blüm, is also the Christian Democrats' designated challenger for the prime minister's office in Northrhine-Westphalia, the largest West German federal state which is now firmly controlled by Social Democrats – again, a significant difference if compared with Britain where "wet" and "one nation" Conservatives have been virtually eliminated from government posts and party leadership.

30 Cf. Alber, "The West German welfare state in transition," p. 111: "Labor force participants passed through the austerity period in, relatively, the most favorable terms."

31 Both Social Democratic and Christian Democratic governments have been remarkably sensitive to the evidence that cuts did occasionally turn out to be detrimental to their respective electoral prospects, in which cases reversals or compensatory measures were quickly adopted. A case in point is a measure that severely cut the amount of cash payments made available to the inmates of old-age homes. After this cut drew wide publicity, payments were quickly restored to the original levels. Cf. A. Windhoff-Héritier, "Sozialpolitik der mageren Jahre," in *Sparpolitik. Ökonomische Zwänge und politische Spielräume*, ed. H. Mäding (Opladen: Westdeutscher Verlag, 1983), pp. 77–99, especially p. 86.

32 This consensual nature of consolidation policies was not only based upon inter-party agreements and forms of collaboration, most importantly in the drafting of the old-age pension reform passed by the Bundestag in 1989. The consensus was also engineered through a specific corporatist arrangement for the health sector, the "health sector concerted action," in which all major organized

potential conflict, a polarized politicization of social policy issues could not emerge. Cuts were made acceptable to the electorate by virtue of their coming in small doses and at the expense of highly diverse social categories, rather than in the form of vehement and sudden assaults upon specific groups. The government that programmatically insisted upon cuts and introduced them was reelected[33] both in 1976 and in 1987.

But the absence of open and polarized political conflict was not only due to the tactics of its containment. The potential for conflict and the rational disposition of large parts of the population to defend the welfare state and to advocate its further growth was much more limited than many critics of the consolidation policies tend to assume. The success of conflict containment must then be partly explained by the fact that there was not much conflict potential to be contained in the first place. According to this hypothesis, the conspicuously smooth course of events reflects the fact that collectivist priorities and encompassing solidarities had widely vanished in the electorate. Positive individual incentives to defend the welfare state, its maintenance and further expansion, were weakened as fewer and fewer groups could expect to be in a position to make an unequivocal redistributive net gain. At the same time the negative collective incentive lost much of its persuasiveness as the West German society was exposed to the experience that large-scale and lasting unemployment and rapidly increasing numbers of people dependent on social assistance did not constitute, as had been widely feared, a threat to social peace.

In sum, the smoothness of the adaptation process must be accounted for not only in terms of the skillful management of possible conflict through political elites, but also in terms of changing perceptions and priorities on the part of large segments of the electorate which correspondingly have "good reasons" to comply with and even advocate austerity policies, rather than to engage in social and political protest over it. The declining allegiance to collectivist ideas about generous and further increasing levels of welfare state spending must in turn be seen in the context of the ongoing labor market restructuring described before.

"The contemporary welfare state has become a strategic environment

---

interests relevant to that sector were involved. Cf. H. Wiesenthal, *Die Konzertierte Aktion im Gesundheitswesen* (Frankfurt: Campus, 1981), and D. Webber, "Krankheit, Geld und Politik: Zur Geschichte der Gesundheitsreform in Deutschland," *Leviathan*, 16 (1988), pp. 156–203.

33 Alber, "The West German welfare state in transition," p. 115, quotes survey data according to which the "percentage of stern welfare state defenders had drastically declined by thirty percentage points between 1975 and 1983." Confronted with the alternative of either having to pay for higher taxes and contributions in order to maintain levels of transfers or having to cut both, increasing numbers of people were rationally disposed towards giving priority to the latter alternative.

in which people operate as calculating entrepreneurs."[34] The ongoing policy discourse on the need for austerity and consolidation measures has certainly sensitized people to their own position and the pay-offs connected with it within the social security game; it has thus undermined attitudes of both "trust in others" and "trust in the future" that together make up a conventionalist and collectivist orientation to social security issues. As people begin to calculate and to compare, some portion of rational support is likely to decline. This applies both to the individual and collective levels, and within both the upper middle class and the lower working class.

Increasing portions of the upper middle class can, with good economic reasons, adopt the perspective that they do not really need and depend upon much of the social security provisions that they are entitled to as members of the system. They are therefore inclined to object to the fiscal burdens the welfare state imposes upon their income.

At the same time, an increasing portion of the working class, particularly of workers in the lower income brackets, loses its rational reason for supporting the income-graduated social security system because the level of benefits that they will eventually derive from it is not substantially higher than the level of social assistance benefits to which they would be entitled even without having made any contributions. To them the social insurance differential is individually[35] unattractive.

Nor does the opposition to, or at any rate lack of strong support for, the social security system to which these two very diverse social categories are rationally disposed necessarily remain a matter of opinion and resentment. It can translate itself in collective as well as individual action. On the collective level, "tax resistance" and "welfare state backlash" are political syndromes on which rightist populist parties and movements have thrived not just in highly developed welfare states such as Denmark and Norway but also in Britain. Apart from the now rather obsolete approach of Victorian moralizing,[36] such political forces can either, in their more benign version, invoke meritocratic and market-liberal principles of property rights, or they can openly rely on racist, xenophobic, and sexist sentiments. The common logic of these approaches is to question the legitimacy of entitlements to transfers and services, be it those of working mothers, foreign workers, "welfare scroungers," farmers, civil servants, the unemployed, or some other supposedly "undeserving" social category.

---

34   de Swaan, *In Care of the State*, p. 229.
35   Although, obviously, a "fallacy of composition" is involved in this argument; it is true on the individual level, but becomes meaningless if all the lower working class would rely on social assistance, thus dramatically lowering the per capita funds available through it.
36   L. Mead, *Beyond Entitlement: The Social Obligations of Citizenship* (New York: Macmillan, 1986); M. Spieker, *Legitimationsprobleme des Sozialstaats* (Bern: Haupt, 1986).

In the German case, the neo-conservative populist approach has constituted a noticeable ingredient of the political discourse of the 1970s and 1980s without assuming anything like the hegemonic role it enjoys in Britain.[37] This approach was accompanied by active efforts, on the part of governing political elites, to promulgate issues and themes which served to distract attention from the older collectivist agendas and thereby disorganize and discredit large-scale collectivities and bonds of solidarity within civil society through a cross-cutting and cross-coding "politics of interpretation".[38] These semantic and symbolic forms of politics are designed to dramatize nonclass issues of either an all-inclusive ("moral order," "national identity," terrorism, "technological competitiveness," ecological issues) or a particularizing variety (focusing on particular institutions – such as the family – or isolated issues such as drugs or AIDS, or specific groups such as asylum-seeking foreigners or *Aussiedler*).

The legal and administrative treatment of the unemployed – and the change of rules that was adopted in Germany in the period we consider here – is a more specific case in point. First, the rules of the unemployment insurance are set up in such a way that a sort of zero-sum game of the employed against the unemployed emerges under conditions of a more than moderate level of unemployment and long-term unemployment, particularly if the perceived probability of one's self becoming unemployed is highly differentiated according to branch of industry, age, region, and other criteria.[39] That is, workers who are employed and who expect to remain so will take an interest in lowering or at least not having increased the amount that is deducted from their wages as their contribution to mandatory unemployment insurance, while unemployed workers will have the reverse interest. More generally, some of the unemployed perceive – or are led to believe by successful rightest populist

37 The basic insight that this political approach seeks to promulgate is nicely captured in a statement by Margaret Thatcher that is noteworthy for its explicitness, its absurdity, and its cleverness: "There is no such thing as society. There are individual men and women, and there are families."

38 As an illustration of what I call "politics of interpretation" I would cite a chief analyst of the Federation of German Employers' Associations who maintained that about half the present number of the unemployed are not in fact unemployed but unemployable, due to their suffering from irreversible physical, mental, or skill deficiencies. This redefinition of unemployment suggests a dissociation between "us" (i.e. normal people, employed or unemployed) and "them," who suffer from special handicaps that cannot conceivably be overcome by collectivist strategies. The implication is clear: if this code is accepted as valid, demands for policies aiming at full employment become meaningless. For a contrasting use of the "politics of interpretation" in this area, one might look at the Swedish practice of coding all persons who are presently undergoing retraining or are employed on nominal or "protected" jobs as "wage earners."

39 That is, if the "veil of ignorance" becomes thin; cf. for an application of this Rawlsian metaphor to social policies J. Elster, "The possibility of rational politics," *Archives Européennes de Sociologie*, 28 (1987), pp. 67–103.

campaigns – their interests to be opposed to those of the employed, as wage increases successfully fought for by the latter will push the price of labor up and diminish the prospects of the unemployed finding jobs. These intra-class conflicts and the concomitant distributional conflicts among workers are exacerbated by policies which virtually abolished state subsidies to unemployment insurance. Furthermore, the cuts have taken the highly and intentionally divisive form of differentiating the claims of unemployed persons according to their age, family status, employment record, and duration of unemployment, thus individualizing the condition of unemployment and not only pitting the employed against the unemployed but also fragmenting the interests of the latter. A similar logic of division and fragmentation seems to apply in recent reforms and developments in the health system and with regard to the income of old-age pensioners where we also find an almost endless variation of individual cases, conditions, and the rules that apply to them, thus making the definition of a collectively shared interest and its organizational representation much more difficult than it otherwise would be.

As a result of these strategies and developments, one can anticipate the emergence and consolidation of a class-divided society in which each class is defined by its relation not to the means of production but to the state-organized resources of welfare, and therefore by the differing degree to which it is vulnerable to being deprived of its share.[40] Let me propose the following five-class model. The upper class within this system is made up of the public sector employees, foremost the civil servants (*Beamte*); the latter enjoy a rather unique combination of privileges, such as old-age pensions without prior deduction of contributions, job security, and extensive coverage of their health expenditures through public funds. The second and largest class consists of "normal" employees – "normal" in the (both descriptive and slightly moralizing) sense that they have full-time and relatively stable jobs, live in equally stable families, enjoy the advantages of a strong representation through unions, and are covered by the mandatory social security systems. A third class is made up of all those who have been in employment but are presently no longer so because of old age, invalidity, or unemployment; they are less numerous and much less well organized than the second class and hence more vulnerable to cuts, but are still able to defend themselves against the worst attacks. In the fourth category, we find the disparate and heterogeneous group of those who depend on means-tested social assistance transfers and/or (as clients and patients) state-organized services. Finally, there is the lower class of the welfare state made up of people who (as refugees, foreign workers, illegal aliens, or

40   The notion of society being divided into several "welfare classes" was first used by R. M. Lepsius, "Soziale Ungleichheit und Klassenstrukturen in der Bundesrepublik Deutschland," in *Klassen in der europäischen Sozialgeschichte*, ed. H. U. Wehler (Göttingen: Ruprecht, 1979), pp. 166–209.

asylum seekers) do not unequivocally enjoy the basic privileges that are tied to national citizenship. Needless to say, such a class system is vastly regressive in its distributional impact, as it privileges the middle classes enjoying stable employment in the public and private sectors at the expense of virtually everyone else.[41]

In economic terms, this decline of class politics can be explained by the fact that by the mid-1970s the model of the Keynesian welfare state was rendered a highly unpromising one by the changed realities of the international economy. Major advances seemed no longer feasible and probably counterproductive, as they would involve budget increases and rates of inflation that no major social and political group would be willing to advocate. From a sociological point of view, the largely homogeneous *Arbeitnehmergesellschaft* (society of employees) had given way, in the eyes of political elites, and probably to some extent in reality, to a fragmented social structure generating a multiplicity of issues, cleavages, and identities which could no longer be responded to by politics in terms of social class, economic growth, and political redistribution. As early as 1976, the Christian Democrats came up with a widely appealing populist political formula. The axis of conflict was no longer labor versus capital but the organized against the unorganized – and, most emphatically, women, children, and families versus male-dominated and employment-centered corporate actors.[42] Much less appealing was the Social Democratic response which emphasized economic decline, rising unemployment, new poverty, and the "two-thirds society", with one-third of the population allegedly marginalized and excluded from prosperity. This formula, accurate though it certainly was and still is to some extent, makes little sense from the point of view of politics. It appeals to benevolence rather than to the interests of the majority of the electorate which still lives under conditions of prosperity and will not easily be mobilized by social policy demands favoring small disadvantaged groups.

The failure of the Left to regain the social policy initiative is a further element of our answer to the question how the massive socioeconomic shocks experienced by the West Germans in the course of the late 1970s and 1980s could be absorbed as smoothly as was actually the case. The victorious Kohl campaigns in both 1983 and 1987 failed to pay more than occasional lip service to a problem that as late as 1982, the last year of the Schmidt government, was generally assigned the position of the

41   Zacher, "Der gebeutelte Sozialstaat in der wirtschaftlichen Krise," p. 5.
42   In fact, it is probably no exaggeration to observe that during the 1980s a new ideological formation and policy orientation has evolved within the Christian Democratic Party that can be described as "conservative state feminism." As a consequence, social policies focusing on the social security status of women were virtually the only area within social policies where not cuts, but substantial improvements – such as the granting of pension claims for mothers, graduated by the number of children – prevailed. Cf. Schmidt, *Sozialpolitik*, pp. 89–90.

single most important social and economic problem that the Germans had to face, namely unemployment, which had risen to 2.5 million registered (and about another 1.5 million unregistered) people without jobs who wanted jobs. This abrupt transformation of a dominant issue into a virtual nonissue must be attributed, according to my analysis, to the three interrelated factors that I have discussed in this chapter, namely:

1   the perceived job security and social security of those within employ-
    ment, as they had as much to lose as they had little to fear and could
    afford to acquiesce in the economic and social condition of their less
    fortunate fellow citizens;
2   the growing heterogeneity of interests, values, and identifications
    within the social structure which became manifest in the rise of issues
    and demands having to do with regional interests, age categories,
    gender categories, health, and agriculture, among numerous others;
    this centrifugal and "disorderly" pattern of political issues dominat-
    ing domestic politics over the last decade was not suitable for integra-
    tion into a coherent and potentially hegemonic program of social
    reform (such as might have been expected from the political Left);
3   the fact that this multiplicity of cleavages, issues, and identities could
    only be – and was in fact quite effectively – over-arched, as it were,
    by the political Right's populist and partly nationalist advances and
    its general emphasis on "moral" rather than social and economic
    reform and leadership, with a particular emphasis on austerity as the
    fiscal equivalent to populism.

7

Postindustrial Cleavage Structures: A Comparison of Evolving Patterns of Social Stratification in Germany, Sweden, and the United States

Gøsta Esping-Andersen

Introduction

Over the last few decades, most labor movements in the Western capitalist democracies have experienced crisis and decline. Trade unions have been weakened in terms of their capacity for cohesive collective action and, in some cases, have suffered fragmentation and eroded membership. Except in the Mediterranean basin, the social democratic or labor parties have been facing (sometimes devastating) electoral decline, increased incapacity to forge governing coalitions, ideological flux and programmatic impasse, and frequently even decomposition.[1]

We can attribute these problems to a host of factors, but the ongoing transformation in the class structure must surely count as decisive. Virtually all labor movements emerged as a response to the rise of industrialism, and logically built their organizations, programs, ideology, and mobilization strategies on the image of the industrial mass-worker. However, what is distinctive of our epoch is the rapid, and even revolutionary, decline of the "Fordist" model of industrial mass production. Within the shrunken manufacturing economy, the organization and

---

1 For an examination of the labor movements in Scandinavia, see G. Esping-Andersen, *Politics against Markets* (Princeton, NJ: Princeton University Press, 1985).

division of work is being recast; service employment is burgeoning and/ or we find growing joblessness and mass unemployment.[2]

These changes are producing a new occupational structure. Everywhere, industrial mass production workers are in decline and professionals are on the rise. However, within this broad trend, nations diverge; in some, like the United States, we see the birth of a new low-paid service proletariat in the consumer industries; in others, like Sweden, there is also a burgeoning new service proletariat, but concentrated in relatively well-paid and secure welfare state jobs. In Germany, postindustrialism is producing joblessness rather than services.

We can therefore identify two broad trends. The first is a *common* structural transformation: the decline of industry, the expansion of services, an overall skill upgrading and professionalization. The "Fordist" stratification system is in eclipse. The second is a *contingent* structural transformation whose shape depends ultimately on the institutional and political framework within which postindustrialization occurs. Because of institutional differences, nations embark upon distinct postindustrial trajectories.

The labor movements are likely to be seriously affected by both the common and contingent types of transformation, not only because they alter patterns of social stratification, but also because they are certain to spur the emergence of new social divisions, new forms of collectivity, new identities and, in the end, new axes of conflict.

The main purpose of this chapter is to examine, comparatively, the emerging patterns of stratification in the era of "postindustrialization," and to suggest how these result in new cleavage structures. This, in my view, is a precondition for addressing the larger question of emerging political alliances. Our focus is on three countries that follow decisively different trajectories: Germany, Sweden, and the United States.

Models of Stratification in Postindustrial Society

The literature on postindustrial societies and the new service economy is often preoccupied with the problem of class, precisely because its goal is to understand the prospects for equality and democracy. Postindustrial theory has its pessimistic and optimistic class scenarios. These scenarios are either implicitly or explicitly the basis for political extrapolations.

In Daniel Bell's generally optimistic model, the rise of science and information technologies creates a postindustrial society which is dominated by service employment and professional–technical cadres. Power and privilege derive from the control of scientific knowledge and hence

2 For a discussion of the concept of Fordism and post-Fordist alternatives, see R. Boyer (ed.), *The Search for Labor Market Flexibility* (Oxford: Oxford University Press, 1988).

meritocracy will become pre-eminent and the salience of class will decline. In his vision, the control over information will emerge as a principal axis of society. His model does not envisage the emergence of a new postindustrial proletariat. Much of the literature on "post-Fordism" and flexibility shares Bell's positive view, although its emphasis is on skill upgrading and the declining hierarchy within industry.[3]

There are essentially two pessimistic versions. One predicts that modern automation and technology cause the emergence of a workless society. Gershuny argues that the service economy will grow only marginally since households will engage in "self-servicing" via purchased material commodities. Thus emerges the possibility that the "service society" may engender mass joblessness rather than service employment.[4]

The jobless growth model is also envisaged in the Baumol theory of unbalanced growth, which argues that high wage costs in the less productive services will produce a cost-disease problem.[5] Following the Baumol model, mass unemployment can be averted if government "subsidizes" service jobs (i.e. welfare state jobs), or if service workers are willing to accept low wages.

If a large share of the service economy expands on the basis of low wages, we might anticipate the emergence of a new service proletarian class divide. Alternatively, as van Parijs argues, a postindustrial economy without job growth might result in an insider–outsider cleavage: a closed labor market of (upgraded) insiders enjoying high wages and job security (efficiency wages), and a swelling army of outsiders including youth, long-term unemployed, early retirees, and discouraged workers. Jobs, themselves, may become the key asset over which distributional struggles will center.[6]

The second pessimistic version emerges from the literature on de-industrialization. The argument here is that industrial decline generates redundancies mainly among the erstwhile well-paid unionized labor force; this is accompanied by a downward pressure on wages. The result is the "declining middle" and heightened labor market polarization

3 D. Bell, *The Coming of Post-Industrial Society* (New York: Basic Books, 1976). Representative examples of the optimistic post-Fordist view are M. Piore and C. Sabel, *The Second Industrial Divide* (New York: Basic Books, 1984); H. Kern and R. Schumann, *Das Ende der Arbeitsteilung? Rationalisierung in der Industrielle Produktion* (Munich: C. H. Beck, 1984); see also Boyer, *The Search for Labor Market Flexibility*.
4 See, for example, J. Gershuny, *After Industrial Society* (London: Macmillan, 1978), and J. Gershuny, *Social Innovation and the Division of Labour* (Oxford: Oxford University Press, 1983).
5 W. Baumol, "The macro-economics of unbalanced growth," *American Economic Review*, 57 (1967), pp. 415–26.
6 P. van Parijs, "A revolution in class theory," *Politics and Society*, 15 (1987), pp. 453–82. Incidentally, a parallel insider–outsider model was developed by Max Adler in his analyses of mass unemployment during the 1930s Depression. See M. Adler, "Wandlung der Arbeiterklasse," *Der Kampf*, 26 (1933), pp. 367–82.

between the top and the new proletarianized bottom. A rather similar model is found in the pessimistic variant of the flexibility literature which suggests the possibility of a "Napoli model" of flexibilization, where firms combine an internal upgraded labor force with a pool of peripheral, "numerically" flexible, labor.[7]

The nature of the welfare state is clearly important in shaping the patterns of postindustrial stratification. As the Baumol logic suggests, welfare state employment is an alternative to mass unemployment or to a low-wage job trajectory. As we shall see, the welfare state "option" has mainly been followed in the Scandinavian countries, accounting for almost all net job growth in the past decades. The Swedish welfare state labor market today accounts for 30 percent of total employment, and it has allowed female participation to increase phenomenally. This contrasts sharply with the transfer-biased Continental European countries where, because of fiscal overload or Christian Democratic preference, social service employment has grown only marginally.

Welfare state institutions also influence the structure of labor supply and the conditions for employment.[8] Opportunities for paid leave from work (ranging from sick pay and maternity to paid leave for education or trade union participation) decide women's capacity to work and pursue careers, and are thus instrumental in narrowing gender-based employment differentials. Yet, the high costs and risks that absenteeism impose on employers may have the adverse effect of inducing "statistical discrimination" in employer hiring strategies. There is little doubt that the extraordinarily high Swedish female participation rates *and*, as we shall see, gender segregation are attributable to Sweden's liberal absenteeism policies.

While paid leave enhances female employment, education and retirement schemes can drastically reshape and reduce the supply of labor. Education delays employment entry, and early retirement schemes have in some cases drastically curtailed the normal age of exit. In countries like Germany, early retirement was used to lure the older unskilled labor force to retire as a means to accelerate industrial rationalization. In other words, retirement schemes have been the midwives of manual worker decline and, in countries like Germany, have been instrumental in nurturing a latent insider–outsider axis.

Welfare states differ sharply in their labor market bias and, as we shall see, this affects emerging stratification patterns. Hence, the nature of the welfare state will dictate the ways in which our traditional manufacturing economy is reorganized, the growth and shape of the service sector,

7   On the impact of de-industrialization, see B. Harrison and B. Bluestone, *The Great U-Turn* (New York: Basic Books, 1988). The pessimistic post-Fordist scenario is presented in Boyer *The Search for Labor Market Flexibility*, and Piore and Sabel, *The Second Industrial Divide*.

8   See, for example, G. Esping-Andersen, *The Three Worlds of Welfare Capitalism* (Cambridge: Polity Press; Princeton, NJ: Princeton University Press, 1990).

the distribution of employment, and also how households organize social reproduction and their use of leisure time.

The Problem of "Classes"

Virtually all varieties of class theory were formulated with the industrial capitalist order in mind. Their target was to provide an understanding of the division of labor and the social hierarchies associated with the industrial divide. Since our task is to understand an emerging "post-industrial" order, I shall shun classical theory and, instead, construct "classes" in a purely heuristic way.

The following analyses of employment change are based on census and survey data for the period from 1960 to the 1980s, a period which is long enough to permit us to identify decisive structural shifts.[9] The analyses focus on three nations that are equally advanced economically and technologically, but which represent three distinct kinds of welfare state and industrial relations system: Germany, Sweden, and the United States.

The weakness of virtually all existing research is that it has focused on either sectoral employment shifts (the rise of jobs in services) or, less commonly, occupational change. In order to identify the outlines of a new stratificational order, we need to combine the two. This we shall undertake in the form of occupation–industry matrices.

The classification of industries

It is possible to divide the economy into two broad logics. In one we find the traditional activities associated with the Fordist system of mass production and mass consumption of standardized commodities. Leaving aside the primary sector completely, the principal sectors engaged in the Fordist industrial economy include manufacturing and distribution (wholesale and retail, transportation, utilities, infrastructure, and administration). One can speak of an internal organic interdependence between these sectors in the sense that the logic of mass industrial production necessitates mass distribution linkages, and vice versa.

In the other, we find the "postindustrial" service sectors whose vitality derives from fundamental changes in societal reproduction. We distinguish three service sectors, each identified by its unique role in

9 For the United States, many would argue that the degree of employment change has been much more powerful in the 1980s than throughout the whole 1960–80 period. Since we have data for 1960, 1980 *and* 1988, we are able to identify whether this is indeed the case. In essentially *all* cases, both the industry and occupational structures are quite stable between 1980 and 1988. The two years are therefore substitutable.

The data in the following tables derive from the 1961 Census and the 1985 Mikrocenzus (Germany), the 1960 and 1980 Census (Sweden), and the 1960 and 1980 Census and the 1988 (March) *Current Population Survey* (United States).

reproduction. Firstly, *business services* mainly provide intermediate, nonphysical, inputs into industrial production and distribution (management consultancy, architectural/engineering services, software programming and systems design, legal and accounting services, financial services, and the like). Their growth is mainly fueled by growing demand for nonphysical, often tailormade, professionalized-scientific inputs into the production process. Business services emerge because industries are less willing to self-service.

Secondly, the growth of *social services* (health, education, and welfare services) reflects household export of the tasks associated with social reproduction, i.e. a decline in "social" self-servicing. The rise of social services is directly tied to the emerging "postindustrial" life cycle: the participation of women in the economy, the equalization of career profiles, the reallocation of household time-use, the shrinking size of households, the phenomenal rise in one-person units, and also the changing demographic profile of modern societies.[10] Social services release time for paid employment and for leisure. They can be exported into the market or into the welfare state.

Thirdly, *consumer services*, like the two previous services, are an alternative to self-servicing, in this case associated with leisure reproduction. On one hand, their growth is connected to the work–social reproduction nexus: when women also work, households are more likely to visit restaurants and send their laundry out. On the other hand, their growth is also connected to the extension of leisure time and the income capacity to purchase entertainment and fun. It is in the consumer services that the Baumol logic, or self-servicing, is most likely to arrest employment growth, since it is in these activities that the commodity option is most available (microwave ovens, dishwashers, video machines, and so on).

The classification of occupations

Detailed occupational titles provide us with a reasonable description of the human capital, responsibilities, and work tasks of a person. Parallel to our sectoral classification, we distinguish a set of occupational classes. In one set, we group those that represent the traditional industrial division of labor; in the second set, we group those that are representative of the "postindustrial" division of labor. For each set, we can then classify occupations according to their place within the Fordist and postindustrial hierarchy, respectively. Our study once again will omit the primary sector occupations (farmers, etc.) entirely and also the military. We thus arrive at the following "classes."

1   The Fordist hierarchy:
    (a)   managers and proprietors (includes executive personnel and the "petite bourgeoisie");

10   See F. Block, *Postindustrial Possibilities* (Berkeley, CA: University of California Press, 1990), for a discussion of the new life cycle.

  (b)   clerical, administrative and sales workers (engaged in the more routine tasks of control, distribution, and administration);

  (c)   manual production workers, subdivided between skilled/craft and the unskilled (these, of course, include also transport workers and other manual occupations engaged in manufacture and distribution, such as packers, truck drivers, haulers, and the like).

2   The postindustrial hierarchy:

  (a)   professionals and scientists;

  (b)   technicians and semi-professionals (school teachers, nurses, social workers, laboratory workers, technical designers, etc.);

  (c)   service workers, subdivided between skilled (cooks, hairdressers, etc.) and unskilled (cleaners, waitresses, bartenders, baggage porters, etc.).[11]

It will be noticed that in each group the hierarchy reflects both a human capital structure and a kind of command/authority structure (managers command, clericals administer commands, and workers execute), although the command structure is less clear-cut within the postindustrial hierarchy. In traditional industrial capitalism, the unskilled manual laborer constituted the archetypal proletarian position; we shall especially focus on the unskilled service worker in our assessment of the proletarianizing and polarizing potential of postindustrial economies.

Three Postindustrial Trajectories

To examine the trends in our three countries, we use 1960 as a benchmark since it marks generally the high point of the "Fordist" industrial epoch. In 1960, there were significant national differences (the United States being somewhat more managerial and service biased), but overall the countries were rather similar; all were basically dominated by the traditional industrial economy. The sectoral trends displayed in table 7.1, however, show that the nations have followed divergent employment paths.

The countries have all experienced a marked shift towards services, but the pace and direction of change differs importantly. In Germany, industry remains much more prominent than elsewhere while the social services are comparatively very underdeveloped. In fact, industry and, generally, the Fordist economy has declined very modestly in Germany.[12] In Sweden, virtually the entire change has been driven by

11   Our operational definition of the unskilled service proletariat is that it involves a job that anyone of us could do with no prior qualifications.

12   The high growth rates for services in Germany are mainly a function of their extremely low initial stage. Similarly, the American growth rates for all three service sectors appear modest, but we must remember that their initial stage was very high.

Table 7.1   The distribution of employment by industry in the 1980s, and the annual average percentage rate of change, 1960–1980s (in parentheses)

	Germany	Sweden	United States
Primary sector	4.9 (−2.6)	5.8 (−2.9)	3.1 (−2.0)
Industry	39.7 (−0.7)	31.5 (−1.3)	25.4 (−1.0)
Distribution	20.7 (+0.4)	20.4 (0.0)	22.7 (−0.1)
Total "Fordist" economy	65.3 (−0.8)	57.7 (−1.2)	51.2 (−0.8)
Government administration	7.8 (+2.7)	4.3 (+2.4)	4.8 (−0.2)
Consumer services	6.4 (+0.4)	5.5 (−1.6)	11.9 (+0.2)
Social services	12.0 (+6.2)	25.5 (+8.7)	20.9 (+3.2)
Business services	7.8 (+5.0)	7.1 (+7.2)	11.2 (+2.3)
Total service economy	26.2 (+3.5)	38.1 (+4.3)	44.0 (+1.8)

the social services – consumer services have, indeed, declined sharply. And, in the United States, the service sector is very large, but with a comparatively heavy bias towards consumer services; still, it comes as a surprise that this welfare state laggard nation's social services are almost twice the size of their German counterpart.[13]

These shifts must be understood on the backdrop of labor market conditions which have been radically different in the three countries. In Germany, total employment has been stagnant, and women's participation has grown relatively little (it remains at about 55 percent). Sweden has experienced considerable overall employment growth, almost all of which is accounted for by the increase in women's employment (from about 60 percent in 1960 to about 82 percent today). Moreover, virtually the entire increase in Swedish women's participation (75 percent) occurred

13   The point is that the United States is a welfare *state* laggard, but has produced an enormous (tax-financed) private welfare and education sector. When this is added to the public share, the total American welfare package absorbs almost the same amount of gross domestic product as does the typical European.

Table 7.2   Occupational distribution of employment in the 1980s, and average annual percentage rate of change, 1960–1980s (in parentheses)

	Germany	Sweden	United States
Managers	4.5 (+1.4)	4.8 (−0.6)	9.1 (+0.6)
Clerical/sale	29.6 (+1.1)	20.4 (+1.1)	28.3 (+0.8)
Manual	33.3 (−0.7)	29.2 (−1.3)	23.1 (−1.2)
All "Fordist" occupations	68.7 (+0.1)	54.4 (−0.6)	60.5 (−0.3)
Professional	5.9 (+4.3)	5.8 (+3.1)	8.8 (+2.3)
Semi-professional	11.4 (+4.9)	20.6 (+5.2)	9.3 (+1.8)
Skilled service	5.5 (+5.8)	3.1 (−0.4)	6.6 (+2.0)
Unskilled service	4.5 (−1.9)	10.5 (+1.7)	11.7 (−0.1)
All "postindustrial" occupations	26.1 (+1.5)	40.0 (+3.0)	36.4 (+1.1)

in welfare state jobs (health, education, and welfare services). The United States has experienced a virtual job explosion over the two decades (almost a doubling of the labor force) with a rate of female increase that follows closely behind Sweden's.

In Germany, low female participation coincides with stagnant social services. But one should not jump to the conclusion that the social services are the only possible inroad for women workers. Women's employment growth in America has *not* been sectorally biased.[14] The stagnation and even decline in consumer services in *both* Germany and Sweden is best ascribed to Baumol's cost-disease problem.[15] While average hourly earnings in American eating and drinking establishments are only 44 percent of manufacturing wages, they are 65 percent in Germany and 80 percent in Sweden.

In table 7.2, the occupational data suggest even greater differentiation between the countries. Germany remains a very "workerist" society; its share of manual workers in the 1980s is equal to the American share in the 1960s! Within its overall jobless growth context, the German trajectory is unique in the degree of pervasive occupational upgrading and the

14   For a more detailed analysis of women's employment in the services, see Esping-Andersen, *The Three Worlds of Welfare Capitalism.*
15   For an econometric test of the cost-disease problem in our three countries, see G. Giannelli and G. Esping-Andersen, "Labor costs and service employment," European University Institute Working Papers, 1989.

very marginal importance of the service proletariat. Combining the share of manual and administrative occupations, we see that the German occupational structure remains heavily "Fordist."

In the 1960s, Sweden's occupational mix was not very different from Germany's; today, the two are almost opposites. Sweden has experienced a significant decline in manual workers (mainly among the unskilled), while the strongest growth has occurred among the semi-professionals and the new service proletariat (two groups, incidentally, heavily female biased). Sweden has comparatively very few administrative jobs. The single most surprising fact is the substantial growth of the new service proletariat – as we shall see, heavily concentrated in the welfare state.

Contrary to what the de-industrialization literature tells us, the momentum of the United States is clearly towards occupational upgrading. While the United States has become even more overmanaged/administrative than earlier, its proletarian component has declined, and the United States is a leader in professionalization.[16]

So far, our data on employment change suggest a number of important hypotheses. First, the Baumol cost-disease effect seems to apply principally to the lower-skilled jobs in the consumer services. The low wages among these groups in the United States are probably the best explanation for their much larger size. And, vice versa, high labor costs in Sweden and Germany make employment growth here prohibitive. The Baumol effect reflects institutional differences in industrial relations systems; strong and comprehensive trade unionism in Sweden and Germany has imposed greater wage equality and higher indirect labor costs (social contributions) across all employment categories.

Second, the data suggest that the marginal effect of an expansion in the service sectors is to increase the relative share of service proletarian jobs. Sweden has a huge service proletariat because social services have expanded so much; the United States, because the consumer services are so large. As we move towards the postindustrial economy, we may very well face a trade-off between strong job growth with a concomitantly large service proletariat, or employment stagnation with a better occupational mix (but probably also joblessness). Our subsequent analyses bring this "size effect" out much more clearly.

The Occupational Structure in the New Service Economy

As we now turn to the distribution of occupations within the new service sectors, we can begin to confront some of the main propositions in the literature. Is the postindustrial structure benign or malign? Is it following

16 Note, however, that the data supporting the declining middle thesis for the United States are based on earnings, not occupations. Our contradictory results suggest the real possibility that the traditionally stable relationship between jobs and earnings is being undone.

Table 7.3 Hierarchy and polarization in manufacturing and the new service economy: the share of select occupations, 1980s

	Germany	*Sweden*	*United States*
Manufacturing			
Managers	2.7	2.3	9.3
Professional/ semi-professional	11.5	15.8	10.7
Unskilled workers	31.7	34.1	37.3
Unskilled per manager + prof. 1960	4.0	3.3	3.4
1980	2.2	1.9	1.9
Service economy			
Managers	5.2	2.7	11.1
Professional/ semi-professional	36.0	49.6	29.0
Unskilled service	12.8	24.5	24.0
Unskilled per manager + prof. 1960	0.8	0.8	1.0
1980	0.3	0.5	0.6

Unskilled workers combine unskilled manual and unskilled service workers; the professional group also includes technicians. The 1980 data refer to 1985 for Germany, 1980 for Sweden, and 1988 for the United States.

the professionalism scenario of Bell or the proletarianization model of Harrison and Bluestone? Can we expect the new social order to repro-duce the kind of class divide and polarization that characterized the old industrial order? In table 7.3, we examine occupational polarization in traditional manufacturing and in our three postindustrial service sectors combined. The table shows, first, that manufacturing is de-proletarianizing and professionalizing, indicating that traditional Fordist hierarchies are fading. While management has more or less stagnated, professionals have doubled over the period. The share of unskilled work-ers has declined significantly. This is the trend in all three countries.[17] The consequence is a sharp reduction in our "polarization ratio" of proletarians per managers/professionals. Being more heavily industrial, it was to be expected that the German ratio is more "workerist."

National variations are more accentuated within the service economy. In Germany and Sweden, the share of managers is very small (and in

17 Because of space limitations we have not provided detailed occupational breakdowns for both 1960 and the 1980s. The discussion is thus based on data not shown here.

decline); in the United States, large (and growing). The services are heavily professional and, in all cases, increasingly so. The differences, however, are dramatic, especially between the 50 percent share in Sweden and the 29 percent in the United States. And, third, the size of the unskilled service proletariat is similar in the United States and Sweden, but only half as large in Germany. We can see that the polarization ratio has declined markedly in all three countries and that, anyhow, the new service economy is much less proletarian (and decreasingly so) than the traditional "Fordist" economy.

The occupational mix of the service economy differs sharply by sector. In Sweden, where the service economy is so heavily slanted toward the social services, it has produced a paradoxical combination of, on the one hand, an unusually high professional (mainly semi-professional, though) content and, on the other hand, a huge social service proletariat. Vice versa, the low American professional share has to do with the relative dominance of consumer services.

Hence, there are two sources of proletarianization. In the United States, it is the consumer service industry (twice as large as in Sweden) which furnishes heavy proletarianization; in Sweden, the same occurs in the social service sector. In Germany, where neither of these service sectors has grown significantly, proletarianization is substantially less. Consumer services constitute a core in a possible proletarianized post-industrial society, but this depends essentially on how large they are permitted to grow. The powerful proletarian element in the Swedish social services is clearly not the consequence of low wages. Rather, our "size effect", in the case of social services, means that each marginal increase in social services favors additions of low-skilled manpower. Or, put differently, the welfare state is liberating women from the traditionally self-serviced social activities (care of the elderly, for example) that involve a heavy dose of unqualified labor.

The services can nurture a sizable growth in traditionally "Fordist" jobs. In Germany and especially the United States, the social services include a very large managerial–administrative labor force. In the former case, this is primarily due to the decentralized, "Lander-based" system of service delivery; in the latter case, private sector dominance in social protection, with its proliferation of private plans, compels a multiplicity of administration. In contrast, Sweden saves on administrative and control personnel because of its consolidated and centralized welfare state, and because means testing (requiring control) plays such a marginal role.

While the business services are quite professionalized, they are also occupationally speaking much closer to the Fordist model, and show less cross-national variation. If the Cohen and Zysman thesis is correct, the convergence found here is not very surprising.[18] Business services largely

---

18 See S. Cohen and J. Zysman, *Manufacturing Matters* (New York: Basic Books, 1987).

cater to externalized manufacturing functions which show much less variation across countries than do the services.

The data suggest that there is very little empirical support for the pessimistic postindustrial theories. The trend is almost universally towards de-proletarianization and depolarization, most dramatically (and surprisingly) so in the United States where the total proletarian share declined by 24 percent (14 percent in Germany and 18 percent in Sweden). The consumer services are certainly a basis of proletarianization but, still, the American experience suggests that the proletarian element can decline (by 23 percent from 1960 to 1988). The only real case of increased proletarianization is found in Swedish social services (a full 33 percent increase).

A proletarian decline should produce less labor market polarization, and this is brought out quite clearly in our data. Our findings therefore sharply contradict the de-skilling and polarization theses. The postindustrialization of labor markets is generally producing job upgrading and less job polarization, especially within the new service industries.

Germany by and large exhibits the most favorable job structure in the new service economy, but this is basically because it is so small. Its favorable occupational mix is, so to speak, bought at the expense of a large "outsider" population, unable to enter into the labor market.

It is much more surprising that upgrading is so powerful in the United States, where employment growth has been both explosive and unregulated by either the welfare state or comprehensive trade unions. However, accumulated empirical evidence shows that the American upgrading process has been accompanied by growing earnings inequalities and a large base of low-paid jobs. As the data of Harrison and Bluestone and of Levy show,[19] there are sharp differences in the profile of job growth over the decades we study: the well-paid jobs exploded in the 1960s and 1970s, while the low-paid jobs dominated the growth profile of the 1980s. But the earnings data and the job data nonetheless show opposite trends, even for the 1980s. Thus, what we can surmise for the United States is a strong decoupling process at work between occupation and earnings. This is almost certainly attributable to the weak and dualistic system of trade unionism.

Finally, what the American labor force data do not show is the concomitant evolution of a new "outsider" population, akin to the situation in Germany. In the American case, however, the outsiders are especially weighted with highly vulnerable groups such as single mothers and black youth. Since, for reasons of education or social position, these groups are structurally barred from full labor market participation, and since the American welfare state fails to assure a comprehensive social safety net, the result is a harsher and more targeted dualism. Whereas

---

19 Harrison and Bluestone, *The Great U-Turn*; F. Levy, *Dollars and Dreams* (New York: Norton, 1988).

poverty is a marginal phenomenon in the German "outsider" population, it is unusually concentrated in the American.[20]

Paradoxically, the social services in Sweden have contributed to a trend towards proletarianization and polarization. Relying on the welfare state to produce a socially benevolent postindustrial order may have secured maximum female labor force participation and certainly also a more favorable earnings structure, but at the cost of a large service proletariat and female ghettoization within the welfare state labor market. Today, almost 70 percent of total public employment is female.[21]

Social Cleavages in Postindustrial Societies

Different structures are likely to give life to different kinds of inequalities, segmentation, and dualisms. The shape of emerging conflicts and alignments will depend to some extent on emerging cleavages.

In this section, we shall examine the "democratizing" effects of postindustrialization by focusing on the relative position of women and, for the United States, also the black and Hispanic minority population (we can undertake limited comparisons with foreign workers in Germany).[22] These are the traditionally most disadvantaged labor market groups. Our method is simple: we shall examine their degree of over- or underrepresentation in order to assess how they have fared in the distribution of jobs.

In table 7.4, we compare the degree of over- or under-representation among women within key service occupations for our three nations, from 1960 to the 1980s. Parallel data are presented in table 7.5 for blacks and Hispanics in the United States.

The new postindustrial economy appears quite favorable for women in the United States, where their traditional under-representation in the professions and over-representation in the unskilled service jobs is close to being eliminated. In Sweden, postindustrialization via the welfare state seems actually to reinforce gender segmentation. Women here do less well at the top, are becoming heavily over-represented within the bottom (social service proletarian) jobs, and remain concentrated in the middle layers of traditionally female jobs. In Germany, women have

---

20   For comparable data on poverty, see D. Mitchell, "Income transfer systems: a comparative study using microdata," Doctoral Dissertation, Australian National University, Canberra, 1990; J. Palmer, T. Smeeding, and B. Torrey, *The Vulnerable* (Washington, DC: The Urban Institute, 1988).

21   This compares with about 46 percent in the United States and less than 40 percent in Germany.

22   The following discussion follows the analyses developed in Esping-Andersen, *The Three Worlds of Welfare Capitalism.*

Table 7.4   Women's over-/under-representation in select postindustrial occupations, 1960s–1980s

	Germany		Sweden		United States	
	1960	*1980s*	*1960*	*1980s*	*1960*	*1980s*
Professionals and semi-professionals[a]	−18	−12	−23	−20	−14	−6
Nurses and teachers	+29	+29	+40	+34	+46	+36
Skilled service workers	+23	+37	+37	+28	+6	+7
Unskilled service proletariat	+49	+36	+42	+68	+38	+19

[a] We have excluded nurses and teachers from the professional/semi-professional class, since these are traditionally heavily female occupations and warrant separate analysis.

Negative values indicate under-representation. The index measures the number of percentage deviation points above/below gender parity, adjusted for the relative proportion of women in the total labor market (39 percent in Germany, 46 percent in both Sweden and the United States).

Table 7.5   The degree of over-/under-representation of blacks and Hispanics in select postindustrial occupations: the United States, 1960–1980s

	Blacks		Hispanics	
	1970	*1980s*	*1970*	*1980s*
Professionals and semi-professionals	−20	−14	−15	−19
Nurses and teachers	−3	+12	−18	−18
Unskilled service workers	+10	+20	+1	+11
Skilled service proletariat	+31	+28	+15	+24

The data are to be read as in table 7.4. Note that also here we adjust for the relative share of blacks and Hispanics in the labor market.

made some headway in the professions and have reduced their level of concentration in the unskilled service jobs. But German women are increasingly over-represented in the nonprofessionalized, skilled service jobs (assistant nurses, hairdressers, cooks, and the like).

Another way of gauging the openness of the postindustrial economy is to compare our indices against those that pertain to the traditional "Fordist" economy. Generally speaking, gender segregation and women's under-representation remains much higher in the traditional industrial economy. In both Sweden and Germany, women's under-representation among managers remains much higher than among professionals, and the trend does not indicate improvement. In the United States, however, the process of gender equalization extends also to management, where female under-representation has declined from −19 to −8 over the period.

The results are more ambiguous for racial and ethnic minorities. For those who *do* obtain employment, the service economy has been quite favorable to blacks, but not to Hispanics. Yet, Blacks in America have not benefited as much as women. They show a noticeable improvement in the professions and in the unskilled service jobs, but the data indicate that the main road for black job mobility lies in the middle layers of service occupations. The profile of Hispanic occupational development suggests that they may have become the ethnic basis of the new post-industrial proletariat; their under-representation among professionals has actually risen, as has their over-representation within the unskilled service proletariat. It is possible that Hispanics, as the latest large immigrant population, are filling the bottom end of the labor market vacated by women and blacks.

Still, the minority bias of postindustrialism seems even stronger in Germany. We should remember that a large proportion of the German foreign workers have limited work-permits, allowing them only to work in certain jobs for a specified amount of time. This alone helps account for their very heavy concentration in traditional industries (63 percent, compared with only 20 percent among American blacks and 23 percent among Hispanics). But it is also clear that, in Germany, when immigrants enter the service economy they do so overwhelmingly at the bottom end. They are exactly twice as likely as a German to fill the unskilled service jobs.

In both Germany and the United States, minorities are much more likely to become part of the "outsider" population. If we examine only open unemployment, in Germany their unemployment rate (1987) was about 15 percent, or 66 percent higher than for Germans; in the same year in the United States, black unemployment was 14.5 percent and Hispanic 10 percent (compared with 6 percent for whites).

In conclusion, the democratizing impact of postindustrial change on employment is mixed, being positive mainly for women (with the partial exception of Sweden) and less so for minorities.

Social Cleavages and Political Alignments in Postindustrial Societies

The process of employment restructuring is recasting traditional social cleavages. Each nation's realignment is also unique. In the concluding section, we attempt to extrapolate the consequences of the new cleavage structures for the labor movements.

The labor movements' traditional mode of mobilization is being eroded, not only by the diminishing size of the industrial working class, but also by its recast class character. The service economy is being reorganized in tandem with the de-proletarianization of industry. The general trend towards professionalization means greater individualization around credentials and human capital. In both Sweden and Germany, the new professional and semi-professional cadres tend to be unionized, but along much narrower and, in a sense, more syndicalist lines. Other large service sector groups – the unskilled service proletariat especially – are much more difficult to organize collectively. In the United States, their existence is more or less a function of trade union *absence*. In Sweden, of course, the unskilled service workers in welfare state jobs are thoroughly unionized, but since they are typically part-time workers their degree of identification with the labor movement is likely to be weaker.

In brief, across all our countries the heterogenization, professionalization, and differentiation that is characteristic of the general trend is almost certain to weaken the capacity for unity and mass mobilization characteristic of the traditional labor movements. But, since the trajectory of change diverges so dramatically from one country to the next, our discussion should properly take place within the national context.

Germany

Germany is, in a sense, the odd-man-out. Since postindustrialization has been weak, the result is an economy that very much retains the classical industrial axis. Yet, industrial Germany is being "de-Fordized" from within as the unskilled worker mass declines and the skilled workforce is upgraded.[23] However, similar trends unfold also in the relatively smaller industrial sector of Sweden and United States.

German industrial restructuring has gone hand in hand with general employment stagnation and thus lack of service dynamism. The entry of women has been modest, while the exit of (mainly older) males has been dramatic. Owing to high wage costs, the consumer services cannot grow;

23   For an empirical analysis of these trends in German manufacturing, see especially Kern and Schumann, *Das Ende der Arbeitsteilung? Rationalisierung in der Industrielle Produktion.*

owing to the anti-service bias of the welfare state, social service employment has been unable to compensate. With blocked opportunities for female employment growth, the net result is a society in which the household retains its classical role of self-servicing its social and leisure activities. Generally speaking, it may be argued that the nexus of family, market, and welfare state in Germany remains within the logic of the traditional industrial order.[24]

The German trajectory may therefore produce a combination of two social axes: in the first, we should expect to see a reproduction of the industrial "class axis," although de-Fordization coupled with declining industrial hierarchy may help erode the traditional frontlines of industrial conflict. If we can generalize from studies such as those by Kern and Schumann, future industrial relations may be characterized by less managerialism, greater "class collaboration," and "micro-corporatist" bargaining. However, if the old mass-worker axis is fading for the native *German* labor force, indications are that *foreign* minority workers still occupy the classical role of industrial reserve army. Thus may emerge an ethnicity/nationality-based labor market segmentation (and possibly also conflict) of the American kind.

Germany's slim postindustrial economy has produced deproletarianization and pervasive upgrading. The services are small, but not polarized. It is in the growing divide between the insiders and outsiders that a second, new axis may evolve. In the context of employmentless growth, the high wages and strong job tenure rights that are enjoyed by the insiders actively helps reinforce the barriers to job entry; and with a strong helping hand from welfare state transfer programs, the outsider population of early retirees and long-term unemployed has been added to the large proportion of housewives and other groups discouraged from the labor market.

Whether the insider–outsider axis becomes political reality depends, of course, on a host of variables (including the unpredictable consequences of unification). It could become conflictual because of the fiscal strains of supporting a welfare-state-subsidized surplus population. On the other hand, it is difficult to imagine that such a heterogeneous and fragmented surplus population, composed of housewives, students, the unemployed, and retirees, will be able to engage in concerted collective action.

The fragmented nature of the outsider populations suggests, however, that a return to the political dualisms (the party of the unemployed and

24 The absence of a large social service economy implies that households (i.e. women) remain wedded to a self-serviced mode of social reproduction, be it in the care of children or the aged. Women's functional imprisonment in household social reproduction helps to explain their low rates of labor market activity, *notwithstanding* the extremely low German fertility rates.

In the field of leisure consumption, we must qualify our statement concerning self-servicing. Germany (and Sweden too) are extreme cases of leisure import in the form of tourism. Germans go abroad for their "fun" consumption, creating consumer service jobs in Italy, Greece, and Bangkok.

the party of the employed) described by Max Adler in the 1930s is unrealistic. In Germany there is no evidence that any particular political party is emerging as the representative of "outsiders." What is more likely is an intensification of distributional conflicts in which the object-ive interest of the insiders is to diminish the fiscal burden of supporting the outsiders, via either tax or benefit reductions.[25] Their high level of job security means that their degree of identification with social welfare programs may diminish; there is a clear trend in Germany towards bargained fringe benefits (like private pensions) among the insiders. If this trend is allowed to accelerate, general support for the welfare state may erode. The outsiders, in contrast, will most likely have to struggle to maintain public support for social programs. Given the Social Demo-cratic Party's traditional position as the main defender of welfare state commitments, we could expect that the net result is a gradual erosion of social democratic support among the insiders, while the Social Demo-cratic Party emerges as the coalition representing a diverse outsider population.

Sweden

Swedish postindustrialization is dominated by welfare state services. In a double sense, this has revolutionized the life cycle and the family. The services free households of their traditional social reproduction respon-sibilities, and they permit women to style their life cycle and career patterns closer to the males (while male life cycles are encouraged to approach women's). Since the social services also constitute the principal female labor market, the Swedish welfare statist, postindustrial logic becomes circularly self-reinforcing.

We have discovered that a welfare statist model does not prevent the rise of a new service proletariat – on the contrary. The Swedish welfare state proletariat is nonetheless qualitatively different from the large American consumer service proletariat. On one side, it can count on good wages and job security; on the other side, the active labor market policies of Sweden allow, at least in principle, retraining and thus sub-sidized outward mobility.

It is entirely possible that proletarianization in the social services fuels a new postindustrial class divide. Yet, what appears more likely is a gender-overlaid public–private divide. In Sweden, welfare state jobs account for about one-third of the entire labor force, and its composition is almost entirely female. Sweden's labor market is probably the most gender segregated of all.[26] The public sector has emerged as a genuine female-employment-ghetto.

25 This theme has also been developed by Claus Offe in his *Contradictions of the Welfare State* (London: Hutchinson, 1984) and *Disorganized Capitalism* (Cam-bridge, MA: MIT Press, 1985).
26 See, for example, G. Standing, *Unemployment and Labor Market Flexibility: Sweden* (Geneva: ILO, 1988).

This produced two concomitant effects: a gender-based dual "class structure," with a female hierarchy in the welfare state and a largely male hierarchy in the private economy; the evolution of distributional conflicts around the public–private axis – the welfare state is compelled to restrain public employee wages since they are entirely tax financed, and this leads to intense wage-inequality problems between public and private sector job equivalents. It is clear that private sector clerical workers now refuse to accept wage solidarity with their kindred in the welfare state. During the 1980s, Swedish strike rates have been among the highest in Western Europe, and the lion's share of strikes have been over wage differentials between public and private sector workers. Indeed, it is between public and private sector unions representing equivalent workers (say, clerical workers) that the most intense conflicts are found.

The repercussions of this new divide are increasingly clear. Both the central confederations of trade unions (LO and TCO) and the Social Democratic Party have been forced to more or less abandon the principles of wage equalization that have characterized their program since the 1930s. And there is very little doubt that the serious decay in Social Democratic Party support over the past years is closely related to its incapacity to harmonize interests between the public and private sectors: it is structurally dependent on high taxation and wage equality for the sustenance of the welfare state; yet, it is forced to give in to the private sector's demands for sharp tax reductions and wage inequalities. The gender-based public–private divide is also influencing electoral coalitions. Recent data show that the large (and electorally decisive) white collar mass is increasingly divided into a social democratic clientele, largely composed of (female) public employees, and a nonsocialist – even anti-public-sector – clientele, composed of (male) private sector employees.[27]

The United States

The American trajectory has very little in common with either the German or the Swedish. Its service economy has been extraordinarily dynamic with less of a particular bias, although the consumer services are internationally large. The substantial degree of social service growth, much of it in the market, has produced heavy managerialism and administration but not proletarianization, as in Sweden. The vitality of the consumer services implies considerable proletarianization and polarization, in terms of both jobs and wages.

The American pattern suggests a far-reaching reorganization of household reproduction, with a considerable externalization of both social and leisure reproduction; this is, of course, both the cause and consequence

---

27   See S. Holmberg and M. Gilliam, *Valjare och Val i Sverige* (Stockholm: Liber Forlag, 1987), and Esping-Andersen, *The Three Worlds of Welfare Capitalism.*

of substantial female employment growth. American women are less likely to work part-time than the Swedish, and are also much less job segregated. The price they pay for this, however, is lower earnings.

Comparatively speaking, the United States exhibits a favorable trend in postindustrial job development, strong professionalization, and de-proletarianization *without* the jobless growth problem inherent in the German model, or the ghettoization problem of the Swedish model. The important point, however, is that occupational improvement has coincided with the emergence of a very group-specific labor market "outcast," the emergence of a new (heavily Hispanic) reserve army, and with sharply increased earnings inequality in general and poverty-level wages in particular.

Indeed, one challenging hypothesis that emerges from the American experience is that (without unions as an institutional filter) the long-term stable association between jobs and earnings that characterized American Fordism has become uncoupled. Moreover, in the new postindustrial economy, job upgrading is going hand in hand with a possibly stronger degree of earnings polarization. The continued institutional centrality of collective bargaining mechanisms in both Germany and Sweden are of critical importance in explaining, respectively, their jobless and welfare statist biases. Neither mechanism engenders significant earnings polarization or poverty. The reign of the market, in its American form at least, produces a fairly positive employment profile, but at the cost of vast inequalities.

The postindustrial employment trend in the United States has been surprisingly favorable to women and, to a lesser degree, also to blacks. Job-wise, both groups have experienced a process of integration into the traditionally white–male–dominated occupational structure. They do so, however, at the price of earnings differentials.

Hence, one might expect that some of the traditional minority-based cleavages will weaken in the United States: the overlap of being female/black and in a poor job is becoming undone. With this trend, it is very possible that gender- and race-based cleavages weaken in terms of job hierarchies, although they may actually be reinforced in terms of earnings conflicts. On the other hand, we notice that the outsider population in the United States is extraordinarily weighted by the same two kinds of groups: single mothers and young black males. Indications are that divisions *within* the black and female population may grow.[28]

There are principally two kinds of losers in the American trajectory: the employed underclass (increasingly Hispanic) within low-paid service jobs, and the outsiders of single mothers and unemployed (heavily black)

28 The trend towards rising intra-minority group inequality is documented in household statistics. Thus, the share of blacks earning $35,000 plus (in constant 1986 dollars) rose from 10.9 percent in 1970 to 17.1 percent in 1986. Concomitantly, the percentage with less than $10,000 rose from 23.6 to 26.2 percent (*Statistical Abstract of the United States*, 1988, table 690).

youth. A broad coalition of these groups is unlikely. First, a large section of the service proletariat fill the bad jobs on a very temporary basis; they are recent immigrants, or youth utilizing such jobs as a "bridging" mechanism between schooling and careers.[29] Second, even if they constitute a permanent "class," their capacity for trade union organization and collective action is chronically low. Third, the degree to which this rather heterogeneous loser population can express itself politically is likely to remain marginal because of its notoriously low levels of electoral participation.

Conclusions

It is difficult to reach anything approximating firm conclusions from a study deliberately focused on societies in flux. What we can offer, instead, are some hypotheses.

First, developments *so far* suggest that we should not expect a fundamentally convergent pattern of postindustrialization. Certainly, there are trends that go in the same direction, but there are many more important ones that diverge.

This leads us to the second hypothesis. The welfare state and the system of industrial relations are decisive in terms of explaining postindustrial variation. In these two institutions lie both barriers and catalysts in realizing postindustrial employment potentialities.

Differences in welfare states have been important in blocking or spurring overall employment expansion. The transfer-biased German welfare state, hostile to collective service provision, has helped block job growth and has encouraged labor force exit; the service-biased Swedish, the opposite. When we take into account the enormous degree of tax subsidization of private social services in America, we have also identified an important source of their growth (and its heavy burden of administrative personnel).

From our comparisons emerge the outlines of a terrible dilemma. Our size effect hypothesis suggests that a marginal extra growth within the new services produces more service proletarians. In contrast, a no-growth labor market appears to hinder their emergence. If this is truly the case, the choice appears to be between a German-style insider–outsider scenario or a Swedish American-style expansionary but proletarianizing scenario (in the former, in terms of jobs; in the latter, in terms of earnings).

29 For the argument that such jobs are "bridges," see V. Oppenheimer, "Life-cycle jobs and the transition to adult occupational careers," Working Paper 168, Institute of Industrial Relations, University of California at Los Angeles, 1989.

8

Electoral Politics and Economic Control in Israel

Asher Arian and Ilan Talmud

Introduction

The Labor Party, under various names, was Israel's dominant party from the 1930s through most of the 1970s. Its elite focused on state building; unavoidably, they also structured the social, economic, and political realities of Israel. The party was eclipsed in 1977. Labor had failed to free itself from the limitations of the structures which had allowed it to rule for so long, losing votes steadily after 1981 (table 8.1).

The sources of the electoral decline of the Labor Party are complex and varied. Duverger had pointed out years before that "the dominant party wears itself out in office, it loses its vigor, its arteries harden. It would thus be possible to show ... that every domination bears within itself the seeds of its own destruction."[1] Very close election results and the creation of the national unity government as a form of mutual survival for minority parties had kept Labor in the government. After the 1988 elections, however, the party was left with the forlorn hope of being able to reinvigorate the industrial and service activities of the Histadrut (labor union federation) by either overseeing the finances of an overextended economy or parliamentary opposition. In another grasp at extending life, the former dominant party chose to retain some semblance of governmental power, rather than joining the opposition.

We shall explore some of the complicated and distinctive ways in

Our thanks to Raphael Ventura for assistance with the data analysis.

1   M. Duverger, *Political Parties* (New York: Wiley, 1963), p. 312.

Table 8.1   Knesset and Histadrut election results for Labor and Likud, 1965–1988 (percent)

Knesset/Histadrut election years	Knesset		Histadrut	
	Labor[a]	Likud	Labor[b]	Likud
1965/1966	36.7[c]	21.3	65.4[d]	15.2
1969/1969	46.2	21.7	62.1	16.9
1973/1973	39.6	30.2	58.3	22.7
1977/1977	24.4	33.4	55.3	28.2
1981/1981	36.3	37.1	61.9	26.4
1984/1985	34.9	31.9	65.8	22.4
1988/1989	32.5[e]	31.1	64.1[f]	27.4

[a] Including Mapam except in 1965 and 1988.
[b] Including Mapam except in 1966.
[c] Mapam accounted for 6.6 percent of the total.
[d] Mapam accounted for 14.5 percent of the total.
[e] Mapam accounted for 2.5 percent of the total.
[f] Including Mapam, which ran alone and won 9 percent.

which the domination of the Labor establishment in Israel bore within itself the seeds of its own destruction. The four related factors leading to the party's electoral decline upon which we shall focus are as follows: (a) the fact that the clarity of the labor movement's message was muted from the outset because of the unique circumstances faced by the Israeli Labor Party in simultaneously undertaking challenges of nation building and class formation (first section); (b) that political dominance was made possible by control of the economy, the unintended political consequence of the dominance being the development of a service class whose policies and affinities were more closely in line with the Ashkenazim (Jews of European background) than with the Sephardim (Jews of Asian and African background), so that the resulting image of the Labor Party was of "Establishment," paradoxically fostered by the success of the Histadrut and the services which it provided and which the Labor Party established and dominated (second section); (c) thus the party was unable to retain the loyalties of the Sephardi immigrants, and especially their children (third section); and (d) the emergence of a strong alternative to Labor in the form of the Likud, a party which tapped the ethnic resentments, the religious sentiments, and the nationalistic yearnings of many of the workers in a much more successful manner than did the Labor Party (penultimate section).

The Double Agenda of
Building Nation and Class

Historically, the Labor Party[2] perceived itself as much more than a
working class party, claiming from the 1930s onwards that it possessed
the appropriate solutions for the nation as a whole. While labor parties
are generally conceived to be the political vehicle of the working class, in
the Israeli case the situation was much more complicated. Consistent
with Zionist ideology, the labor movement in Israel was a class organizer
and a nation-builder at one and the same time, from the very beginning
of the Zionist experience. This stands in contrast with the historical
experience of European labor parties, which gained legitimation or political control after long and violent, sometimes revolutionary, events.
European organized labor movements rebelled against the old regimes
and became contenders for state power, whereas the Israeli one founded
a new political entity which it dominated from its formative period.
Moreover, the Zionist labor leaders brought to pre-state Israel ideological
and organizational models developed in Europe, but the language and
organizing strategies of European social democracy reflected a very
different class structure than existed in Israel. Palestine was not an
industrial country, and did not evolve in ways that matched European
development. While social class has always had a respected place in the
political rhetoric of the country, in terms of political reality its role was
marginal.

Class formation in Israel was concurrent with the foundation of a new
political entity – the Jewish state in the land of Israel.[3] The double
agenda of building both a nation and a class dictated the very forms of
political struggle as well as the content of economic policies initiated by
the Labor Party. The Israeli Labor Party lacked support of a historical
working class.[4] This made the party and the social structure unique
among welfare states, since the Labor Party fashioned a welfare state in
Israel without having the social base generally associated with the

2   At that time called Mapai, the Hebrew acronym for the Workers Party in the
Land of Israel. Earlier, it was known as Ahdut Haavoda, meaning the Unity of
Labor. For a history of the pre-state period see W. Laqueur, *A History of Zionism*
(London: Weidenfeld & Nicolson, 1972), and N. Lucas, *The Modern History of
Israel* (New York: Praeger, 1974).
3   Cf. G. Esping-Andersen, R. Friedland, and E. O. Wright, "Modes of class
struggle and the capitalist state," *Kapitalistate*, 4–5 (1976), pp. 186–220.
4   See an opposite example in E. P. Thompson, *The Making of the English Working
Class* (London: Penguin, 1968). On the gradual integration of the British class
with the polity, see T. H. Marshall, *Class, Citizenship and Social Development*
(Westport, CT: Greenwood Press, 1973).

development of such an arrangement.[5] Labor was a "dominant party," and as such was a crucial component of the political system both ideologically and in terms of its pivotal political location.[6] When an influx of Sephardi immigrants came soon after Independence, the Labor Party was ideally positioned to absorb them, socialize them, and to demand and receive their votes. Thus, the capacity of the centrist and right-wing opposition to provide an effective ideological and organizational response to the dominance of the labor movement was paralyzed.

The building of the new state coincided with the geopolitical conflict between the Arabs and the Jews regarding the land. This conflict contributed to the cohesion of the political community in Israel, and to the leadership's capacity to enforce its rule even in a nonsovereign society. There was also convergence between the symbols of the pioneering Zionist settlers and the Socialist workers in the dominant ideological value system.[7] Unionization strengthened the internal cohesion of the labor movement, and the external conflict with the Arabs reinforced the political hegemony of the party.

David Ben Gurion summed up the synthesis of sectoral and general goals: from class to nation. Speaking in 1929 to the Council of the Histadrut (the General Confederation of Jewish Labor in the Land of Israel), he said, "The question of Hebrew labor in the land of Israel is not a class question, but a Zionist question.... The economic value of labor in the nation's existence determines the social value of the worker in the nation's life. The actualization of Zionism conditions and obliges the working class in the land of Israel to greatness."[8] Through its revolution, the Jewish working class would be more than a vanguard for the beleaguered Jews of the Diaspora; it would also achieve a metamorphosis in Jewish life by transforming itself from a working class to a working nation.

Ben Gurion reflected his assessment of political realities. When he led the World Zionist Organization in the 1930s and early 1940s, Mapai dominated the nonsovereign political organizations in the Yishuv, the pre-state community. Managing the financial capital of the Jewish

---

5 Cf. T. J. Pempel and J. Williamson, "Welfare spending in advanced industrial democracies, 1950–1980," *American Journal of Sociology*, 93(1988), pp. 1424–56; W. Korpi, "Power, politics, and state autonomy in the development of social citizenship: social rights during sickness in eighteen OECD countries since 1930," *American Sociological Review*, 54 (1989), pp. 309–28.

6 On dominant party systems and their structural and ideological implications see Duverger, *Political Parties*. On pivotal power as a source of domination see A. Etzioni, "Alternative ways to democracy: the example of Israel," *Political Science Quarterly*, 74 (1959), pp. 196–214. On the symptoms of diffusion of political hegemony throughout society, see A. Gramsci, *Selections from the Prison Notebooks* (New York: International Publishers, 1980), pp. 12–13, 55–60, 397–408.

7 S. N. Eisenstadt, *Israeli Society* (Jerusalem: Magnes, 1967), chs 1, 2.

8 Cited in M. Cohen, *Zion and State: Nation, Class and the Shaping of Modern Israel* (Oxford: Basil Blackwell, 1987), pp. 85–6.

people enabled the labor movement to wield political power through its control of the import-capital economy.[9] Labor leaders thought that in a "colonial country" class conflict was meaningless. The establishment of an independent Jewish state, they asserted, would liberate the Jewish people in terms of class and nationhood, thus creating a new kind of a Jew, emancipated both as a worker and as a citizen. The role of the labor movement in this setting was labeled "constructive Socialism"; by this they meant building institutional and economic infrastructures as a potential base for the prospective state.

The 1930s was a period of national consolidation. Mapai attained control over the voluntary institutions which represented the Zionist movement and the Jews living in Palestine, and it was positioned to manage the capital imported through fund-raising efforts of the Diaspora branches of international Jewish political organizations. Managing the entire web of this institutional setting is still one of the principal steering methods of Mapai and its successors.[10]

The interlocking labor unions, and other national institutions, and their key economic activities introduced a corporatist decision-making structure in pre-state Israel, which has persisted to this day. Since its foundation, the Histadrut has claimed "national responsibility" and has often chosen to moderate wage demands accordingly.[11] An effective and service-providing labor union, control over the national institutions (the functional equivalent of the national government in the pre-state period), and the Histadrut enterprises were welded into a dominant party – Mapai and its successor, the Labor Party.

Meanwhile, political discourse was almost exclusively focused on the security situation and on the Israeli–Arab conflict. While security questions sometimes led to fierce partisan skirmishes, the manner in which the economy was organized and especially the strong role of the state was generally accepted. This remarkable consensus, diffused throughout Israeli society, was part of the hegemonic ideology which emerged, subordinating economic and social issues to security object-ives.[12] In this context, class struggle appeared illegitimate. It is certainly

9 See A. Foster, *Banking – Theory and Practice* (Jerusalem: Reuven Mass, 1961) (in Hebrew); N. Gross, N. Halevi, E. Kleiman, and M. Sarnat, *A Banker and a Renewal Nation: the History of Bank Leumi Le-Israel* (Ramat-Gan: Massada, 1977) (in Hebrew).
10 Y. Shapiro, *The Formative Years of the Israeli Labor Party* (Beverly Hills, CA: Sage, 1976), and *Israeli Democracy* (Ramat-Gan: Massada, 1978) (in Hebrew). On the economic context see N. Halevi and R. Klinov-Malul, *The Economic Develop-ment of Israel* (New York: Praeger, 1968), ch. 3; H. Barkai, *The Formative Years of the Israeli Economy* (Jerusalem: The Falk Institute, 1983).
11 Z. Karmi, *The Labor Union in Israel and Abroad* (Tel Aviv: Mesilot, 1959) (in Hebrew).
12 I. Talmud, "'Between politics and economy': public consent versus ideolo-gical distinction in Israel," M. A. Thesis, Department of Sociology, Tel Aviv University, 1985.

ironic that Shimon Peres was willing to enter the government formed in 1988 as Finance Minister – and not in his usual foreign policy role. He did so as much to pump funds to the Histadrut to save its industrial firms, collective settlements, and service providers lest they collapse, and, with them, Labor's power base. In addition, of course, he also claimed to be dedicated to promoting growth in the national economy.

Economic Control as a
Vehicle for Political Control

The historic role of the labor movement in setting up the institutional-ized economic arrangements was critical in determining later political developments.[13] Even in the pre-state period, the labor parties and the unions controlled the allocation of publicly provided material goods. They were especially responsive to the demands of the middle class in order to gain its support.[14]

After Independence, the logic of Labor hegemony dictated that it adopt policies to continue its rule, regardless of the ideological implica-tions of these policies. Israel absorbed an immigrant population three times larger than its original population size,[15] most of them from countries of Asia and Africa, and they were settled in temporary housing and later in developing towns. For example, in order to overcome the scarcity which resulted from the huge immigration, an austerity eco-nomy was initiated but was then cancelled. In 1951 some of the veteran Ashkenazi electorate shifted to parties of the center and right.[16] The government abandoned more egalitarian policies in favor of middle class politics.

The role of the government in the economy of Israel is unprecedented among democratic regimes; the involvement of political actors in the economy is enormous, and has increased over the years.[17] Most critically,

13   See H. Etzioni-Halevi, *Political Culture in Israel* (New York: Praeger, 1977), p. 40; Y. Shapiro, *Israeli Democracy*, pp. 127–44.
14   A. Gonen and S. Hason, "Public housing as a geographical–political means in Israeli cities," *State, Government and International Relations*, 18(1982), pp. 27–37 (in Hebrew); D. Horowitz and M. Lissak, *Origins of The Israeli Polity* (Tel Aviv: Am Oved, 1978), p. 181 (in Hebrew); S. Netser, *Excerpts from My Notebook* (Tel Aviv: Am Oved, 1980) (in Hebrew).
15   The original population size was approximately 600,000. The total immigra-tion was almost 940,000. See D. Potenkin, *The Israeli Economy: The First Decade* (Jerusalem: The Falk Institute, 1967), p. 20, table 1.
16   For full documentation see Y. Shapiro, *An Elite Without Successors: Generations of Political Leaders in Israel* (Tel Aviv: Sifriyat Hapoalim, 1984) (in Hebrew).
17   D. Horowitz, *Structure and Trends in the Israeli Economy* (Ramat Gan: Massada, 1964) (in Hebrew). Yair Aharoni, a close observer of the Israeli economy, estimates that the impact of the government and its policies on the economy's performance is 90 percent. A. Arian, *Politics in Israel: The Second Generation* (Chatham, NJ: Chatham House, 1985), p. 32.

the government has monopolized the capital market. Direct government activity is very high, a phenomenon which is permitted by the flow of capital from outside the country. By the late 1980s, Israel was receiving $3.2 billion annually from the US government, compared with $71 million in 1970. In 1970 only $1 million was in grants; in 1988, more than half of the total was. This aid has expanded eighty-seven times between 1968 to 1979 (in real dollar terms) as endowment, and twelve times as credit.[18] The party in power had a tremendous resource at its disposal.

Government activity calculated on the basis of total resources comes to about 50 percent. A time series examination of the relations between the general Israeli government consumption and the gross national product (GNP)[19] reveals that the ratio was between 0.33 and 0.36 until the 1960s; it then contracted to about a quarter, and rose above 40 percent after 1967.[20] American economic aid contributed to the expansion of the public sector and, moreover, to the political power of the government *vis-à-vis* other actors.

A large part of public consumption went to security, which was a quarter of the GNP in 1980.[21] The civil nonmilitary component of security consumption was 44 percent in 1982, and 23 percent of the industrial export in 1982 was security production.[22] The percentage of the gross domestic product (GDP) which went for governmental consumption in 1980 was 38.3 (in comparison with 17.6 percent for the United States, an average 16.1 percent for market economies, a 17.0 percent average for developed market economies, and an average 13.0 percent for developing market economies).[23]

Attempts to resolve the problems of economic scarcity, unemployment, security, and integration of the new immigrant groups were driven by perceived political needs. The logic of employment policy, for example, postulated the importance of full employment rather than productivity. The service sector expanded over the years, in both the private and public sectors, but especially in the latter.[24] A third of the nation's employed people worked in jobs for which the government was either the direct or indirect employer, including the armed forces, teachers, employees of municipalities and local authorities, the Jewish Agency,

18 H. Barkai, *The Cost of Security from a Retrospective Outlook* (Jerusalem: The Falk Institute, 1980), table 3; D. Kokhav, "Security costs and their impact on the Israeli economy," *Maarakhot*, 287 (1983), table 3 (in Hebrew).

19 This measure estimates only the direct share of the government, not the weight of Histadrut or the national institutions.

20 *Statistical Abstract of Israel, 1985*, p. 176.

21 Barkai, *The Cost of Security from a Retrospective Outlook*, table 2.

22 Kokhav, "Security costs and their impact," table 4.

23 *National Accounts Statistics: Analysis of Main Aggregates, 1985* (New York: United Nations, 1988), pp. 231, 234.

24 See H. Pack, *Structural Change and Economic Policy in Israel* (New Haven, CN: Yale University Press, 1971), p. 162; and *Statistical Abstracts of Israel* for 1968, 1969, 1978, and 1983.

workers of government corporations, the Histadrut's sick fund, and civil servants. In addition, the salaries of many workers (such as the 30,000 workers in the Histadrut's Koor) were influenced by the national wage agreement.[25] This makes the Israeli economy somewhat immune to the fluctuations of the international economic system that affect most of the industrialized world, but dependent on the ability of its leaders to procure the revenues needed to maintain the public budget.

The Histadrut network provides much of the explanation of the Israel Labor Party's early success and institutionalization; political control over the market was established and maintained through its enterprises; it deserves credit for Labor's persistence near power during the period since 1977; but it must also be seen as part of the explanation of Labor's decline.

The Histadrut has been the major continuous power base of Labor and, as such, it has symbolized Labor as "Establishment." Despite being out of power or sharing it with the Likud for the last dozen years, this "Establishment" image is prevalent, especially among the Israel-born voters of Sephardi background who associate it with the difficult (and some say discriminatory) practices which their parents endured when they arrived in Israel forty years ago.[26]

The structure of the Histadrut had changed little since the pre-state years, although there were instances of activities being transferred to or transformed by the state. The Histadrut's economic activities were historically significant because it was willing to pioneer in sectors that would not attract capitalist investors. Since the ideology was to develop the economic basis of the homeland and to create a class of Jewish workers in the land of Israel, the Histadrut was often prepared to take economic risks.

Histadrut enterprises manufactured about 20 percent of the GNP in 1988, employed a little more than 20 percent of the labor force, and owned about 10 percent of the national economy.[27] The Histadrut's role in the economy included its large bureaucracy which oversaw the work of its executive committee, workers councils, trade unions, *Davar* (the Histadrut's newspaper), and the social welfare activities, the pension plans, and the sick fund;[28] its economic enterprises, including industrial, commercial, building, banking, and insurance; cooperatives including department stores, supermarkets, and food suppliers;[29] and the cooperat-

---

25 *Statistical Abstract of Israel, 1985*, pp. 330–1. On the workers' enterprise as a labor-intensive employer, see I. Barzilai, "Weight of the workers' enterprises in the national economy," *Economic Quarterly*, 20 (1974), p. 141 (in Hebrew).

26 Arian, *Politics in Israel*, p. 153.

27 Y. Aharoni, *Structure and Behavior in the Israeli Economy* (Tel Aviv: Tcherikover, 1976), pp. 213–14.

28 The sick fund alone employs about 30,000 people and is a major consumer of medical supplies and other commodities.

29 In 1980, Tnuva supplied two-thirds of the country's fresh agricultural produce. In all, the agricultural sector affiliated with the Histadrut produces 84 percent of Israel's produce.

ive kibbutz and moshav movements, and other cooperative ventures.[30] Histadrut control over its members extended to many spheres of life: among its activities, the Histadrut had publishing houses, sports associations, libraries, an autonomous school system, and teachers' seminars.

Membership in the union was very broad: the Histadrut's 1.5 million members comprised more than 80 percent of the employed working force of the country and three-quarters of the Knesset electorate. Until the 1960s, parties that competed were workers parties or lists that did not reject socialist ideals. Since the 1966 Histadrut elections, however, the anti-socialist Likud (then called Gahal) also competed in Histadrut elections, i.e. most of the parties that compete in the Knesset elections, with the important exception of the major religious parties, also compete in the Histadrut elections. The Histadrut elections have increasingly been seen as a mid-term national election.

The Histadrut member voted many times: (a) in the national convention, (b) for the workers council for the city or region, (c) for the trade union council in craft or profession, and (d) for the workers committee at his/her workplace. Women also voted for *Naamat*, a women's workers council. The national convention and workers councils were elected using a proportional representation fixed-list system similar to that used to elect the Israeli parliament.[31] The elections for the convention were based on a single national constituency, and that was usually the case with the trade unions. Some of the national trade unions and most of the workers committees, however, were elected on a plurality basis. The latter system promoted the election of visible and popular leaders; the former system retained the processes of selection and promotion in the hands of the labor establishment. A clear sign of the growing disparity between the labor leadership and the rank and file was the different compositions of the leadership elected by the different types of elections. The national lists of convention and council tended, until the mid-1980s, to retain in power older Ashkenazi leaders, while the plurality votes of the workers committees tended to place younger and increasingly Sephardi leadership in the spotlight.

The hierarchical structure of the Histadrut and the control of this structure by Labor Party leaders were major explanations for the

---

30 Cooperative enterprises employed some 21,000 workers, but less than 10,000 of them were members of cooperatives. Difficult ideological problems are faced because the norm is against exploiting hired labor. Egged and Dan, for instance, transportation cooperatives that account for 80 percent of the country's passenger movement, are periodically plagued with tensions between drivers who are cooperative members and drivers who are salaried employees. Another example is the eleven regional enterprises set up by the major kibbutz movement: of the 6,000 workers, 1,200 are kibbutz members.

31 In Knesset elections, the minimum percentage needed to win representation is 1 percent; for the Histadrut national convention, the minimum has been 2 percent since the 1981 elections. In 1977 it was 1 percent, and before that time no minimum was required.

continued dominance of the establishment elite and the conservative image of the Histadrut in the public mind.[32] While more dynamic and younger leadership emerged in the workers committees, this was less likely to happen in the national bodies and the important workers councils. The power of the leaders at the national level rested in their ability to nominate. The closer to power, the more likely they were to call for list elections in all the Histadrut elections.[33]

In the elections to the national convention, the Labor Party (now the Labor–Mapam Alignment list) had always won an absolute majority (see table 8.1). Control of the Histadrut was a central lever of Labor control over the economy, patronage, and power. This was especially obvious in the years before 1977 when the Labor Party was always in control of the government. Its leadership then enjoyed a great deal of power in preventing developments deemed undesirable.[34] The leadership was able to structure power relations in the society; thus, the opposition and newcomers to the system could not mount sustained political resistance.[35]

Through the Histadrut, the Labor Party enjoyed a central position in managing and mediating demands for wage increases. The collective bargaining process was more cooperative than conflictual.[36] But its long history and the high visibility of Labor officials in shaping economic and social policy reaffirmed its image as the Establishment and it became a natural target for channeling feelings of frustration.

The economic and service institutions of the Histadrut, weighted down by enormous deficits, were seen by some Labor activists in 1988 as an economic burden rather than an ideological imperative or a political boon. While unlikely to abandon this power base, Labor was challenged to rejuvenate this labor bastion for its own sake, the sake of the party, and (not incidentally) the sake of the nation and its economy.

The intimate relations which the Histadrut and the government developed regarding economic matters and regarding the provision of

32   S. Bahat, "Structural relations between trade unions and labor parties – a comparative study" (Hebrew), M. A. Thesis, Department of Labor Studies, Tel Aviv University, 1979.
33   In an interview with Israel Kaisar, the Secretary-General of the Histadrut argued in favor of more national control over the selection of the heads of local and regional workers councils. Tel Aviv, October 29, 1988.
34   Arian, *Politics in Israel*, pp. 28–34.
35   P. Bachrach and M. S. Baratz, "Two faces of power," *American Political Science Review*, 56 (1962), pp. 947–52. On power as a structural phenomenon see S. Lukes, *Power: A Radical View* (London: Macmillan, 1975).
36   A. Arian, *Political and Administrative Aspects of Welfare Policy in Israel* (Tel Aviv: Institute for Social and Labor Research, 1978); Y. Reshef, "Political exchange in Israel: Histadrut–state relations," *Industrial Relations*, 25, 3 (Fall, 1986), pp. 303–19; E. Kleiman, "The Histadrut economy of Israel," *Jerusalem Quarterly*, 41 (Winter 1987), pp. 77–94.

services blurred the lines between the labor union sector and the governmental sector in the public mind. The Histadrut, after all, was a major employer and was the major provider of health care in the country.[37] As the industrial enterprises continued to accrue enormous debt in the 1970s and the 1980s, the attendant fear of unemployment grew. And as the health services increasingly deteriorated, mostly because of budgetary limitations, it was natural to point an accusing finger at the Histadrut.

The Labor Party in 1988 was faced with a twofold struggle: it had to secure government funds, credits, and guarantees for its over-extended industries, cooperatives, and service providers. Only then would it be in a position to again use the Histadrut as a vehicle to regain political power. The wheel had turned. For forty years, Labor wielded political power by controlling the economy; in 1988, its hope was to restructure the economy (Peres called it "growth") in a way which would save the economic future of the Histadrut and the political future of the Labor Party.

As Labor leaders were increasingly voted out of national roles, they eclipsed the union elite by taking over positions recently dominated by the Histadrut leadership. Thus, the Labor Knesset list in 1988 was comparatively weak in leaders of the Histadrut. Three Histadrut activists who were members of the outgoing Knesset were not replaced by others.[38] In addition, the 1988 Labor election campaign largely kept the Histadrut leadership from the Labor television commercials and from public view. In light of all this, it was not surprising that the huge reservoir of personnel and vehicles which the Histadrut institutions controlled were employed during the campaign in an uninspired manner.

Ethnic Voters and Status Politics

In the new community being built in the land of Israel, there was no bourgeoisie against which to fight. Most of the early immigrants and their leaders came from Eastern Europe and were petit-bourgeois in their origins.[39] More to the point, the immigrants came to the land of Israel in successive waves. Each wave elevated the previous wave in the social system. The expanded bureaucracies of the Jewish community absorbed a great many of the new immigrants and created a wide

---

37   Arian, *Politics in Israel*, pp. 229–32.
38   Specifically, Amir, Hacohen, and Harel. Related in an interview with Labor Party activist Shmuel Bahat, interviewed in Tel Aviv, November 4, 1988.
39   M. Roshwald, "Political parties and social class in Israel," *Social Research*, 23 (1956), pp. 199–218.

"service class,"[40] peopled mainly by Ashkenazim providing services to everyone else and, especially after Independence, to the Sephardim.

As new immigrants, absorbed by the machine–party–organization which characterized the dominant-party system, the plurality of Sephardi voters who arrived after Independence supported the Labor Party. By the 1960s, however, many Sephardim shifted their support to the right-wing parties, in particular to Herut, the hawkish and pro-capitalist party.[41] This trend revealed an interesting paradox: the Sephardim, who suffered from an inferior standing in the stratification system, voted for a capitalist list, while the veteran Ashkenazim, who enjoyed a relatively advantageous social position, voted more heavily for the "workers party."

Sephardim today make up about 60 percent of Israel's Jewish population, and the Ashkenazim about 40 percent. But because the family size and the average age of these groups differ, the proportion of the groups in the electorate generates distinct patterns. In 1988, Ashkenazim and Sephardim were of roughly equal size in the electorate. Table 8.2 presents further information about them, their development since 1969, and their electoral impact.

European- or American-born voters and their Israel-born children constituted a majority of the electorate in 1969, but by 1988 they had the potential for electing the same number of Knesset members as the Asian and African voters and their Israel-born voting children – forty-seven for each group. The shrinking of the Ashkenazi base is evident compared with their potential in the 1969 elections: fifty-nine for the Ashkenazim, forty-three for the Sephardim. Moreover, those of Sephardi background have a larger voting reserve as measured by children who have not yet reached voting age. Their potential will be realized when their children who are under voting age (47.6 percent for the Israel-born children of Asian and African background, 37.1 percent for the Israel-born children of European and American background) begin voting and when the Ashkenazim, who tend to be older and who have fewer children, make up an increasingly larger share of the electorate.

It is more helpful to think of Israeli politics as parties striving to recruit voters in terms of their policy positions, party identifications, and

40 On the definition and the social and political consequences of the service class, see R. Dahrendorf, "The service class," in *Industrial Man*, ed. T. B. Harmonsworth (London: Penguin, 1969), pp. 140–50; for a general overview see N. Abercrombie and J. Urry, *Capital, Labour and the Middle Classes*, Controversies in Sociology, vol. 15 (London: Allen & Unwin, 1983). A comparative approach to the relations between the state and the class and its formation is in J. Kocka, *White Collar Workers in America: 1890–1940* (London: Sage, 1980).
41 In 1965 Herut and the Liberal Party formed a joint list. The Liberals were for a free economy and stressed the role of individual entrepreneurship. This act increased the legitimacy of the stigmatized Herut. In 1967, the inclusion of Herut in the first National Unity coalition widened its legitimation.

Table 8.2   Voting potential of the Jewish population in Israel, by place of birth, 1969 and 1988

	Percent in population		*Percent under 18*		*Knesset seats*[a]	
	1967	*1986*	*1969*	*1986*	*1969*	*1988*
Israel-born; father Israel-born	6.5	19.5	62.3	74.7	4	8
Israel-born; father Asia- or Africa-born	18.7	25.7	81.6	47.6	5	22
Israel-born; father Europe- or America-born	16.4	16.2	49.1	37.1	13	16
Asia- or Africa-born	27.8	17.2	11.5	2.4	38	27
Europe- or America-born	30.6	21.4	3.6	5.8	46	33
Total	2,344,877	3,561,400	31.6%	34.1%	106	106

[a] Assuming 80 percent participation; 12,000 votes per seat in 1969; 17,600 votes per seat in 1988.
Source: *Statistical Abstract of Israel, 1969*, pp. 42–3; *Statistical Abstract of Israel, 1987*, pp. 73–5.

ethnic affiliations, rather than in terms of their class membership. In Weber's sense, both Likud and Labor represent "mixed types" of parties,[42] because the parties represent status group interests even though the rhetoric of the parties is in a sense class oriented.[43]

The gap between the rhetoric and reality has enabled the Likud to appear as a "free market" and welfare state proponent representing

42   M. Weber, *Economy and Society*, ed. G. Roth and C. Wittich (Berkeley, CA: University of California Press, 1968), vol. 1, pp. 302–7; vol. 2, pp. 926–40.
43   The Likud is more inclined to capitalism and Labor to socialism. Nonetheless, issues such as the nature of the welfare state and other economic issues are simply not part of the political debate. See Talmud, " 'Between politics and economy.' "
   The connection between left-right position and attitude regarding specific policy issues is weak. However, differences are more apparent regarding security and foreign affairs issues. See A. Arian and M. Shamir, "The primarily political functions of left–right continuum," *Comparative Politics* (January 1983), pp. 135–58.

independent lower status groups and liberated from the control of the
Labor Party. Israeli electoral politics is best understood in terms of the
political action of groups attempting to achieve prestige or control within
the society for its distinctive lifestyle, symbols, and culture.[44] Thus
the dominant Ashkenazim, fearing that their position is threatened,
have attempted to employ exclusionary practices against Sephardi
contenders.[45] This is a much more relevant understanding of politics in
Israel than a notion of class politics, wherein organized class interests
are articulated through the party system.

While there are those who conceive of class and ethnicity as
synonymous,[46] we conceptualize class and status (in terms of ethnicity)
as two analytically different aspects of social stratification which may
empirically coincide.[47] This distinction allows us (a) to differentiate
between material bases and cultural manifestations of social control and
(b) to link electoral behavior and organizational control in Israel.[48]
Scrutinizing the group identification of the Israeli electorate, it is clear

44   A good example of a study of status politics is J. R. Gusfield, *Moral Crusade:
Status Politics and the American Temperance Movement* (Urbana, IL: University of
Illinois Press, 1968). For other studies employing the concept, see W. Scott,
"The Equal Right Amendment as a status politics," *Social Forces*, 64, 2 (Decem-
ber 1985), pp. 499–506; C. H. Harper and K. Leich, "Religious awakening and
status politics," *Sociological Analysis*, 45, 4 (Winter 1984), pp. 339–53; M. Moen,
"School prayer and the politics of life-style concern," *Social Science Quarterly*, 65, 4
(December 1984), pp. 1065–71; A. Zuckerman and M. I. Lichbach, "Stability
and change in European electorates," *World Politics*, 29 (1977), pp. 523–51; A.
Zuckerman, *The Politics of Fraction: Christian Democratic Rule in Italy* (New Haven,
CT: Yale University Press, 1979).
45   See N. Elias, *The History of the Manners*, vol. 1, *The Civilizing Process* (New
York: Pantheon, 1978); A. de Tocqueville, *Democracy in America* (New York:
Mentor Books, 1956), pp. 26–38, and *The Old Regime and the French Revolution*
(New York: Doubleday, 1955), pp. vii–xv; on status politics outside the political
sphere see M. Regev, "The musical soundscape as a contest area: 'Oriental
music' and Israeli popular music," *Media, Culture and Society*, 8 (1986),
pp. 343–55.
46   M. Hechter, *Internal Colonialism: The Celtic Fringe in British National Development, 1536–1966* (London: Routledge & Kegan Paul, 1975).
47   See R. Norton, "Ethnicity and class: a conceptual note with reference to the
politics of the post-colonial societies," *Ethnic and Racial Studies*, 7, 3 (July 1984),
pp. 426–34. See also W. J. Wilson, *The Declining Significance of Race* (Chicago, IL:
University of Chicago Press, 1980); N. Danigelis, "Race, class and political
involvement in the U.S.," *Social Forces*, 61, 2 (December 1981), pp. 532–50.
48   See P. Cohen, "Ethnicity, class and political alignment in Israel," *Jewish
Journal of Sociology*, 25, 2 (December 1983), pp. 119–30; Y. Yishai, "Israel's
right-wing proletariat," in *Politics and Society in Israel*, ed. E. Krauz (New Brunswick, NJ: Transaction 1985), ch. 12; M. Hechter, "The political economy of
ethnic change," *American Journal of Sociology*, 79, 5 (March 1974), pp. 1151–78.

that ethnicity is an independent and nonspurious variable, although correlated with social position.[49]

Labor and Likud voting is weakly correlated with class, but each party clearly represents the interests of different status groups. More nearly coinciding with reality, it is useful to think of Labor and Likud as ethnic parties. The first mobilizes the dominant Ashkenazim and the latter the emergent Sephardim. In 1984, Labor was more ethnic than the Likud;[50] in 1988, each respective ethnic group (the Ashkenazim for Labor, the Sephardim for the Likud) contributed about two-thirds of the votes for the two parties.

Our hypothesis is that in the Israeli case there is a very weak association between class structure and party vote, and a much stronger connection between status group (or class disposition or ethnic affiliation) and party vote. We can test this hypothesis by examining election surveys conducted over the years and, on the one hand, studying the relationship between vote for Likud or Labor and class when controlling for ethnicity and, on the other, assessing the affinity between vote and ethnicity while controlling for class.

This examination is presented in table 8.3. Using analysis of variance (ANOVA), we test the hypothesis that the group means of the dependent variable are equal. In this case, we test, for example, whether respondents who identify themselves as workers have the same mean scores of voting (a) Labor and (b) Likud regardless of whether they are Ashkenazi or Sephardi; similarly we check the vote score by ethnic group, controlling for class.

It is evident from table 8.3 that in Israel the importance of ethnicity is much greater than that of class.[51] Furthermore, for each point of examination, there is a strong effect of ethnicity on the vote. Class identification plays a role in the Israeli political system, but a very limited one. Comparing the η coefficients over time indicates that the association

49 E. Cohen, "Ethnicity and legitimation in Israel," in *Politics and Society in Israel*, ed. E. Krauz (New Brunswick, NJ: Transaction, 1985), ch. 15; S. Deshen, "'The business of ethnicity is finished!'?: the ethnic factor in a local election campaign," in *The Elections in Israel – 1969*, ed. A. Arian (Jerusalem: Jerusalem Academic Press, 1972), pp. 278–302; S. Deshen, "On signs and symbols: the transformation of designations in Israeli electioneering," *Political Anthropology*, 1 (1976), pp. 83–100; E. B. Rafael, *The Emergence of Ethnicity in Israel: Cultural Groups and Social Conflict in Israel* (London: Greenwood Press, 1985). See also C. Ragin, "Class, status and 'Reactive ethnic cleavages': the social bases of political regionalism," *American Sociological Review*, 42, 2 (1977), pp. 438–50.

50 Ethnicity and class indicators are not strongly correlated in Israel. See M. Shamir and A. Arian, "The ethnic vote in Israel's 1981 elections," *Electoral Studies*, 1 (1982), pp. 315–31. See also Y. Peres and S. Shemer, "The ethnic factor in the 10th Knesset elections," *Megamot*, 28 (1984), pp. 316–31 (in Hebrew).

51 This is seen by comparing the *F* ratios within each year.

Table 8.3   Class and ethnicity by two-party vote: analysis of variance
with main effects reported

| | | F critical value | | η coefficient | |
| | | Class | Ethnicity | Class | Ethnicity |
Date	N	(df = 3)	(df = 2)	(df = 3)	(df = 2)
Sept 1969	664	0.808	8.183**	0.05	0.15
Oct 1969	944	7.919**	25.118**	0.14	0.22
May 1973	1044	n.a.	9.509**	n.a.	0.13
Mar 1977	569	2.315	30.870**	0.11	0.31
Mar 1981	747	0.758	20.044**	0.07	0.23
Apr 1981	554	0.919	38.234**	0.07	0.35
Jun 1981	769	2.157	30.470**	0.11	0.28
Jul 1984	730	0.845	118.866**	0.06	0.50
Jan 1986	626	2.236	31.954**	0.15	0.32
Dec 1987	589	3.226*	31.851**	0.14	0.32
Jun 1988	631	n.a.	67.470**	n.a.	0.42

*, $p < 0.05$; **, $p < 0.001$.
n.a., unavailability of the question in that sample; df, degrees of freedom.

between vote and ethnicity is high and consistent; the relationship between vote and class is much lower and much less stable. This is clear
evidence of the "unawareness" class as such; ethnic identification is
prominent and growing over the years – in short status politics, and not
class politics.[52]

Ethnicity and economic control are joined in a fascinating manner in
the Israeli case. The high levels of economic concentration and the role
of the bureaucracy made the influence of political actors inevitable at all
levels of the economic system.[53] In such a controlled system, mobility
was often dependent on one's contacts or background. Accordingly,
alternative routes of social mobility led through sectors less controlled by
the State, such as the small private sector. Per capita income, for
example, grew over the years, but income differential between the veteran Ashkenazi and the newcomer Sephardi groups also widened. As a

[52]   The patterns held for Histadrut employees as well. In 1981, in the period
before the election, a sample was drawn from a list of employees provided by
Hevrat Ovdim, the Histadrut holding company. The sampling and interviewing
were conducted in July 1984 by the PORI Research Institute. Only the *F* test for
ethnicity was statistically significant. In addition, the η coefficient for ethnicity
was high (0.33), in contrast with the negligible η coefficient of class (0.02).
[53]   Y. Aharoni, *Structure and Behavior in the Israeli Economy* (Tel Aviv: Tcherikover, 1976), pp. 213–14 (in Hebrew).

result, a sense of relative deprivation arose among the less-advantaged group.[54] This increasing gap was an outcome of different modes of accumulation between the advantaged and the disadvantaged and increased the original advantage of the Ashkenazim in relative terms: the gap is explained in terms of different levels of education, differential networking in the labor market (especially among employees), and differential occupational opportunity structures associated with geographic location (center versus periphery).[55] Moreover, since 1969, the number of noncitizen Arabs (from the territories) in the labor force has tripled, from about 2.5 percent to about 8 percent. This process contributed to an improvement in the position of the Sephardi workers, but in relative terms the Ashkenazi groups gained even more.[56]

Labor's previous ability to coopt Sephardi parties and activists became less and less successful.[57] Sephardim, because of their growing numbers, have made their sense of relative deprivation electorally effective. The patterns of symbolic domination, status politics, and patterns of economic control, so tightly linked in the early decade of statehood, broke down because the Likud emerged as a viable political alternative. Among the self-employed, moreover, the average income of the Sephardim was *higher* than that of the Ashkenazi group. Nonetheless, the Sephardim tended to fill *lower* prestige occupations and hence this "alternative route of social mobility" was partial at best.[58] On the other hand, Sephardim were more exposed to employment instability.[59] Hence, the bureaucratic control of the Labor Party, as the party of the bureaucratic middle class, was challenged by both "new winners" and the "new losers" of the occupational changes in Israel.[60]

54   See R. Williams, "Relative deprivation," in *The Idea of Social Structure*, ed. L. Coser (New York: Harcourt Brace Jovanovich, 1975), pp. 355–78; J. Urry, *Reference Groups and the Theory of Revolution* (London: Routledge & Kegan Paul, 1973).

55   Y. Nahon, *Patterns of Educational Expansion and the Structure of Occupational Opportunities – the Ethnic Dimension* (Jerusalem: Jerusalem Institute for Israeli Research, 1987), pp. 61–80 (in Hebrew).

56   M. Semyonov and N. Levin-Epstein, *Hewers of Wood and the Drawers of Water: Noncitizen Arabs in the Israeli Labor Market* (Ithaca, NY: Institute for Labor Relations Press, 1987).

57   H. Herzog, *The Ethnic Lists to The Israeli Kennest* (Tel Aviv: Am Oved, 1983) (in Hebrew).

58   But it does not occur at random. In 1961, the Ashkenazi controlled the self-employed sector, but by 1983 the ethnic share of this sector was equal. See Y. Nahon, *Self Employed Workers: The Ethnic Dimension*, Research Paper 30 (Jerusalem: Jerusalem Institute for Israeli Studies, 1989) (in Hebrew).

59   See V. Lavy, *Unemployment in Israel's Developing Towns*, Research Paper 29 (Jerusalem: Jerusalem Institute for Israeli Studies, 1989) (in Hebrew).

60   E. Yuchtman-Yaar, "Differences in ethnic patterns of socioeconomic achievement: a neglected aspect of structured inequality," *International Review of Modern Sociology*, 15 (1985), pp. 99–116.

A Political Alternative

The analysis to this point has focused on the Labor Party. But since electoral strength is the result of interaction in a political situation, the alternative to the Labor Party must also be considered. Put differently, there must be a political force poised to take advantage of a faltering dominant party.

This vacuum was filled by the Likud led by Menachem Begin. After running eight times unsuccessfully, the party finally emerged victorious in 1977. The failure of preparedness in 1973, the crisis of leadership within Labor, evidence of corruption, the successful emergence of an upstart party (the Democratic Movement for Change) which siphoned off many Labor votes, and the emergence of a young and growing electorate angered by the style of Labor's immigrant absorption policies applied to the Sephardi waves of immigrants all fueled the fall. But these developments also coincided with a major reassessment within the electorate.[61]

The emerging outlook was one which had a curious mix of nationalist and religious symbolism, on the one hand, and rational and professional considerations on the other. Deep-seated beliefs about the nature and destiny of Israel and the Jewish people were core beliefs for many Israelis. There emerged a basic coexistence between a rational model of security policy which posited predictable relations between means and ends, on the one hand, and mystic beliefs which denied basic tenets of instrumental rationality, on the other. Israelis seemed to be successful in blending these two kinds of beliefs.[62]

The Likud was more successful in representing these viewpoints than was the more moderate, more pragmatic Labor Party. Moreover, by agreeing to participate with the Likud in a national unity government for seven of the last twenty-one years (until 1989), Labor was further weakened. It could not promote a clear definition of itself, except for the short period before elections. But having the government on hold did not prevent change in Israel. By forging a minimal common denominator, the unity government defined the consensus of the middle. After the 1984

61 For other treatments, see A. Gonen, "A geographical analysis of the elections in Jewish urban communities," in *The Roots of Begin's Success: The 1981 Israeli Elections*, ed. E. Guttman, D. Caspi, and A. Diskin (New York: St Martin's Press, 1984), pp. 59–87; A. Arian, "Competitiveness and polarization: elections 1981," *Jerusalem Quarterly* (1983), pp. 139–58; M. Shamir, "Realignment in the Israeli party system," in *The Elections in Israel – 1984*, ed. A. Arian and M. Shamir (New Brunswick, NJ: Transaction, 1986), pp. 267–96; Y. Shapiro, "Political sociology in Israel: a critical view," in *Politics and Society In Israel*, ed. E. Krauz (New Brunswick, NJ: Transaction, 1985), pp. 6–16.
62 A. Arian, I. Talmud, and T. Hermann, *National Security and Public Opinion in Israel* (Boulder, CO: Westview Press, 1988), ch. 4.

elections, the army withdrew from Lebanon, inflation was controlled,[63] and the Lavi project was abandoned, all by joint agreement. But beyond that, the symmetry broke down in favor of the Right. In the areas of foreign policy (such as willingness to talk with the Palestine Liberation Organization or to conceive of transforming the territories they were ready to cede into a state) and in the support they agreed to give to the settlements in the territories, Labor accepted mild versions of the Likud platform.

The 1988 elections reinforced these conclusions and witnessed the further slide of the Labor vote. The data in table 8.4 testify to the inability of the Labor Party to penetrate the demographic groups which are growing most quickly. Table 8.4 presents the results of a survey conducted in the last weeks of October 1988, days before the election. Respondents were asked to choose between Labor and Likud in terms of their effectiveness in dealing with three policy issues – the economy, negotiations with the Arabs, and the intifada (Arab uprising against Israeli occupation). The results show that, with regard to the economy, Labor had a slight edge; but in the other policy areas the Likud was favored. Moreover, Labor's clear advantage was among that segment of its supporters which was shrinking fastest, the European-born over the age of 30. Notice that the assessment that Labor was better able to deal with the problems was strong within that group regardless of the religious observance of the respondents. Among their Israel-born children, however, Labor was assessed as better only among the secular. The Israel-born of Ashkenazi background who were religious gave the Likud higher marks.

The reverse pattern was not symmetrical. The Likud was highly preferred by the Asian- and African-born, and much more so by those who were religious, although seculars also favored the Likud. For their children who were born in Israel, the pattern persisted: the Likud was preferred, regardless of religiosity, although the secular were more moderate in their support for the Likud. Labor did not have majority support from the fastest growing group (the Israel-born Sephardim). From its traditional constituency (Israel-born Ashkenazim), Labor managed to retain the support only of the secular.

Labor has been unable to generate the remarkable leadership which it provided during the early decades of statehood. That leadership led the nation to historic feats which in turn have posed grave problems for the state. The accomplishments of Labor and its organizational structures have had perverse consequences for the Labor establishment. While Labor perfected the organizational mediation which allowed it to control the economy and the society, its leadership extracted resources for the party's institutions. The visibility of this action has been growing, and this leads to an inevitable contradiction in the political goals of the

63   H. Barkai, "Israel's attempt at economic stabilization," *Jerusalem Quarterly* (Summer 1987), pp. 3–20.

Asher Arian and Ilan Talmud

Table 8.4   Assessment of party effectiveness for major groups,[a] by place of birth, age, and religiosity[b]: percentage who think, can better deal with, . . . [c]

	N	Economy		Negotiations with the Arabs		Intifada	
		Likud	Labor	Likud	Labor	Likud	Labor
AA/-50/rel	(95)	61	15	72	18	75	6
AA/-50/sec	(73)	40	38	47	43	56	26
Eur/+30/rel	(84)	29	46	31	43	40	40
Eur/+30/sec	(169)	29	48	25	59	28	49
Is-AA/-50/rel	(144)	59	23	65	20	74	15
Is-AA/-50/sec	(112)	46	37	53	37	55	28
Is-Eur/-50/rel	(45)	46	26	67	22	63	20
Is-Eur/-50/sec	(153)	16	61	21	68	26	60
Is-Is/-50/sec	(91)	28	52	26	62	31	52
Total	(966)	39	40	47	35	42	42

[a] Based on a national survey conducted by the Dahaf Research Institute during the last week of October 1988. The groups reported here comprise 966 of the 1,166 respondents, or 82.8 percent of the sample.
[b] Place of birth: AA, Asia–Africa born; Eur, Europe–America born; Is-AA, Israel born, father Asia–Africa born; Is-Eur, Israel born, father Europe–America born; Is-Is, Israel born, father Israel born. Age: −50, below 50; +30, above 30. Religiosity: rel, religious and traditional; sec, secular.
[c] The difference between the sum of the two percentages for each group and 100 is the percentage of respondents who responded that neither party would be better than the other in handling the problem. For example, 61 percent of the first group thought the Likud would handle the economy best, 15 percent thought Labor would, and 24 percent (100 − (61 + 15)) thought there would be no difference between the two parties.

leadership. They must maintain the party's institutions and patronage from which its original strength came, but by so doing they have alienated themselves from growing segments of the population.

This dilemma must be faced by the Labor Party leadership during a period in which the Israeli economy strives for renewed growth and when the implications of Israel's extended military commitment in the region and in the territories make the situation more dire. Living in a psychological atmosphere of constant threat and perceived insecurity has been an important unifying dimension among Israel's Jews and has been a major factor in the leadership's ability to rule. During the early years, the halo effect of effective national leadership accrued to the Labor Party. But more recently, the public seems to have adopted the position that it is the Likud which has the ability to lead the nation in both war and peace.[64]

In addition to the inherent contradiction between the Labor's rhetoric and praxis in domestic policy, the party has faced a similar discrepancy in security and foreign affairs. The Labor movement incorporated nationalism with social democracy, lenient diplomacy with the belief that deeds are more important than words in national confrontation, humanistic ideology with tough security postures. These dual messages of Labor have put the Likud in a better position to capitalize on feelings of fear and discontent.

The impact on domestic alignments of living under protracted tension has been to give the Likud an asymmetric advantage. In reality, there has been a great deal more consensus than real conflict in Israel regarding policy toward the territories and the Arab states. Similarly, consensus is the rule regarding productive and distributional arrangements in the country. Yet, the atmosphere of Israeli politics is confrontational, and in this struggle, at this moment in time, the Likud is better equipped to display the type of flexibility which can be translated into political success.

Conclusion

The Labor Party established and refined most features of Israel's political economy. It fashioned mechanisms for recruiting the support of substantial parts of the electorate. The social and economic choices which Labor made meant excluding increasing groups of the electorate while favoring its veteran elements. The rival Likud adopted the rhetoric of the welfare state while retaining economic control at the political level. This is what Labor had done before, but now the Likud was dealing with the growing sectors of the electorate. The Likud adopted patterns of symbolic expression regarding the state of permanent security tension which were consonant with the fears and anxieties of the population. Labor was not successful in regaining momentum. Labor could not abandon its past, nor could it regain its future.

---

64   See Arian, Talmud and Hermann, *National Security and Public Opinion in Israel*.

9

Facing Economic Restructuring and Constitutional Renewal: Social Democracy Adrift in Canada

Neil Bradford and Jane Jenson

Introduction: The 1988 Election as Precipitant

The election of November 1988 was a crucial decision point for Canadian society. It unveiled the difficulties of the federal New Democratic Party (NDP) at the same time as it revealed a new expression of popular power in a coalition of social movements and interests, including unions, the organized women's movement, churches, nationalists, and intellectuals. This coalition led a consistent assault against the Free Trade Agreement (FTA), which emerged as the single issue of the election. The Canadian Left – incorporating this popular coalition, the NDP, and parts of the Liberal Party – castigated the "deal" as the mechanism by which the Progressive Conservative government was importing a neo-liberal, anti-welfare state, anti-labor response to economic restructuring. Forces opposed to the FTA argued that, in the guise of responding to the necessities of international economic trends generally and American protectionism particularly, the partisan Right and Canadian business were actually pursuing a broad-based assault on the traditions of Canada's "exceptionalism" in North America: that is, its long-standing acceptance of state intervention, higher levels of state spending than in the United States on social programs such as universal health care

Support for this work came in part from the Center for International Affairs, Harvard University and the Social Science and Humanities Research Council of Canada.

and pensions, and labor legislation somewhat more supportive of collective bargaining rights and the labor movement.

With an unprecedented level of activity from corporations and business organizations on the side of the FTA, the election took on an unfamiliar cast. Not only did it focus on an important issue – instead of the usual talk of "leadership," "time for a change," or undebated economic proposals – but it also saw a massive mobilization of popular opinion and attention. Passions ran high. Eventually, 57 percent of the population voted against free trade. However, given the division of this vote between two parties and the distributional effects of the first-past-the-post electoral system rewarding regionally concentrated support, the government won a substantial majority and the FTA is now in place.

For the federal New Democrats this was an election which provoked much internal controversy. After four years of riding high in the polls– indeed appearing at times to be the second party (and, for a moment, the first) rather than the third that it had always been – their party plummeted to its customary distant third place. Moreover, during the campaign the NDP lost the high ground of opposition to free trade to the Liberals, while the Pro-Canada Network, which was an organizational expression of the popular coalition, emerged as a more visible representative of the anti-deal forces. Within days of the election, conflict erupted inside the NDP. Leaders of the labor movement (long the party's major financial backer as well as its link to the working class) launched blistering criticisms of the campaign strategy, faulting the NDP for its electoralist reluctance to develop economic alternatives. Critics claimed that this reluctance followed from a mistaken assumption that such discussion would reduce the NDP's electoral appeal. In addition, they were angered by what they saw as the party's unwillingness to address the fears of labor about free trade or to work with it in its highly motivated and mobilized coalition with the other social movements. Again, this reluctance to appear "too close" to labor arose from electoralist calculations.

Yet this internal conflict over the direction of the NDP and its place in Canadian society did not fall from the sky during and after the 1988 election campaign. It was simply another manifestation of the strategic dilemma of this social democratic party which has never succeeded in winning more than a fifth of the votes of the Canadian federal electorate (table 9.1). If the election precipitated conflict within the party and between the labor movement and the parliamentary wing, such fallout was only another example of the New Democrats' on-going difficulties.

The NDP's vulnerabilities in 1988, and the form which the internal conflict took, reflect the inability of the party to consolidate a strategic position representing an alternative to the "bourgeois" parties in the evolving debate over Canada's economic and constitutional future. The NDP has always been an important actor in such debates but it has not been able to provide or sustain a clear alternative to the formulations set out by other parties, social movements, and state managers.

Table 9.1 New Democratic Party election results in federal elections

Election year	Vote (%)	Seats/ Total
1962	14	19/265
1963	13	17/265
1965	18	21/265
1968	17	21/264
1972	18	31/264
1974	15	16/264
1979	18	26/282
1980	20	32/282
1984	19	30/282
1988	19	43/295

In this chapter we argue that the NDP's current troubles, and particularly the disputes over its strategy of *contentless populism* based on electoralism and parliamentarism, follow in part from the internal pluralism which has made any consistent response to economic restructuring and constitutional change very difficult for it to mount. The NDP's difficulties arise from the ways in which the two crucial dimensions of recent political conflict in Canada – constitutional and economic – cut into the internal alliance of the party. Evolving disputes around these two dimensions severely divide the fragile coalition which the federal NDP has always been.[1]

However, as an organization acting within a competitive party system, the NDP obviously responds to more than internal pluralism. Its strategic choices are also influenced by the behavior of the other parties – most evidently, the Liberals. At times the left-wing of the Liberal Party has succeeded in pulling that party quite close to positions of "right-wing social democracy" and the predicament of the NDP has been to distinguish itself from its main competitor.

Therefore, our explanation for the NDP's reliance on "contentless populism" proceeds by tracing the impact of electoral competition to demonstrate how the party's strategic choices over time have addressed both its own pluralistic currents and the external challenges arising from competition with the other parties. But all this occurred in a particular context. Political conflict in the postwar years has centered around disputes over regional economic power, continental trading relations, constitutional arrangements, and competing national identities.

1 For another discussion of the effects of internal pluralism on a divided Left, to which this analysis obviously owes some debts, see G. Ross and J. Jenson, "Pluralism and the decline of Left hegemony: the French Left in power," *Politics and Society*, 14, 2 (1985), pp. 147–83.

Canada's "Permeable Fordism": The Interlocking of Continentalism and Federalism

As in other countries Canada's postwar economy developed with high rates of economic growth based on the deep extension of mass production and consumption. Yet it had its particularities.[2] First, it was very *permeable* to international effects, responding to continental forces, exporting resources, and importing capital for both resource development and manufacturing. Second, a political compromise between capital and labor organized through the party system and/or tripartism, familiar in West European social democracies, did not characterize Canada. Instead, the Canadian union movement confined its militancy to workplace actions and appeared in everyday politics as just another lobby for concessions from the state, when its demands could not be extracted through collective bargaining. In the postwar years labor support for the social democratic Cooperative Commonwealth Federation (CCF) was weak and much disputed.[3]

A discourse of nation building was more important than that of class. The welfare state was the product of state-initiated policies rather than political exchange.[4] Therefore, new citizenship rights were not proclaimed. Keynesian programs grew out of the Depression era and wartime bureaucracies which saw the solution to the problems of the Canadian economy residing in a strong central government endowed with the will to intervene in the economy in a countercyclical fashion. The social compromises and institutionalized relationships of the Canadian welfare state were rationalized in terms of the needs of the federal system. Further, an economic discourse constructed around the exporting of staples more than mass production identified Canada's immense natural resources rather than its workers as the source of its economic greatness.

Although the Canadian economy expanded dramatically after 1945, it quickly exhibited the vulnerabilities which troubled its subsequent history. Reliance on relatively unprocessed natural resources as the leading sector, domestic manufacturing sustained in a branch-plant system, a high level of capital and goods imports, a state that spent comparatively

2 For the development of the notion of "permeable Fordism" see J. Jenson, " 'Different' but not 'exceptional': Canada's permeable Fordism," *Canadian Review of Sociology and Anthropology*, 26, 1 (1989).

3 The CCF transformed itself into the NDP in 1961. On the unions' postwar relationship with the CCF, see J. Brodie and J. Jenson, *Crisis, Challenge and Change: Party and Class in Canada Revisited* (Ottawa: Carleton University Press, 1988), pp. 227–45.

4 J. Myles, "Decline or impasse? The current state of the welfare state," *Studies in Political Economy*, 26 (1988).

little on social programs and left labor–management relations to the arena of private collective bargaining was an unstable mix.[5]

Keynesian-inspired macroeconomic policy tools were severely limited in a small, open economy with high levels of foreign ownership. Repatriation of profits and global strategies of multinational corporations meant that the Canadian economy never achieved the employment-creating or developmental possibilities of high growth levels. Moreover, Keynesian countercyclical spending did not overcome the profound structuring effects of a resource-based economy where prosperity was distributed largely by geographic lottery. Uneven regional development continued. In short, permeability called forth state strategies supplementing Keynesianism to alter regional disparities, to combat structural unemployment, and to maintain investment flows to balance outflows resulting from profit repatriation.

In these ways Canada's specificity almost guaranteed a politics centered on conflict over regional development strategies and continental integration. Indeed, an aspect of all economic policies quickly came to be intergovernmental battles stemming from disputes about resource ownership and control. The provinces had constitutional jurisdiction over resources but the federal government needed to shape the disposition of resources if it was to direct economic development. Moreover, an economic strategy of resource exporting provided space for provincial governments to pursue their own "province building" projects. Fluctuations

---

5 Canada's economy after 1945 marked the transition from the interwar dominance of agricultural exports to the new staples industries. Its shape was a consequence of deliberate state development strategies as well as trends in the international economy, which transformed Canadian capitalism's international connections. The state strategy emphasized exports, organized by multinational corporations, of the highly desirable resource staples; a commitment to the pursuit of more open international trade relations, especially through the General Agreement on Tariffs and Trade; an effort, albeit somewhat feeble, to maintain full employment through the use of macroeconomic fiscal mechanisms; and satisfaction of pent-up consumer demand through imports of manufactured goods or goods produced in Canada by American corporations investing in branch plants. This package has been termed the Second National Policy. See D. V. Smiley, *The Federal Condition in Canada* (Toronto: McGraw-Hill, 1987), p. 179. Any imbalances in trade which might result from goods imports were to be offset by the import of capital, for both the resource sector and consumer-goods manufacturing, and by the export of resources. Moreover, the Canadian state continued its century-long practice of underwriting the costly infrastructural requirements of the new staples. The Trans-Canada Highway, the Trans-Canada Pipeline, and the St Lawrence Seaway were all begun before 1955. See W. Clement, "Canada's social structure: capital, labour and the state, 1930–1982," in *Modern Canada: 1930–1980s*, ed. M. Cross and G. Keeley (Toronto: McClelland & Stewart, 1984); D. Wolfe, "The rise and demise of the Keynesian era in Canada: economic policy, 1930–1982," in *Modern Canada: 1930–1980's*, ed. Cross and Keeley; and C. Yates, "From plant to politics: the Canadian U.A.W., 1936–1984," Ph.D. thesis, Political Science, Carleton University, 1988.

in world prices for primary products further fragmented the Canadian economy, providing the mobilizational underpinnings for provincial challenges to the postwar "nation building" strategy.

Increasingly complicated federal–provincial relations were bound to result.[6] Not only was the regulation and management of resource industries a provincial responsibility, but labor relations and almost all areas of social spending for state welfare belonged constitutionally to the provinces, either exclusively or shared with the federal government. It followed, then, that federalism would become a pivotal arena of conflict.

Canadian politics from the mid-1960s until the present has been dominated by cultural and regional disputes which have focused on federalism as a distributive system. Provincial governments question the fairness of outcomes organized by the federal government. From the Royal Commission on Bilingualism and Biculturalism (1967) to the Royal Commission on Canada's Economic Union and Development Prospects (1985), the nation building discourse and strategy of the federal government has been disputed. Conflicts erupted over the identity of the nation, the costs and benefits of continued association in a single economic unit, and the self-definition of the nation in cultural terms. New actors contest the idea of a "single nation" and celebrate province-based loyalties. New political forms – cooperative federalism, executive federalism, regular federal–provincial conferences – have emerged as the decision making center of the state. As a result of the interconnection of economic development and constitutional responsibilities, then, the politics of economic crisis and restructuring also brings rethinking about national identities.

No federal political party has escaped the consequences of this dual crisis. Throughout the 1970s and 1980s the NDP faced the familiar problems of social democracy everywhere – accusations of statism, disputes over the role of labor and new social movements, the frustrating inability to find a replacement for Keynesianism. In addition the party staggered in the face of internal conflicts as it responded to the politics of constitutional renewal and continental economic restructuring. Its internal coalition has disintegrated, while it has also lost its ability clearly to distinguish itself from the Liberals. Unable to arrive at a coherent

---

6 The first crack appeared in the 1960s when the Quebec government, led by its strategy of *maîtres chez nous*, insisted on that province's right to implement an interventionist development strategy based on resource expansion to drive industrialization. But, it also required that the province gain control over the basic instruments of the Keynesian welfare state. Therefore, demands for "opting out," wrapped in the discourse of cultural development for Francophones and Québécois, appeared on the agenda of federalism. See J. Jenson, "Economic factors in Canadian political integration," in *The Integration Question: Political Economy and Public Policy in Canada and North America*, ed. J. H. Pammett and B. W. Tomlin (Toronto: Addison-Wesley, 1984), pp. 58–9.

alternative for the new conditions, the NDP has relied instead on a defensive electoral strategy of contentless populism.

The New Democratic Party's Pluralism

The NDP came into existence in 1961 to respond to the weaknesses of its predecessor, the CCF, created by an alliance of organized farmers, labor, and socialist intellectuals in the 1930s. The CCF embraced a version of Fabian socialism modified to suit a party whose primary electoral base was independent commodity producers. Despite the party's determined efforts, links with organized labor remained tenuous until the 1950s.[7] Throughout the 1930s and the war, the CCF's *Regina Manifesto* had been an important source of political ideas and pressure for greater state responsibility for social and economic conditions and a more regularized relationship between capital and labor. From the CCF's perspective, implementation of such reforms depended upon a strong federal government directing a united country. Therefore, while justification for its proposals arose from its distinctive social democratic theory of the state and society, the CCF did link up with the themes of the Liberals' and Progressive Conservatives' straightforward nation building discourse.

The CCF's particular founding coalition contained several tensions which remained at the heart of the party throughout the postwar years. One was between those who emphasized the populism of the western experience and those who looked to the labor movement, not simply for financial backing, but also as the correct base of a social democratic party. A second cleavage divided those who sought a more radical, movement-oriented transformatory politics and those who interpreted the postwar conditions as requiring a revision of the past radical discourse and analysis. Thus although the CCF's political worldview came together in support of statism, centralized federalism, and identification with organized labor, it reflected more an uncertain compromise than a widely shared commitment amongst party members.

In maneuvering through the cleavages inherited from the CCF, the NDP plumped for the labor movement and opted for revisionism. Although it did not banish proponents of alternative positions, the party's choices were reinforced by external factors such as the continuation of postwar affluence, the discrediting of the ideology of the Left worldwide, and the overall decline of CCF voting support, especially among farmers in the late 1950s. Through this process of social democratic "renewal," the NDP claimed a role in constructing and managing the conditions of postwar affluence and turned its electoral sights not only towards unionized workers but also to the expanding middle strata. The revisionism of the NDP was intended precisely to address the situation of

7 D. Lewis, *The Good Fight: Political Memoirs 1909–58* (Toronto: Macmillan, 1981).

the late 1950s from the left, by recognizing that affluence did indeed exist but serious distributional problems persisted nonetheless. Guiding all the arguments surrounding the creation of the NDP was the view that the postwar experience with Keynesianism demonstrated both the technical superiority and political advantages of economic fine tuning and selective market interventions.[8]

The intent of this strategy was to modernize the NDP's statist orientation to the economy, substituting new modes of supply and demand management for the shopworn orthodoxies of comprehensive planning. Similarly, on the thorny question of federalism, the NDP's founding document departed from traditional CCF dogma by introducing "cooperative federalism." The party was seeking to indicate its recognition of the federal character of Canadian *society*. However, any notion that the institutions of federalism might become the forum for challenges to the central government's ability to act nationally was absent in what can be termed the NDP's "society-centric" view of constitutional questions.[9]

In organizational terms, the NDP was a federation of provincial parties. Relationships of authority and funds moved from provincial bodies to the national office. The alliance with organized labor also allowed union locals to affiliate with the party, bringing trade union leaders into the governing councils of the NDP *ex officio*. These arrangements provided money and other resources which, at last, enabled Canada's social democratic party to mount viable national election campaigns.

It is evident, then, that the NDP was pluralistic from the beginning. While electoral progress in Ontario remained painfully slow, the presence of the unions, located in the central provinces of Ontario and Quebec, provided an access point for central Canadian perspectives to the party machinery. At the same time, however, the federal form of organization and the long-standing ability of the western provincial wings to retain and increase support meant that prairie populist forces

8 N. Bradford, "Ideas, intellectuals, and social democracy in Canada," in *Canadian Parties in Transition*, ed. A. G. Gagnon and A. B. Tanguay (Toronto: Nelson, 1988), pp. 85–6.
9 Despite a willingness to use provinces (especially Saskatchewan) as "laboratories for reform," the federal government remained the focal point for implementing social change. Moreover, the crucial conflictual questions of federalism were supposed to remain in the "de-politicized" context of fiscal arrangements. Pierre Trudeau was influential in convincing the NDP to abandon the unexamined centralism of the CCF and to move towards cooperative federalism, recognizing the "federal nature of Canadian society" (Bradford, "Ideas, intellectuals and social democracy," p. 86). Indeed, Trudeau, who left the NDP in 1964 to run for the Liberals and to rise mercurially to become Prime Minister, spent the rest of his career trying to reconcile the tension between recognizing a federal society while maintaining a central government which was not overwhelmed by provincial governments. He lost much of this battle, as the story of federal–provincial relations in the 1970s and 1980s demonstrates.

remained strong. Thus, the potential for conflict between western and central Canadian perspectives, between populism and laborism, persisted. Moreover, the move to liberal progressive revisionism did not vanquish the extra-parliamentary socialists and that strategic dispute was destined to continue.[10] The effects of internal pluralism institutionalized in the organizational structures of the NDP emerged with increasing clarity and force as political and economic crisis intensified.

Confronting Quebec and the Waffle

In fact, the NDP did not enjoy many years of grace before it experienced the first signals that even its new perspectives might not resolve its difficulties. The two major faultlines of Canadian postwar politics also cleaved the NDP, whose policy debates highlighted them clearly. The first of these faultlines was created by the state's economic strategy of continentalism. Concern about the impact of continentalism began to surface in the late 1950s, and by the mid-1960s the NDP had responded with a program for domestic capital formation calling on the federal government to ensure that investment (whether public or private) serve the interests of Canadians. From this statist approach to the problem of American control over the domestic economy followed a parliamentary strategy stressing the NDP's capacity to govern in the national interest, employing various supply-side policy instruments to monitor foreign investment and facilitate "Canadianization."

The second faultline involved federalism and the overarching national identity. Weakening support for centralized federalism reverberated through the NDP as controversy erupted over Quebec's place in Confederation. With the emergence of Quebec nationalism, pressure was placed on the NDP to adapt by discarding the "One Canada" assumptions brought to the party by its historically important Anglophone Quebec intellectual elite. Throughout the 1960s, the party wrestled with whether it should recognize Quebec as a nation, accepting the logic that this might lead to fundamental modifications in state institutions, or whether a compromise of "special status" was appropriate.

It was the Progressive Conservative party after it came to power in 1957 under John Diefenbaker's leadership which first confronted these issues. Indeed, Diefenbaker's defeat of the King–St Laurent Liberal

10 This split had existed almost from the beginning in the CCF and became particularly important in the 1950s. W. Young, *The Anatomy of a Party: The National CCF 1932–1961* (Toronto: University of Toronto, 1969). By the mid-1960s, the radicals gained new purchase with the development of the "creative politics" movement which argued the time was ripe to reorient Canadian politics away from regionalism and around class-based identities; a reorientation which, its proponents argued, would strengthen the national project by reducing regional and linguistic divisions. Bradford, "Ideas, intellectuals and social democracy," pp. 89–90.

regime owed much to the Tories' populist mobilization around growing fears about continentalism and the threat posed to Canadian unity by rising Quebec nationalism. However, the economic uncertainties and strains within federalism soon exposed the hollowness of the Diefenbaker sweep. Prairie-based economics, sensitive to regional concerns of commodity producers and spiced with anti-Americanism, clashed with the party's traditional power brokers concentrated in Ontario's business community. In addition, the election of the new Liberal government in Quebec in 1960 and the energies released by the Quiet Revolution revealed the limitations of Diefenbaker's "unhyphenated Canadianism" as a response to evolving demands for new accommodations with Quebec.[11]

In the context of electoral competition, the legacy of the Diefenbaker interlude had very different effects on the two other parties. The failures of the Diefenbaker government set the stage for renewed Liberal dominance of the federal party system and the continued marginalization of the NDP. As the Progressive Conservatives divided over the Quebec question, the Liberals recruited influential provincial figures to develop a more convincing framework for renewed federalism, propelled by novel language and cultural policies aiming to renovate a national identity. At the same time, on economic issues, the Liberals, increasingly subject to the influence of their progressive reform wing, refashioned themselves as the sponsors of modern *dirigiste* planning and intervention very much in vogue in Western Europe.[12] By the mid-1960s the Liberals consolidated an agenda properly labeled "right-wing social democracy." Often the subject of dispute between the party's reform and business wings, right-wing social democracy in the Pearson and early Trudeau years was characterized by four key policies: bilingualism, cooperative federalism, extended social programs, and selective nationalistic economic measures.[13]

Throughout the 1960s, the NDP was stalled by popular perceptions that its responses to the changing conditions within the federation and the economy were little more than a left-wing version of those implemented by the governing Liberals. Moreover, for the NDP, Diefenbaker's defeat and the conditions which eroded the government's credibility presented other constraints. Not only did Diefenbaker's continued strength as a prairie populist appeal to the NDP's traditional western constituency, but his reference to anti-American and antinuclear themes neutralized much of the NDP's distinctiveness in pivotal urban areas of

11 D. Smith, "Party government, representation and national integration in Canada," in *Party Government and Regional Representation in Canada*, ed. P. Aucoin (Toronto: University of Toronto, 1985), pp. 25–9.

12 R. Campbell, *Grand Illusions: The Politics of the Keynesian Experience in Canada* (Peterborough, Ont.: Broadview Press, 1987), ch. 6.

13 P. Newman, *The Distemper of Our Times* (Winnipeg: Greywood, 1968); Wolfe, "The rise and demise of the Keynesian era," pp. 144–6.

central Canada.[14] In addition, the evident collapse of the "One Canada" approach to national unity questions revealed an NDP as divided over constitutional issues and bereft of organizational resources in Quebec as the Tories.

Thus, with the Liberals managing to reestablish their Quebec stronghold, and with the Progressive Conservatives continuing to stress populist themes in the hinterlands, the NDP had little room for maneuver. The particular plight of the NDP in the federal party system was evident: internal party divisions over policy and strategy were compounded externally by the Liberals' selective appropriation of the revisionist social democratic program and by the Tories' populism.

While the four elections of the 1960s had left the NDP mired in uncertainty, a turnaround seemed possible in 1972. The reforming impulse which had animated the Liberals in the 1960s was running its course and by the early 1970s the Liberals had reassessed their social spending commitments in conjunction with a well-publicized series of tax concessions to corporations. Therefore, in his first campaign as leader, David Lewis could lambast "corporate welfare bums": those identifiable large corporations whose tax breaks were "ripping off" ordinary Canadian taxpayers and the government.

As the 1970s began, the economic and constitutional debates within the NDP began to overlap. Increased recognition of the weakening economy merged with the intensifying conflict over Quebec's place in Confederation. At this point, the tensions of internal pluralism crystallized as the Waffle faction appeared inside the NDP to advocate an alternative to the mainstream of party policy.[15] The Waffle advocated an independent socialist Canada to be achieved by "two nations in one struggle." Making use of a more ringing discourse of socialism, the Waffle took radical positions on the economy and constitutional questions which ran roughshod over the delicate balance of the party's internal pluralism. The Waffle's economic analysis claimed that independent socialism was impossible *until* the major threat to Canadian survival, American control of the economy, ended.[16] Moreover, given that the fundamental threat was external capital, the Waffle proposed that the NDP mobilize a broad-based alliance of classes and groups.[17] Reflecting its roots in the New Left of the late 1960s, the Waffle's conception of social change privileged neither the labor movement's claims

---

14 D. Morton, *The New Democrats 1961–1986: The Politics of Change* (Toronto: Copp Clark Pitman, 1986), p. 40.

15 Why the group was called the Waffle is lost to history. Nevertheless, the most convincing version is from Morton who writes: "... the [Waffle] document rejected concessions to consensus radicalism: if it waffled, it would 'waffle to the left'" (*The New Democrats*, p. 92).

16 Brodie and Jenson, *Crisis, Challenge and Change*, p. 273.

17 For the other intellectual roots of Waffle arguments, in the emerging "new Canadian political economy," see Bradford, "Ideas, intellectuals and social democracy," pp. 91–2.

nor the incrementalism of the legislative process. It tried to foster a more participatory, society-centered politics, denigrating parliamentarism.

This emphasis on grassroots politics appealed to socialists who had never been comfortable with unexamined parliamentarism. The call for a broad-based social alliance was also welcomed by those activists who felt that the preoccupation with organized labor was undercutting other strategic perspectives emerging from the middle strata and new social movements on which the party's expansion would largely depend. But, not surprisingly, the Waffle intervention met hostile reaction from organized labor and from those who were uncomfortable with its willingness to recognize a new place for Quebec. As a crucial subtext of their attack on American capital, Wafflers argued that Canadian unions should replace the internationals. They followed up with a call for "democratization" aimed at the union leaders, whose fears that dramatic efforts to expropriate foreign capital would have negative employment effects made them chary of Waffle stances.

Internal conflict played itself out at the 1971 leadership convention when David Lewis – the key architect of the party's parliamentarism and alliance with organized labor – met the unexpected although ultimately unsuccessful challenge of the Waffle's candidate. When efforts at policy and personal mediation were unsuccessful, the unions combined with many of the party's elected parliamentarians to expel the Waffle group in 1972.[18] In disciplining the Waffle, the NDP reconsecrated its state-oriented, social democratic discourse and organizational forms.

These years of intense internal struggle around economic development strategies and approaches to federalism left a legacy of distrust and bitterness within the NDP and the broader Left. It was at this difficult juncture in the party's history that an electoral strategy presented itself which would address the failure to make incursions into areas of Liberal vote, particularly among the middle strata and in urban areas, while rendering less urgent any resolution of the deep-seated divisions on policy and strategy. The new leadership struck on a chance discovery of

---

18 Because it kept a separate mailing list, issued its own statements, and ran Waffle-identified candidates in elections, the NDP could charge it with constituting a "party within a party," and use that as the constitutional grounds for winding down the Waffle (Brodie and Jenson, *Crisis, Challenge and Change*, p. 278). On the details of the conflict and its long-term costs inside the NDP, see Morton, *The New Democrats*, pp. 130ff. One probably completely unanticipated consequence was that there was a serious rift between the NDP and the most critical and active young intellectuals that lasted well into the 1980s, thus cutting the NDP off from new understandings of Canadian society as they developed in the academy (Bradford, "Ideas, intellectuals and social democracy," pp. 92–3). And the level of antagonism among the unions and the Wafflers – with, for example, union leaders accusing the Wafflers of being social misfits and Wafflers returning the swipes in kind – meant that Canadian unions entered the 1970s with little chance of engaging in intellectual debates outside the movement. The timing of such a brutal conflict was unfortunate.

the electoral rewards from a new form of populist discourse, one which masked the fundamental internal disputes about economic direction and constitutional politics.[19]

The "corporate welfare bias" slogan also defused the issue of American ownership of the economy because many of the companies on the daily "hit list" were American multinationals or their branch-plant subsidiaries; nationalists could take heart that the question of foreign domination was being addressed. In essence, the 1972 campaign represented a new confirmation of Keynesian style economics, packaged in populist rhetoric which bridged some of the deep fissures that had opened inside the NDP. And it seemed to work; the NDP not only discovered a more distinctive identity from the Liberals, but it won ten more seats and assumed an important role in the ensuing situation of minority government.

Thus, the NDP entered the mid-decade with several painfully learned lessons. First, searching for an alternative framework to interpret the conditions created by Canada's political and economic crisis was divisive and potentially paralyzing. The better part of valor was to damp down controversy among the party's competing tendencies whenever possible. The second lesson was that the labor unions were a powerful force within the party, and any new orientations would have to address their perception of the situation as well as accommodate their needs. The experiences of the early 1970s had shown that the labor movement remained a quite conservative force, still unwilling to rethink traditional positions on economic nationalism, two nations, and mobilizing strategies for Left politics. The one bright spot in this period was that populism had the double advantage of not escalating these internal tensions and of delivering modest but real electoral success. The party organization stored that lesson away for the future.

The New West and Industrial Strategy

Since the mid-1970s, Canada has experienced an economic crisis with as profound restructuring effects as any other. Moreover, throughout these years, provincial governments had been mobilizing their resources. This was not simply the result of growing Quebec nationalism nor of the perversity of "power-hungry" politicians and bureaucrats in the provinces. Rather, it was in large part a reflection of the differentiated ways that capitalist restructuring affected manufacturing and resource-producing economies. The fact of economic openness had quite different implications for resource producers and manufacturers. Given the geography of economic activity in Canada, the central provinces (and increasingly only Ontario) had the bulk of manufacturing while the peripheries, especially the western provinces and Quebec, depended on

19 On populism as a chance discovery see Morton, *The New Democrats*, pp. 141–3.

resource production.[20] From the first response to the energy crisis region-al competition was assured, as the federal government kept domestically produced oil below the world price in order to cushion the shock for eastern manufacturers and consumers. It thereby limited western pro-vinces' windfall profits. This competition was fought out in the arena of intergovernmental relations.

Organized labor and the NDP have both continued the search for an effective response to the changed economic and political environment. After suffering the impact of the Liberal's unilateral imposition of wage controls in 1975 the Canadian Labor Congress (CLC) and several of its large affiliates recognized that the new conditions demanded a departure from the strategies of collective bargaining and occasional forays into lobbying which had guided them in the postwar decades. Initially attracted to a version of social corporatism, the CLC moved to provide more sustained electoral and programmatic support for the NDP.[21] Moreover, it began to formulate a strategy for industrial restructuring, one which rejected continentalism, favoring instead more processing of natural resources and research and development in Canada, enhanced regulation of foreign investment, and the improvement of social pro-grams.[22] While decidedly labor-focused, this plan dovetailed with many of the policy initiatives being undertaken by the NDP.

In the 1974 election, the electorate had difficulty distinguishing the NDP's oppositional politics from those of the Liberals. Two years of Liberal minority government had produced several nationalist policies, reflecting in part demands made earlier by the NDP as well as the left-wing of the Liberal Party. Trying to cope with the "identity crisis" thereby generated, the NDP committed itself to finding a policy response for the post-Keynesian future.[23] In this search, there was a return to the concerns first elaborated by the Waffle and now echoed by the CLC

20 Brodie and Jenson, *Crisis, Challenge and Change*, pp. 298–9.
21 This initiative by organized labor was, in many ways, a legacy of wage controls, when the Liberal Party flagrantly reneged on its campaign promise to protect labor. The CLC set out to convince the rank and file that the old-line parties had proven themselves, once again, to be only the friends of big business and that unionists had no alternative but to support "their party," the NDP. As the 1979 federal election approached, the CLC executive decided to increase its funding of the NDP and to press union locals to mobilize their members into a voting bloc. In a campaign termed "Canadian Labor Calling," the CLC set up telephone centers in target ridings where volunteers and union votes were plenti-ful. The telephone campaign stressed the realities of shrinking pay checks, unemployment, the erosion of trade union rights under the Liberal government, and the need for a new and comprehensive industrial strategy. Labor continued its partisan activity in support of the NDP in 1980, 1984, and 1988 but the effects on electoral outcomes were limited.
22 R. Mahon, *The Politics of Industrial Restructuring* (Toronto: University of Toronto Press, 1984), p. 213.
23 Morton, *The New Democrats*, p. 192.

about technological backwardness and export impotence associated with a branch-plant industrial structure. Of course, the party's use of the Waffle's intellectual legacy was selective: advocacy of an "independent socialist Canada" was replaced with a much narrower political analysis of adjustment problems and investment strategy in a small, open economy. By the late 1970s, then, the NDP offered its "industrial strategy" for productivity and innovation in response to neo-liberal claims that the Canadian economy's problems stemmed from social expenditures, state intervention, and insufficient market influence.[24] Like the CLC's restructuring strategy which was primarily tailored to the needs of Ontario, where de-industrialization was hitting hardest, the NDP's proposal relied on strong leadership from the central government to direct the anticipated restructuring. How this aspect of the post-Keynesian agenda would mesh with the concerns of the party's western wing remained unclear.

In 1980, the reelected Liberal government, emboldened by its defeat of the Tories' program for a more decentralized federation and by the withering of Quebec nationalism after the referendum on sovereignty-association that year, elaborated an ambitious set of policies termed the Third National Policy.[25] The Liberal package of resource, industrial, and constitutional proposals envisioned a large role for the federal government in the economy, both in organizing the internal market and regulating external investment flows. This program also reasserted the centrality of a national identity expressed through institutional reforms aiming to strengthen citizens' loyalties to the central government. However, this statist–nationalist response to the evolving crisis was shipwrecked economically by plummeting commodity prices and was politically stalemated by the effects of more than a decade of constitutional conflict led by rebellious provincial Premiers.

For the NDP any policy initiative presupposing a strengthened federal government was immediately viewed with suspicion since the leaders of the western provinces and many of their constituents saw the new industrial strategy as another effort to bolster Ontario at the expense of the west. In the 1970s, New Democratic provincial Premiers directed their anger against the federal Liberal government's efforts to rescue a national economic strategy from the crumbling edifice of postwar continentalism. However, by the early 1980s, as the federal wing of the NDP sided with the Liberals on each of the major issues of Canadian politics which pitted the center against the west, the centralizing implications of

---

24　In this analysis the NDP found an ally within the Canadian state, which led the charge for some sort of "industrial strategy." For the story of internal state conflict over industrial strategy or continentalism see G. Williams, *Not For Export: Toward a Political Economy of Canada's Arrested Industrialization* (Toronto: McClelland & Stewart, 1984), ch. 7, and Mahon, *The Politics of Industrial Restructuring*, ch. 8.

25　Smiley, *The Federal Condition*, p. 187.

the party's post-Keynesian economic analysis set in motion a "western revolt."

The NDP was doubly damned. Its opponents accused it of suffering the same ills as social democracy elsewhere – outdated statist responses to productivity crises, protectionism in the face of competitiveness challenges, and careening public expenditures. These critics cited the troubles of the British economy in the 1970s and the dramatic failures of the French Socialists after 1981 as evidence confirming the bankruptcy of Canada's social democratic alternative. Yet, as New Democrats struggled to sort through these broadsides – so common to social democracy at the time – they were also embroiled in internal debates about constitutional politics.

Indeed, constitutional politics, fought after 1980, crystallized many of the intra-party tensions and exposed the extent to which constitutional and economic questions in Canada had become closely intertwined. When the Trudeau government announced an amending formula for the Constitution and an entrenched Charter of Rights, the federal NDP indicated support for the Trudeau initiative based on a long-standing adherence to the concept of a national bill of rights.[26] This commitment wrecked havoc within the party. Provincial leaders and western federal caucus members found threatening the increased role of the Supreme Court and the dilution of parliamentary sovereignty which would follow from an entrenched Charter. They were also adamant that provincial control over resources must be treated as nonnegotiable in any compromise. Furthermore, social movements, especially women and native peoples, objected to specific items in the proposed Charter, which weakened their rights. They mounted successful campaigns outside Parliament to force a more acceptable outcome and such appeals were taken up by those New Democrats whose own notion of politics – reminiscent of the Waffle – were less party directed and more open to popular alliances. Even the labor movement was divided over whether to pursue constitutional recognition of the right to strike. Supporters of parliamentary sovereignty aligned with unionists from Quebec to block any sustained efforts in that direction.

In the several years of intense controversy that it took to rewrite the Constitution, these divisions swirled through the NDP. The discontent, evident among the party's rank and file, parliamentary wing, and provincial leadership, erupted at the party's national conventions in 1981 and 1983, where party leaders from western Canada rejected the federal NDP's economic policies and gained space for provincial diversity and resource-driven economic development.

In many ways, the NDP had been caught by its failure, first, to assess the political consequences of the westward shift in economic activity throughout the 1970s and, second, to recognize how these transformations

26 J. Richards and D. Kerr (eds), *Canada, What's Left?* (Edmonton: NeWest, 1986).

would organize conflict around the new Constitution. Despite the western domination of the federal caucus, with its constituencies increasingly antagonistic toward both federal power and Ontario's historic dominance in the Canadian economy and politics, the party's electoral strategy continued to focus on developing support in Ontario. Thus, on most of the major political issues of the 1980s, the party was paralyzed by the choice of appealing to the center and alienating its power base in the west or the reverse.[27]

Yet the objections raised by the western party leaders were never confined to federalism and regional economics. They incorporated a critique of Keynesianism, disputing the NDP's preoccupation with organized labor's desire for protection of jobs in mature and declining industries. Westerners' basic economic proposals called for an incomes policy, based on a new social contract featuring greater restrictions on adjustment-retarding industrial assistance. This idea would require considerable explaining to a labor movement weathering a severe economic recession at the same time that the Liberal government was imposing wage controls on the public sector. Not surprisingly, labor saw a clear threat to its social power in the westerners' view of labor as "just another interest group."

Towards 1988:
The Return of Contentless Populism

Ironically, the main thrust of these western objections was buttressed by the positions of an influential party figure long associated with the Ontario wing and a central Canadian analysis of national economic problems. James Laxer, in a departure from the federal party's traditional pro-labor parliamentarism, published an economic polemic offering a rationale for expunging any remaining traces of Keynesian demand-side stimulative spending from the party's analysis and encouraging tactical support for the Liberals.[28] Embracing the language of neo-liberalism, Laxer believed that the NDP had to impress on the public consciousness that it too was prepared to restrain the labor movement and streamline state expenditures to steer the country through the "leaner and meaner" 1980s and 1990s. For Laxer, the NDP's target constituency was domestic business and middle class technocrats, rather than workers, organized or unorganized.

Identifying this constituency made Laxer's economic analysis quite compatible with the positions of the western faction whose government

---

27 By contrast, the Liberals, with their electoral stronghold in Quebec, could mobilize decisively around a center-oriented economic–constitutional package without fear of serious internal conflict.

28 J. Laxer, *Rethinking the Economy: The Laxer Report on Canadian Economic Problems and Policies* (Toronto: Lorimer, 1984).

experience and focus on province-based development strategies earned them the label "prairie capitalists." Nor was Laxer's economics incompatible with the populist, almost *autogestionnaire*, thrust of the westerners; only Laxer's politics – his recommendation in favor of the Liberals – jarred with the western position.

Entering the 1984 election, then, at least two camps were shaping up inside the NDP, with different visions of economic strategy, of representational targets, of labor's role in the social democracy of the future, and of federal–provincial relations. As controversy again rocked the NDP, no coherent position could be presented to the electorate. Therefore, as the 1984 election approached, the NDP scrambled to find a message which would allow it to maneuver against the other parties while still divided over policy. Party leaders developed the populist theme of appealing to "ordinary Canadians," but with little substantive discussion about what ordinary Canadians might hope to gain from electing the NDP. Missing from the strategy was any reference to the economic restructuring proposals which had at least framed the 1979 and 1980 campaigns.

In making this choice the NDP leadership relied on a populism born of desperation but also one which was consciously chosen. Drawing on sophisticated polling and marketing techniques, the proponents of contentless populism argued that the majority of voters were alienated by the party's insistence on using the language of social democracy. More fundamentally, however, after the conflicts over the Constitution and post-Keynesianism, it was obvious to the party elite that any attempt to construct a program-oriented campaign risked alienating many traditional New Democrats as well. The particular form of populist discourse which the party settled on in 1984 reflected as much an uncertainty about the future direction of the social democratic project in Canada as a conscious decision to substitute image for substance.

The 1984 election, like 1972, was interpreted as a victory of sorts for the NDP.[29] Suffering no loss of seats, the party was reassured that the years of constitutional–economic debate had not been fatal to its electoral fortunes. Rather, armed with its populist slogan the party held its ground while the governing Liberals were decimated. Of course, the most remarkable feature of the 1984 election was the success of the Tories. In marked contrast with the divisive effects visited upon the NDP and the Liberals by the crisis and restructuring the Mulroney Conservatives gained new opportunities to meld formerly competing intra-party tensions. The Royal Commission on Canada's Economic Union and Development Prospects, which became the guiding economic document for the new government, recommended that Canada face the future with a market-driven continentalist strategy rather than an interventionist–nationalist one. The subsequent free-trade initiative appealed to business elites across the country by promising less federal

29 Some people had even feared that the NDP would drop below the twelve-seat level which gave it status as an official party in Parliament.

interference in the investment process and in provincial jurisdictions and reduced social welfare expenditures. Significantly, it also contributed to the unhinging of Liberal dominance in Quebec by responding to the provincial government's desire to secure a continental resource export market. Furthermore, the quick accommodations made with the energy-producing provinces in the Western and Atlantic Accords, and the formal recognition of Quebec's "special status" in the Meech Lake Agreement of 1987, signaled the institutionalization within the Conservative party – and by implication within Canada's federal structures – of regional identities. A neo-liberal economic strategy and a decentralizing approach to federalism not only have permitted the Tories to mobilize a unified party and successful interregional electoral coalition; they also amount to a strategic redefinition of the "national interest," one designed to consolidate the Conservatives' position as the governing party for the future.

In this new political environment, the NDP has moved again to address the tensions and divisions left unresolved from the pre-1984 period. Responding to the enthusiasm for the popular mobilizations which accompanied the process of Constitution-making and the Solidarity movement in British Columbia, as well as the growing interest in more decentralized, democratic-social-movement styles of political representation, the NDP published *Canada Unlimited*.[30] Countering the notion that social democracy means statism and centralized bureaucracies, the NDP highlighted the possibilities for community initiatives, local investment funds, and self-directed, self-reliant economic development. It called for a new partnership between the national and local governments, evading the crucial questions of provincial participation and federalism. This document announced a new kind of policy formation process, organized around consultation via "democratic engagement" with social movements, voluntary bodies, local labor councils, public-interest think tanks and so forth. *Canada Unlimited* clearly represented an effort to address concerns about statism and narrow parliamentarism; however, it remained rather ambiguous about the content of a new national economic strategy as well as the intergovernmental reforms required for its implementation. Therefore, on its own it could not serve as a blueprint for the future.

Virtually simultaneously with the *Canada Unlimited* initiative, growing enthusiasm emerged within the NDP for a revamped statist approach to economic development. Economist Diane Bellemare gained support for a strategy modeled on the social democracy of small European states which rely on national direction of labor-market and regional-adjustment programs to sustain full employment.[31] This proposal mapped out new institutional structures of federal–provincial cooperation, designed to institutionalize community input into national econo-

30 New Democratic Party, *Canada Unlimited* (Ottawa: NDP, 1985).
31 D. Bellemare, "The birth of a Canadian economy," New Democratic Party, *Forum 2000 Theme Papers* (Ottawa: NDP, 1986).

mic strategies. Appealing in its coherence and sweep, the proposal also depended on the willingness of provincial governments to surrender some of their autonomy and commit themselves to support for cooperative solutions.

Neither of these two initiatives was workable by itself, then. The *Canada Unlimited* position did not adequately address constitutional questions, basically submerging them into calls for local participation and generalized decentralization, overseen by the federal government. Despite the political promise of the party's announced openness to popular groups and local struggles, only the most optimistic of democrats could believe that decentralized community development initiatives would succeed in overcoming the problems of a small open economy. This approach essentially left open the question of building a solid foundation for opposing free trade in the name of Canadian economic autonomy. On the other hand, Bellemare's economic national strategy presupposed a political will not only of a party but also of the state. The constitutional implications of Bellemare's full-employment strategy modeled on the unitary states of Sweden, Austria, and Norway suggest that there must be a way to recentralize not only the sponsoring political party but also the institutions of federalism. That such a strategy can be initiated by a party with the NDP's internal pluralism is difficult to imagine.

Thus, in 1988, faced with two appealing but still unmerged views of the future, the NDP was immobilized on programmatic matters and its immobilization brought it back to the 1972 and 1984 strategies of contentless populism. This time the campaign was organized around the themes of "fairness," "honesty," and the integrity of the party leader; choosing to avoid broad economic issues, any references to a social democratic alternative were absent. Not surprisingly, the impression was created that the New Democrats were simply running to catch up with the Liberals in opposing free trade, despite the fact that the NDP was the only party which had mounted a principled criticism of further continental integration for years.

This position was extremely costly in an election when the *only* issue was free trade, and when it mushroomed to incorporate concerns and policy matters far beyond narrowly economic ones, substantially increasing opposition to the "deal." It was also flawed because the constituencies traditionally targeted by the NDP – organized labor and the urban middle class of central Canada – became major actors in the anti-free-trade coalition. As the debate over free trade erupted, the NDP found itself marginalized, the consequence of relying on contentless populism in an election when there was a burning issue and no opportunity to tar the other two parties with the same brush.

Conclusion

In this chapter we have argued that to understand the failure of the NDP to make its anticipated breakthrough in 1988 and the conflict which emerged immediately after the election, it is necessary to situate the campaign design in historical context by revealing its location in an on-going pattern of strategic compromise engendered by almost two decades of internal policy uncertainty. The campaign reflected a pattern of compromise responding in the first instance to the diversity of internal pluralism in the party, a diversity which followed from the ways in which postwar politics crumbled in the face of new conditions. From this perspective, the resort to pollsters, "sound bites," issueless campaigns, and the stress on leadership can be seen more as a symptom of the NDP's difficulties than as a satisfactory explanation. It is necessary to ask *when* such an electoral strategy gains ascendancy and banishes proposals for coherent alternatives to the sidelines. The answer is obvious: when the party is uncertain about the way ahead. Equally obvious is the conclusion that the strategy's "success" hinges on factors beyond the NDP's control – the positioning of the other major players in the partisan struggle. Therefore the question becomes one of *why* the NDP has experienced such problems in offering a coherent response to changing postwar economic and political conditions. The Canadian story, it is suggested, is a story in which two questions – national economic development and federalism – have combined to pose not simply a double challenge but challenges which intertwine so as to undo the NDP even more than if each had to be faced separately.

Yet, the resort to contentless populism, as the 1988 election and its aftermath demonstrates, is not a viable social democratic strategy and there is the risk now that it will generate even further internal conflict, rather than defuse tensions. Indeed such debate is already emerging in the NDP, turning on familiar themes although with interesting new combinations. The labor movement has questioned the NDP's sensitivity to what its campaign strategists interpreted as western Canada's opinion on free trade. It also claims that the party refused to pay attention to labor's advice "from the ground" during the campaign. New in such criticisms, however, is the suggestion that the labor movement may be willing to play a leading role in constructing a less parliamentarist and more movement-oriented representational strategy for Left politics.

These emerging perspectives provided an important focal point for the debate in the leadership contest of November 1989. Once again the party's long-standing internal pluralism came to the fore. The two leading candidates – former British Columbia Premier Dave Barrett and federal Member of Parliament Audrey McLaughlin – in their policy orientations, supporting coalitions, and images of the party, offered delegates rather discordant packages. Barrett emphasized protection of the western electoral base through strategic focus on provincial victories, underpinned by federal party politics sensitive to the regional economic grievances of "prairie capitalists," resource-sector workers, and farmers. In contrast, McLaughlin's representational targets were the new social movements, feminists, and central Canadian trade unionists seeking to build new coalitions with the so-called "popular sector." Moreover, electoral breakthrough in Quebec remained central to McLaughlin's strategic focus. Beyond their shared opposition to the FTA and the Meech Lake Accord, then, the Barrett and McLaughlin campaigns divided along lines reflecting the NDP's basic cleavages. Not surprisingly, the convention expressed these internal tensions rather than providing any authoritative resolution through policy or programmatic innovation. Indeed the narrow margin of victory for the McLaughlin forces combined with their leader's reluctance to offer broad policy visions leaves unstated the NDP's long-term adjustment strategy for the new conditions.

The task remains to elaborate and mobilize around a progressive adjustment agenda, sensitive to Canada's peculiar relationship between federalism, a regionalized national economy, and continental integration. Required to find not only an economic strategy for the free-trade future but also a set of arrangements for federalism, the NDP's task is a difficult one. But finding such a political alternative is essential if Canada is not to be absorbed quietly into the neo-liberal agenda of its continentalizing capitalists.

10

The Democratic Party and City Politics in the Postindustrial Era

Alan DiGaetano

In this chapter we shall examine the "urban" dimension of recent Democratic Party restructuring. Given the highly decentralized nature of American state structure, state and local party organizations have played a much larger and more independent role in party politics in the United States. Big city Democratic organizations, and the changes they have undergone since the 1930s, therefore constitute an essential part of the story of Democratic Party decline in the postindustrial era.

Typically, urban party decline or adaptation is said to result from nonpartisan reform structures and the rise of new organizational forms in the electoral process such as political action committees or candidate-centered campaign organizations.[1] There are some important exceptions to these organizational explanations of party transformation, however.[2] Robert Kuttner, for example, ascribes Democratic Party decline to the failure of its leadership to promote "progressive populist" policies and programs that hold the Democratic electoral coalition together:

> I use the term "progressive-populist" to describe the modern Democratic Party philosophy that began with the New Deal, which also incorporated several antecedents and resonated with the in-tuitively egalitarian strain in the American character. It

1 See B. D. Jones, *Governing Urban American: A Policy Focus* (Boston, MA: Little, Brown, 1983), p. 246; A. Ware, *The Breakdown of Democratic Party Organization, 1940–1980* (Oxford: Clarendon Press, 1985); S. Welsh and T. Bledsoe, *Urban Reform and its Consequences: A Study in Representation* (Chicago, IL: University of Chicago Press, 1988).
2 T. B. Edsall, *The New Politics of Inequality* (New York: Norton, 1984).

appropriated the demand for economic justice from the populists; it embraced and enlarged several regulatory interventions from the Progressive era. It defined the modern mixed economy. It added the idea of macroeconomic management by the federal government, as well as direct federal spending in a variety of areas dedicated to the betterment of the common American. It included a social-democratic welfare state, and a dose of economic planning. It contained a salutary whiff of class warfare whenever "economic royalists" sought to resist its forward movement.[3]

By viewing progressive populism as the ideological trademark of the Democratic Party inscribed by the realigning election of 1932, we can assess the degree to which urban Democratic politics have adhered to or deviated from its ideological *raison d'être*.

The urban wing of the Democratic Party became a crucial partner in the party's majority coalition that emerged in the 1930s under the banner of Franklin Roosevelt's New Deal. At the national level, congressional urban Democrats continued to fight for liberal urban programs during and after the Depression of the 1930s. At the local level, however, local Democratic leaders pursued more conservative policies in the area of urban redevelopment. A "new convergence of power" in urban politics, as Robert Salisbury called it,[4] situated mayors at the center of governing alliances among downtown business interests and professional administrative officials, and, in some cities, labor unions. These alliances are usefully viewed as elements in a "regime."[5] Regimes, according to Todd Swanstrom,[6] are modes of governance which include the formal and informal arrangements among political actors, the patterns of policy-making and implementation, and the means by which regimes are legitimized and how they mobilize electoral support. In the post-Second World War period, executive-centered urban *regimes* coalesced around the common concern of revitalizing central city business districts.[7]

3 R. Kuttner, *The Life of the Party: Democratic Prospects for 1988 and Beyond* (New York: Penguin Books, 1987), p. 7.
4 R. Salisbury, "Urban politics: the new convergence of power," *Journal of Politics*, 26 (November 1964), pp. 775–97.
5 See S. Elkin, "Twentieth century urban regimes," *Journal of Urban Affairs*, 7 (1985), pp. 11–28; C. N. Stone, "Summing up: urban regimes, development policy, and political arrangements," in *The Politics of Urban Development*, ed. C. N. Stone and H. Sanders (Lawrence, KS: University Press of Kansas, 1987), pp. 269–90.
6 T. Swanstrom, "Semi-sovereign cities: the politics of urban development," *Polity*, 2 (1988), pp. 83–110, especially p. 109.
7 See J. H. Mollenkopf, *The Contested City* (Princeton, NJ: Princeton University Press, 1983), ch. 4; S. S. Fainstein and N. I. Fainstein, "Regime strategies, communal resistance, and economic forces," in *Restructuring the City: The Political Economics of Urban Redevelopment*, ed. S. S. Fainstein and N. I. Fainstein (New York: Longman, 1986), pp. 245–82.

Table 10.1   Emergence of a democratic urban electorate: twelve largest cities

Year	Net party plurality
1920	1,540,000 Republican
1924	1,308,000 Republican
1928	210,000 Democratic
1932	1,791,000 Democratic
1936	3,479,000 Democratic
1940	2,112,000 Democratic
1944	2,230,000 Democratic
1948	1,481,000 Democratic

The cities included are New York, Chicago, Philadelphia, Pittsburgh, Detroit, Cleveland, Baltimore, St Louis, Boston, San Francisco, Milwaukee, and Los Angeles.
Source: D. Judd, *The Politics of American Cities: Private Power and Public Policy*, 3rd edn (Boston, MA: Scott, Foresman, 1988), p. 127

Moreover, this new convergence of power eclipsed party rule in America's larger cities. The remainder of the chapter is divided into three parts, each analyzing a different period of postindustrial urban Democratic regime formation in relation to progressive populism.

Postwar Progrowth Regimes and the Politics of Consensus, 1945–1964

Al Smith's presidential candidacy in 1928 and Franklin D. Roosevelt's New Deal administration facilitated the partisan realignment that made the Democratic Party the majority party in the postindustrial era.[8] As table 10.1 indicates, big cities became one of the major pillars of Democratic Party support during the 1930s. In the pre-1930s period, political control of cities had been divided between Democratic and Republican machines. Table 10.2 shows that in 1929 Republicans controlled a clear plurality of mayors' offices in America's major cities (100,000+ in 1930). In 1932, however, Democratic and Republican positions reversed abruptly, with the Democrats winning a plurality of 44 percent or better of mayoral offices from 1932 to 1942. In sum, the 1932 partisan realignment pushed major cities into the Democratic camp, allowing local Democratic parties to dominate urban politics in the 1930s and afterward.

8 W. D. Burham, *Critical Elections and the Mainsprings of American Politics* (New York: Norton, 1970).

Table 10.2   Party control of Mayor's Office for selected years, cities over 100,000 population, 1930

	1929	1932	1935	1938	1942
Republican					
Number	45	21	17	14	16
Percentage	48.9	22.8	18.4	15.2	17.4
Democratic					
Number	23	43	45	42	41
Percentage	30.4	46.7	48.9	45.7	44.5
Third party					
Number	2	1	4	3	2
Percentage	2.2	1.1	4.4	3.3	2.2
Nonpartisan and city manager					
Number	14	23	23	33	30
Percentage	15.2	25.0	25.0	35.8	32.6
No information					
Number	3	4	3	0	3
Percentage	3.3	4.4	3.3	0.0	3.3
Total					
Number	92	92	92	92	92
Percentage	100.0	100.0	100.0	100.0	100.0

Source: B. Stave, *Socialism in the Cities* (Port Washington, NY: Kennekatt, 1975), p. 159

Roosevelt's New Deal congealed the Democratic Party's urban electorate. In the throes of the Great Depression, public relief and public works programs provided subsistence and jobs to the impoverished and unemployed. Also, the Roosevelt administration extended governmental protection to labor union organizing activities. These and other social reform initiatives consolidated Democratic loyalty among the urban poor and working class. What is more, government assumed a new role under these progressive populist reforms, as guarantor of economic opportunity and security for the economically disadvantaged. The Democratic Party reaped the benefits of these changes, for Democrats authored the policies and programs that created this nascent welfare state.

The formation of progrowth regimes

The passage of the 1949 Housing Act, which created what has been commonly known as the urban renewal program, was initiated by the liberal urban wing of the national Democratic Party under the rubric of the Truman administration's Fair Deal. The urban renewal program was the only major piece of urban legislation proposed by Truman in his inaugural address of 1949 to survive the battlegrounds of Congressional politics. The conservative coalition of Republicans and southern Democrats, which played a much stronger role in shaping legislation after 1938, defeated almost all of Truman's twenty-one domestic policy proposals, which included national health insurance, fair employment practices, and middle-income cooperative housing. The only program initiative for which liberal Democrats mustered sufficient support was the urban renewal program.[9]

Urban renewal originally represented a potential for building local progressive–populist coalitions around the issue of central city housing. This potential, however, was never realized. Instead a compromise was struck between the conservative and liberal wings of the Democratic Party which would ultimately blunt the thrust of the progressive–populist agenda established earlier by the New Deal. Liberal Democrats traded off some of the more progressive elements of the original draft of the legislation in order to secure its passage in the face of an intense lobbying drive by real-estate interests to block the public housing component in the program. Conservatives won use of government subsidies to private developers as the means for redeveloping blighted urban areas, rather than relying on public construction of housing as originally intended, in exchange for retaining a public housing component in the renewal program.[10] As a result, urban renewal came to furnish the financial support and political infrastructure that facilitated the emergence of coalitions intent on revitalizing central business districts. The emphasis was on public subsidization of private development, not housing for the urban poor and working classes.

What John Mollenkopf refers to as "progrowth coalitions" gradually displaced local Democratic Party organizations in this period as the center of power in urban politics.[11] Urban progrowth coalitions united big city mayors, business interests, professional planners, and bureaucratic city officials, and even labor union leaders in some cities.[12] Labor, however, was only a junior partner. It was downtown business associations that played the prominent role in developing local renewal programs. Pittsburgh's Allegheny Conference on Community Development, the New Boston Committee, the Central Atlanta Improvement Committee, and San Francisco's Blyth–Zellerbach Committee were all business

9 Mollenkopf, *Contested City*, pp. 72–82.
10 Mollenkopf, *Contested City*, pp. 77–81; D. Judd, *The Politics of American Cities: Private Power and Public Policy*, 3rd edn (Boston, MA: Scott, Foresman, 1988), pp. 263–73.
11 J. H. Mollenkopf, "The postwar politics of urban development," in *Marxism and the Metropolis: New Perspectives in Urban Political Economy*, ed. W. K. Tabb and L. S. Sawers (New York: Oxford University Press, 1978), pp. 117–52.
12 Mollenkopf, "The postwar politics of urban development."

associations participating directly in the formation of their respective city's growth regime.[13]

Given this consortium of interests, then, it is hardly surprising that Democratic city regimes in the postwar period were not guided by principles of progressive populism. From the 1950s on, Democratic mayors developed urban renewal programs encased in conservative market-based ideology rather than progressive populism. The federal urban renewal program, which was ostensibly designed to create opportunities for the construction of low- and moderate-income housing, became a tool for the urban progrowth coalitions to rebuild central city business districts. Moreover, some Democratic constituencies were the primary losers, as poor, working class, and minority residents were displaced by the renewal programs which emphasized commercial and upper-income housing development.[14]

The redevelopment strategy employed during this phase of progrowth politics emphasized wholesale clearance of designated renewal sites and construction of new housing and commercial structures. Between 1949 and 1961, the urban renewal program demolished 126,000 housing units, but built only 28,000 new units to replace them.[15] Moreover, as Paul Kantor relates, "For the majority of cities, residential reuse of the cleared land was not prominent, accounting for only about one-fifth of the planned use of central city urban renewal lands between 1949 and 1966; commercial, industrial, public institutional, and public infrastructure accounted for the remainder."[16] City leaders were trying to use federal urban renewal grants to subsidize private downtown development in the hope that this would catalyze a transformation of older industrial cities into corporate centers for the postindustrial economy.[17]

Progrowth regimes encountered relatively little opposition in the 1950s and early 1960s. Opposition was isolated, while powerful forces marshalled progrowth coalitions to accomplish the task of downtown redevelopment. Typically, progrowth coalitions targeted politically weak neighborhoods inhabited by poor, working class, and minority residents. At first, these groups put up little resistance to the destruction of their neighborhoods. Moreover, in accordance with federal renewal requirements, local development agencies were empowered with extraordinary land-use authority and often operated independently from city government. Judd describes renewal agencies as

---

13 Judd, *The Politics of American Cities*, pp. 371–82; P. Kantor, *The Dependent City: The Changing Political Economy of Urban America* (Glenview, IL: Scott, Foresman, 1988), pp. 253–62.

14 Judd, *The Politics of American Cities*, pp. 371–82; Kantor, *The Dependent City*, pp. 253–62.

15 Judd, *The Politics of American Cities*, p. 273.

16 Kantor, *The Dependent City*, p. 256.

17 See Fainstein and Fainstein, "Regime strategies, communal resistance, and economic forces."

semiautonomous bodies with vast amounts of independent legal, financial, and technical resources. They are generally independent of municipal government, having their own boards of directors. They also possess the power of eminent domain, which is essential to the redevelopment process because it enables the agencies to assemble large sites by taking land, through compensation, away from individual owners. This land assembly power is absolutely necessary, because business corporations, if attempting land assembly on their own, must buy from "willing" sellers and thus pay a high price for valuable urban real estate.[18]

Thus, vesting independent local renewal agencies with extensive land assembly powers enabled progrowth coalitions to overwhelm politically weak neighborhoods, and also made it possible to shield potential developers from speculative market forces set off by the renewal program.

The case of Philadelphia illustrates the inner workings of postwar progrowth regimes. The administrations of reform, Democratic mayors Joseph Clark and Richardson Dilworth (1952–62), coalesced with the city's independent Redevelopment Authority; the Greater Philadelphia Movement, a leading renewal advocacy business association; and the Philadelphia Housing Association, a nonprofit organization that specialized in housing development and urban planning. Under the auspices of the federal urban renewal program, Philadelphia's progrowth coalition restructured the city's central business district. To anchor the renewal plan, the old terminal of the Pennsylvania Railroad was torn down and replaced by a large commercial-office complex dubbed Penn Center. This initiative produced a redevelopment domino effect: the historic district was rehabilitated; skyscrapers mushroomed throughout the central business district; an array of restaurants and retail shops appeared on the scene; and luxury housing returned to the downtown area.[19]

To make way for this downtown renewal, the Philadelphia Redevelopment Authority demolished 9,000 homes; by 1963, only 3,000 replacement units had been constructed. As in other cities, Philadelphia's postwar progrowth regime displaced primarily poor, working class, minority neighborhoods near the central business district, and facilitated the construction of middle class and luxury apartments for white collar workers and corporate executives who worked in the revitalized downtown economy.[20]

18 Judd, *The Politics of American Cities*, p. 379.
19 N. Kleniewski, "From industrial to corporate city: the role of urban renewal," in *Marxism and the Metropolis: New Perspectives in Urban Political Economy*, ed. W. S. Tabb and L. Sawers, 2nd edn (New York: Oxford University Press, 1984), pp. 205–22.
20 Kleniewski, "From industrial to corporate city."

The electoral base of postwar progrowth regimes

Progrowth governing coalitions, despite their success in achieving consensus on their renewal programs, could not remain in power without legitimizing their political regime through the election process. To generate electoral support, progrowth governing coalitions relied on local Democratic Party organizations to mobilize the predominantly Democratic urban electorate in municipal elections.

Big city Democratic organization in the 1940s and 1950s developed primarily along two lines. In some cities, New Deal programs and postwar urban programs provided the political resources for building or reviving Democratic Party machines. In other cities, particularly ones where nonpartisan election systems had been set in place, labor unions provided the political muscle for boosting local Democratic Party fortunes. Both urban Democratic machines and labor-linked party organizations worked on behalf of urban progrowth coalitions in local elections.

In the first type of city, local Democratic Party leaders took advantage of the partisan realignment of the 1930s and the new federal activism in domestic policy-making to build or revive urban Democratic Party machines. In Pittsburgh, widening support among the city's working class voters and the defeat of the long-standing Republican machine in the mid-1930s opened the way for Democratic Party boss David Lawrence to erect a powerful Democratic machine. Using New Deal public works programs as sources of patronage, Lawrence consolidated the local Democratic Party position among working class voters and fashioned a citywide machine to maintain control over local government.[21] Similarly, Democratic Party bosses Ed Kelly and Patrick Nash constructed a dominant machine in Chicago on the foundation of New Deal programs and a newly aligned Democratic majority.[22]

Urban renewal and other federal programs continued to feed patronage to these surviving Democratic machines in the 1950s and 1960s.[23] Democratic mayors David Lawrence in Pittsburgh, Richard Daley in Chicago, Richard Lee in New Haven, and John Kenney in Jersey City assumed dual roles as heads of Democratic machine organizations and

21 B. Stave, *The New Deal and the Last Hurrah* (Pittsburgh, PA: University of Pittsburgh Press, 1970).
22 See L. Dorsett, *Franklin Roosevelt and the City Bosses* (Port Washington, NY: Kennekat, 1977); S. P. Erie, *Rainbow's End: Irish-Americans and the Dilemmas of Urban Machine Politics, 1840–1985* (Berkeley, CA: University of California Press, 1988).
23 See Dorsett, *Franklin Roosevelt and the City Bosses*; J. M. Allswang, *Bosses, Machines, and Urban Voters*, revised edn (Baltimore, MD: Johns Hopkins University Press, 1986); and Erie, *Rainbow's End*.

progrowth governing coalitions. Using patronage to manage conflict, these progrowth bosses insulated their regimes from political controversy. At election time, the neighborhood-based machine organizations ground out majorities in much the same way as they had done in the past.[24]

Roosevelt's New Deal also catapulted organized labor into the political arena. Pro-labor legislation solidified the alliance between the Democratic Party and labor unions. The Congress of Industrial Unions (CIO), for instance, spent substantial sums for campaign literature and media advertising, supplied large numbers of campaign workers, and held political rallies on behalf of Roosevelt in 1936, 1940, and 1944. As Piven and Cloward note, "the unions came to constitute a parallel infrastructure [to the Democratic Party organization] to mobilize voters."[25]

In those cities where political reforms precluded the rebuilding of party machines, local CIO political action committees, referred to as Committees for Political Education (COPE), infiltrated local Democratic Party organizations and, in some places, became the dominant faction. Labor unions played a particularly important role in nonpartisan cities, where Democratic machines had long disappeared. These labor-linked Democratic Party organizations mobilized Democratic voters in support of progrowth mayoral candidates.[26]

COPE activities in nonpartisan Detroit between 1940 and 1965 illustrate how labor-union-linked local Democratic parties could work as effective campaign organizations. The dominance of a single union, the United Auto Workers (UAW), according to David Greenstone, explains COPE's successful revival of a long-neglected local Democratic Party apparatus.[27] UAW leaders gained control over the local COPE operations. Then, through COPE, UAW political activists secured leadership positions in the local Democratic Party. Using COPE as a resource base, labor leaders furnished considerable funding and a permanent campaign organization to the local Democracy. In the 1950s, Detroit's labor-linked Democratic organization supported progrowth mayoral incumbents Albert Cobo and Joseph Mariani in city election contests.[28]

---

24 See Erie, *Rainbow's End*; Allswang, *Bosses, Machines and Urban Voters*; and A. Talbot, *The Mayor's Game: Richard Lee of New Haven and the Politics of Change* (New York: Harper & Row, 1967).
25 F. F. Piven and R. Cloward, *Why Americans Don't Vote* (New York: Pantheon, 1988), p. 132.
26 J. D. Greenstone, *Labor in American Politics* (New York: Alfred A. Knopf, 1969).
27 See Greenstone, *Labor in American Politics*; R. Conot, *American Odyssey* (Detroit, MI: Wayne State University Press, 1986).
28 Greenstone, *Labor in American Politics*.

Restructuring Urban Progrowth Regimes, 1965–1980

Federal urban renewal programs served as the vehicle for carrying out the progrowth coalition's agenda between 1950 and 1965. These regimes, however, sowed the seeds of their own demise. Urban disorder and the rise of community resistance to urban renewal projects in the mid-1960s forced Democratic governing coalitions to alter the institutional underpinnings of their progrowth regimes to insulate redevelopment decision making from popular control and political conflict. Also, postwar economic restructuring and demographic shifts, facilitated in part by the urban renewal activities of the 1950s and early 1960s, eroded the electoral base for machines and labor-linked Democratic organizations. In the aftermath, Democratic mayors assembled personal campaign organizations to maintain the legitimacy of their progrowth regimes. I now turn to these changes in central city Democratic regimes.

Community resistance, economic restructuring, and progrowth regimes

The political turbulence of the 1960s forced progrowth governing coalitions to modify their development regimes. First, the urban turmoil of the 1960s shattered the politics of consensus that had reigned during the 1950s. The mass migration of blacks to large cities created fissures in the urban Democratic electorate along racial and class lines.[29] In the 1960s, these tensions erupted in a wave of riots that rocked most of the nation's larger cities. The Johnson administration's Great Society programs, such as the antipoverty Community Action Program, were designed as a response to the social crisis at the root of urban disorder.[30] Johnson's "War on Poverty" also served as a strategy to incorporate urban blacks into the national Democratic coalition.[31] Some mayors used these social programs to broker among the racial and poor constituencies at the local level. However, the Democratic urban electorate often split over these redistributive social policies, with blacks favoring antipoverty programs while white ethnic working class voters often viewed such measures with suspicion. In other words, urban disorders and the Johnson administration's expansion of the welfare state, because it narrowly targeted poor

---

29   Kantor, *The Dependent City*, pp. 179–84.
30   See F. F. Piven and R. Cloward, *Regulating the Poor: The Functions of Public Welfare* (New York: Vintage Books, 1971), ch. 8; Judd, *The Politics of American Cities*, ch. 8.
31   F. F. Piven, "The urban crisis: who got what, and why," in *The Politics of Turmoil: Essays on Poverty, Race, and the Urban Crisis*, ed. F. F. Piven and R. Cloward (New York: Pantheon Books, 1974), pp. 314–51.

and minority constituencies, often hardened divisions within the urban electorate.

Second, progrowth policies compounded the polarization of the urban electorate. Politically weak, poor, minority, and working class neighborhoods served as targets for the progrowth coalition's urban renewal bulldozers, thus evoking disaffection for local Democratic regimes among previously staunch Democratic constituencies. Many of these political discontents turned to protest and other antirenewal strategies in the 1960s and 1970s, causing setbacks for progrowth regimes in cities like San Francisco and Boston.[32]

In reaction to urban unrest and neighborhood-based challenges, many progrowth coalitions erected institutional buffers, such as independent quasi-public development authorities and special development districts, to insulate development-policy-making from popular control.[33] Development agencies and programs, furthermore, were kept "structurally segregated" from redistributive programs to avoid further politicization of the development process.[34] Finally, through the establishment of separate community service programs, like Kevin White's Little City Halls program in Boston and Coleman Young's Neighborhood City Halls, and the distribution of federal grants to selected community groups,[35] Democratic mayors garnered enough neighborhood support to put together majority electoral coalitions. These new institutional arrangements worked to shield progrowth regimes from popular control and mute conflict in development politics.

To compensate for the erosion of progrowth political consensus, Democratic governing coalitions also shifted their redevelopment strategies to accommodate economic changes. First, by the early 1970s, the American system of cities, structured by what Kantor calls a "multilocational" economy, had become much more competitive.[36] The mobility of capital, a product of the multilocational corporate structure, generated intense pressure on city governments to enter into fierce rivalries with each other in order to capture private economic development. Further, the introduction of New Federalism under the Nixon administration eliminated the urban renewal program and replaced it with a Community Development

32 See Mollenkopf, *Contested City*, pp. 180–212; C. Hartman and R. Kessler, "The illusion and reality of urban renewal: San Francisco's Yerba Buena Center," in *Marxism and the Metropolis: New Perspectives in Urban Political Economy*, ed. W. S. Tabb and L. Sawers (New York: Oxford University Press, 1978), pp. 153–78.

33 Kantor, *The Dependent City*, pp. 246–50.

34 R. Friedland, F. F. Piven, and R. R. Alford, "Political conflict, urban structures, and the fiscal crisis," in *Comparing Public Policies: New Concepts and Methods*, ed. D. Ashford (Beverly Hills, CA: Sage, 1977), pp. 197–225.

35 K. K. Wong and P. E. Peterson, "Urban response to federal program flexibility: politics of Community Development Block Grants," *Urban Affairs Quarterly*, 21 (1986), pp. 293–309.

36 Kantor, *The Dependent City*, pp. 164–70.

Block Grant (CDBG) program. CDBGs required much less federal supervision over the administration of local development efforts than the categorical grant program of urban renewal, thus affording local government officials wider latitude in devising their growth strategies.[37] In reaction to these changes in the political economy context, urban progrowth regimes shifted from the "grand strategy" dictated by the urban renewal program to a more flexible strategy that employed a diverse array of techniques to subsidize private development.[38] The repertoire of urban development subsidy tools proliferated from the late 1960s to the 1980s. Progrowth regimes in this period incorporated tax abatements, industrial revenue bonds, loans, free or cheap land, publicly owned industrial parks, infrastructural improvement, and the use of special tax districts that concentrated the benefits of development in downtown areas to encourage further development.[39] The upshot of all this was that Democratic progrowth governing coalitions in this period expanded the subsidization of businesses, and thus continued to follow a conservative economic logic rather than progressive populism.

The case of Baltimore illustrates how Democratic city administrations after 1965 combined flexible and expanded growth strategies with institutional buffers against political conflict and popular control. Baltimore lost 13.1 percent (119,000 people) of its population between 1970 and 1980, along with 45 percent of its manufacturing base (40,000 jobs). The median household income dropped from 74 to 63 percent of the Standard Metropolitan Statistical Area average.[40] In the midst of this decline, former Mayor Donald Schaefer, first elected in 1971, forged a progrowth governing coalition to rebuild the city's downtown economy. As Marc V. Levine explains, "Between 1971 and 1985, city officials and private investors made three redevelopment priorities the foundation of Baltimore's downtown strategy: Office development, the revitalization of retail and commercial activity, and the promotion of tourism and conventions."[41] Baltimore employed a mix of loans and loan guarantees ($500 million between 1976 and 1986), Urban Development Action Grants, CDBGs, and other grants to subsidize downtown development.[42]

37   P. R. Dommel, *Decentralizing Urban Policy: Case Studies in Community Development* (Washington, DC: Brookings Institution, 1982).
38   Kantor, *The Dependent City*, pp. 254–68.
39   See B. D. Jones and L. Bachelor, *The Sustaining Hand: Community Leadership and Corporate Power* (Lawrence, KS: University Press of Kansas, 1986), ch. 6; C. N. Stone and H. T. Sanders (eds), *The Politics of Urban Development* (Lawrence, KS: University Press of Kansas, 1987); S. Cummings (ed.), *Business Elites and Urban Development: Case Studies and Critical Perspectives* (Albany, NY: State University of New York Press, 1988); Kantor, *The Dependent City*, pp. 226–33.
40   M. C. Levine, "Downtown redevelopment as an urban growth strategy: a critical appraisal of the Baltimore renaissance," *Journal of Urban Affairs*, 9 (1987), p. 107.
41   Levine, "Downtown redevelopment as an urban growth strategy," p. 109.
42   See Levine, "Downtown redevelopment as an urban growth strategy"; R. P.

Baltimore's governing coalition also established institutional buffers and a social control system to manage political conflict. The Schaefer administration erected a massive complex of twenty-four quasi-public development agencies, dubbed Schaefer's "shadow government," that insulated Baltimore's developmental decision making process from popular control.[43] Furthermore, Schaefer established a clientele network with politically allied neighborhood groups through the city's Department of Housing and Community Development and a decentralized service system of neighborhood-based Mayor's Stations. Clientele relations with neighborhood groups were cemented by the distribution of CDBGs to political supporters. As Wong and Peterson explain:

> In order to mobilize community support for his renaissance, Mayor Schaefer allocated portions of the CDBG funds to coopt neighborhood groups. Community groups that supported the administration's renaissance have been getting the lion's share of the many CDBG-funded rehabilitation and Model Cities-type services. Outspoken dissenting groups were said to have disturbed the mayor, who seemed to want to mute public controversy. These organizations received hardly any CDBG projects.[44]

Baltimore's use of quasi-public development agencies removed development decision making from the formal political arena, while the formation of clientele relations through neighborhood programs was used to generate political support for the city's progrowth regime.

Despite the revitalization of downtown Baltimore, the centerpiece of which is the city's Harbor Place commercial area, the benefits of the progrowth regime have not been disbursed evenly. As Levine concludes:

> The Baltimore experience reveals fundamental deficiencies in the corporate center strategy of urban economic development. Despite the omnipresent rhetoric of renaissance, Baltimore's basic economic problems – the loss of quality jobs, lagging per capita income, deteriorating city neighborhoods – remain unsolved. The standard of living for the majority of city dwellers continues to decline as Baltimore has become the archetype of urban dualism.[45]

Stoker, "Baltimore: the self-evaluating city?," in *The Politics of Urban Development*, ed. C. N. Stone and H. T. Sanders (Lawrence, KS: University Press of Kansas, 1987).
43   See B. Berkowitz, "Economic development really works," in *Urban Economic Development*, ed. R. D. Bingham and J. P. Blair (Beverly Hills, CA: Sage, 1984); Stoker, "Baltimore."
44   Wong and Peterson, "Urban response to federal program flexibility," p. 306.
45   Levine, "Downtown redevelopment as an urban growth strategy," p. 118.

Baltimore's progrowth regime heavily subsidized downtown businesses, but did little to equalize the distribution of benefits of downtown development.

Democratic city regimes from the 1960s to the early 1980s struck a balance between subsidizing downtown business interests, particularly developers and large corporations, and servicing selective neighborhood interests through clientele networks. In measuring this against the standard of progressive populism, Democratic city regimes fall short of the mark. Close ties to the business community and an ideologically imbued "economic logic" prevented Democratic city governing coalitions from disbursing economic benefits to Democratic constituencies or from imposing a modicum of planning and regulation on private development through governmental intervention. Instead, Democratic progrowth regimes tailored subsidy packages to the requirements of multilocational corporations and downtown developers. In the meantime, economic disparity between the haves and the have-nots persisted and in some cases increased.

Progrowth regimes and
independent candidate organizations

Demographic restructuring of central cities also disrupted the consensus politics established by progrowth regimes in the 1950s. A "dual migration,"[46] in which relatively affluent whites migrated to exclusionary suburban enclaves while poor and minority groups simultaneously flooded into the inner cities, polarized central cities along class and racial lines.[47] As a result, the urban working class became divided into two cohorts, one made up of traditional blue collar workers who were predominantly white, and another composed of the "new" urban workers who were poorer and largely minority, as table 10.3 suggests. Class and race polarities threatened to undermine the dominance of Democratic progrowth regimes.

Big city elections after 1965, particularly Democratic primaries, often saw rival Democratic constituencies pitted against each other in contests that pivoted on the issue of race. Democratic mayoral candidates adopted two sorts of strategies to navigate the shoals of a racially polarized electorate. First, in cities for which no clear majority emerged among racial groups, Democratic mayoral candidates have often attempted to construct biracial or multiracial electoral coalitions. Democratic mayors Tom Bradley (1974–present) of Los Angeles, William Green (1980–3) of Philadelphia, Donald Schaefer (1971–83), and Kevin White of Boston (1968–83), fashioned biracial political alliances of black and white liberal voters by juggling promises of economic growth and redistribution. However, in cities where one group held a clear majority in

46 Judd, *The Politics of American Cities*, p. 147.
47 Kantor, *The Dependent City*, pp. 180–4.

Table 10.3 Population breakdown of seven selected cities on the basis of class and race, 1980

City	Foreign born (%)	Black (%)	Spanish (%)	Below 125% of poverty level (%)	Per capita median income ($) Whites	Blacks	Below 125% of poverty level Whites	Blacks
Baltimore	3.1	54.8	1.0	28.9	7,619	4,493	17.4	38.0
Boston	15.5	22.5	6.5	27.2	7,448	4,620	21.8	37.3
Chicago	14.5	39.8	14.1	33.2	8,903	4,904	14.3	38.0
Cleveland	5.8	43.8	3.1	27.7	8,770	5,377	8.6	32.7
New York	23.6	25.3	19.9	25.9	8,902	5,014	17.8	36.8
Philadelphia	6.4	37.8	3.8	21.9	8,326	4,658	16.4	39.7
Pittsburgh	5.2	24.0	0.8	22.8	7,926	4,970	15.7	40.7

Source: P. Kantor, The Dependent City: The Changing Political Economy of Urban America (Glenview, IL: Scott, Foresman, 1988), p. 181

the electorate, Democratic mayors tended to calibrate their electoral appeals more narrowly to a single racial group. For example, black urban regimes, as Adolph Reed calls them, targeted black voters as their electoral base by emphasizing the benefits of their policies to the black community.[48] Black mayors Coleman Young (1973–present) of Detroit, Maynard Jackson (1974–81) of Atlanta, and Kenneth Gibson of Newark (1970–86) pursued this single constituency approach.

Racial polarization wreaked havoc on big city Democratic machines. Black leaders, often aligned with white liberals, challenged entrenched white ethnic party bosses for control of City Hall. For instance, Harold Washington, Chicago's first black mayor, mobilized the black community to defeat the Democratic machine's white candidate in the primary and forged a black–Hispanic–white liberal electoral coalition to narrowly edge out the Republican candidate in the general election.[49] In Philadelphia, William Green, a former Congressman, organized a liberal biracial coalition in the 1979 mayoral race that drove the final nail in the coffin of the local Democratic machine.[50] In these and other cases, the local Democratic party organizations splintered under the pressure of polarized urban politics.

The decline of Democratic machines and labor-union-linked Democratic organizations "facilitated candidate independence" from party organizations.[51] The development of new campaign technologies, moreover, replaced labor intensive methods of voter mobilization used by both party machines and labor-union-linked party organizations. Capital intensive campaign techniques, such as phonebanks, computer-generated polling, direct mail fundraising, and mass media strategies obviated large-scale precinct organizations.[52] In this context, mayors at the center of progrowth coalitions formed personal campaign organizations staffed by city hall operatives and worked independently of Democratic Party organizations to mobilize their electoral coalitions. These candidate-centered organizations, funded primarily through contributions from downtown business interests and mayoral appointees, have

48   A. Reed, "The black urban regime: structural origins and constraints," in *Power, Community, and the City: Comparative Urban and Community Research*, ed. M. P. Smith (New Brunswick, NJ: Transaction, 1988).

49   G. Squires, L. Bennett, K. McCourt, and P. Nyden, *Chicago: Race, Class, and the Response to Urban Decline* (Philadelphia, PA: Temple University Press, 1987), ch. 3.

50   B. Ranson, "Black independent electoral politics in Philadelphia and the election of Mayor W. Wilson Goode," in *The New Black Politics: The Search for Political Power*, ed. M. P. Preston, L. J. Henderson Jr, and P. L. Puryear, 2nd edn (New York: Longman, 1987).

51   Ware, *The Breakdown of Democratic Party Organization*, p. 241.

52   B. Ginsberg, "Money and power: the new political economy of American elections," in *The Political Economy: Readings in Politics and Economics of American Public Policy*, ed. T. Fergusson and J. Rogers (Armonk, NY: M. E. Sharpe, 1984), pp. 163–79.

relied on low turnouts and selective bases of support to reelect progrowth mayors.

In Baltimore, which uses partisan elections, former mayor William Schaefer's 1983 reelection bid illustrates how mayoral personal campaign organizations operate. Schaefer's electoral appeal cut across class lines and divided the black vote in the primary race against the black candidate William H. Murphy. First, Schaefer welded together a personal campaign organization out of political appointees in his shadow government. The organization raised over a million dollars, much of which was donated in large contributions from business supporters and political appointees.[53] This campaign chest aided Schaefer in his rout of his black opponent with 71 percent of the vote in a city where blacks comprised 55 percent of the population.[54]

Second, Schaefer's organization mounted a large-scale invasion of the city's neighborhoods. As one report tells the story, "Schaefer's aides made sure that the Mayor followed a tight schedule through the summer that took him into nearly every neighborhood in the city stumping for votes.... The Mayor [also] spent the summer calling press conferences, and stumping at neighborhood meetings, house parties and community rallies."[55] The Schaefer campaign organization also issued marching orders to its army of volunteers to canvass the city. Schaefer's field organization, directed by Michael H. Davis, hit the pavement at election time, knocking on doors and stopping people on the street to get out the vote. Two hundred other political workers manned phonebanks, exhorting voters to cast their ballots for Schaefer. To insure a large victory margin, several hundred cars were commandeered "around the city to drive voters to the polls."[56] In short, despite an active Democratic Party organization in Baltimore, Schaefer relied on a personal campaign organization to win reelection in his mayoral races.

In nonpartisan San Francisco, Democrat Diane Feinstein (1979–87), catapulted into the mayor's office by the assassination of Mayor George Moscone, also developed an independent campaign organization to maintain her progrowth governing coalition.[57] In 1983, Feinstein faced a recall election. To fend off this challenge, Feinstein and her closest political aides engineered the building of a personal campaign organization based on volunteers and money. Feinstein's tough fiscal management policies and her activist approach in the area of economic development had earned her high marks from San Francisco's business community as the outpouring of campaign contributions during the 1983 recall election demonstrated. Of the contributions, 94 percent were for $500 or more,

53 *Baltimore Sun*, September 3, 1983; October 5, 1983.
54 *Baltimore Sun*, September 9, 1983.
55 *Baltimore Sun*, September 8, 1983; September 11, 1983.
56 *Baltimore Sun*, September 8, 1983.
57 S. S. Fainstein, N. I. Fainstein, and P. J. Armistead, "San Francisco: urban transformation and the local state," in *Restructuring the City: The Political Economy of Urban Redevelopment*, ed. S. S. Fainstein and N. I. Fainstein, 2nd edn (New York: Longman, 1986), pp. 202–44; *San Francisco Chronicle*, November 11, 1983.

with most coming from businesses that had "substantial financial dealings with the city."[58]

In addition, Feinstein appointed one of her chief political aides, Fred Ross Jr, to take charge of organizing a large campaign effort to defeat the recall drive. Feinstein's campaign strategy introduced two intriguing innovations to San Francisco electioneering. First, the Feinstein organization orchestrated a massive "vote-by-mail" effort that netted 51,033 absentee ballots – 32.6 percent of the total vote. This was purported to be the largest proportion of absentee voting in election history.[59] Second, campaign chief Ross strategically deployed an army of three-member "Feinstein Brigades" that blitzed 250 selected precincts "trying to find pro-Feinstein voters [to] make sure they [went] to the polls."[60] All told, the Feinstein field organization fielded 2,000 foot soldiers, armed with a campaign chest of $550,000, and easily routed the recall forces by capturing more than 80 percent of the total vote. As Ross chortled after the recall election, "the Mayor now has an organization that's personally loyal to her, and probably the most formidable organization in the city right now."[61] Feinstein reassembled her army of political workers seven months later in the regular municipal election, which repeated its performance.

Independent campaign organizations linked to executive-centered governing coalitions have supplanted local Democratic Party organizations in big city elections. These mayor-centered campaign organizations mobilize the neighborhood clientele of progrowth governing coalitions in election contests, and thus perpetuate progrowth regimes. Mayor-centered candidate organizations are also linked with downtown business interests and developers, as indicated by the fact that Democratic progrowth mayoral candidates receive the lion's share of their contributions from corporate executives and developers. In short, the character of independent candidate organizations reflected the politics of Democratic progrowth regimes, with Democratic mayors balancing downtown interests and selective neighborhood constituencies.

Urban Politics in the 1980s:
The Rise of Progressive Governing
Coalitions

Fainstein and Fainstein identify three patterns of postindustrial urban development: new, old, and converting cities.[62] *New cities* have experienced

58 *San Francisco Chronicle*, April 3, 1983.
59 *San Francisco Chronicle*, April 27, 1983.
60 *San Francisco Chronicle*, April 27, 1983.
61 *San Francisco Chronicle*, April 28, 1983.
62 N. I. Fainstein and S. S. Fainstein, "Restructuring the American city: a comparative perspective," in *Urban Policy Under Capitalism*, ed. N. I. Fainstein and S. S. Fainstein (Beverly Hills, CA: Sage, 1982), pp. 161–89.

the most rapid growth in the postindustrial era, as their economies were based on newer industries such as oil, military, or high technology and therefore did not undergo major restructuring. Examples of new cities include Dallas, Houston, and Los Angeles. *Converting cities* declined during the first three decades of the postwar period, losing most of their manufacturing base, but eventually made successful transitions to the postindustrial structure by converting into corporate headquarter/service centers. Examples of converting cities are New York, Boston, and San Francisco. *Old cities* are the industrial giants of the past that have suffered continuous decline in the postwar period because they have not undergone a successful postindustrial transformation into corporate headquarter/service cities. These cities continue to lose manufacturing, but without the compensating development of a strong downtown economy. Detroit, Buffalo, and Youngstown are examples of old cities.

Urban regimes have reflected these divergent paths. In declining cities like Detroit, Buffalo, and Newark, progrowth regimes continued to dominate local politics.[63] In a number of converting cities, however, urban regimes more aptly characterized as progressive populist have emerged in the 1980s. In this section we examine the appearance of progressive–populist regimes in converting cities during the 1980s.

The emergence of progressive–populist regimes

Urban renewal programs in many big cities galvanized neighborhood organizing and protest that challenged progrowth governing coalitions in the late 1960s and 1970s. These neighborhood groups initially pursued confrontational strategies to halt redevelopment programs that threatened to bulldoze poor and working class neighborhoods to make way for middle class housing and commercial development.[64] By the mid-1970s, however, the local groups had largely turned to accommodationist strategies, which emphasized cooperation with public officials and development interests. Neighborhood organizations have since concentrated their efforts on building or renovating low- and moderate-income housing through community development corporations or providing services to neighborhood residents.[65] In the 1980s, this institutionalized community movement became the political base for the formation of progressive–populist governing coalitions in a number of cities.[66]

Populist and liberal politicians in Minneapolis, San Francisco, Denver, Boston, Santa Monica, and Chicago organized progressive–

---

63   See Reed, "The black urban regime."
64   See R. Fisher, *Let the People Decide: Neighborhood Organizing in America* (Boston, MA: Twayne, 1984), ch. 4; Mollenkopf, *Contested City*, ch. 5.
65   See Fisher, *Let the People Decide*, ch. 5.
66   See P. Clavel, *The Progressive City: Planning and Participation, 1969–1984* (New Brunswick, NJ: Rutgers University Press, 1986).

populist governing coalitions in the 1980s.[67] Drawing their political support from local communities, these regimes attempt to *manage* economic growth in two ways: (a) by redistributing some of the benefits of economic development in the form of jobs and housing programs for poor and working class residents; (b) by controlling the rate and kind of growth to protect the city's physical environment.

The emergence of urban progressive–populist coalitions was spurred, at least in part, by rapid downtown development. Boston, San Francisco, Santa Monica, and Chicago experienced substantial economic growth in the 1980s. Unbridled development, in turn, threatened the quality of life for both the urban middle class and the working class. Urban growth has pushed up the cost of housing, exacerbated pollution and congestion problems, and endangered precious parks and tree-lined avenues.[68] In other words, middle and working class anxiety and discontent about rapid growth provoked demands for growth management.[69] At the same time, the relative prosperity brought about by rapid economic development in these cities has made it possible to fund progressive–populist redistributive programs.

Unlike the liberal city regimes of the 1960s that promoted social reform through the Johnson administration's Great Society programs,[70] progressive–populist urban regimes of the 1980s did not segregate social and economic development policies to shield development decision making from popular control.[71] In fact, progressive–populist regimes have begun to employ zoning and other policy tools (a) to extract concessions from developers to fund construction of low- and moderate-income

---

67 See Clavel, *The Progressive City*; Stone, "Summing up"; D. Judd and R. L. Ready, "Entrepreneurial cities and the new politics of economic development," in *Reagan and the Cities*, ed. G. E. Peterson and C. W. Lewis (Washington, DC: The Urban Institute, 1986); D. S. Daykin, "The limits to neighborhood power: progressive politics and local control in Santa Monica," in *Business Elites and Urban Development: Case Studies and Critical Perspectives*, ed. S. Cummings (Albany, NY: State University of New York Press, 1988), pp. 357–87; T. Swanstrom, "Urban populism, uneven development, and the space for reform," in *Business Elites and Urban Development: Case Studies and Critical Perspectives*, ed. S. Cummings (Albany, NY: State University of New York Press, 1988), pp. 121–52.

68 See D. Keating, "Linking downtown development to broader community goals: an analysis of linkage policies in three cities," *American Planning Association Journal* (Spring 1986), pp. 133–41; D. Muzzio and R. W. Bailey, "Economic development, housing and zoning: a tale of two cities," *Journal of Urban Affairs*, 8 (1986), pp. 1–18.

69 See M. Baldassare, "Predicting local concern about growth: the roots of citizen discontent," *Journal of Urban Affairs*, 6 (1984), pp. 39–49.

70 See J. D. Greenstone and P. E. Peterson, *Race and Authority in Urban Politics: Community Participation and the War on Poverty* (Chicago, IL: University of Chicago Press, 1973).

71 See Friedland et al., "Political conflict, urban structure, and the fiscal crisis."

housing, (b) to mitigate the negative effects of rapid economic growth on the urban environment, and (c) to expand neighborhood participation in the planning process.[72]

Boston's governing coalition exemplifies the resurgence of progressive–populist politics in the 1980s. Democrat Raymond Flynn, who succeeded progrowth mayor Kevin White in 1984, forged a governing alliance between his mayoral administration and the city's well-established community organizations. Flynn, a long-time neighborhood-oriented politician, fashioned a political regime based on growth management rather than on progrowth policies. Three fundamental principles undergird Boston's growth management regime: (a) "economic justice" should be the operational standard for growth policies and programs, whereby some of the benefits of economic growth are to be distributed to the disadvantaged segment of the city's population; (b) government should regulate the rate and kind of growth that takes place in the city; and (c) neighborhood participation in developmental policy-making should be expanded.[73]

Each of these progressive–populist principles is reflected in the Flynn administration's development strategy and programs. First, Boston's growth management regime features an array of programs that redistribute some of the benefits of Boston's downtown development boom to poor and working class neighborhoods. These include a housing and job linkage program, which requires developers of large projects to contribute to an affordable housing and job training trust fund; inclusionary zoning, which enjoins developers to set aside a proportion of housing units in their large complexes for low- and moderate-income residents; a program that transfers publicly owned surplus land to nonprofit neighborhood development corporations who construct affordable housing; and legislation that limits condominium conversions to protect the existing stock of poor and working class housing.[74] These programs have produced substantial results. In 1987, for example, Boston subsidized 2,345 new units of housing, which was nearly five times the average for cities of comparable size, and much greater than the amount of housing subsidization under the previous mayor administration.[75] Second, the Flynn administration has introduced large-scale planning to control the rate and kind of development. Through the creation of planning zones, known as Interim Planning and Greenbelt Protection Overlay Districts, the Flynn administration imposes strict height, size, and open

---

72 See Keating, "Linking downtown development to broader community goals"; Muzzio and Bailey, "Economic development, housing, and zoning"; T. Swanstrom, "Urban populism, uneven development, and the space for reform."
73 City of Boston, *Breaking Ground: A Report on Boston Housing Policy and Performance* (April 1987).
74 City of Boston, *Breaking Ground*; Swanstrom, "Urban populism, uneven development, and the space for reform."
75 *Boston Globe*, February 1, 1989.

space requirements on development.[76] Third, Flynn has created community-based planning boards that review neighborhood development proposals and recommend zoning restrictions, thus partially democratizing the land-use decision making process. It should be noted that these growth management programs have been underwritten (in the case of the linkage program) or provoked (in the case of zoning controls) by Boston's economic development boom in the 1980s.[77]

Boston's growth management regime represents a departure from its earlier progrowth approach in the 1970s and early 1980s. Using government as a tool to regulate economic development and formulating development policies that include elements of redistribution and citizen participation, Boston's growth management regime marks a return to the Democratic Party's progressive–populist New Deal orientation, albeit with a difference. The New Deal formula was in large part based on the need to regenerate the nation's economy to provide jobs and increase prosperity for its urban constituencies.[78] The progressive–populist regimes of the 1980s, in contrast, have been reactions to *problems* provoked by rapid urban economic development. Middle class preservationists have sought to contain what they consider to be overdevelopment, and thus protect their neighborhoods from congestion and other infringements on their quality of life. Poor and working class neighborhood groups, in turn, have demanded protection of affordable housing stock from neighborhood gentrification. In other words, sources of support for Boston's progressive regime in the 1980s have been produced by rapid economic growth, not its absence. On the basis of this more defensive posture of growth management, Flynn has fashioned a workable political coalition as demonstrated by his landslide reelection in 1987.

Postindustrial Urban Regimes and the Democratic Party

The reemergence of progressive–populist regimes in the 1980s holds some promise for uniting polarized Democratic constituencies around issues of economic opportunity and quality of life. First of all, progressive–populist urban regimes offer something to the urban working class, both blue collar and new collar, which had been sorely neglected during the years of progrowth coalition dominance. The redistributive linkage policies and programs that tackle the problems of affordable housing, job creation, and job training resonate with both white and

76 *Boston Globe*, May 22, 1987; May 28, 1989.
77 See Keating, "Linking downtown development to broader community goals"; Muzzio and Bailey, "Economic development, housing, and zoning."
78 See A. Wolfe, *America's Impasse: The Rise and Fall of the Politics of Growth* (New York: Pantheon Books, 1981).

minority working class constituencies. Second, progressive–populist regimes blend the necessary ingredients for constructing cross-class coalitions. The support of middle class environmental activists suggests that
growth management policies furnish the means to bring together different class segments of the local Democratic electorate. In sum, the local
progressive–populist regimes contain the raw material for rebuilding
local Democratic coalitions, at least in some northern and western cities,
on the basis of a social reform program.

Despite these political opportunities for renovating local Democratic
parties on the basis of progressive–populist social reform, daunting
obstacles remain. First, electoral barriers created by reform movements
(nonpartisan elections and direct primaries) in Democratic strongholds,
such as San Francisco, Boston, and Detroit, prevent institutionalization
of progressive–populist regimes in local Democratic organizations. The
dominant electoral organization in big city politics is still the independent campaign organization, which means that urban electoral coalitions
still center on individual candidates, even under populist–progressive
regimes. The defeat, retirement, or death of a mayor, as in the case of
Chicago's Harold Washington, usually spells disaster for biracial or
multiracial urban Democratic alliances.

Second, the polarization of politics along lines of class and race, as
revealed by the recent election in Chicago, continues to fracture the
Democratic urban electorate. The progressive–populist regime engineered by Harold Washington during his first mayoral administration,
which was backed by a multiracial coalition of blacks, Hispanics, and
white liberals, collapsed after his death. The 1989 special mayoral election to choose his successor produced sharp racial cleavages in the voting
results, with Richard Daley Jr capturing 94 percent of the white vote
and, consequently, the Mayor's Office.[79] In other words, progressive–
populist regimes are based on fragile arrangements, and remain vulnerable to the polarizing tendencies in the urban Democratic electorate.

Third, the unevenness of urban development produced by postindustrial urban restructuring means that only converting cities, such
as Boston and San Francisco, will generate the economic growth necessary to support progressive–populist urban regimes. In declining cities,
like Detroit and Buffalo, the formation of such governing coalitions
seems improbable. In these cities, progrowth coalitions remain firmly
entrenched.

In a sense, then, progressive–populist urban regimes are political
reactions to economic restructuring in converting cities, rather than
generalizable political programs for rebuilding the Democratic Party
from the grassroots. For all these reasons, and probably others, the
widespread resurgence of local Democratic parties as political institutions that mobilize voters on the basis of progressive urban appeals is
unlikely, at least in the near future.

79 *New York Times*, April 5, 1989.

11

Structural Constraints and Political Development: The Case of the American Democratic Party

Frances Fox Piven

In this final chapter, I will try to explain the travails of the American Democratic Party. I know I take liberties in treating the Democrats as a labor party, since it has always been more heterogeneous and less programmatic than labor parties elsewhere. Still, during the electoral realignment of the 1930s, the Democrats gained the overwhelming allegiance of most manual workers and their unions. However, if this signaled the emergence of something like a labor party, it did not last. Working class support for the Democrats dropped precipitously in the presidential contests of the 1950s, recovered briefly in the 1960s, and then plunged again, as table 11.1 shows. In other words, working class defections from the American "labor party" began at the very peak of industrialism. Later, postindustrial trends also took their toll, and in the 1970s and 1980s, the ranks of the old working class did indeed begin to shrink. At the same time, however, the numbers of low wage earners were enlarging, not only in the growing service sector but in restructured industrial employment as well. Many of these workers were minorities. Many more were women. And among both low-income people and women, Democratic preferences were increasing, but their voting levels were falling. Not only did the Democrats lose support among older groups of industrial workers, and lose it early, but they failed to mobilize the ranks of this new working class. Clearly, the unraveling of the Democratic party was not a straightforward reflection of postindustrial economic trends, as table 11.1 illustrates.

I want to thank Robert Alford, James MacGregor Burns, Richard Cloward, Jeff Escoffier, Joel Krieger, and Richard Valelly for their comments on an earlier version of this paper.

Table 11.1   Percentage of white major party voters who voted
Democratic for president by union membership, class, and nonsouth

	Union member	Working class	Nonsouth
1944	67	64	–
1948	79	76	–
1952	53	52	39
1956	50	44	36
1960	64	55	46
1964	80	75	65
1968	50	50	42
1972	40	32	33
1976	60	58	46
1980	48	44	36
1984	50	42	37

Source: Extrapolated from P. R. Abramson, J. H. Aldrich, and D. W. Rohde,
Change and Continuity in the 1980 Elections (Washington, DC: Congressional
Quarterly Press, 1983), figures 5–2, 5–3, and 5–4. Based on National
Opinion Research Center polls, which are susceptible to substantial over-
reporting of voting.

Democratic decomposition – by which I mean both slipping vote
totals and rising levels of split-ticket voting – is better explained by
taking account of distinctive American political structures, including a
divided and decentralized state structure, and unique restrictions on the
franchise, which the Democratic party inherited when it reemerged in
the Great Depression as a "labor party." A fragmented and decentralized government meant that the national party was itself fragmented,
without an effective command center to formulate and impose coherent
party strategies. Simultaneously, divided and decentralized government
and the restricted franchise nourished the politics of the southern wing,
and the influence of well-organized business groups. Sectional and
interest group influences in turn worked to promote policies which
inhibited the growth of the party's union allies, and stunted the
expansion of the welfare state programs which had earned the party
popular support in the 1930s. These accommodations left the party's
infrastructure weak, and its constituency support fragile, well before the
onset of postindustrial changes.
    The economic and social transformations of the post-Second World
War period aggravated party weaknesses. But these transformations
were not exogenous to politics, nor to the inherited structures which
mold American politics. A decentered Democratic party collaborated in
national policies that shaped the pattern of postwar industrial growth in
ways that, from the point of view of the national Democratic party, were

entirely perverse. These military, infrastructure, and housing policies, for example, also reflected sectional influence, as well as the heavy hand of investor interest groups. Steadily over a period of three decades, these policies dissipated Democratic support among older constituencies, and aggravated deep-seated constituency conflicts. And this occurred while the party infrastructure fashioned during the New Deal atrophied, inhibiting the party from recruiting new supporters to compensate for the defections generated by disaffection and conflict. By the 1970s, the several sources of weakness of the Democrats were well advanced, paving the way for the ascendance to national power of a revamped Republican party dominated by a temporarily unified business class that had joined in an alliance of convenience with right-wing populists, many of whose constituents were Democratic defectors.

I need to say a word about the weight I give in this explanation to political structures. Surely, Democratic leaders were not entirely constrained by structural arrangements and the sectional and interest group forces privileged by these arrangements. Or at least there must have been particular junctures when they had at least some latitude so that their choices mattered in shaping the course of events. In principle, I believe that structure and agency together shape political life. But I do not attempt here to sift through the tangled history of the past fifty years to try to identify the specific real options available to Democratic leaders, or why they failed to utilize them. The task I have set myself is more modest; if politics rests on some exercise of agency, it is also the case that structures always restrict agency, and it is that dimension of Democratic Party history that I am trying to illuminate. Moreover, I am struck by the evidence that while the panic years of the early 1930s may have expanded the options of Democratic leaders by stilling opposition, even modest recovery revived opposition and constricted latitude. It is chastening to note, for example, the failure of Democratic efforts in the late 1930s to overcome the constraints of sectionalism with a concerted campaign to transform the south. In a series of moves that Steve Fraser calls "political strategy at its grandest," the Congress of Industrial Organizations (CIO) tried to organize the southern textile industry; northern liberals in the congress fought for legislation that would raise wages in the south; and Roosevelt worked to purge congressional reactionaries, particularly southerners, from the party in the primary elections of 1938.[1] But within a few months it was over, and it was the

---

1   S. Fraser, "The labor question," in *The Rise and Fall of the New Deal Order*, ed. S. Fraser and G. Gerstle (Princeton, NJ: Princeton University Press, 1989), pp. 74–5. See also J. MacGregor Burns, *Roosevelt: The Lion and the Fox* (New York: Harcourt, Brace, 1956), pp. 360–2. Roosevelt campaigned personally and vigorously against what he said was the feudal politics of the south, and tried to defeat Senators Walter George from Georgia, "Cotton Ed" Smith from South Carolina, and Millard Tydings from Maryland. All won easily, strengthening the congressional alliance of southern Democrats and Republicans and weakening Roosevelt. I am grateful to Ronald Shurin for a personal communication reviewing these events.

south and not the national party that prevailed, suggesting the great
weight of the inherited structures to which the south owed its power.

Electoral Decomposition
of the Democratic Party

There is no disputing that the Democrats hold on national electoral
politics has slipped badly. The party has won only three presidential
elections in four decades, and the most recent victory was made possible
only by the Watergate scandal and the near-impeachment of a Republican president. Moreover, the Democratic contender has usually lost by
landslide margins in the electoral college, and by very large proportions
of the popular vote as well. After the 1988 election, the *Congressional
Quarterly* summed up the recent record: "In the six presidential elections
since ... 1964, GOP White House candidates have won 264 million
popular votes to 215 for the Democrats, 2,501 electoral votes to 679 for
the Democrats, and 241 states to 54 for the Democrats."

Large-scale defections are part of the reason.[2] Democratic support
has been leaching among groups which had been the core party constituencies since the New Deal, most importantly white southerners and
working class voters.[3] In the election of 1936 that solidified the New
Deal Democratic Party, Franklin Delano Roosevelt won 85 percent of
the white southern vote,[4] and the south was crucial to every Democratic
presidential victory thereafter. By 1976, when the Democrats ran a
presidential candidate from Georgia, only 53 percent of white southerners voted Democratic.[5] And by 1984, 70 percent of white southerners
joined the Reagan landslide,[6] a margin that fell only slightly to 67
percent in 1988.[7]

---

2   One source of defection reflects relatively recent shifts. In the 1960s and
1970s, the Democrats made gains among high status northern whites, which they
lost again in the 1980s as income inequalities widened and the electorate became
increasingly polarized along class lines. I put these relatively fleeting changes to
one side in my analysis.

3   J. R. Petrocik, *Party Coalitions: Realignments and the Decline of the New Deal Party
System* (Chicago, IL: University of Chicago Press, 1981), ch. 6, provides data on
what he calls the "noncritical" realignment resulting from partisan shifts among
different constituency groups.

4   E. C. Ladd, "As the realignment turns: a drama in many acts," *Public
Opinion*, 7, 6 (1985), p. 5.

5   Petrocik, *Realignments and the Decline of the New Deal Party System*, p. 96.

6   P. R. Abramson, J. H. Aldrich and D. W. Rohde, *Change and Continuity in the
1984 Elections* (Washington, DC: Congressional Quarterly, 1986), pp. 136–7,
table 5–1.

7   G. M. Pomper, *The Election of 1988: Reports and Interpretations* (Chatham, NJ:
Chatham House, 1988), pp. 133–4, table 5.2.

Meanwhile, Democratic support also slipped among working class voters. After the losses of the Eisenhower elections in the 1950s, a large majority of working class voters returned to the Democratic Party in 1964, only to desert again in 1968.[8] By the 1980s, Republican presidential candidates claimed firm majorities of the working class vote, and large majorities of the white working class vote.[9] Moreover, despite the efforts of the unions, the Democratic margin even among union families had narrowed to the point where its existence was disputed.[10] And an AFL−CIO poll showed that 52 percent of white unionists under forty had voted for Reagan.[11] Although Bush did less well in 1988 with 49 percent of the blue collar vote,[12] it seems clear that the overwhelming Democratic working class margins of the New Deal are gone.

To be sure, despite these upheavals in the electorate, the Democrats retain their hold on the Congress, and also control a majority, albeit a narrowing one, of positions in state and local governments.[13] A good many of the union members who had voted for Reagan and Bush in the 1980s split their tickets and voted for Democratic candidates for the Congress.[14] Still, Republican domination of the presidency is important, because of the enormous powers of the office, because of the large symbolic significance of the quadrennial ritual of a presidential election in defining the substance and orientation of electoral politics, and because of the very great influence of the president on public opinion

8 Some analysts view the Lyndon Baines Johnson overwhelming victory over Barry Goldwater in 1964 as reestablishing or "reproducing" the Democratic order, and hence date the beginnings of Democratic decomposition much later than I do. See, for example, D. Plotke, "The Democratic political order, 1932–72," Ph.D. dissertation, University of California, 1985, p. 836.

9 Abramson et al., *Change and Continuity in the 1984 Elections*, pp. 136–7, table 5–1.

10 See "Opinion roundup," *Public Opinion* (November–January 1988), p. 21.

11 W. Galenson, "The historical role of American trade unionism," in *Unions in Transition*, ed. S. M. Lipset (San Francisco, CA: Institute for Contemporary Studies, 1986), p. 65.

12 Pomper, *The Election of 1988*, pp. 133–4, table 5.2.

13 In 1988, when Michael Dukakis lost forty states, the Democrats actually increased their majority in the Senate. However, some elected Democrats are switching parties, especially in the south. In 1989, 128 southern elected officials changed parties, including two congressional representatives. See J. Judis, "The Democrats keep on drifting – not Right, not Left, just away," *In These Times* (September 6–12, 1989), p. 8.

14 "American politics has reached a stalemate," write William Schneider and Patrick Reddy. "Democrats can't win the White House.... Republicans can't win a majority anywhere else." "Altered states," in *The American Enterprise*, 1, 4 (July–August 1990), p. 45. In the 1984 AFL–CIO poll cited, 72 percent and 69 percent of the respondents had voted for Democrats for the Senate and House of Representatives respectively. See Galenson, "The historical role of American trade unionism," p. 66.

between elections. Presidential elections, said Schattschneider, "might properly be described as the focus of American politics."[15]

The pattern of split-level voting prevents any quick judgment of a Republican realignment. So too, for a long time, did the overwhelming majority that the Democrats claimed in party allegiance, presidential voting patterns notwithstanding. Thus, even when they lost the presidency in the 1950s, registered Democrats still outnumbered registered Republicans by nearly two to one. However, polls over the past decade report a fluctuating parity between the parties, signaling that Democratic decomposition is proceeding apace. A poll commissioned by the Democrats in 1989, for example, showed that 37 percent of voters think of themselves as Democrats, compared with 30 percent who identify themselves as Republicans. Moreover, party identification seems to have come unhinged from substantive assessments of the parties. Kuttner reports that in 1952 about a third of the voters said they preferred the Democrats because they were the party of ordinary working people, and another third liked them because of their economic policies.[16] But, by 1989, more people trusted the Republican Party to lead the country than the Democratic Party by a margin of 43 percent to 34 percent. And although the Democrats retained a narrowing margin in party allegiance, the Republicans had gained a two to one edge in party identification among white voters under age 35.[17]

The other source of Democratic weakness is falling turnout, especially among the young and less-well-off. To explain the importance of this development, I need to say a word about employment trends in the United States in the last two decades. Alone among the countries discussed in this volume, the United States has witnessed an enormous expansion of low-wage employment. While American politics fits the pattern of a "two-thirds" society, in which a prosperous employed working class allies itself with the better-off against the bottom third, the American economic pattern is somewhat different.[18] The bottom third is not made up of the unemployed and the marginal who according to Claus Offe in this volume typify the German lower strata, but of a growing new working class of low-paid workers, many of them women and minorities employed in the service sector. The US response to intensified global competition in the 1970s and 1980s was to create a kind of third world

15   E. E. Schattschneider, *Party Government* (New York: Rinehart, 1942), p. 83. Lipset underlines the point when he says "The national parties basically have only existed to select a presidential nominee at a national convention every four years." See "The American party system: concluding observations," in *Party Coalitions in the 1980s*, ed. S. M. Lipset (San Francisco, CA: Institute for Contemporary Studies, 1981), p. 429.
16   R. Kuttner, *The Life of the Party: Democratic Prospects in 1988 and Beyond* (New York: Viking, 1987), p. 76.
17   Judis, "The Democrats just keep drifting," p. 8.
18   For the idea of the "two-thirds society" see P. Glotz, "Forward to Europe: A Declaration for a New European Left," *Dissent* (Summer, 1986), pp. 327–39.

labor force within its borders. In principle, this was a Democratic opportunity.

Consistent with what one might expect from sharpening economic inequality, the Democrats have increased their advantage among voters in the lower third of the income distribution, at least in terms of partisan preferences. Taken together with the sharp trend toward Republicanism among the better-off during the 1980s, this suggests that electoral politics is becoming more polarized along class lines, as it was during the New Deal years. The twist, however, is this: the less-well-off were Democratically inclined, but they were far less likely to vote, and their turnout rates were declining.[19] This development is sometimes attributed to the increasing indifference expressed toward both parties by the public,[20] particularly the young, who show sharply declining rates of both political interest and participation according to a number of recent polls.[21] Still, disaffection among voters cannot be understood apart from party performance, so the issue is again pushed back to the failure of constituency-building strategies of the Democrats. An adequate explanation of declining Democratic participation requires consideration of key structural features of the American political system which fragmented and decentralized the party, and also nourished the sectional and interest group forces which took advantage of a decentered party. Political adaptations to these conditions first aborted the development of the Democratic party as a labor party, and later helped to accelerate its decomposition.

Institutional Constraints on Labor Politics

Labor parties everywhere emerged on the crest of industrialization, nourished by the growing numbers of the working class and the expansion of the male franchise which an insurgent working class demanded. In the United States, the Democratic Party became, if not a labor party, at least the party of labor in the 1930s. However, this historic development occurred under conditions quite different from the earlier rise of

19 Thomas Edsall shows that partisan preferences came to be sharply correlated with income categories in the 1980s, seeming to spell the possibility of recreating the partisan polarities along class lines of the 1930s. See "The Reagan legacy," in *The Reagan Legacy*, ed. S. Blumenthal and T. Edsall (New York: Pantheon Books, 1988), p. 22. See also F. F. Piven and R. A. Cloward, *Why Americans Don't Vote* (New York: Pantheon Books, 1988).
20 For a discussion of the erosion of partisan affiliation, see M. Wattenberg, *The Decline of the Political Parties, 1952–1984* (Cambridge, MA: Harvard University Press, 1984).
21 See M. Oreskes, "Study finds 'astonishing' indifference to elections," *New York Times*, May 6, 1990, p. 32; M. Oreskes, "Profiles of today's youth: they couldn't care less," *New York Times*, June 28, 1990, p. D21; and "USA today poll," in *USA Today*, July 3, 1990, p. 11A.

labor parties in Western Europe. In Europe, the winning of the male franchise and the emergence of labor parties more or less coincided. In the United States, white male workers and farmers had achieved the right to vote much earlier, in a long political process that began with the popular mobilizations of the revolutionary war and concluded with the elimination of most property, education, and religious qualifications by the third decade of the nineteenth century. This meant that the mass party system which the unions entered in the 1930s was already highly developed, and heavily freighted with a series of structural arrangements developed in response to popular challenges that had welled up in earlier historical periods. Two kinds of structural arrangements inherited by the New Deal Democratic Party were especially important: the constitutionally fragmented and decentralized organization of the United States government; and class-related restrictions on the exercise of the universal franchise.

The American national government was the thoughtful and deliberate construction of elites in the aftermath of the revolutionary war. Half a century ago, Schattschneider commented on the significance of the Constitution they designed:

> Indubitably geography, history, tradition, and national character have had interesting effects on the parties. . . . But the Constitution has had an influence so important and overwhelming that the peculiarities of the American party system cease to be mysterious once we have begun to look at the Constitution and the parties together.[22]

Schattschneider singles out in particular the elaborate division of powers in the national government, a structure he says was "designed to make parties ineffective . . . [because they] would lose and exhaust themselves in futile attempts to fight their way through the labyrinthine framework. . . ."[23]

The animus of the Founders toward parties of course reflected their fear of a populace that could be mobilized by parties. There was reason to be fearful. The protection once provided to the propertied by the armies of the British Crown was gone, at a time when radical democratic currents stirred by the revolutionary war were strong, among a still-armed population. If it was unwise to simply ignore democratic aspirations, they could nevertheless be blunted and diffused by a system of

---

22 E. E. Schattschneider, *Party Government*, p. 128. S. M. Lipset develops Schattschneider's argument about the constitutional influences on parties in several places. See for example "Radicalism in North America: a comparative view of the party systems in Canada and the United States," *Transactions of the Royal Society of Canada*, Series IV, 14 (1976), p. 37 *passim*; and "The American party system: concluding observations," pp. 424–6.

23 Schattschneider, *Party Government*, p. 7.

"checks and balances" which effectively divided authority for key policies between the congress, the presidency, and the courts, and also made these decision making centers at least partially independent of each other. As Lipset and Rokkan point out, these safeguards against direct majority power limited party influence over officials in government. They encouraged shifting and flexible alliances, and made it difficult to translate election victories into policy.[24] The long-run effect, in short, was not only to fracture the authority of the central government, but to create lasting impediments to coherent party organization.

At the same time, post-revolutionary elites were themselves leery of the new central authority they were creating, in part because of the sharply diverse economies of the thirteen colonies, as famously signaled by the compromise over slavery embodied in the Constitution. The more general compromise, and it had lasting effects, was to structurally decentralize power. This was done in two ways. First, the authority of the new national government was limited to constitutionally specified policies, thus leaving an enormous reservoir of unspecified power to the state governments and to the local governments chartered by state legislatures. Second, the system of electoral representation was designed to give great weight to regions as opposed to persons, both in representation in the Senate and in the arrangement of the electoral college through which the President was chosen. There are obvious parallels here between sectionalism in American political development and what Bradford and Jenson call the "pluralism" of Canadian politics.[25] As in Canada, the strong sectionalism which has always marked American politics had its roots in regional economic differences, and it was nurtured by a political system which both protected regionalism and lent it weight in national government with, as it turned out, lasting implications for American political parties.

The decentralization of government power also fostered the growth of the local clientelist political organizations for which the United States is renowned, and which marked working class politics particularly during the first decades of industrialization.[26] Decentralization meant that local

24 S. M. Lipset and S. Rokkan, "Cleavage structures, party systems, and voter alignments: an introduction," in *Party Systems and Voter Alignments: Cross-National Perspectives*, ed. S. M. Lipset and S. Rokkan (New York: Free Press, 1967), pp. 31–2.
25 See chapter 9 in this volume.
26 On clientelism and working class politics, see A. Bridges, *A City in the Republic: Ante-Bellum New York and the Origins of Machine Politics* (New York: Cambridge University Press, 1984); R. Oestreicher, "Urban working-class political behavior and theories of American electoral politics, 1870–1940," *Journal of American History*, 74, 4 (March 1988), pp. 1257–86; Piven and Cloward, *Why Americans Don't Vote*, ch. 2; M. Shefter, "The electoral foundations of the political machine: New York City, 1884–1897," in *The History of American Electoral Behavior*, ed. J. Sibley, A. Bogue, and W. Flanigan (Princeton, NJ: Princeton University Press, 1978).

government did many things with relative autonomy, and could yield enormous patronage resources. At the same time, the wide distribution of the franchise meant that nineteenth-century artisans and laborers in the immigrant wards of the cities attracted the organizing efforts of clientelist parties. These working men had the votes that could produce election victories for the parties, and control over the patronage resources that local or state government yielded. Both clientelist organization and the wide availability of the vote pre-dated industrialization and the experience of proletarianization. Hence, when an industrial working class emerged, powerful local political organizations which appealed to workers on the basis of ethnic, religious, and individual advantage already existed.

Finally, a fragmented and decentralized state also nourished interest group politics, even as it inhibited the party development which might counter interest group influence. In part this was because a government system with multiple points of access was more exposed to well-organized groups with the resources and tenacity to pursue influence.[27] Interest groups could operate in the several branches of government or at different levels of government to promote the policies they favored or to block policies they opposed. Moreover, since the very structural arrangements which exposed the state to well-organized interests also ensured the fragmentation of the national parties, and their consequent lack of a strategic or programmatic center, there was little resistance from party leaders to the demands of well-organized interest groups. This too is a point Schattschneider saw clearly:

> American legislation, the budget, and public administration everywhere show the handiwork of the pressure groups which have had their way in American government and imposed their will on Congress, the administrative agencies, the states, and the local government at a multitude of points.[28]

27 Ira Katznelson has recently suggested a similar argument, pointing to key features of the American state in explaining the distinctive features of American social policy, including "decentralization and federalism, an institutionally constrained presidency, a porous central bureaucracy, catchall party organizations, a highly autonomous Congress, and the importance of law and the judiciary in policy making and implementation." "Rethinking the silences of social and economic policy," *Political Science Quarterly*, 101 (1986), p. 323.

28 Schattschneider, *Party Government*, p. 108. The literature on the role of interest groups in American politics is of course vast. See especially T. J. Lowi, *The End of Liberalism: Ideology, Policy and the Crisis of Public Authority* (New York: Norton, 1969); A. F. Bentley, *The Process of Government* (Cambridge, MA: Belknap, 1967); E. Latham, *The Group Basis of Politics* (Ithaca, NY: Cornell University Press, 1952); and D. Truman, *The Governmental Process* (New York: Alfred A. Knopf, 1951). On the role of interest groups in the Congress, see R. Bauer, I. de Sola Pool and L. A. Dexter, *American Business and Public Policy* (Chicago, IL: Aldine & Atherton, 1963); D. R. Mathews, *US Senators and Their World* (New

The other set of structural arrangements which had a telling influence on the party-building strategies of the contemporary Democrats evolved a century after the writing of the Constitution, on the eve of industrialization. If the Founding Fathers feared democratic currents, they nevertheless also feared opposing them, and left the issue of enfranchisement to state governments, with the result that the universal male franchise was rather quickly, if somewhat unevenly, established. However, during the closing decades of the nineteenth century, industrialists and Republicans in the north, planters and Democrats in the south, introduced a series of "reforms" into state electoral laws and procedures that effectively disenfranchised many workers and farmers. This effort was especially vigorous in the south, where the disenfranchisement of blacks was linked to the stability of the plantation economy and the serf labor on which it relied. There, new literacy and poll tax requirements, together with onerous personal voter registration requirements, were incorporated into state constitutions, and resulted in the rapid disenfranchisement of the entire black population and of most poorer whites as well. A similar reform effort swept the north, animated less by the race issue and more by elite reactions against insurgent farmer and industrial movements. But the result was similar, if less drastic: in the north, too, literacy tests which had been abandoned half a century earlier were reintroduced, in some states along with a poll tax, and in any case elaborate and obstructive requirements for personal and periodic registration were imposed, at first mainly on the big cities where the immigrant working class, and the clientelist local political organizations which depended on immigrant working class support, were concentrated.

At the same time, the local parties, which might otherwise have worked to subvert these restrictions, came under direct attack by reformers who worked to strip the parties of their patronage resources, and to further fragment the local and sometimes state governments they controlled. These reforms unfolded in the context of the 1896 electoral realignment which reduced party competition in much of the country. Together, these several changes took their toll on voter participation. On the one hand, restrictive rules and procedures made voting difficult, and clientelist local parties had fewer resources to help voters through the process; on the other hand, uncompetitive elections lowered the motive of voters to vote or of parties to enlist them. Voter turnout, which had been consistently high for most of the nineteenth century, steadily

---

York: Norton, 1973); A. Denzau and M. C. Munger, "Legislators and interest groups: how unorganized interests get represented," in *American Political Science Review*, 80 (1986), pp. 89–106; R. H. Salisbury and K. A. Shepsle, "US Congressmen as enterprise," *Legislative Studies Quarterly*, 6 (1981), pp. 559–76; R. L. Hall and F. W. Wayman, "Buying time: moneyed interests and the mobilization of bias in congressional committees," *American Political Science Review*, 84, 3 (1990), pp. 797–820.

declined after the turn of the century, falling to barely half the nationwide electorate by the 1920s.[29]

New Deal Party Building Strategies, or the Labor Party Aborted

These structural constraints were ultimately to prevent the emergence of a labor party, which the upheavals of the Great Depression momentarily made seem possible. By 1932, when economic calamity scuttled Republican domination of the national government, blue collar workers constituted about half the workforce. Meanwhile, a series of widespread protest movements – among the unemployed, farmers, the old, and industrial workers – prompted Franklin Delano Roosevelt, as the leader of the ascendant but unsteady Democratic Party, first to inject the language of class into national political rhetoric and then, as panic stilled political opposition, to inaugurate the first federal welfare state programs. Not long afterwards, pressed by an escalating strike movement, Roosevelt threw his support behind legislation to protect unionization efforts. With that development, organized labor broke with its traditional policy of abstaining from national electoral politics[30] to become a full-fledged partner of the Democratic Party.

The sectional party coalition

These developments, however, did not occur on a fresh slate. The Democrats were now the party of northern labor, but they continued to be the sectional party of the rural south. There is a seeming parallel here to the rise to government power of Scandinavian labor parties through alliances with farmer parties. But, in fact, there is no parallel. The alliance with the rural south was not an alliance with family farmers but with a quasi-feudal political formation. That distinctive regional formation in turn was sustained by the structures to which I am directing attention. The decentralization of governmental authority allowed the

29   For an elaboration of this analysis, see Piven and Cloward, *Why Americans Don't Vote*. On early twentieth-century turnout generally, and among immigrant stock urban workers in particular, see P. Kleppner, *Who Voted? The Dynamics of Electoral Turnout* (New York: Praeger, 1982), especially pp. 63–7. See also K. Andersen, *The Creation of a Democratic Majority, 1928–1936* (Chicago, IL: University of Chicago Press, 1982), especially pp. 48–52; and N. H. Nie, S. Verba, and J. H. Petrocik, *The Changing American Voter* (Cambridge, MA: Harvard University Press, 1976), especially pp. 91–2.
30   A resolution adopted at the 1896 AFL convention asserted that "party politics, whether it be Democratic, Republican, Socialistic, Populistic, Prohibition, or any other shall have no place in the convention of the American Federation of Labor." Quoted in Galenson, "The historical role of American trade unionism," p. 49.

southern oligarchy to construct a political system that shored up the plantation economy, and to defend that system under the banner of "states rights." At the same time, the disenfranchising arrangements of the late nineteenth century (together with the regular use of state sanctioned violence) protected the southern system from electoral challenges from below, by the simple expedient of purging poor whites and blacks from the electorate. Finally, the decentralization of representation, particularly in the Senate and the electoral college, gave this sectional political system a strong grip on the national government. And a system of divided powers in the national government meant that that grip could become a stranglehold on national policy, especially as powerful southern Democrats in the congress allied themselves with northern Republicans.

For a time, the alliance with the south shored up the national Democratic Party. No matter their slight totals in the popular vote, the institution of the electoral college gave the southern states a bloc of votes which became the bedrock of Democratic victories. Moreover, the party's dependence on the southern wing was accentuated by persisting weaknesses in its labor base in the north. True, the rhetorical and programmatic initiatives of the New Deal had for the moment sealed the allegiance of working people to the Democrats. And important new federal programs channeled through city governments became a lifeline for the fading big city machines. Together, the appeals of the New Deal and revived local parties helped raise turnout outside of the south, from 66 percent in 1928 to 73 percent in 1940.[31] The unions contributed to this effort, as I will show in a moment. Still, while the increase in turnout was large, it was not as large as it might have been, because recruitment efforts had to hurdle procedural encumbrances on the franchise inherited from the conflicts of the late nineteenth century, as table 11.2 shows.

A party coalition which embraced the quasi-feudal south and the urban working class north could not last. Indeed, New Deal policies oriented to sectional interests themselves helped to undermine it, by encouraging landowners to take land out of production or to mechanize, while simultaneously allowing the southern states and counties to refuse welfare payments to the millions of sharecroppers, tenants, and laborers who were displaced. Many of them, of course, were black, and they eventually made their way to the cities of the north where already established black communities provided some kind of haven. In the north, blacks gained the vote, and became a factor in Democratic electoral calculations. Their growing voting numbers were concentrated in the heartland of the urban working class, in the industrial states with the largest number of electoral college votes. For over three decades, beginning in 1948, Democratic presidential contenders were forced to choose

31 W. D. Burnham, "The system of 1896: an analysis," in *The Evolution of American Electoral Systems*, ed. P. Kleppner (Westport, CT: Greenwood Press, 1981), p. 100, table 1.

Table 11.2   Presidential turnout percentages, 1924–1940

	South	Nonsouth	National
1924	19	57	49
1928	23	66	57
1932	24	66	57
1936	25	71	61
1940	26	73	62

Source: W. D. Burnham, "The system of 1896: an analysis," in *The Evolution of American Electoral Systems*, ed. P. Kleppner (Westport, CT: Greenwood Press, 1981), p. 100, table 1

and lose. They could defer to their white southern coalition partners who were outraged even at rhetorical inroads on the caste system. If they did, they risked losing black support in the north, and with it perhaps some of the industrial states where Democratic majorities were narrow. Or they could defer to black demands, and the black struggle for civil rights which was gaining allies throughout the north, and risk losing the white south. There was, in short, no way to hold this sectional coalition together.

The Democrats lost the south. By the 1980s, the south had in fact become the staunchest Republican region in presidential contests. But southern influence remained large in the decades during which the coalition unraveled. The structural arrangements which gave the southern section so much power also made its loss especially threatening. Democratic presidential contenders exerted themselves to placate the white south and stem the loss of southern electoral votes, and southern Democrats in the Congress continued to wield extraordinary power over legislation. Moreover, the power of the southern section ultimately undermined the possibility of shoring up working class Democratic support in the north.

A crippled union infrastructure

Everywhere, labor parties are allied with unions. Unions are in fact virtually the infrastructure of the parties, functioning to enlist working people in support of the party. That is why, for example, as Arian and Talmud explain in this volume, the Israeli Labor Party even forfeits its role as the political opposition in an effort to stay in the government where it can ensure the maintenance of the Histadrut. In countries where labor parties have fared better during the disturbances of post-industrialism, union membership is high and the unions are relatively centralized. The American rate of unionization is now one of the lowest in the west. Having reached a peak of about one-third of the workforce at the end of the Second World War, union membership stabilized briefly and then began to decline, to 16 percent of the workforce in 1989.[32] To be sure, union density has begun to fall in other industrial countries as well. But in most countries the loss is recent and relatively modest.[33] In the United States, the decline began several decades ago, and was precipitous. This is surely one reason for the troubles of the Democratic Party. But the low level of unionization in the United States itself has to be explained, particularly in light of the scale and vigor of American labor struggles for the right to organize during the New Deal Democratic Party building period.[34] The search for an explanation takes us back to the role of the south in national politics, to the importance of interest groups, and to the structural arrangements that made sectional and interest groups powerful.

Once legal protection for unionism had been won by mass strikes in the mid-1930s, the new industrial unions rapidly allied themselves with the Democratic Party, and shortly thereafter the craft unions did as well. This development seemed to promise the emergence of an entirely new political formation in American electoral politics. As early as 1936, the newly formed CIO began to work for the Democratic ticket, creating a political arm that performed much like a campaign organization, spending money to stage rallies, print leaflets, and recruit voters in the industrial states where the CIO unions were strong. This was only the beginning of the development of a massive and far-flung CIO campaign apparatus, supplemented in 1948 by a comparable AFL effort, that deployed "armies of trade union precinct workers" and often took the place of the local Democratic Party itself.[35] In the late 1940s, the union

32   See P. Sexton, "Repression of labor," *Democratic Left*, 18, 5 (September–October, 1990), p. 9. Some estimates indicate that union membership will sink to 13 percent of the workforce by the year 2000. See S. M. Lipset, "Preface," *Unions in Transition* (San Francisco, CA: Institute for Contemporary Studies, 1986), p. xvi.

33   On this point, see L. Troy, "The rise and fall of American trade unions: the labor movement from FDR to RR," in Lipset, *Unions in Transition*, p. 76, table 1.

34   For a provocative treatment which stresses the militancy of American labor in comparative perspective, see G. Arrighi, "Marxism and its history," *New Left Review*, 179 (January–February 1990), pp. 29–63.

35   The phrase is in M. Davis, *Prisoners of the American Dream* (London: Verso, 1986), p. 90. On the impact of unions on the Democratic vote, see E. E. Schattschneider, who estimated that unionism added 10 percentage points to the Democratic inclination of the labor vote, in *The Semisovereign People* (New York: Holt, Rinehart & Winston, 1960), p. 50. See also H. Scoble ("Organized labor in the electoral process: some questions," *Western Political Science Quarterly*, 16 (1963), p. 675) who examined this calculation under different assumptions and concluded that union influence could in fact have an even larger impact on the labor vote.

party formation in the United States did not look very different from that in Western Europe: union density levels were not much lower, and the degree of class polarization in voting was as high as in Western Europe.[36]

However, despite the unions' electoral efforts for the Democrats, the support for unionism by party leaders did not last. Within a few years the legislative protections of the National Labor Relations Act were being whittled away and the once pro-labor National Labor Relations Board was reconstituted, largely as a result of the influence of the fatal alliance that developed between southerners and business-oriented Republicans in the Congress.[37] Meanwhile, decentralization permitted the states to undercut the union protections won from the federal government in 1935, and a good many did just that, especially in the south.

The opposition of the southern section was not the whole of the problem. The other part of the problem was the weakness of the union cause in the north, where labor influence was offset by the continuing power in the Congress of local clientelist politicians, by the persisting low turnout of working class voters,[38] and by the growing susceptibility of the Congress to business lobbyists as the threat wielded by the strike movements of the 1930s and 1940s receded.

Democratic presidents did not much resist the assault on unions either, and in some instances even took the lead, for they too were beholden to business lobbyists and especially to southern congressional powerbrokers. As the Second World War approached, Roosevelt threatened to draft striking workers, and Truman did the same during the strike wave that followed the close of the war. To be sure, facing a third party challenge from the Left in the 1948 election, Truman vetoed the anti-union Taft–Hartley Act of 1947. However, when the Congress overrode his veto, Truman used the powers it granted him twelve times in the first year after its passage. The margin of votes needed to override the veto was, consistently, provided by southern Democrats in the

36 On class voting, see R. Alford, *Party and Society: The Anglo-American Democracies* (Chicago, IL: Rand McNally, 1963).

37 Lipset ("Labor unions in the public mind," in *Unions in Transition*, pp. 287–322), argues vigorously that the decline in union density in the United States is a reflection of declining public support for unions. But the evidence he provides of a correlation between declining public approval of unions and loss of membership does not say anything about the direction of causality.

38 In a 1959 study, Harold Sheppard and Nicholas Masters found that the UAW had registered 90 percent of its members, and 87 percent of them voted ("The political attitudes and preferences of union members: the case of the Detroit Auto Workers," *American Political Science Review*, 53 (1959), pp. 437–47). However, if this was accurate, it was not typical. Sidney Lens reports that in the late 1950s the director of the AFL–CIO's political arm estimated that, overall, only 40 percent of union members were registered voters. A survey by the Amalgamated Clothing Workers found even fewer registrants. Cited in Davis, *Prisoners of the American Dream*, p. 98.

Congress. And also consistently, for the next two decades, Democratic presidential contenders simply ignored their union allies and made no move to overturn the restrictions of Taft–Hartley.

These reversals marked the end of labor's brief political flowering. The "free speech" rights granted employers under Taft–Hartley were matched by new curbs on strikes, and the outright prohibition of such solidary tactics as sympathy strikes, secondary boycotts, and mass picketing. Noncommunist affidavits required of union officials spurred a long wave of union fratricide. Perhaps most important, the Act explicitly allowed state open-shop laws which were especially prevalent in the south. These several provisions set the stage for the failure of Operation Dixie, the southern organizing drive launched by the CIO in 1946, which ran aground on union infighting and intransigent southern opposition.[39] This meant that as new plants dispersed to the sunbelt in subsequent decades, the unions did not follow. It was not until the late 1970s, when the bleeding of the unions was well advanced, that a Democratic president threw his weight behind legislation to restore some of the union protections of the 1930s. Business and southern influence again combined to ensure that the initiative was defeated.

These events go far toward explaining the decline of union membership.[40] Like the dissolution of the Democratic party, union decline began too early to be attributed to contracting smokestack industries. Later, of course, the old industries did decline, and new plants and people shifted to the sunbelt. The failure of union organizing efforts there was not simply a reflection of postindustrialism either, or for that matter of the conservative political culture of the south. The sorry record of union organizing in the south had a good deal to do with the way the ground rules had been changed in the 1940s, by representatives of the southern sectional establishment and northern business interests whose power was lodged in the structural arrangements which the twentieth century inherited from the nineteenth and eighteenth.

Party building and the welfare state

The main American welfare state programs were also inaugurated during the party-building era of the New Deal. But the US programs trailed behind those of Western Europe in benefit levels and scope of coverage and, after the Second World War, a number of the limited programs that

---

39   The CIO attempted to penetrate the south early, and had scored some local organizing successes during the war. See N. Lichtenstein, "From corporatism to collective bargaining: organized labor and the eclipse of social democracy in the postwar era," in *The Rise and Fall of the New Deal Order*, pp. 135–7. On the failure of Operation Dixie, see also Davis, *Prisoners of the American Dream*, pp. 92–4.

40   Michael Goldfield attributes the decline of union membership more to employer opposition than to either the contraction of smokestack industries or the shift of industry to the sunbelt. See "Labor in American politics – its current weakness," *Journal of Politics*, 48 (1986), pp. 2–29.

had been inaugurated in the 1930s were allowed to languish. Meanwhile, new programs proved impossible to win in the Congress, owing to the vigorous resistance of southern Democrats and business-oriented Republicans on the one hand, and the desultory support of northern Democrats who were also influenced by business interests and by the local clientelists parties to which many congressmen remained beholden.

During the crisis months when Roosevelt first took office, elites everywhere, shaken by the depth of the economic crisis and by mounting protest among the unemployed, supported emergency measures, including emergency relief, and so too did southern congressmen, whose impoverished region had been especially hard hit by the economic calamity. Even so, however, objections from the south to national relief programs that overrode local wage scales or interfered with caste arrangements began early. And when the Social Security Act of 1935 replaced emergency relief, southern representatives who dominated the key committees in the Congress carried great weight.[41] So too did business leaders who organized to oppose the Act because they feared income support programs would interfere with low-wage labor markets. Together with southern representatives, they used the political leverage guaranteed them by divided and decentralized government to ensure that the new national welfare state programs would conform with sectionally and sectorally diversified labor markets.[42]

The intricate provisions of the Social Security Act reflected this confluence of forces. On the one hand, whole categories of low-wage workers were excluded from the old-age and unemployment insurance programs, and in any case eligibility was conditional on a history of steady

41 Both the House Ways and Means Committee and the Senate Finance Committee were chaired by Southerners. For discussions of the role of the south in the New Deal, see V. O. Key, *Southern Politics in State and Nation* (New York: Alfred A. Knopf, 1984); G. B. Tindall, *The Disruption of the Solid South* (Athens GA: University of Georgia Press, 1965); F. F. Piven and R. A. Cloward, *Poor Peoples' Movements: Why They Succeed, How They Fail* (New York: Pantheon Books, 1977), ch. 5; L. J. Alston and J. P. Ferrie, "Resisting the welfare state: southern opposition to the Farm Security Administration," in *The Emergence of the Modern Political Economy*, ed. R. Higgs (Greenwich, CT: JAI Press, 1985).

42 The key group in formulating the main provisions of the Social Security Act is widely agreed to have been the American Association for Labor Legislation (AALL). While the AALL is often defined as a civic reform organization, G. William Domhoff's analysis makes clear that the organization drew its support from business leaders associated with the National Civic Federation. See *The Power Elite and the State: How Policy is Made in America* (New York: Aldine de Gruyter, 1990), pp. 44–64. On the influence of different factions of business on the Social Security Act, see also J. Quadagno, "Welfare capitalism and the Social Security Act of 1935," *American Sociological Review*, 49 (October 1984), pp. 632–47; and J. C. Jenkins and B. G. Brents, "Social protest, hegemonic competition, and social reform," *American Sociological Review*, 54, 6 (December 1989), pp. 891–909.

employment. Moreover, a good deal of authority over the unemployment insurance program, and over the "categorical" or welfare programs, was ceded to the states and even to the counties, where local employers could ensure that conditions of eligibility and benefit levels were calibrated to their requirements.[43]

On the other hand, the inauguration of national welfare state programs under the Social Security Act was primarily a response to the demands of working people who were potential Democratic voters, and it is the bearing of the programs on constituency building that is my primary interest here. Two features of the American welfare state deserve scrutiny in this respect. One is that a complex system of sharply differentiated programs nourished divisions among Democratic constituencies, a feature of the system that became especially pernicious when the programs were enlarged in the 1960s, partly in response to the black movement. White working class taxpayers were especially resentful of categorical programs identified with the minority poor, and perhaps particularly so because they carried the brunt of the steeply regressive state and local taxes which helped fund the categorical programs. This aspect of the American programs has in fact often been remarked upon, and is similar to the pattern of institutionally patterned fragmentation that Offe says in this volume increasingly characterizes German welfare state programs, with devastating consequences for class political solidarity.

Another feature of the American welfare state was perhaps even more important for its ultimately perverse effects on Democratic party-building efforts. Simply put, there was too little of it. The Social Security Act was not the beginning of a process of welfare state development. For a long time, it was the high point. After the Second World War, the new industrial unions expanded their sights not only to demand higher social security payments, but to demand national health insurance, child care facilities, government housing, and so on. They got none of this from a Congress dominated by southern Democrats and business-oriented Republicans. And so a still-militant and still-strong labor movement used workplace power to bargain with employers for health and old-age protections, and later to bargain for supplementary unemployment benefits as well.[44] The result was that, over time, core working class groups looked less to government for the measures that would guarantee their security, and more to the market place. For example, without a national

43   For a fuller discussion, see F. F. Piven and R. A. Cloward, *Regulating the Poor* (New York: Pantheon Books, 1971), and "The historical sources of the contemporary relief debate," in *The Mean Season: The Attack on the Welfare State*, ed. F. Block, R. A. Cloward, B. Ehrenreich, and F. F. Piven (New York: Pantheon Books, 1987), pp. 3–44.

44   For an analysis, see B. Stevens, "Labor unions, employee benefits, and the privatization of the American welfare state," *Journal of Policy History*, 2, 3 (1990), pp. 233–60.

health program, most Americans relied on employers for health protections. In turn, a government that did less was less likely to generate confidence or affection. And a party that did less was also less likely to hold the allegiance of its constituency over time.

Democratic Party Policies and Postindustrialism

All of the rich industrial nations of the west have had to adapt to intensifying international competition, especially in the auto, steel, electronics, and machine tools industries whose workers formed the core base of labor parties. Inevitably, those adaptations have been troubling for labor parties built on constituencies and organizations formed in an earlier industrial era. But labor parties have not only suffered the impact of those adaptations; they have also helped to shape them.

As is becoming increasingly obvious, strong labor parties, high union density, and developed welfare states have imposed political limits on the options of investors responding to the new international economic order. When the large-scale industrial disinvestment and wage and social benefit cuts that are the hallmarks of the American adaptation are politically unfeasible, investors are more likely to turn to competitive strategies emphasizing increased capitalization, technological and production innovations, and active labor market policies.[45] In the United States, however, weak unions and a politically compromised and meager welfare state facilitated rapid and wholesale disinvestment from older industries and a virtual explosion of speculation on the one hand, and campaigns to lower wages, break unions, cut welfare state spending, and roll back government regulatory protections on the other. Partly as a result, average weekly earnings began to fall in the early 1970s, and average household income remained more or less stable only because married women flooded into the labor market to shore up family income by filling the jobs in the enlarging service sector industries. (In the 1980s, a more regressive tax system and cuts in social programs exacerbated these market income trends.) But the conditions which made these large changes in the economy possible were as much political as economic, as I will explain when I turn to the business mobilization that began in the 1970s.

Politics was in command of postindustrial trends in another sense too. While shifts in international markets encouraged the spatial decentralization of industry, the United States led the way among industrial

---

45　For measures of the impact of social democratic corporatist arrangements on economic growth, see sources in chapter 1, footnote 18. See also A. Hicks and W. D. Patterson, "On the robustness of the left corporatist model of economic growth," *Journal of Politics*, 51 (1989), pp. 662–75.

countries in the extent of decentralization.[46] In any case, international markets did not dictate the specific geography of decentralization or its political consequences. A series of national policies, some dating from the New Deal, others inaugurated later, played a major role in this respect. But rather than using their influence on national policy to moderate the impact of postindustrial change on the party, its infrastructure and its constituencies, Democratic Party leaders happily sold their influence to sectional interests in the south, and to local party bosses and business interest groups in the north. As a consequence, the Democrats supported policies that were perhaps rational from the perspective of particularistic sectional and business interests, but which were entirely irrational from the perspective of the longer run interests of the national Democratic Party, and perhaps from the larger perspective of the national economic well-being as well.

Before I make the case for the large role of sectional and interest group politics in shaping the geography of the contemporary American economy, let me summarize the more usual view. In the United States, the industrial centers of the north and midwest were the mainstays, together with the largely rural south, of the New Deal Democratic Party. These centers were overwhelmed and transformed by the shift of industrial production to low cost areas and the rise of a multifaceted service economy, both at least partly the result of global economic developments. Shifts in investment, in turn, changed the kinds of work people do and the conditions under which they do it, the places where they live, and their political identities and allegiances. Not only did the ranks of industrial workers shrink and a new service sector workforce grow, but as the geography of new investment shifted in response to changes in market advantage, people and enterprises moved from the solidly Democratic central cities to the now Republican suburbs, and from the predominantly Democratic northeast and midwest to the increasingly Republican states of the south and west.[47] Together, these trends both reduced the numerical strength of a core constituency of the New Deal Democratic Party and eroded its political cohesion.

All of this happened, of course, and the impact on the old industrial centers was enormous, as Alan DiGaetano points out in his chapter. The city of Detroit, for example, fabled bastion of the United Auto Workers, lost half of its people and most of its businesses in the years since

---

46 See S. Lash and J. Urry, *The End of Organized Capitalism* (Cambridge: Polity Press), p. 109.

47 Loïc Wacquant describes the impact of de-industrialization on the Democratic bastion of Chicago. In 1954, over 10,200 manufacturing establishments in the city had provided half a million blue collar jobs. By 1982, the number of establishments had been halved, and blue collar employment had fallen to 172,000. See "The ghetto, the state, and the new capitalist economy," *Dissent* (Fall, 1989), pp. 510–11.

the Second World War;[48] Chicago lost half of its manufacturing establishments and more than half of its manufacturing employment.[49] But this happened not simply as a result of investor adaptations to new market conditions, but as a result of market conditions that were at least in part the result of government policies promoted by sectional and investor interests. In fact, and as I have already noted, long before the decline of the mass production industries which we associate with post-industrialism, a series of federal policies tilted economic development toward the south. These policies included not only the welfare and labor policies which ratified regional disparities in labor costs, but an array of federal activities which accelerated in the 1960s, including military installations, defense and aerospace contracts directed to the districts of powerful southern congressmen, and, to make these and other enterprises possible, an enormously costly federally financed infrastructure, particularly in highways and water projects.[50] In other words, while the shift of mass production industries to low wage areas was a global trend, a pattern of federal – and Democratic – policies created specific additional incentives encouraging the movement of new investment and people away from the urban concentrations of the northeast and midwest and into the south and the southwest.

Much the same point should be made about the shift of economic activity and people to the suburbs which now contain a majority of the nation's voters, and a majority that is turning out to be a major base for the Republican Party.[51] While the prevailing view attributes suburbanization simply to changes in the locational requirements of business investors and to the attractions of home-ownership for the middle class, federal policies were a crucial component of this development as well. Again, federally subsidized highways, and water and sewer grants, enormously enhanced the locational advantages of outlying areas, while federal tax laws created incentives for investment in new facilities rather than the refurbishment of old ones.[52] Meanwhile, federal housing policies which provided low cost mortgages and tax benefits for mainly suburban home-owners vastly overshadowed the modest programs

---

48 See I. Wilkerson, "Giving up the jewels to salvage the house," *New York Times*, September 10, 1990.

49 See Wacquant, "The ghetto, the state, and the new capitalist economy."

50 On this point, see F. F. Piven, "Federal policy and urban fiscal strain," *Yale Law and Policy Review*, 2, 2 (Spring, 1984), pp. 291–320; A. Watkins, "Good business climates: the second war between the states," *Dissent* (Fall, 1980); and P. Ashton, "The political economy of suburban development," in *Marxism and the Metropolis*, ed. W. Tabb and L. Sawers (New York: Oxford University Press, 1978), pp. 64–89.

51 On this point, see T. Edsall, *Chain Reaction* (New York: Norton, 1991), ch. 1.

52 On the impact of highway subsidies, see J. Mollenkopf, *The Contested City* (Princeton, NJ: Princeton University Press, 1983), pp. 14–144.

directed to low cost housing in the cities.[53] What the cities did get, as DiGaetano explains, was urban renewal programs promoted by local "progrowth" coalitions of real estate and downtown business interests and their local political allies, with the result that whole neighborhoods, and often Democratic neighborhoods, were decimated as those who could joined the exodus to the suburbs, those who could not crowded into further impacted slums, and local conflict escalated.[54]

Finally, even the divisive impact of racial conflict on Democratic ranks has something to do with the policies which Democrats themselves promoted. I do not want to overstate this. The race issue is deeply rooted, and in the main the unfortunate Democrats inherited it. White–black conflict was part of the reason the party lost the south, and the Democrats were then torn apart again by racial conflict in the cities. But the several party strategies I have described made race conflict sharper and more telling than would otherwise have been the case. Race conflict was surely worsened by the scale and precipitousness of the displacement of blacks from the south, which in turn had a good deal to do with Democratic agricultural and welfare policies. The failure of the Democrats to shore up unions also mattered, for it deprived the party of an infrastructure that might have worked to moderate racial conflict.[55] And a white working class that felt itself to be getting very little from its party or government was that much more likely to be resentful of programs directed to blacks. Finally, the combination of programs which spurred the great migration to the suburbs of the past three decades may also have worsened race conflict, both by stripping the older cities of employment opportunities and public revenues, and by reifying racial separation in political jurisdictions, so that race polarization came to be seen as a conflict between devastated and pathology-ridden black municipalities and prosperous white suburban jurisdictions.

Not all postindustrial trends necessarily had to work against the Democratic Party. If the ranks of the old working class were reduced and

53 There is an obvious parallel here to the promotion of owner-occupied housing by the British Conservatives. See Lash and Urry, *The End of Organized Capitalism*, p. 102.
54 The role of real-estate and banking interests in these several housing and redevelopment policies has been very important. A study of business political action committees in 1990 showed that political contributions from these interests were by far the largest of any category. See R. Berke, "Study confirms interest groups' pattern of giving," *New York Times*, September 16, 1990, p. 26.
55 While I think a stronger union structure would have worked overall to moderate race conflict, unions were also the focus of conflict, especially in the construction trades. On this point, see J. Quadagno, "How the war on poverty fractured the Democratic Party: organized labor's battle against economic justice for blacks," unpublished paper presented to the Workshop in Political Economy, Florida State University, September 1990.

dispersed, new potential constituencies were also being created, among the enlarging numbers of people, many of them young and minorities, who were doing worse, and also among increasingly politicized women. However, the party has done little to recruit either group. Just as this constitutionally fragmented party did not override sectional and interest group influences in order to protect the party's base, neither does it seem capable of strategic action to expand the party's base.

As I noted at the outset, people at the bottom of the income distribution have become increasingly Democratic by preference. Sharply polarizing economic conditions seem to be recreating something of the pattern of political polarization of the New Deal era. Some of the new have-nots are in the industrial sector where the attack on unions and job restructuring had smoothed the way for sharp wage cuts. Many more are in the service sector where the fastest growing occupations – cashiers, nurses, janitors, retail workers – are concentrated.[56] And some are the marginally employed or the never employed who depend on the welfare state. Of course, just how large a Democratic margin this reservoir would actually produce in a given election, and whether it can turn a presidential election, depends on other factors in the contest. For the moment, however, that is beside the point, since the very strata that are turning to the Democrats are also those who are least likely to vote.[57]

The New Deal Democratic majority was made possible by the mobilization of new voters. An unusual concatenation of circumstances and organizations made this possible. On the one hand, economic calamity and rising politicization motivated people to vote; on the other, the new unions, together with big city Democratic organizations temporarily revived by New Deal largesse, helped new voters to hurdle the inherited procedural barriers that had depressed turnout since the turn of the century. In the last two decades, however, this mobilizing infrastructure atrophied, its place taken by media-dominated campaigns associated with particular candidates, as DiGaetano explains. But media campaigns do not give people voter registration cards, and the decline of face-to-face recruitment efforts made the procedural barriers inherited from the nineteenth century more telling in their effects. As a result, outside the south where the civil rights revolution had raised registration and turnout, registration levels fell, especially among the low-income strata who were becoming more Democratic in their preferences. Turnout

56   Bennett Harrison and Barry Bluestone cite Bureau of Labor Statistics data showing the ten fastest growing occupations, as well as changes in the distribution of workers by type of employment and wage category. See *The Great U-Turn* (New York: Basic Books, 1990), pp. 70–1, tables A.1 and A.2.

57   According to Harold Meyerson, sales, technical, service, and administrative workers now constitute 28 percent of the voting age population, but only 11 percent of the electorate. Blue collar workers, who are more likely to be unionized, do a little better, constituting 18 percent of the voting age population and 13 percent of the electorate. See "Why the Democrats keep losing," *Dissent* (Summer, 1989), p. 306.

levels fell even faster, from the twentieth century high of 65 percent in 1960 to 51 percent in 1988.[58] As the procedures inherited from the nineteenth century steadily eroded the Democratic base, and the party infrastructure atrophied, a decentered party of loosely connected entrepreneurial politicians exposed to a myriad of special interests remained paralyzed; it could not or would not recruit Democratic voters.

The Democrats have also done little to take advantage of the other large opportunity associated with postindustrial trends, the politicization of women and their shift to the Left. As Therborn points out in this volume, gender politics is at the core of postindustrial political change. In the Scandinavian countries, as the social democratic parties move vigorously to recruit women, offering them new programs and high levels of representation in the parties, gender is becoming a new axis of party alignment.[59]

That the Democratic Party has taken no comparably large steps is not because women do not constitute a potential target constituency of large importance. To the contrary: women have come to significantly outnumber men in the electorate, both as a result of demographic trends, and because the long-term decline in voter turnout is sharper among men than among women. At the same time as their voting numbers have increased, women have remained more Democratic, while men have veered sharply toward the Republicans. This gap in gender partisanship first became evident in the 1980 election, and since then it has more or less held.[60] Moreover, gender differences in policy preferences are far wider than gender differences in partisan preferences, with women differing from men particularly on issues of war and peace, the environment, and social welfare. These differences in political opinion probably reflect the complex influence of the large-scale entry of women into low-wage and more irregular employment, their increasing involvement with welfare state programs as two-parent family structures weaken and wages fall, and the lingering influence of more traditional "maternal" values.[61] Whatever the reasons, the emergence of a distinct gender politics in the

58 On registration and turnout data for this period and a discussion of the biases they contain, see Piven and Cloward, *Why Americans Don't Vote*, appendices A, B and C.

59 On European patterns, see P. Norris, "The gender gap: a cross-national trend?," in *The Politics of the Gender Gap*, ed. C. M. Mueller (Beverly Hills, CA: Sage, 1988), pp. 217–34.

60 Female voting patterns also diverged from male patterns in the 1950s, although then women tilted to the right. See H. C. Kenski, "The gender factor in a changing electorate," and A. Miller, "Gender and the vote," in *The Politics of the Gender Gap*, pp. 38–60, 258–82.

61 On the institutional changes which underlie gender differences in politics, see F. F. Piven, "Women and the state: ideology, power and the welfare state," in *Gender and the Life Course*, ed. A. Rossi (Hawthorne, NY: Aldine, 1985), pp. 265–87; and S. Erie and M. Rein, "Women and the welfare state," in *The Politics of the Gender Gap*, pp. 173–91.

United States has become quite plain. The bungled 1984 nomination of a woman for the vice-presidency aside, the Democrats have not done much to mobilize their gender advantage. They have not championed the issues which incline women toward the Democratic Party, and they have not exerted themselves to represent women prominently in Democratic councils.[62] Perhaps this is why the gender gap broadens between elections, but narrows as each election draws near.

To sum up so far, working class allegiance to the Democratic Party weakened rapidly after the Second World War as a result of the failure of the party to shore up a union infrastructure or to promote welfare state policies oriented to the working class. The economic and demographic trends of the next three decades aggravated the weaknesses that had already developed in the Democratic Party. However, these trends were not simply the result of exogenous market forces. Rather, they were also the result of policies promoted by a centerless Democratic Party. Beholden as it was to sectional and interest group forces, the Democratic Party itself had promoted the dispersal of New Deal Democratic strongholds, and contributed to the growth of the suburban and sunbelt areas that were becoming the base of a revived Republican Party. To be sure, economic transformation was also generating new targets of electoral opportunity for the Democratic Party, both among the enlarging pool of have-nots and among politicized women. But the Democratic Party remained frozen, without a center that could move strategically to mobilize these constituencies in the face of inherited institutional obstacles and the weaknesses in infrastructure that resulted from earlier Democratic Party accommodations to sectional and interest group forces.

Postindustrial Political Strategies: Republican Countermobilization and Democratic Paralysis

I have so far emphasized the weight of institutional features of the American political system which inhibited Democratic Party building strategies. Those institutional arrangements are a kind of dead politics, the heritage of past political conflicts and the strategies they generated which then come to encumber contemporary actors. But strategic politics continues nevertheless within these constraints, as the Republican–business initiatives of the 1970s and 1980s demonstrate.

62 The decentralization of the heated abortion controversy in the United States, however, is prodding some state and local Democratic candidates to headline the right to abortion. In general, women's rights issues appear to have been especially salient as predictors of political preferences among nonvoters, suggesting at least congruence between the potential Democratic constituencies that I am discussing. See J. W. Calvert and J. Gilchrist, "The disappearing American voter," unpublished paper presented at the 1990 Annual Meeting of the American Political Science Association, San Francisco, 1990.

The progressive fragmentation of the Democratic Party paved the way for the resurgence of a modernized Republican Party backed by an increasingly politicized and at least temporarily unified business class. There will be disagreements about the turning point. Perhaps it was the election of Richard Nixon in 1968, at the close of a decade of conflict which wracked the Democratic Party. To be sure, the Nixon regime fell in disgrace as a result of the Watergate scandals, but even as it collapsed, business interests and Republican strategists were organizing a new bid for national ascendance.

Indeed, it is not hyperbole to say that, in the 1970s, American business temporarily overcame its usually fractured interest group politics and began to act like a political class. The problems which prompted this transformation were considerable: intensifying competition from Europe and Japan, and later from newly industrializing countries; rising commodity prices demanded by Third World suppliers as dramatized by the oil shocks of the 1970s; and the apparent inability of the administration to stabilize spiralling prices. Prodded by these developments, American business leaders set about developing a political program to shore up profits by slashing taxes and business regulation, lowering wages and welfare state spending, and building up American military power abroad. To that end, they created new organizations to promote the business outlook and revived old ones, poured money into business-oriented think tanks to provide the intellectual foundations for the business program, and set about modernizing and centralizing the Republican Party, using the pooled money of mobilized business contributors to overcome, at least for a time, the usual centrifugal forces of American party politics.

The first results were evident in the toughened stance of employers toward unions in the 1970s. Then, by the end of the decade, business lobbyists succeeded in rolling back regulatory controls, increased military spending, and defeated virtually all of the Carter initiatives on social spending, as well as his modest effort to roll back some of the limits on unions contained in the Taft–Hartley Act. But the real fruits of the business–Republican mobilization were harvested after the election of 1980. The new Republican regime – backed by a now virtually unanimous business community and only weakly resisted by congressional Democrats oriented to sectional and business interests – rapidly slashed taxes on business and the better-off, sharply increased military expenditures, accelerated the deregulation of business, launched a fierce attack on unions with the highly publicized destruction of the air controllers union and a far less publicized series of hostile appointments to the National Labor Relations Board, and, finally, inaugurated a decade-long attack on welfare state programs.

The impact of these several developments was both economic and political, and each reinforced the other. As the decline of the mass production industries proceeded apace, industrial job loss combined with welfare state program cuts to create pervasive economic hardship and insecurity. Under these conditions, new forms of employment spread easily, including "two-tier" hiring arrangements which paid new cohorts of workers sharply less, and increased reliance by business on homework and temporary employees. Of course, these arrangements undercut the unions, already reeling under the impact of employer anti-union campaigns, and union membership continued to drop. Strike levels fell precipitously, reaching their lowest levels in half a century in the 1980s,[63] and average wages continued their downward slide. By the end of the decade, something like a reordering of the class structure had been effected, as the income share of the top 1 percent rose by 87 percent, while the poorest 20 percent lost 5 percent, and most Americans barely stayed even.[64]

These developments did not, however, excite the outrage that might have benefited the Democratic Party. Part of the reason was that while a good many people were doing worse, almost as many were doing better, and these were not only more likely to be voters but were also the more visible participants in a consumer culture. At least as important, however, was the "hegemonic project" which was promulgated along with the new public policies. This was perhaps the most innovative aspect of the Republican–business mobilization, the revival in the 1970s and 1980s of the nineteenth-century doctrine of *laissez-faire*. The obvious evidence of industrial decline laid the groundwork for a propaganda campaign in which government and business leaders joined with think tank experts to define the policies of the 1980s as the necessary and inevitable response to global economic restructuring. To survive in a competitive international economy, US entrepreneurs had to be stimulated by higher profits and released from government regulation and union constraints. Only then will foreign penetration of the American economy be slowed and domestic economic growth restored, along with the good jobs, high wages, and public programs that economic growth will make possible.

Nineteenth-century *laissez-faire* naturalized the depredations of nineteenth-century capitalists, defining them as merely the working out of "market laws." Just so does this neo-*laissez-faire* naturalize the policies that promote US postindustrial strategies, defining these policies as the inevitable adaptation demanded by international markets, no matter

---

63 In 1978, more than a million workers were involved in stoppages; in 1988, the number of striking workers fell to 118,000. See K. Moody and J. Slaughter, "New directions for labor," *Dollars and Sense*, 158 (July–August 1990), p. 21.

64 The income share of the poorest fifth of the population fell to 4.6 percent, the lowest share since 1954. The next poorest fifth fell to 10.7 percent, and the middle fifth fell to 16.7 percent, both shares the lowest on record. Meanwhile, the share of the top fifth rose to 44 percent, the highest ever. See Center on Budget and Policy Priorities, "Poverty rate and household income stagnate as rich–poor gap hits postwar high," (Washington, DC: Center on Budget and Policy Priorities, October 20, 1989). It is worth noting that a similar polarization of income occurred under Thatcher. See P. Hall, *Governing the Economy* (Cambridge: Polity Press, 1986), pp. 123–6.

that other nations have adopted quite different policies to encourage different postindustrial strategies. Still, this argument is hard to answer. Not only does it resonate with the familiarity of ancient doctrine, but it gains confirmation as people shop for Japanese electronics or Korean clothes, watch foreign investors buy landmarks like Rockefeller Center, and all this while American factories shut their doors.

Still, if some concrete experiences shore up neo-*laissez-faire*, others contradict it, suggesting that the doctrine is vulnerable. Most important, after a decade with business in command, neo-*laissez-faire* is not producing its promises of increased prosperity for most people. To the contrary, real wages continue to slide, while public programs become more niggardly, and deficits rage out of control. Meanwhile, the evidence is overwhelming that business-oriented policies have unleashed more greed than entrepreneurialism, with the result that, a long-term boom notwithstanding, American productivity rates have lagged, while income to capital has soared.[65] And, of course, if world capitalist markets collapse, so will the doctrine of neo-*laissez-faire*.

My main point, however, is a different one. The exceptional success of neo-*laissez-faire* and the policies it justifies in the United States itself has to be explained. The explanation obviously has a great deal to do with the political weakness of labor-based political formations, which allowed the business–conservative mobilization of the last two decades to proceed without significant resistance. The historic weakness of American labor, in turn, is traceable to distinctive political structures which allowed sectional and business interests to cripple unionism and the welfare state, and ultimately to prevent the emergence of a labor party.

Conclusion

The political moral of the American story seems clear. The strength or weakness of labor politics matters greatly in humanizing adaptations to the new international economy, and perhaps in rationalizing national adaptations as well. There is a parallel here to the transition to industrial capitalism itself. The imposition of markets disrupted traditional communities, violated ancient rights, and destroyed the subsistence resources of the peasantry. But where traditions were vigorous and older bases of cohesion remained intact, popular resistance to the "new political economy" was also strong. And resistance mattered. The French peasantry won rights to land during the French Revolution, with the result that they could not easily be displaced from the countryside, and industrialization in France was retarded for a century and a half. Similarly, the food riots which spread across Europe in the wake of the introduction of unregulated markets into the countryside significantly

65 Again, the parallels with the British pattern are noteworthy. See Hall, *Governing the Economy*, pp. 115, 123.

moderated the effort to redistribute foodstuffs from the localities to the growing markets of the cities. In these instances, popular resistance moderated some of the cruelties of the transition to capitalism. In just this way, where the labor politics rooted in the mass production industries and the ascendant nation state is still vigorous, its traditions strong, and its bases of cohesion intact, so has it succeeded in moderating the cruelties of the transition to a global economy.

Still, the film cannot be run backwards. If the institutional context of American politics inhibited the political development of labor during the heyday of industrialism and the nation state, the postindustrial context is even less likely to promote labor politics, at least in its familiar union and electoral forms. New popular political struggles will emerge, to be sure, shaped by the new conditions and new understandings generated by postindustrialism. Perhaps in countries where labor politics remains strong, these new political currents will be absorbed into older labor formations, as environmentalists and feminists are being absorbed into some European labor parties. In the United States, however, the Democratic Party remains a bulwark of entrenched interests that is unlikely to yield or adapt unless assaulted by protest movements in the future.

About the Contributors

Asher Arian is Distinguished Professor of Political Science at the Graduate Center of the City University of New York, and Professor of Political Science at the University of Haifa. He has published widely on voting behavior, political parties, and public opinion in Israel, including *Politics in Israel: The Second Generation*. His forthcoming book, *Changing New York City Politics* (with Arthur Goldberg, John Mollenkopf, and Edward Rogowsky), will be published by Routledge.

Neil Bradford teaches in the Department of Political Science and History, Huron College, University of Western Ontario. He has written about differences in representational forms in Canada and Sweden, as well as on intellectuals in politics.

Ivor Crewe is Professor of Government at the University of Essex, England, and co-director of the *British Journal of Political Science*. His recent publications include *Decade of Dealignment* (with Bo Sarlvik), *British Parliamentary Constituencies* (with Anthony Fox), and *Electoral Change in Western Democracies* (co-edited with David Denver). He is currently completing a study of the British Social Democratic Party and is also engaged on a comparative study of popular conceptions of citizenship in Britain and the United States.

Alan DiGaetano is Assistant Professor of Political Science at Baruch College of the City University of New York. He has written on American city politics and is currently conducting research comparing urban politics in the United States and Britain.

Gøsta Esping-Andersen is Professor of Political and Social Sciences at the European University in Florence, Italy. He is the author of *Politics against Markets* (1985) and *The Three Worlds of Welfare Capitalism* (1990).

Jane Jenson teaches political science at Carleton University and is a research affiliate of the Center for European Studies, Harvard University. Recently she has been the co-author of *Crisis, Challenge and Change: Party and Class in Canada Revisited* (1988) and *Absent Mandate: Interpreting Change in Canadian Politics* (1991), as well as articles on French and Canadian politics.

Joel Krieger is Professor of Political Science at Wellesley College. He is author of *Reagan, Thatcher and the Politics of Decline* (1986) and co-author of *European Politics in Transition* (1987, second edition forthcoming).

Claus Offe was born in Berlin in 1940. Since 1988 he has been Professor of Political Science and Sociology at the University of Bremen. His publications in English include *Contradictions of the Welfare State* (1984) and *Disorganized Capitalism* (1985).

Frances Fox Piven is Distinguished Professor of Political Science at the Graduate Center of the City University of New York. She is co-author (with Richard Cloward) of *Regulating the Poor* (1971), *Politics of Turmoil* (1974), *Poor Peoples' Movements* (1977), *The New Class War* (1982), *The Mean Season* (1987), and *Why Americans Don't Vote* (1988).

George Ross is the Morris Hilquit Professor of Labor and Social Thought at Brandeis University and Senior Associate of the Center for European Studies, Harvard University. His publications include *Workers and Communists in France* (1980) and *The View from Inside: A French Communist Cell in Crisis* (1984, co-authored with Jane Jenson). He is also the co-editor of *The Mitterrand Experiment* (1987) and *In Search of the New France* (1991). His current research interests include the role of the European Commission in the construction of Europe 1992.

Ilan Talmud is a Paul F. Lazarsfeld Fellow in Sociology, and an Interdisciplinary Fellow at the Center for the Social Sciences, Columbia University. He co-authored *National Security and Public Opinion in Israel* (1988). His main interests are economic sociology and political control, and he is completing a dissertation on the strategic response of big European corporations to trade dependence.

Göran Therborn is Professor of Sociology at the University of Gothenburg, Sweden. His books include *Science, Class and Society, The Ideology of Power and the Power of Ideology*, and *Why Some Peoples Are More Unemployed Than Others*.

Index

Index compiled by Jackie McDermott